Paul Tillich

Paul Tillich

A New Catholic Assessment

Monika Hellwig
Thomas Franklin O'Meara, O.P.
Ronald Modras
Julia A. Lamm
John C. Dwyer
Kenan B. Osborne, O.F.M.
Raymond F. Bulman
George H. Tavard
Jean Richard
Mary Ann Stenger
Anthony A. Akinwale, O.P.
Sebastian Painadath, S.J.
Frederick J. Parrella
Claude Geffré, O.P.
Langdon Gilkey

Raymond F. Bulman
Frederick J. Parrella
Editors

A Michael Glazier Book
† THE LITURGICAL PRESS
Collegeville, Minnesota

A Michael Glazier Book published by The Liturgical Press

Cover design by David Manahan, O.S.B.
Cover photograph: Paul Tillich with Cardinal Suenens at the Divinity School
of the University of Chicago in 1964. © Archie Lieberman.

1   2   3   4   5   6   7   8   9

Library of Congress Cataloging-in-Publication Data

Paul Tillich : a new Catholic assessment / Monika Hellwig . . . [et al.];
   Raymond F. Bulman, Frederick J. Parrella, editors.
     p.   cm.
   "A Michael Glazier book."
   Includes bibliographical references and index.
   ISBN 0-8146-5828-8
   1. Tillich, Paul, 1886–1965. 2. Theology, Doctrinal—
History—20th century. 3. Catholic Church—Doctrines.
I. Hellwig, Monika. II. Bulman, Raymond F. 1933-   .
III. Parrella, Frederick J.
BX4827.T53P29 1994
230'.092—dc20   93-34711
                                                  CIP

*To our colleagues in the
North American Paul Tillich Society
in appreciation for their
friendship and support*

Contents

The Socialist Tillich and Liberation Theology

Paul Tillich and the Feminist Critique
of Roman Catholic Theology

Tillich's Method of Correlation and
the Concerns of African Theologians

Paul Tillich's Theology of Prayer:
An Indian Perspective

Tillich and Contemporary Spirituality

Paul Tillich and the
Future of Interreligious Ecumenism

A Protestant Response

Appreciation and Reply.

"It is indeed a great honor for me that a book ~~large~~ about my theology with contributions by a large group of outstanding Roman Catholic theologians is to be published, and it is an expression of generosity and openness that I have been asked to write an answer to some of the criticisms made by the contributors ~~at the end of the book~~. I gladly follow this invitation allthough I am aware of the limitations that a short ~~answer~~ reply to so many weighty problems ~~must have~~ necessarily has. ...

... I want to start with a general statement that ~~is to all contributions~~ applies to all articles in some way or the other: A large part of the criticisms ~~made~~ are an expression of the basic difference ~~the Ro~~ between the Roman Catholic and the Protestant ...

... of Christianity and even of the nature of religion ..."

("Reply" of Paul Tillich to *Paul Tillich in Catholic Thought* [1964])

Foreword

A volume in which Paul Tillich's contribution to Catholic thought is evaluated and appreciated in retrospect is most opportune and most welcome. This is all the more so when the contributors are themselves noteworthy scholars who were influenced by this remarkable thinker. Tillich himself once wrote that there should never have been Protestant Churches; what was needed was the Protestant principle within the Catholic Church. If he himself embodied the Protestant principle in a new and more radical way, he achieved something of what he thought should always have been true, because his thought has influenced contemporary Catholicism more extensively and intensively than he could possibly have predicted.

There were, of course, contemporary Catholic thinkers—foremost among them Karl Rahner—who shared with Tillich the turn to the subject in the post-war existentialist world, and shared it with deep conviction. Yet it is a fact that anyone acknowledging the authority of the Catholic *magisterium* simply did not enjoy the freedom for speculative theology in the new mode that could be claimed by a liberal Protestant scholar with the heritage of the German universities. Tillich wrote with unfettered creativity of extraordinary scope and simplicity, holding himself in relation to the shared experience of Christian life and tradition, while refusing to be confined by past philosophical interpretations. And in this he squarely met the deeply-felt need on the part of modern Catholic intellectuals for intelligibility in their faith and beliefs.

It was particularly in the non-personal, non-individuated image of the Triune God that Tillich touched Catholic imagination, with its traditional acceptance of paradoxical combinations of the positive and the negative in the approach of the human mind to the divine. The brilliant conceptualization of the three-in-one God as ground of being, as expressive being, and as unitive being certainly preserved orthodox continuity with the ancient councils, but it also spoke a very encouraging word to Catholic intellectual anxiety over the evident and unchallenged tritheism dominating contemporary Christian piety.

Perhaps another aspect of Tillich's work that appealed to Catholic minds was that he accomplished what Rahner was hesitant to do and Karl Barth roundly condemned. He produced a *summa* for our times in his three-volume *Systematic Theology,* working out both an entire theological world view and a comprehensive spirituality that showed the coherence of Christian faith in our times and its applicability to all aspects of the human situation as we know it. Because of the traditional and deeply ingrained Catholic expectation of continuity between faith and reason, there was a great hunger for a comprehensive system such as Tillich's. Previous attempts, of course, had already been made by such great Catholic thinkers as Matthias Scheeben in the nineteenth century and neo-Thomists in the twentieth, but not with the intellectual boldness that Tillich brought to the project. Tillich's system came to the Catholic community at a time when the search for new meanings was a crucial issue.

A third way in which Tillich met the needs of the time within the Catholic community (as indeed elsewhere) lies in the acuity of the psychological perception which he brought to questions about faith and doubt and the struggle to pursue ultimate truth beyond the boundaries of our ability to understand. What was particularly helpful in such works as *Dynamics of Faith* was the sympathetic presentation of the necessity of continually unmasking and transcending idolatries. Of the existence of such idolatries the modern Catholic intellectual was becoming increasingly and painfully aware. The fact that this constitutes the general condition of historical life for human beings, including Christians, was an encouraging message that had not generally occurred to us.

There are many reasons why contemporary Catholic theologians should be remembering, appreciating, and thanking Paul Tillich, and it is a distinct pleasure to welcome this volume in which such a task is being accomplished.

Monika Hellwig

Acknowledgments

The editors wish to express their special appreciation:

To the University Seminars at Columbia University for assistance in the preparation of the manuscript for publication. Some of the ideas presented have benefited from discussions in the University Seminar on Studies in Religion.

To Dr. Bella Hass Weinberg of St. John's University, New York, for her professional expertise in preparing the index, as well as for her many helpful suggestions in producing the manuscript.

To Michael Niemczyk and Jennifer Redwitz for their careful proofreading of the manuscript and to Madeleine E. Beaumont for her assistance in translating the article of Claude Geffré from French.

To Mark Twomey, Managing Editor of The Liturgical Press, for his wise and patient advice and his confidence in the project from its inception.

To Archie Lieberman for permission to use the photo of Paul Tillich and Cardinal Suenens on the cover and to Jerald C. Brauer, Dean Emeritus of the Divinity School of the University of Chicago, for both suggesting and locating the photograph.

To Thomas F. O'Meara, O.P., for his suggestions in the planning of the manuscript and his encouragement and enthusiasm for a new volume on Tillich by Catholic theologians.

To Erdmuthe Tillich Farris for permission to use a handwritten letter of Paul Tillich in the front matter, and even more, for her enthusiastic support of this volume.

Introduction

If Protestant theologian and philosopher Paul Tillich had lived to see
and evaluate the reception of the Second Vatican Council in the last
quarter of a century, had he witnessed the transformation of the Catholic Church from the *societas perfecta* of the Pian era to the *communio* and
sacramentum salutis mundi of today, he might not be at all surprised.
In 1963, he was aware of the changes that Pope John XXIII and the
Second Vatican Council *could* make in Catholic life and theology. The
issue for Tillich was the degree and the effectiveness of the revival of
what he called the "principle of reformation" within Catholicism.[1] If
Tillich were with us today to examine the present status of Catholicism and its theology, his reaction, we suspect, would be quite pre-
dictable. First, he would certainly be concerned about the renewal of
heteronomous power within the Church's institutional structures in
the last fifteen years. But, more important, he would be unabashedly
pleased, as Ronald Modras says in one of the essays to follow, with
"the widespread and continuing growth of Catholic self-criticism." Perhaps he would be quite surprised at the extent, as Modras puts it, to
which "the prophetic and Protestant principle continues to survive in
the Catholic Church."

Tillich's death in 1965, the last year of the Second Vatican Council,
coincided with the beginning of a new era in Catholicism. During
his education and early career in Germany in the first decades of
the twentieth century, Tillich was acquainted with a very different
Catholic Church, the post-Reformation, ultramontane Catholicism of
the post-Pius IX era.[2] The ecclesiology of this time saw the Church as
a society based on a state model structured like a pyramid, with the
Pope and the hierarchy enjoying unquestioned authority at the top.
This Church, as Yves Congar writes, was like "an organization where
Christ intervened at its origin as the founder, and the Holy Spirit as
the guarantee of its authority."[3] Thus, Tillich's encounter with Catholicism and Catholic theology was Tridentine in both form and content—
that is, anti-historical, apologetic, and highly suspicious of modern
historical and scientific thought. Catholic theology, from 1878 onwards,
was primarily Neo-Scholastic—made all the more inflexible and defen-

sive by the ecclesiastical reaction to modernist thinking in the years
before World War I. In spite of its systematic strengths and singular
coherence, the neo-scholastic approach lacked sensitivity to time and
history, was closed to adaptation and development except in logical
forms, and used the writings of Scripture and the Church Fathers not
as rich sources of life and tradition, but as proofs for a priori theological theses.

After World War I, the first winds of change in Catholic theology
took place in France and Germany with the earliest critique of Neo-
Scholasticism emerging from within the tradition itself. The renewal
of interest in Scripture, the return to the writings of the Church Fathers,
and the rediscovery of mystery within the liturgy marked the theological revival between the world wars. Despite a temporary setback
with Pius XII's condemnation of the "new theology" in his 1950 encyclical *Humani Generis*, both the method and the content of Catholic
theology was beginning to leave the safe harbor of neo-scholasticism
forever. After four decades of evolution and transition in theology, the
Second Vatican Council marked the final break with Neo-Scholasticism
as the best or only way of doing theology.[4]

Catholic theology after the council was marked by a pluralism of
methods, the use of contemporary existentialist and personalist philosophy, and more integration and adaptation of non-theological disciplines, especially sociology, psychology, and history. In spite of a
kind of post-conciliar theological eclecticism, a number of common
characteristics became clear. First, historical consciousness took root
at the heart of theological thought and with this consciousness came
a new emphasis on Scripture as the historical foundation and norm
of faith. In the often-cited words of Vatican II: "The human race has
passed from a rather static concept of reality to a more dynamic, evolutionary one."[5] Richard McBrien, just a few years after the council,
commented that "the implications of this sentence cannot easily be
exaggerated."[6] Theology was now free to exist in history, not in eternity. Put differently, the Church began to understand itself not as a
community above history but as a pilgrim Church; it recognized, to
paraphrase Piet Schoonenberg, that theology above history was in itself historically conditioned, since it belonged to that period of history
which was not sufficiently aware of its own historicity.[7] The formal
reception of this historical consciousness in the life of the Church has
marked Catholic theology and Catholic life for the past three decades.

Second, Catholic theology was also characterized by a turn to the
human subject and subjectivity in which experience as the starting point
of the theological enterprise triumphed over older, objective, non-

historical truths. Before Vatican II, experience as a factor in theology appeared too subjectivist, too selective, too threatening to the normative objective tradition, with its understanding of truth as absolute and unchanging. With *Gaudium et Spes*, however, Catholicism acknowledged that the Church must continue to reinterpret doctrinal formulations in light of the gospel.[8] Theology was thus understood from a radically different perspective. As Dermot Lane says: "Theology, from beginning to end, is about the critical unpacking of the revelation of God that takes place in human experience through faith. This means that our faith understanding of God must be critically informed by, based on, and received from experience."[9] Theology thus moved from an almost exclusive focus on its transcendent object to a new awareness of the importance of the human subject and its relative and historical place. In other words, theology required both anthropology and history to perform its task.[10]

In the early years after the council, the full implications of a biblical-historical, experiential, and eclectic framework for doing theology were often lost both by many conservatives in the Church who clutched to the old world views and by some liberals who agitated for change often without critical theological reflection. Perhaps the most important problem for the Church was the failure of the bishops to educate the members of the Church about the breadth and depth of the transition taking place.[11] As St. Éxupéry admonishes, we lack perspective for the transformations that go deep. That perspective is now much more clear, almost thirty years later. Vatican II heralded a fundamental change in epistemology, in the interpretation of Christian symbols, in the meaning we give to the terms God, Christ, Church, grace, and eternal life. Vatican II was the beginning, not the end, of reform. Ecclesiologically, the notion of ongoing moral reform in *Lumen Gentium* also applies to the epistemological framework of theology: ". . . the Church, embracing sinners within her bosom, is at the same time holy and always in need of being purified. . . ."[12] Theology learned that it had to make the absolute message of the gospel relative to its reception in a particular time, place, and culture.

The reception of Vatican II, or the response of the community with its mind and heart to the conciliar documents, has been in process during the more than quarter of a century since Paul Tillich's death. He witnessed Catholicism on the brink of change, but he did not see the change itself nor its positive and negative implications. If, as J. M. R. Tillard tells us, it is a factor of crucial theological importance that non-Roman Catholic Churches—Protestant, Anglican, and Orthodox—have also "received" the documents of the council, the hypothetical question of how Tillich would have "received" the decrees of Vatican II in his own mind and heart should be of great interest to Protestants and Catholics alike.[13] How would Tillich have interpreted the council in the re-shaping of the Catholic tradition? While he proclaimed himself a Lutheran theologically and was an energetic exponent of the Protestant principle, Tillich's interest and affection for Catholicism is also well documented. In the first of his autobiographical reflections, he states that his opposition to Roman Catholicism "was never directed . . . against dogmatic values or liturgical forms of the Roman Catholic system but rather against Catholicism's heteronomous character with its assertion of dogmatic authority. . . ."[14] Put differently, Tillich was more outspoken in his rejection of the "Roman" rather than the "Catholic" aspect of the tradition.

In some ways, the essays that follow are answers to this hypothetical question. We cannot have access to Tillich's response directly, of course, but we do have something akin: Catholic theological reflection which moves and takes form in and through Tillich's theological thought. Hence, we are afforded a glimpse of how Tillich might have received the changes in Catholic theology by an examination of how Catholic theologians themselves have continued to receive Tillich within the confines of their work. In 1964, two Dominicans, Thomas O'Meara and Donald Weisser, edited an earlier volume on Tillich and Catholic thought.[15] This work (which was so successful that it was reprinted by Doubleday in 1969) was a collection of articles written between 1950 and 1964, including essays from some of America's most distinguished Catholic theologians, including Gustav Weigel, Avery Dulles, and George Tavard. A pioneer work in ecumenical theology, it continues to have vital significance.

Some twenty-five years or so after the O'Meara work, the two editors of the present volume sought out original essays on Tillich's thought by Catholic theologians that would enlarge the spirit of ecumenism of the first volume as well as reflect the very different world of Catholic theology and Tillich scholarship in recent decades. In an attempt to cast as wide a net as possible, we asked potential contributors the following questions: What does Tillich's theology look like under the scrutiny of post-conciliar Catholic theological eyes? What is the explicit or implicit value of Tillich's theology for the Catholic theologian in the last decade of the twentieth century? How has Tillich's thought been applied to new and pressing areas of Catholic theological concern? Each essay in the present volume reflects the topic that is of special interest to the individual author. Some traditional Catholic topics appear more important to the contributors of this volume than the first and others, such as revelation, Scripture, and Christological doctrine, are hardly covered at all. Likewise, some of Tillich's themes—symbol, theonomy, idolatry, Protestant principle, and Catholic substance—are understandably more visible in these essays than others such as estrangement, courage, and an interpretation of history.

As these Catholic theologians "receive" and apply the conciliar decrees, they also continue to employ Tillich's theology as a source of inspiration and enrichment. Thus, these essays reflect a kind of two-fold "reception": first, of conciliar theology and its application to the modern world; second, of Tillich's theological heritage by a second generation of Catholic theologians committed to his thought. In this volume, a number of common characteristics are discernible in all the essays. First, none of the present chapters present a critique of Tillich's theology from a post-Tridentine perspective. Unlike the 1964 book, which contained several articles comparing Saint Thomas and Tillich, no such comparative theme is operative today because of the eclectic mood of post-Vatican II theology. Indeed, as Ronald Modras says, "anything like a single Catholic standard for measuring his thought" no longer exists, given the pluralistic framework of Catholic theology.

Second, the authors of this volume are no longer aloof or cautious about Tillich; they all appropriate and apply Tillich's theological perspective to their topic in a most positive fashion. Thus, we witness a shift in the Catholic theological response to Tillich: no longer is he an object of evaluation and critique (not to mention suspicion) as much as a subject and source of theological insight. In these essays, his theology provides a kind of unique hermeneutic to such questions as Church and sacraments, especially the Eucharist, prayer and spirituality, liberation theology, and Christian eschatology. Put differently, Tillich is no longer an outsider within the Catholic house. His role and place in Catholic theology has evolved since the sixties from friendly stranger to not-so-strange, indeed welcome, friend and colleague.

Third, these essays expand the topics which concerned Tillich in his own time; they bring Tillich into the nineties by appropriating his categories of thought to the theological, political, and cultural questions that he himself could not have imagined during his lifetime. Mary Ann Stenger's feminist critique of Tillich, Jean Richard's appropriation of Tillich's socialist writings for liberation theology, and the essay on contemporary spirituality are cases in point. Finally, the essays are no longer restricted to Western theological concerns. Anthony Akinwale's application of Tillich's method of correlation to answer the concerns of African theologians and Sebastian Painadath's theology of prayer from an Indian perspective and its usefulness in a Hindu-Christian dialogue are fascinating signs of Tillich's enduring strengths and the flexibility of his thought. Always a lightning rod for interconfessional ecumenical dialogue among the Western Christian Churches, Tillich's understanding of Christ as the Concrete Universal and religion as ultimate concern now serves, as Claude Geffré's essay demonstrates, as a fruitful framework for interreligious dialogue among world religions, including those of the East.

In conclusion, the fact that Catholic theologians continue to read, reflect upon, and discuss Tillich's philosophical and theological thought in their own work today is noteworthy enough. But the deeper significance of these essays lies precisely in the positive contribution to Catholic theology Tillich continues to make when specific theological questions are explored through Tillichian lenses. Perhaps it is something of an anachronism today to work with such divisions as "Catholic" and "Protestant" in the theological enterprise—realistically, since Vatican II, the theology (though not the politics) of the Churches have drawn much closer together. While it may be wise to heed Julia Lamm's suggestion in her essay that appropriating those themes in Tillich that are so congenial to Catholicism—ontology, mysticism, immediate awareness, culture, etc.—can sometimes be self-serving, still older historical and thematic distinctions between the two traditions fade before the new age in which all of us live and the new configuration given to theological issues that we all confront in the post-modern culture. But even those major parts of Tillich's system which remain permanently in tension theologically and philosophically with the Catholic tradition still play a prophetic role within the Catholic heritage. Thus Lamm also reminds us that the " 'Protestant principle' [is] not something foreign to Catholic thought and spirituality (thus to be at best tolerated) but as integral to it." Tillich's life work was directed to making the eternal message of the gospel relevant to contemporary Christians. Catholic theologians delight in Tillich's theology not only because of his Catholic appeal but precisely because he was also Protestant and continued to point out to both traditions the extent to which they need one another. Tillich appreciated and understood history, accepted the importance of experience, and proclaimed the prophetic principle—in this way, he anticipated many of the theological changes which took place at Vatican II. Likewise, his understanding of the Church resonates with a Catholic spirit: "The Church antecedes individual piety, it is not the result of it. The Church is not a creation of religious individuals, but religious individuals are products of the Church. Not the moral standard of the congregation makes the holiness of the Church but the holiness of the Church makes its members holy. . . . The

Church represents the presence of the Divine which is given before any experience or activity. . . ."[16]

If one theme could be singled out from the pages to follow, it is a thoroughly Catholic appreciation of the Protestant principle—"the refusal to divinize any element of human or historic reality," as Claude Geffré will describe it. At the same time, the Catholic substance remains forever as the "the affirmation of God's spiritual presence in everything that is." This is the source of the sacramental world view, the font of all Christian confidence and consolation, and, as Tillich very well knew, the essential truth that the Protestant Churches must relearn from the Catholic tradition.

David Tracy reminds us that we must always correlate "the meaning and truth of the Christian fact with the meaning and truth of our contemporary experience."[17] This was the true task of the Second Vatican Council and the vocation of Catholic and Protestant theology alike in the face of a secular and profane world on one side and new idolatrous forms of Christianity on the other. This remains the continuing work of the Catholic Church in its ongoing reception and application of conciliar theology as well as its effort to expand and adapt the conciliar tradition to create a theology that answers the questions of the next millennium. As these essays will reveal, Catholic theologians, and indeed the Churches of all traditions, are fortunate to have Tillich as a prophetic colleague and friend, and his theological system as a source of wisdom in the journey to come.

Raymond F. Bulman
Frederick J. Parrella

Notes

[1] Paul Tillich, *Systematic Theology*, vol. 3 (Chicago: The University of Chicago Press, 1963) 168.

[2] See Paul Tillich, "The Permanent Significance of the Catholic Church for Protestantism" *Protestant Digest* (New York) 3, 10, (February–March, 1941) 24.

[3] Yves Congar, *L'Eglise du Saint Augustin à l'époque moderne* (Paris: Les éditions du Cerf, 1970) 382–383.

[4] See T. Mark Schoof, *A Survey of Catholic Theology 1800–1970* (New York: Paulist Newman, 1970) 146–151. Many examples exist in the conciliar documents but perhaps none more striking than the dramatic change in the interpretation of Revelation in *Dei Verbum* (the Dogmatic Constitution on Divine Revelation) from the

propositional approach in neo-scholastic theology to the biblical/interpersonal understanding of revelation in the conciliar documents.

⁵ *Gaudium et Spes,* par. 5.

⁶ Richard McBrien, *Church: The Continuing Quest* (New York: Newman, 1970) 28.

⁷ Piet Schoonenberg, *Man and Sin. A Theological View.* (Notre Dame: University
of Notre Dame Press, 1965) 192.

⁸ *Gaudium et Spes,* par. 4; the often-cited phrase is "scrutinizing the signs of the
times."

⁹ Dermot Lane, *The Experience of God. An Invitation to Do Theology* (New York:
Paulist, 1981) 3.

¹⁰ See William E. Hill, "Theology," in *The New Dictionary of Theology,* edited by
Dermot Lane, Mary Collins, and Joseph Komonchak (Wilmington: Michael Glazier,
1987) 1011–1027.

¹¹ See Richard McBrien, *The Remaking of the Church. An Agenda for Reform.* (New
York: Harper and Row, 1973) 67–68.

¹² *Lumen Gentium,* art. 8.

¹³ J.-M. R. Tillard, "Did We Receive Vatican II?" *One in Christ* 21 (1985) 278. On
this issue, see also Acerbi, A. "Receiving Vatican II in a Changed Historical Context." In *Where Does the Church Stand? Concilium* 146 (1981) 77–84. And Alberigo,
G., Jossua, J.-P., and Komonchak, J., eds., *The Reception of Vatican II* (Washington:
The Catholic University of America Press, 1987).

¹⁴ Paul Tillich, *On the Boundary* (New York: Scribners, 1966 [1936]) 39. In this
same passage Tillich also remarks that in the light of National Socialism in Germany, he once considered becoming a Catholic.

¹⁵ Thomas O'Meara and Donald Weisser, eds., *Paul Tillich in Catholic Thought,*
Dubuque: The Priory Press, 1964.

¹⁶ "The Permanent Significance of the Catholic Church for Protestantism," 26.

¹⁷ David Tracy, "The Catholic Model of Caritas: Self-Transcendence and Transformation," *Concilium* 121 (New York: Seabury, 1979) 101.

Paul Tillich in Catholic Thought: The Past and the Future

Thomas Franklin O'Meara, O.P.

An Early Catholic Appraisal

In the autumn of 1961, an ecumenical *kairos*, a new and unexpected atmosphere, was rapidly extending its influence in the United States. That time of ecclesial change—in a country long marked by prejudice— had been prepared by the meetings of the World Council of Churches, and it looked forward to the ecumenical council, Vatican II, about to begin. I was then a Dominican seminarian in Dubuque, Iowa. During the previous decades there had been no contact in that small mid-western city between the Catholic seminary for Dominican and diocesan priests, and the Lutheran and Presbyterian seminaries. Suddenly, stimulated by a visit from the Danish theologian K. E. Skydsgaard, a first ecumenical cluster of seminaries took shape. Professors attended theological colloquia, and students were introduced to theologians from other church traditions. I was assigned a paper on the incarnation, and the faculty and library of Wartburg Lutheran seminary introduced me to the theologies of Karl Barth, Emil Brunner, Gustav Aulen, and Paul Tillich. If I found Tillich's Christology in the second volume of the *Systematic Theology* foreign in its existentialist reduction of the Logos in Jesus, still the presentation of theological method, the comprehension of the history of philosophy in theology as well as the pattern of autonomy, heteronomy, and theonomy made a lasting impact. The explanation of theology as correlation was a revelation to a Dominican who was trying after seven years of classes on Aristotle, Thomas Aquinas, and Neo-Thomism to find out how theology served Church and society. Here was a view of theology which was pastoral and theoretical, historical and cultural, psychological as well as metaphysical.

Given permission by my superiors (access to books on religion by Protestants was then forbidden to a Catholic) and then protected by a universal rescript from an office deep in the Vatican, I studied dur-

ing my last two years of seminary some of the great Protestant theologians of the 1950s and 1960s, particularly Paul Tillich. Journals and
special volumes honoring Tillich showed me that there were essays
written on him by Catholics. The Jesuit Gustave Weigel was a pioneer
of ecumenism and of a Roman Catholic understanding of Tillich. Amazingly his first article on Tillich had appeared in 1950. He viewed Tillich as a high-point in Protestant theology and of particular interest
to Catholics because of his appreciation of the history of philosophy,
intellectual research, and the work of correlation which sought to make
Christianity coherent. Weigel's subsequent essays, however, also asked
whether Tillich's existentialism did not eliminate tradition and content, and whether his theory of symbols was adequate to express with
any degree of literal meaning historical events and religious truths. Still
the two theologians appreciated each other greatly, and Tillich wrote
responses to Weigel's articles.[1]

In the summer of 1962, as I was beginning my last year in the Dominican *studium*, it occurred to me one morning that there could be a collection of Roman Catholic essays on Tillich. The book of essays by
C. W. Kegley and R. Bretall was my model.[2] I wrote brief letters to
Avery Dulles, Kenelm Foster, George Tavard, Weigel, and others asking to reprint essays already published, and they quickly responded
affirmatively. Then I solicited some new essays, and the Dominican
publishing house The Priory Press accepted the book. Thus came into
existence in a few weeks *Paul Tillich in Catholic Thought*.

The director of The Priory Press, Thomas Donlan, was enthusiastic
about this early volume of ecumenical theology and was responsible
for its attractive format and international success. In September 1963,
as I was leaving for doctoral studies in Germany, the publisher suggested that a Dominican who had helped me in the project assume
responsibility and become co-editor: Donald Weisser.[3] J. Heywood
Thomas, a Welsh theologian whose *Paul Tillich: An Appraisal*[4] had just
been published, wrote a foreword.

I wrote in the introduction to the volume:

> The following pages represent an appraisal by contemporary Catho-
> lic theologians of Dr. Tillich's theology. . . . These studies, arranged
> in an order somewhat similar to his theological system, touch upon
> the fundamental areas of his thought: the nature of revelation and
> theology; its relationship to human thought; Jesus Christ; the Church
> and the Christian. The purpose of the volume is not, ultimately, crit-
> ical; its purpose is to explore the truth and relevance of a theologian's
> understanding of Christianity and the causes for his success in form-
> ing our contemporary scene.[5]

Tillich was "the heir of German philosophical and theological trends from the past century and beyond." Just as he struggled "to make Christ meaningful to our culture," Catholics should break out into new worlds of theology.

> Tillich's ideas and terms are new and, as he wishes, contemporary. The judgement of right and wrong in relation to Catholic theology should be made only after the meaning behind the words is explored. Dr. Tillich's desire to be relevant, his prominence, and his respect for coherence should lead us to expect that he has something to offer anyone interested in shepherding the space age. The Catholic reader may recall that Paul Tillich has been asked to speak as today's theologian before many eminent gatherings because he has worked for the present and the future. The tragedy of being out of touch with man and his life can never prevail over the revelation of Christ. But irrelevance is a perennial threat to theologians.[6]

In May of 1963, Tillich had been invited to address 250 guests at the celebration of the fortieth anniversary of *Time* magazine. A few months later Weisser contacted Tillich at the University of Chicago about writing a response to the essays by Catholic theologians, and he agreed with enthusiasm to do it. Tillich worked on "An Afterword: Appreciation and Reply" during the first months of 1964, even writing down some responses to the different theologians when he was occasionally hospitalized; Hannah Tillich said it was something Paulus wanted to do, but the piece was still incomplete in June. It was eventually completed, and *Paul Tillich in Catholic Thought* appeared in late autumn, 1964. Tillich began his overview of the authors with these lines:

> It is indeed a great honor for me that a book about my theology, consisting of contributions by a large group of outstanding Roman Catholic theologians is to be published. And it is an expression of generosity and openness that I have been asked to write an answer to some of the criticisms made by the contributors. I gladly accept this invitation, although I am aware of the limitations that a short reply to so many weighty papers has. . . . A large part of the criticisms are an expression of the basic differences between the Roman Catholic and the Protestant understanding of Christianity, and even of the nature of religion. This is unavoidable. It is the consequence of that interaction between destiny and decision which determines the religious condition of every human being.
>
> It seems to me that there are three main points in which this contrast appears directly: objectivity against subjectivity; authority against autonomy; analogy against symbol.[7]

The "Afterword" (among the last of his many writings) ends with the words:

> I want to repeat that I did this reply with the same joy about a fruitful dialogue with which I read the articles. One thing I learned in doing so is the necessity that we learn more about each other's thought, the classical as well as the contemporary. . . . But fundamental differences cannot be removed and must be acknowledged. Only the divine Spirit and historical providence can overcome the splits amongst those representing the Spiritual Community which transcends every particular church and every particular religious group. A dialogue, done in "listening love," can be a tool of providence and a channel of the divine Spirit.[8]

The book was launched with a reception in Hyde Park at a Dominican house which was the headquarters of The Priory Press; the volume was also published in England,[9] and it was said that measures by Franco blocked its publication in Spain. In a circular letter in December, 1964, sending German-speaking friends greetings for Christmas and the New Year, Tillich wrote:

> In 1964 three books by me have appeared: the third volume of sermons with the title, *The Eternal Now,* just appearing in German as *Das Ewig im Jetzt;* second, five articles under the title *Morality and Beyond;* thirdly *Systematic Theology Vol. III.* Moreover two new books have appeared on my theology. The first is from a young American theologian who studies under Barth, *The Systematic Theology of Paul Tillich* with an interesting "Foreword" from Karl Barth. The second is *Paul Tillich in Catholic Thought.* It is edited by Dominicans, and contains fifteen essays by various Catholic authors and an extensive response by me. It was recently dedicated with a "Cocktail Party" at the Dominican house.[10]

Lectures during the academic year 1964/1965 saw Tillich looking more and more physically drained, and in August, 1965, he began his eightieth year. A few days after a last lecture in Chicago on the significance of the history of religion for systematic theology, he died on October 22, 1965.

To look at *Paul Tillich in Catholic Thought* is to see a particular period in theology and ecumenism, one which is not so distant and yet one which is clearly past. Some essays are Roman Catholic in a static and unimaginative way, and a few compare Tillich with some aspect of Neo-Thomism; all were written before the second session of Vatican II. The focus is often philosophical rather than theological, Scholastic rather than historical. The act of dialogue, however, was then new and was more important than the ideas in the fifteen essays. The book's project was its achievement. The meeting of American Catholic theology (many of whose representatives had been educated in Roman schools) with an internationally famous Protestant theologian, a conversation between professors in medieval or Tridentine Scholasticism and a theologian who had been on the cover of *Time* magazine four years earlier—this was significant. Ecumenism had emerged; change in the Catholic Church had begun. Tillich spoke of a new moment, "a *kairos*, a moment full of potentialities, in Protestant-Catholic relations. . . ."[11]

The Appeal to Catholics

Paul Tillich's *Systematic Theology* took seriously different periods in the history of Christianity. Both idealist and Aristotelian categories were discussed and employed. In most Protestant writers Catholicism was still more or less ignored, but Tillich had a positive word for Aquinas and Bonaventure. Indeed, Protestantism could not just be critique: the Protestant principle needed the Catholic substance. "The Protestant principle is an expression of the conquest of religion by the Spiritual Presence and consequently an expression of the victory over the ambiguities of religion, its profanization, and its demonization. . . . It alone is not enough; it needs the 'Catholic substance,' the concrete embodiment of the Spiritual Presence."[12] American Roman Catholics, educated in only Neo-Scholastic theology up to Vatican II, were not attracted to Tillich because he offered pantheist expressions of dogmas like incarnation and Trinity, or because he occasionally chose a demythologizing program like Rudolf Bultmann's. The form of this theology rather than its content—the theological method and the dynamics of a transcendental-existential anthropology, particularly the circle of themes in religion, culture, and philosophy—led a number of Catholics, first in America and then in Europe, to see possibilities for modern theological expression.

Tillich helped to reawaken a sleeping Catholicism (anesthetized by a timeless ontology) to theology as a co-relation to two poles: the revelation of God, and the situation in which the Christian lives or speaks. What was taught in books and classes should speak to the issues of daily life and the culture of an epoch. "Theology, as a function of the Christian Church, must serve the needs of the Church. A theological system is supposed to satisfy two basic needs: the statement of the heart of the Christian message and the interpretation of this truth for every new generation."[13] This had in fact been the approach of, among others, Origen, Thomas Aquinas in the "Prologus" to the *Summa theologiae,* and Luther.

"Theonomy" expresses this transparency of the cultural form to the transcendent, an openness of the finite and the existential for what was called "New Being" or the "Power of Being." Culture—from modern art to psychology—was not an enemy but a channel for the divine presence. "Religion is the substance of culture, culture is the form of religion."[14] Tillich's view of Roman Catholicism was hardly always positive. Didn't the Catholic Church tend to a heteronomy, to a human and arrogant subjugation of people to unquestioned authorities? The positive essence of Catholicism, the sacramental, easily became corrupted in the idolatrous, the superstitious, and the magical. To this Tillich added a third critique of Tridentine Catholicism (one less noted): the immobility and pretended timelessness of a static institution.[15]

Tillich was not the first Protestant theologian to attract Catholic interest. That distinction belonged to Karl Barth thundering forth out of little Switzerland in lusty denunciations of Rome. Barth seemed to be free of the apparent pantheisms and relativisms of Protestant liberal theology. By 1962, Jerome Hâmer, Hans Urs von Balthasar, and Hans Küng had written positively and creatively on Barth. The Barthian mindset, however, separated the finite and the infinite, nature and grace. In its attempt at system, a pageant of biblical and historical figures and ideas moved across a landscape whose topography was alien, even hostile to the Catholic synthesis of divine and human activities. In the orders of being and grace Aquinas had concluded: "God has given us the gift of being real causes."[16] But Barth found creaturely cooperation with grace—in a saint, in Mary, in the Church— to be so central to the Catholic mind as to be the source of its errors.[17] Since Barthian theology was so opposed to what was essential in Catholicism—sacramental mediation and graced activity—dialogue could only go so far.

Why did Tillich have such success among Roman Catholics? He was a mentor of the modern: in modern philosophy, in nineteenth- and twentieth-century Protestant theologies, but also in the realms of art and psychology, he put modernity in a positive light. Tillich was viewed in mid-century as an existentialist, but he was also very much an idealist from the previous century. In the long run Tillich's correlation between revelation and culture and his exposition of theonomies would prove more attractive to Catholics than Barth's encyclopedia of words on the Word. An affinity between Catholicism and Tillich's theology appears in four areas: sacramentality, metaphysics, culture, and mysticism.[18]

In some ways theonomy is similar to the ''sacramental'' essence of Roman Catholicism. Often the Catholic spirit or thought-form (Catholic substance) brings together the human and the divine, admits of degrees of participation, and seeks ministerial cooperation by the finite in the infinite's gracious presence. Tillich's dialectic was not ashamed of finite modes, varieties of ''symbols,'' in which the divine Logos is present in nature, mind, and revelation. ''Grace is really grace only if grace is present.''[19] Moreover, to the shock of many Protestant pastors and academics, he dismissed the pretense that Protestant theology was kept immune from philosophy. Tillich's thought employed philosophy and explained analogy. Philosophy was the expression of culture, the language of each theology. Tillich called his theology ''belief-ful realism,'' and the multiple traditions of Western Christianity focused in Aquinas proceeded from the principle that both creation and God's new creation were real and intelligible.

The God of philosophy and culture is the God of revelation; the Logos in Jesus Christ is the Logos of the multiple structures of the world. Catholicism is a heavily cultural entity. Its drive towards incarnation and universality is nourished by the visual and structural, by art and liturgy. Tillich valued a universal, incarnational, essential dynamic (Catholic substance). Catholicism is always struggling with cultural forms which it imagines to be eternal but which are the creators and bearers of time. Theonomy is a search, a liturgy, not a museum or a mosaic. Tillich was a critic but not a puritan judge of mediation and image. The pages on formative power in *The Protestant Era* offer a theology of forms, transparencies, and critiques of grace which are closer to contemporary Catholic theologians than to Lutheran ones.[20]

Mysticism is faith and grace in the intuitive key. Tillich's interest in art and psychology showed his attraction to the intuitive, the mystical, as did his preference for the Platonic strain in the history of Christianity, his work on Schelling and Boehme, and his European acquaintance with spirituality and monasticism. He had already concluded in 1925: ''All aspects of knowing are essentially conditioned by intuition. . . . Both sacramentalism and mysticism are directed toward the present Unconditioned: sacramentalism through given, concrete forms, and mysticism beyond every form.''[21]

Looking back, it seems that Catholics early on saw their own Tillich. In the auditoriums of Harvard and Chicago, Tillich was a liberal Protestant, an existentialist, a German celebrity of the magisterium of the university, the systematician synthesizing German metaphysics of 1900, existentialisms of 1930, and American psychology of 1950. If for some Protestants his system drew Jesus' life and message into a psychological ontology, for Catholics Tillich pointed to ecumenical, wider cultural directions, to an appreciation of the self and of history. He helped American Catholic theologians understand their own ethos, one not so much of statues as of sacramentality, not one of rubrics but of theonomy. They were already looking beyond Karl Adam and Romano Guardini toward Hans Urs von Balthasar and Karl Rahner, toward more modern forms which could stimulate theology without extinguishing revelation. One could expand Christianity beyond Neo-Scholasticism into the world of Rudolf Otto or of C. G. Jung. Theonomy disclosed new being in wider circles, in wider modes of revelation, even in a latent Church. Correlation was never viewed as revelation's answer to existential questions or as the derivation of revelation from existence; rather, correlation sought out the thought-forms (which are always within issues and problems) of a cultural era in which a distinct but never separate revelation could be expressed. Despite a Teutonic vagueness, one could see in Tillich's final pages the reign of God struggling to find its pulse and form in history; these ideas resembled the themes of Teilhard de Chardin, whose books were just being published in these years after his death in 1955.

If existentialism did not fully describe Tillich's *Systematic Theology*, in *Paul Tillich in Catholic Thought* and in the decades after Vatican II Catholics turned to the Tillich on either side of a Christological existentialism: to the Tillich of the history of theology, of a conversation between Greek and medieval categories, and modern thinkers; and to a Tillich of mystical and sacramental principles like theonomy and symbol, to a theologian whose origin in Schelling's cosmic processes of divine presence was still largely unknown to Americans but which was reappearing in the *Systematic Theology*. The ecumenical influence of Tillich became broader than his reputation in the 1950s suggested. The thinker of the *System der Wissenschaften* with its panorama of modes of *Geist* would appear beyond the efforts of the existentialist therapies, and his theology would draw upon the history of metaphysics and idealist beginnings. He brought more and more into his system the philosophy of his youth and a Christian interest beyond a general philosophy of religion; a theology of Spirit and history along with its foundations in God and being, revelation and culture would sustain an ecumenical influence.[22]

Tillich engagingly introduced English-speaking Catholicism to aspects and possibilities of a theology of existence and ambiguity, polarity and process. The ecumenical conversation begun in the 1950s between two theologies became more than a gingerly meeting between existentialist and Neo-Scholastic theologies. Rather it became three encounters: between Reformation and baroque cultural theologies, between Protestant and Catholic forms of idealism and romanticism, and between Augustinian and Thomistic interpretations of reason and mysticism. Tillich knew about earlier dialogues between Catholic professors and modern philosophers, about figures like J. M. Sailer in Bavaria and J. S. Drey in Tübingen, and about the later theologians like Herman Schell caught between kaiser and pope.[23] How interesting that the subject of his two dissertations, Schelling, would be an exceptional source for Catholic theologians in the nineteenth century, would, through Yves Congar influence the ecclesiology of Vatican II, and then, after 1960, would be the subject of studies by Xavier Tilliette, Walter Kasper, Klaus Hemmerle, Emilio Brito, and Marc Maesschalck.

Tillich and Przywara

The dialogue between Tillich and Catholic Theology began in the youth of Tillich's career. In the years after the publication of these early essays on Tillich, unplanned circumstances of research and life unpredictably led me more than once to a lesser-known thinker who had appeared in *Paul Tillich in Catholic Thought:* Erich Przywara.

When I was collecting essays for *Paul Tillich in Catholic Thought*, I came across only one essay written by a European Catholic. A Jesuit with a curious name had contributed in 1959 to Walter Leibrecht's volume, *Religion and Culture, Essays in Honor of Paul Tillich.*[24] In the early 1960s in America his few pages were little noted, but today they strike the reader as particularly original. Noting Tillich's roots in Schelling, Baader, and Boehme, Erich Przywara's appreciation of Tillich stood apart from American and British concerns with analogy or existentialism. Tillich, he said, was developing a Christian grammar: its root terms were *kerygma, mysterium, kairos,* and *oikonomia*. This grammar "culminates in the *kairos* around which his whole thought moves."[25] Przywara discussed briefly root terms in the New Testament, in theologians of the early Church, and in Luther. He saw the worlds of idealist philosophy, theosophy, and Russian mysticism influencing Tillich's conviction that "the Holy must be understood as an intrusion through the realm of meaning which is its abyss and its ground." Both theism and atheism are rooted in the divine ground and abyss. But Przywara concluded that the fourth root-term of *oikonomia*—the activities of the Trinity on earth within the freely directed eschatology of the history of graced humanity—can respond to some of the abstractions in Tillich's thought. The truly godly God is not caught in a Manichean struggle nor is God's Logos and prophet Jesus trapped in an uncertain verticality. "For this reason Catholicism has this Christian root-term *oikonomia* as its most fundamental term . . . and sees the dialectical character and double significance of the *kairos* as rooted in the final Christian root-term *oikonomia* and represented in the ordering of the Church through ecclesiastical office-holders."[26]

Who was Erich Przywara? A mysterious figure of some romantic Slavic origin? A refugee from Hitler or Stalin? In the Munich bookstores and university libraries, I came across in 1964 volumes from a new edition of his works. Since World War I, he had carried on a wide-ranging conversation with the issues of modern philosophy and culture; he seemed a speculative Romano Guardini. Erich Przywara was born in 1889 in Kattowitz, Silesia, not far from Breslau, where Tillich would receive his doctorate in philosophy. He entered the Jesuits in 1908 and studied theology in Valkenburg until his ordination to the priesthood in 1921. After four years as prefect of music at the Jesuit *Gymnasium* in Austria, Stella Matutina, he was from 1922 to 1941 on the staff of the Jesuit periodical of culture and theology, *Stimmen der Zeit.* For ten years after 1941 he gave lectures to various circles; after 1951 he lived near Murnau and became increasingly ill. In 1963 he wrote me briefly mentioning his other essays on Tillich; I asked Karl Rahner about him in 1965, and he responded sadly that he was still alive but was ill and mentally not in contact with the world around him. He died in 1972 at the age of 83.

Like Tillich, Przywara saw new opportunities for Christianity after the great war. Among his eight hundred publications are a *Religionsbegründung* from 1923 (in dialogue with Max Scheler), books on Kierkegaard, Kant, and Augustine, a philosophy of religion from 1929, and the influential study on analogy of 1931. He composed books on God and the cross, on the old and new covenants, and on Ignatian spirituality and the Gospel according to John. Since culture and philosophy should not exist without prayer, contemplation, and worship, there were popular books on the church year, conversion, Eucharist, and work. A book on "the Christian pathway" appeared in 1925, and one on "true heroism" in the fateful year 1936.

Przywara rejected cultural isolationism and pursued dialogue with truth wherever it could be found. Pioneering the Catholic dialogue with philosophy, Protestantism, and literature, he wrote in conversation with Aquinas, Ignatius, Luther, Kant, and Newman, but he also explained and critiqued the lectures and writings of Husserl, Heidegger, Buber, and Barth. Both he and Tillich were knowledgeable in the history of theology, and both were engaged in an appreciation and critique of modern philosophy from Schelling to Heidegger. Systematicians by instinct, they lived on the boundary lines of faith and culture.

While Przywara was studying the later works of Schelling and responding to the work of Max Scheler, he was also introducing Reformation themes into Catholic theology. Composing studies on justification and the *theologia crucis*, he became friends with Karl Barth at the universities of Bonn and Münster from 1927 to 1929 and led the Reformed theologian to a deeper interest in the theme of Church. Przywara wrote in 1923: "The period of the history of religions and of religious psychology is dying," and the school of Barth and Gogarten may be effecting "a primal, authentic rebirth of Protestantism."[27] The Jesuit saw ecumenical differences as something to be pondered and resolved, for their origins lay in a single principle, which for Catholics was the axiom that grace did not destroy but led nature to its destiny. Barth led Przywara to explore the relationship between the positive anthropology of Catholicism and the cross of Christ, but also to see how ecumenical differences were grounded not so much in church dogma but in the deeper theological mentality of analogy. Long conversations in 1928 explored the transcendence of God. Both men proceeded from the dialectic of God's work and human work, but disagreed over its intensity of realization in liturgy and life (Barth bemoaned how Przywara bubbled over the descriptions of the many presences of God's grace). Przywara had his critics: some found his interpretation of Aquinas too positive an anthropology; others found his appreciation of Barth uncritical.

Perhaps the unravelling of the common front of dialectical theology or a realization that Barth was unyielding in his separation of God from creature led the Jesuit from 1928 to 1930 to review such of Tillich's writings as *Kairos, Zur Geisteslage und Geisteswendung, Protestantismus als Kritik und Gestaltung,* and *Religiöse Verwirklichung.*[28] "Paul Tillich sees himself one with Karl Barth in what one can call the consequent radicalism of the Protestant teaching of single causality . . . a 'prophetic critique,' i.e., a destructive critique on all that presents itself as an absolute representation of God on earth (church, sacrament, etc.). . . . But Tillich emphasizes against Barth something that one might be inclined to call 'Catholic': 'the transcendent being as present . . . is the being of grace.' "[29] Przywara did not object to a Tillichian theology in which Christ crucified, Michelangelo's Last Judgement, or Paul confronting Peter were leitmotifs, for he also found there the importance of a theology of God's presence. This theology, including its "religious socialism," did not exclude dynamic if critical exploration of some harmony between personality and grace, traditional in their sources among great minds but contemporary in their vocabulary and dynamic re-expression.

Several times Tillich and Przywara shared a podium: perhaps their most significant conversation occurred in 1928 at one of the important cultural seminars in Davos, Switzerland. Tillich's advocacy of a theology of grace beyond modern German philosophies of religion and his motif of theonomy drew the Jesuit's sympathy. But to some Protestants like Gerhardt Kuhlmann reporting on the dialogue, Tillich's positive view of the knowing subject's access to God was not "radical Protestantism" but a Thomism in disguise.[30] In his report on the meeting, Przywara said that Tillich was fashioning his theology within a polarity drawn from the thought of Boehme, Baader, and the late Schelling, between differentiated cosmic processes and primal ground. This emphasis leads creation back into God, a move the Jesuit did not accept. Still, this intense divine presence, active in creation, history, and revelation, gives Tillich's thought, at least at first reading, a rather "Catholic" accent. And yet, this theology, because it is rather bound to an ontology of transcendentality and symbol, is in danger of becoming gnostic.[31]

Przywara, like Tillich, viewed Neo-Scholastic Catholicism as stuck in a static mediocrity and mediation. Przywara was not only a pioneer but also a versatile master in the conversation with modern culture. Rising from the anti-modernist condemnations of Pius X, from the condition of being a minority in the Prussian *Reich*, and from the ruins of the world war, German Catholicism was seeking a positive appreciation of science, art, and philosophy. Przywara pondered not only the relationship of contemporary philosophy of religion to past figures but also the voices of the holy and the transcendent in literature. He distinguished modernism (an ideology, or a projection of integralist and ultramontane clericalism) from a critical Catholic exploration of modernity. "There inevitably exists a remarkable correlation between the public face of a particular age (its visible surfaces were expressed in various political and social movements) and its metaphysical core, its invisible spirit. The practical face of an age can be read in the great debates which unfold from day to day. The metaphysical heart discloses itself in the philosophies and theologies which are emerging in this period. The observer and interpreter of the present will not neglect either. For what is decisively important for knowing God also has its particular meaning for the temporal: the invisible is known in the visible."[32] For Przywara, philosophy is itself an approximate theology, the ultimate form of the obediential potency reaching tentatively toward the mystery of the supernatural. Theologies pondering God's activity on earth arrange themselves on a line between Augustine (the desire to know God in a primarily hierarchical cosmos) and Thomas (the respectful service before God in a world whose levels emerge as non-divine being and beings before the mystery of God). The Platonic-Augustinian type emphasizes that God is all, the Aristotelian-Thomistic that the creature is a true nature with its own activity. For Augustine the question about the origin of religion means the participation worked by God in God through love; for Thomas a fabric of actions is woven by spirit and world participating in a higher life. Theology does not end with logic but with a physics and a metaphysics of creation and human persons. The sovereign dignity of human action bursts forth in Aquinas' theological axiom, "grace brings nature to completion." This basic proposition has a dual form, for it implies harmony both in the order of grace and of belief. "Grace does not extinguish nature, faith does not extinguish reason; each becomes a new vital form of nature or reason. The creature appears not as perfect nature in itself but as something which one can designate in an unusual expression as an existing-being-of-grace."[33] Thomas's theology rejoices in active creatures; God is not jealous of their "secondary causality." "Thomas' basic law of the *causae secundae,* the untouchable heritage of classical Catholicism,"[34] was for Przywara "Catholic radicalism"; the fullness of God's being was displayed in creatures' individuality and action.

Przywara refused to choose between God over all and God in all. According to the principle of the *analogia entis,* the proper inner life of God transcends all human ideas and through faith this life corresponds a little to what the teaching about the triune forces of the divine Trinity would communicate. Human nature is full preparedness for God, a capability of receiving the special revelation of God. The creature is a true agent fashioning its own forms, but the measure by which God communicates divine being to the creature is determined by God. Creation and redemption are, as Aquinas showed, processions *ad extra.* "God is not an ultimate, final rhythm of created reality; God is the content and the reality from which all content and all reality exist. Life with God is religion as the ultimate content-giving content of all contents. . . . But God is equally the content and the reality in created contents and forms and realities."[35] The supernatural is not deduced from nature nor is it just an object for faith.

Like Tillich, Przywara returned often to the dialectic of "religion" and "culture." Justin and Tertullian, Tillich and Barth. Was culture the opposite of religion or was religion the power of culture? "The nineteenth century," he wrote, "at its beginning and at its end sees an impasse between autonomous science and culture, and religion. Emerging from the Catholic romanticism there is an ideal of a science and culture which have their immanent ideal modes in religion, in Christianity."[36] The mistake of the modern period is to take one side (the finite) of the dialectic, and to turn self and process into a monistic prison; and then to derive whatever there is of the holy and the divine solely from finite consciousness.

Przywara was never a professor nor a founder of any school, but Karl Rahner and Hans Urs von Balthasar were proud to call themselves his students. Von Balthasar worked with him on the Jesuit journal, *Stimmen der Zeit,* and, as Przywara was becoming almost unknown in the wake of the council, he wrote:

> Erich Przywara's extraordinary theological mission—hardly comparable with any other of this age in depth and breadth—could have been the decisive means of salvation for our Christian thought today. The age took the easier way, not to dialogue with him; but that is not his fault. He had always perceived an opening in the church to the all that is, that opening which the Council has brought. . . . [He was] the greatest spirit I have had the privilege to meet.[37]

When Przywara received the Obersilesian Culture Prize in 1967, Karl Rahner said in the "*Laudatio*": "We, the generation after him, and the coming generations still have important, beneficial lessons to learn from him. The total and true Przywara is yet to come. He stands on a point in the pathway which many in the church must still pass by."[38] Rahner placed Przywara in the company of Teilhard de Chardin.

As we hear one Jesuit praising an older one, it may occur to some that Przywara is not without his similarities to Rahner. An openness to philosophy in the twentieth century, a rich comprehension of the history of theology, a deep understanding of Aquinas along with a creative alternative to Neo-Thomism, a gift for speculation and system joined to a ceaseless involvement in practical issues—these are present in both Jesuit theologians. Tillich also shared many of these same insights. It is surprising that few pages comparing Przywara and Tillich have been written, and that few studies comparing Rahner and Tillich (their similarities could occupy many books) have appeared. As we go forward in the conversation between Tillich and Catholicism, perhaps it is fruitful also to return to the little-known, perhaps little-understood conversation of an earlier period.

Religions and Culture

How does culture draw forth theology? Tillich's insights still speak to us. He remains informative and inspirational not because he resolved how a divine revelation emerges from finite consciousness or because his Christology escaped the rapid decline that enveloped existential theologies in the 1960s, but because his insights into the history of theology, his patterns of understanding religion and Christianity, still open up approaches to culture and philosophy realizing revelation and grace. To illustrate Tillich's lasting presence, we might turn briefly to some of his views written twenty-five to fifty years ago on Protestantism, Roman Catholicism, and the world religions. Their ideas and programs still seem insightful.

Protestantism

Tillich published an essay in 1937 called "Protestantism in the Present World Situation" and this appeared a few years later in *The Protestant Era* as "The End of the Protestant Era?"[39] The piece began by stating that Protestantism is facing a difficult struggle because the previous era, a Protestant era, is either coming to an end or is undergoing fundamental changes. The challenges come from secularism, mass collectivism, and paganism. Will Protestantism in its traditional forms outlast the period marked by the end of early capitalism, by massive centers of urban life and mobile populations, and by superficially beneficent economic and social controls? The Protestant principle stands in contradiction to these tendencies, as it insists upon the majesty of God and the personal responsibility of the individual. But the forms assumed by minister, sermon, and Church are increasingly weak and open to disintegration. Static oppositions to modernity and liberalism (Barthianism and fundamentalism) cannot offer true alternatives. If Catholicism fights against social totalitarianism and personal disintegration with authorities lodged with the papacy and Neo-Thomism, still its sacrifice of freedom and adaptability is likewise not the answer. Interestingly, Tillich finds one new way of "fundamental change" in Protestantism in the direction of sacramentality: "[Protestantism] must obtain a new understanding of symbols and all those things which we have called 'sacred objectivities'. . . . It has to remodel its form of life, its constitution, its rites, and its individual and social ethics."[40] Nevertheless, it should retain resources which lie outside of Catholicism and not accept cleavages between the sacred and the profane or be trapped in tendencies toward superstition or magic. It should ponder how the kingdom of God acts continuously in history rather than in holy institutions. Thus Protestantism will retain its prophetic form, its prophetic protest against the political forces that dehumanize society in the name of some form of collectivity.

The difficulty in his program did not escape Tillich. If Protestantism introduces certain Catholic elements, does it not lose its identity? If not, does it not lose popular appeal? "Hence to say that Protestantism, if it is to maintain itself, must draw certain lessons from the history of Catholicism does not mean that it should learn in the ordinary way of imitation and repetition. It must seek a new foundation if it is to survive at all in its essential aspects."[41] Is there a third way? Tillich imagined it as a prophetic spirit "without ecclesiastical conditions, organizations, and traditions," a force of integration in a disintegrating world. The metamorphoses of Protestant Churches into wider and deeper forces of renewal would imply that the Protestant era has not ended. Protestantism would escape its danger, a replacement of "the abundance of the *complexio oppositorum* by the poverty of sacred emptiness (in this point following Judaism and Islam)."[42]

What impact did this forecast have fifty years ago among church leaders as it anticipated the pastoral problematic of Churches of the word in a society of media and information systems? Decades past these ideas were already focusing not on speculative hermeneutics but on social and pastoral renewal, and today they address Protestant Churches where sacramentality little existed or where it is being rediscovered in the liturgical movement. A new crisis for liberal Protestantism appeared in the 1970s and has not ceased for over two decades to bring decline to the parish life of the mainline Protestant Churches in the United States.[43] Is this a further stage in the challenged era which Tillich described years earlier?

Roman Catholicism

For the first decades of his life Tillich feared and criticized Rome, which he saw as a particularly potent system of religious heteronomy.[44] The *Systematic Theology* had in mind a pre-conciliar Catholicism, but even from that perspective it contained some abrupt and exaggerated negative judments. By 1945, however, Tillich saw positive aspects in the sacramentality of Catholicism and the Catholic principle.[45] "The church as the community of the New Being is the place where the new theonomy is actual. But from there it pours into the whole of man's cultural life."[46]

Tillich was prophetic in locating heteronomy in a monarchical, domineering authority, one which acted without justification and without appeal. ''The basis of a genuine heteronomy is the claim to speak in the name of the ground of being and therefore in an unconditional and ultimate way. A heteronomous authority usually expresses itself in terms of myth and cult because these are the direct and intentional expression of the depth of reason.''[47] Today Catholicism has renewed its liturgical life, expanded its theological horizons, restored the place of the Scripture, learned from Protestant theologians, and pursued some worldwide inculturation. Its all too prominent difficulties, however, lie in the area of ecclesial structure. The decision to accept some broader modes of collegiality beyond the solitary papacy, to employ synods, committees, pastoral councils, and bishops' conferences repeatedly erupts in well-publicized conflicts. These are signs and manifestations of the persistence of heteronomous authority. From a historical point of view this time of difficulty is not so surprising. After four centuries of emphasis upon a centralized, universal authority, the *kairos* of Vatican II has directed the dynamics of the ecclesial community back toward the local Church. This is a shift away from a pyramidical Church into whose pinnacle the Pian popes drew every office and every responsibility. Since ecclesial unity and tradition are to be maintained amid global diversity, it is not surprising that this new direction has not been accomplished in a few decades but has only just begun. In some impositions of church authority there remains an ignorance of history, an organizational rigidity, a fear of process and consultation, and personal neuroses—the prodigal children of heteronomy. Certainly the ongoing struggles between authoritarianism and adult Christian life (part of a laborious shift from the baroque to a participative society) underscore the insightfulness of Tillich's evaluation of Catholicism.[48] Tillich remarked in the midst of the council and not long before his death, ''If through the Second Vatican Council, the Roman Catholic church revives the principle of reformation within itself, the question remains as to how far such a reformation can go. . . . Only the future can show to what degree the principle of reformation will become effective within the Roman church through an interpretation under the guidance of the prophetic Spirit.''[49]

World Religions

During the last years of his life, particularly in a journey to Japan, Tillich experienced worlds beyond European and American Protestantism. His theology had been prepared for this by the figures of Rudolf Otto and Ernst Troeltsch, and his system had already explored wider modes of presence for the ground of being, revelation, and new being.

> What is the Spiritual Community's relation to the manifold religious communities in the history of religion? . . . The concrete occasion for the distinction between the latent and the manifest church comes with the encounter of groups outside the organized churches who show the power of the New Being in an impressive way. . . . In the state of latency there must be actualized elements and elements not actualized. And this is just what characterizes the latent Spiritual Community. There is the Spiritual Presence's impact in faith and love.[50]

Religious groups outside of explicit Christianity are "teleologically related" to the Spiritual Community, "unconsciously driven toward the Christ" even if they reject him in the concrete forms of the Churches. Latent groups can in some ways well represent the Spiritual Community, and they can also be its implicit critics.

In the Bampton lectures for 1961 Tillich focused his attention upon the world religions. Beginning with some motifs from Scripture, he notes that the eschatological judgment of Jesus in Matthew 25 offers a standard of life and salvation which is not religious ritual or dogma but love. Love is "the substance of every moral law." The Gospel according to John locates Christ, certainly the center of this Gospel, in the wider sphere of the Logos, "the universal principle of divine self-manifestation." To human religion Jesus brings adoration "in Spirit and in Truth" (John 4:23). Paul and early theologians dealt with religions dialectically—and Tillich went on to offer a historical tour of Christian theologies of wider grace. Then he located Asian religions in the midst of contemporary social and smaller religious movements. The religious spectrum of a Japan or a Taiwan was not so exotically different from a country in the West: secularism, Marxism, religious indifference, and fundamentalisms were all present. Christianity existed largely in the forms of the West, but they did not necessarily compose a criterion of superiority. What was the future purpose of missionary activity? Protestant liberal theology ("My own teacher, Ernst Troeltsch, asks most radically the question of the standing of Christianity among the world religions"[51]) was struggling with Barthianism, while Catholicism, despite its admirable rejection of fascism and Marxism, lived within but still rejected modernity. In Tillich's view Roman Catholicism was not pursuing a new understanding of Asian religions—a position in which he was mistaken.[52]

Tillich next developed a theological dialogue which on the Christian side centered on the kingdom of God. The differences in religious terminologies and cultural mentalities with the East were significant, but conceptual contrasts did not mean that a dialogue of mutual learning was impossible. Nor did this theologian of the pervasive critique of justification by faith think that basic Christian ideas were fully absent from Buddhism (nor Buddhist ones from Christianity). One must search for manifestations of the Spirit at a deeper level than has been done heretofore and be open to finding the most basic biblical ideas of God's presence in life and history by learning from the East.

An On-going Dialogue

In this century, especially in the key moments of 1925, 1945, and 1965, Catholicism has pursued tentatively and erratically its conversation with modernity. Hesitantly its theology left the Neo-Scholastic and legal melange with which the official Pian Church up to Vatican II expressed itself. That world might be described in words borrowed from Tillich's sketch of religious art in the nineteenth century: "An ideal, but one without a foundation in reality, is set up against an encountered reality which is only beautiful and corrected in terms of its conformity to the ideal in a manner which combines sentimentality and dishonesty . . . the low taste of a culturally empty period."[53] A hesitant Catholic appreciation of modernity—going beyond the Enlightenment, living from its own past sources in idealism and romanticism, retaining its traditions of realism and revelation—sought first not systems and methods but renewal in liturgy and spirituality, expression in literature and transcendental philosophy. By the 1930s Catholic theologians were studying Barth, Brunner, and Tillich. The Catholic dialogue with Tillich is an outstanding example of how and what Catholicism in its openings to modernity learned from liberal Protestantism. Here theology was not, in fact, drawn into the vortices of feared and supposed pantheisms and relativisms, but it found an example of modern approaches and thought-forms.

Tillich could and can be instructive for Catholics throughout the world because he sought to understand and not to banish religion. After World War I, Tillich affirmed that religion flows not from secular history but from God's presence amid human life and fragmentation. Tillich's theology flourished within the university, but his lectures were complemented by culture: by the style and images of psychology and art in the twentieth century. So his theology was never a contentless structure (steel girders framing glass windows), a warehouse of objectless methods. Galleries of culture drew the transcendent into the material and the concrete, and they fashioned theology's applications in preaching and worship. While Catholicism has been learning to critique its array of sacramental forms in light of the event of Christ,

Protestantism is learning to let Reformation theologies do more than condemn human religion. God is not distant and hidden but imma- nent and revealing. The role of individual transcendence and the place of Jesus Christ in a long history of religions remain two great theologi- cal issues of our time.

Do not, however, ambiguous existence, New Being, media of reve- lation, and symbol suffer from the very universality and vagueness which has sustained Tillich's influence in many fields? In the long run, he could explain history to Catholics, critique autonomies, and sug- gest thought-forms, but his theology resulted in a Christianity which was rather austere. The transcendental self was a source of divine reve- lation but the distinctness of God's presence was left vague, and vari- ous revelations were not convincingly distinguished from psyche or history, or centered in Christ. "The revelation of ultimate import is the revelation of the ontological ground of all meaningfulness."[54] The- onomies never escaped the shadow of finitude threatening to turn the limitations of being into sin. Symbol permitted Tillich to affirm a tradi- tional teaching or sacrament without clarifying that form's contact with grace or truth. Despite their limited Neo-Scholastic mentalities, some of the authors in the first volume on Tillich were struck by these theo- logical principles left unresolved in the swirl of self and culture. Out- side of academia, human beings can tolerate in religion only small dosages of abstraction and vagueness.

What is frequently ignored (to the detriment of an ecumenical under- standing of the Catholic mind) is this: Tillich and German Protestant theology often describe in the categories of believing, transcendental knowing, that which Catholic theology pursues, beneath words, in the realm of graced life. Whether in Thomas Aquinas, Teresa of Avila, or Karl Rahner, grace contacts the entire personality, and its basic and essential emergence occurs not first or solely in religious ideas but in an individual life. There salvation invites, redemption happens, and love inspires. Tillich and Rahner pondered various presences of the divine and special presences in Christ: for the Protestant, there was general and special revelation; for the Jesuit, general and special salvation-history. Rahner's topography of circles of implicit divine pres- ence, "a world of grace," was easier to discern in a world of religious forms and simultaneously it was less constrained in verbal and men- tal categories. A brief comparison of Rahner with Tillich points to es- sential differences between liberal Protestantism and post-conciliar Catholicism, differences which Catholic fundamentalists and disillu- sioned Protestants of the left or the right ignore. Catholic theology (apart from some figures prominent in the media), while embracing personal and historical approaches, has not proffered to the worldwide Church a reduction of traditional beliefs. Since Vatican II there has been little if any controversy over dogma: the areas of conflict are ecclesial forms and ethics. "Liberal" in post-conciliar Catholicism means not the demythologization of the supernatural in Christianity but heated discussions over pastoral forms. "Postmodern" for Protestantism means either a more intense form of existential hermeneutics (monuments decorated with literary bouquets) or a nostalgia for a biblical world from the past. For Catholicism the term means a critique of ecclesiastical structures from 1560 to 1960 and an advocacy of trans-European realizations of church life and liturgy. Catholicism is not in fact leaving behind modernity or entering fully postmodernity, but is still emerging from the baroque.

In the months before death ended his long journey in philosophy and theology, Tillich said that he was still learning. Books, articles, and conferences—and particularly this volume—indicate that Catholic theologians are still learning from Tillich. But theology has its historical life and one *kairos* does not last permanently. Having profited greatly from ecumenism, Catholicism and Protestantism are now generally focused, and rightly so, upon their own identities; significant ecumenical dialogue succeeded and came to a halt. Now every Church faces serious, pastoral challenges at both the local and international levels. Catholicism has accepted into its life much of the Reformers' renewal, but, from another point of view, Catholicism is still not much beyond incipient conversations with modernity. It is clear, however, that its journey will not reproduce the history of Protestantism in the past century or two.

Tillich and his Catholic students have been concerned with the Greek, medieval, and modern worlds. Curiously, both the post-conciliar Catholic communion of increasingly varied Churches preoccupied with praxis, and the Protestant theologian whose multi-layered theology lay beyond Schelling, Troeltsch, and Barth, might be called postmodern.

Notes

[1] See P. Collins, *Gustave Weigel, A Pioneer of Reform* (Collegeville, The Liturgical Press 1992) 209ff.

[2] C. W. Kegley and R. Bretall, *The Theology of Paul Tillich* (New York, 1961).

[3] For Weisser's interpretation of the dialogue with Tillich, see his "Paul Tillich: A Roman Catholic Appreciation," *The Christian Advocate* 11 (February 10, 1966) 7ff.

[4] J. Heywood Thomas, *Paul Tillich: An Appraisal* (London, 1964).

[5] *Paul Tillich in Catholic Thought* (Dubuque: The Priory Press, 1964) xxf.

[6] Ibid., xxiii.

[7] Paul Tillich, "An Afterword: Appreciation and Reply," 301ff.

[8] Ibid., 311.

[9] London: Darton, Longman and Todd, 1965.

[10] Paul Tillich, *Ein Lebensbild in Dokumenten, Briefe, Tagebuch-Auszüge, Berichte*, eds. R. Albrecht and M. Hahl (Stuttgart, 1980) 362.

[11] O'Meara and Weisser, *Catholic Thought*, xxi.

[12] Paul Tillich, *Systematic Theology*, vol. 3 (Chicago, 1963) 245.

[13] Paul Tillich, *Systematic Theology*, vol. 1 (Chicago, 1951) 3.

[14] Tillich, *Systematic Theology*, 3:158.

[15] Paul Tillich, *The Interpretation of History* (New York, 1936) 66.

[16] *Summa theologiae*, 1.22.3.

[17] Karl Barth, *Church Dogmatics* 1/2 (Edinburgh, 1956) 17ff.

[18] See T. O'Meara, "Tillich and the Catholic Substance," in *The Thought of Paul Tillich* (San Francisco, 1985) 290ff.

[19] Paul Tillich, *Political Expectation* (New York: Harper and Row, 1971) 30.

[20] Paul Tillich, *The Protestant Era* (Chicago, 1948) 206ff.

[21] Paul Tillich, "Religionsphilosophie," in M. Dessoir, ed., *Die Philosophie in ihren Einzelgebieten* 2 (Berlin, 1925) 771, 812.

[22] See J. Richard, "Théologie et philosophie dans l'évolution de Paul Tillich," *Laval Théologique et Philosophique* 42 (1986) 167ff.

[23] See Paul Tillich, *Christianity and the Encounter of the World Religions* (New York, 1963) 50.

[24] Walter Leibrecht, *Religion and Culture: Essays in Honor of Paul Tillich* (New York, 1959).

[25] Erich Przywara, "Christian Root-Terms: Kerygma, Mysterium, Kairos, Oikonomia," in "O'Meara and Weisser, *Catholic Thought*, 197ff.

[26] Przywara, "Christian Root-Terms" 204.

[27] W. H. Neuser, *Karl Barth in Münster, 1925–1930* (Zürich, 1985) 41ff.

[28] Darmstadt, 1926; Darmstadt, 1929; Berlin, 1929. Sections from these books appeared in *The Protestant Era* and *The Interpretation of History*.

[29] Erich Przywara, "Kairos," *Stimmen der Zeit* 119 (1930) 230.

[30] Gerhardt Kuhlmann, "Radikaler Protestantismus? Antwort an Paul Tillich," *Theologische Blätter* 9 (1925) 225f.

[31] See Erich Przywara, "Protestantische und katholische Ur-Einstellung," *Theologische Blätter* 9 (1925) 226; "Protestantismus: II. Beurteilung vom Standpunkt des

Katholizismus," in *Die Religion in Geschichte und Gegenwart,* 2d ed., (Tübingen, 1930) vol. 4, cols. 1600ff.

32 Erich Przywara, "Tragische Welt?," *Stimmen der Zeit* 111 (1926) 183.

33 Erich Przywara, "Der Grundsatz 'Gratia non destruit, sed supponit et perficit naturam.' Eine ideengeschichtliche Interpretation," *Scholastik* 2 (1942) 183.

34 Erich Przywara, "Katholischer Radikalismus," *Ringen der Gegenwart* 1 (Augsburg, 1929) 82.

35 Erich Przywara, "Zwischen Religion und Kultur," *Weg zu Gott, Ringen der Gegenwart* 1 (Augsburg, 1929) 93.

36 Ibid., 91.

37 H. J. Schultz, ed., *Tendenzen der Theologie im 20, Jahrhundert* (Berlin, 1966) 354. "Hans Urs von Balthasar," *Christliche Philosophie,* 3 (Graz, 1990) 286.

38 Karl Rahner, "Laudatio auf Erich Przywara," *Gnade als Freiheit* (Freiburg, 1968) 272; see H. Fries, "Erich Przywara," *Catholica* 17 (1973) 69ff; K. H. Neufeld, "Vertiefte und gelebte Katholizität. Erich Przywara, 100 Jahre," *Theologie und Philosophie* 65 (1990) 161ff.; a complete bibliography of Przywara's writings has been published by L. Zimny.

39 The later text is slightly altered from the version in the *American Journal of Sociology* 43 (1937) 236ff.

40 Paul Tillich, "The End of the Protestant Era?" in *The Protestant Era,* 222ff.

41 Ibid., 232.

42 Tillich, *Systematic Theology,* 3:170.

43 Along the same lines see Paul Tillich, "Nature and Sacrament," in *The Protestant Era,* 94ff.

44 "I have long been opposed to the most expressly heteronomous religious system, Roman Catholicism. This protest was both Protestant and autonomous. It was never directed, in spite of theological differences, against the dogmatic values or liturgical forms in the Roman Catholic system but rather against Catholicism's heteronomous character with its assertion of a dogmatic authority that is valid even when submission to it is only superficial" (Paul Tillich, *On the Boundary* [New York, 1966] 39).

45 Paul Tillich, "The Permanent Significance of the Catholic Church for Protestantism," *Protestant Digest* 3 (1941) 23ff. In terms of the Catholic substance, Schelling wrote at the end of his *Philosophie der Offenbarung:* "Catholicism must be granted that it has the thing (*Sache*), and still has it; its merit is to have preserved this, the historical connection with Christ. On the other hand, one must say the Roman church has the thing, but not the understanding of it" (*Werke,* 14:322).

46 Tillich, *Systematic Theology,* 3:148.

47 Ibid., 1:84. "During the high Middle Ages a theonomy (Bonaventura) was realized under the preponderance of heteronomous elements (Thomas)" (p. 85).

[48] Ironically, Protestantism has produced recently and unexpectedly a plethora of ecclesiastical heteronomies. These extreme reactionary groups are intent upon politics and Church, and their fundamentalist spirit threatens to diminish and to confuse all Churches. Would Tillich have been surprised at the resurgence of fundamentalisms of all sorts after 1980? Perhaps less so than others.

[49] Tillich, *Systematic Theology* 3:168.

[50] Ibid., 3:243f.

[51] Tillich, *Christianity and the Encounter* 43ff. For Tillich's wide theological perspective in his earlier writings of the 1920s, see J. L. Adams, *Paul Tillich's Philosophy of Culture, Science and Religion* (New York, 1970) 261ff. On Tillich's theology of the world religions see the publications of T. Thomas.

[52] Tillich apparently was ignorant of the pioneering efforts by so many European Catholics like Charles de Foucauld, Louis Massignon, Jules Monchanin, Henri Le Saux, Bede Griffiths, and Hugo La Salle to fashion Christian monastic, contemplative, even liturgical forms in Asian forms. Six years after this remark Thomas Merton died at a large meeting of representatives from Asian monasteries considering from diverse experience the same issues Tillich raised in his lectures; see T. O'Meara, "Exploring the Depths. A Theological Tradition in Viewing the World Religions," *In Verantwortung fur den Glauben (Heinrich Fries Festschrift)* (Freiburg, 1992) 375ff.

Catholic theology and life begin with grace as the free presence of God in an individual self. Teaching, Church, and liturgy serve as incarnations of grace but do not exhaust them. Ecumenical dialogue is a conversation not ultimately about theodicies or ethics but about similar ways in which people have experienced the triad of grace, sin, and personality. In Aquinas's theology the "new law" is ultimately the presence of the Holy Spirit in an individual life and "secondarily" teachings and sacraments (*Summa theologiae*, 1-2.106.1). All this helps to explain the Catholic tradition since the exploration of the Americas that grace exists outside of Christian belief and baptism.

[53] Tillich, *Systematic Theology* 3:77.

[54] Paul Tillich, "The Philosophy of Religion," *What Is Religion?* (New York, 1969) 58.

Catholic Substance and the
Catholic Church Today

Ronald Modras

By reducing it to one, far-reaching principle, Tillich was credited with making all of Protestantism luminous.[1] The same can be said of his theology of religious symbols with respect to Catholicism. His thinking on the sacramental element in all religion clarifies what it means to be Catholic and arguably has become the most influential aspect of his philosophy of religion. Neither Catholic substance nor the Protestant principle can be correctly understood in isolation from the other, and I shall not attempt to do so here. Considered together, however, these polar categories illuminate what may at first appear as unrelieved chaos in the Roman Catholic Church today. I would also say that they allow us to assign a positive assessment to what may at first look like disintegration in the Catholic Church, if not institutional suicide.

Early Writings

Even though ecclesiology, and certainly not the time-worn issues of Catholic-Protestant *Kontroverstheologie*, was not a central consideration for Tillich, religion was a major concern, particularly its relationship to modern secular culture.[2] Out of that concern Tillich developed the categories he came to call Catholic substance and the Protestant principle. As early as 1923 and throughout his career up to his final lecture, the Catholic-Protestant dialectic, interpreted as principles that transcended not only inter-Christian polemics but Christianity itself, pervaded his thinking.

Tillich's first public presentation of his own creative thought was in 1919 in Berlin, when he spoke "On the Idea of a Theology of Culture." There he first contended that religion is the substance of culture and culture the form of religion.[3] His thesis that religious experience must not be separated from the secular, though original to his Protestant audience, would come to find a congenial hearing from Catholics, since it was rooted in Catholic, especially Ignatian, spirituality. Though it later would be developed along different lines by Karl Rahner, for Tillich, meeting with religious socialists in Weimar Germany, the challenge was to create an alternative to secular autonomy and the heteronomy of traditional religion by way of theonomy. Writing on "Kairos" in 1923, Tillich described theonomy as uniting the absolute and the relative: the demand that everything relative become the vehicle of the absolute and the insight that nothing relative can ever become absolute itself. Here, to my knowledge, is Tillich's earliest expression of the Catholic-Protestant dialectic: "Everything can be a vessel of the unconditional, but nothing can be unconditional itself."[4]

Writing that same year on the "Basic Principles of Religious Socialism," Tillich distinguished between the sacramental attitude that lacks historical consciousness and the rational attitude that is historically critical. He defined the sacramental attitude as a consciousness of the presence of the divine, whether in all of finite creation or in certain objects and actions. Here, he wrote, lie the roots of sacred symbols. In contrast to the sacramental attitude, the rational critical attitude stands in detachment from the immediacy of the holy, rejecting it when irrational and unjust. Combining the sacramental and critical elements in a higher form of both tendencies was the "prophetic attitude" of theonomous religion. Tillich interpreted the prophets' struggle against idolatry and social injustice as a struggle against "sacramental demonries." No absolute claim may be raised on behalf of any symbol, confession, Church, or religion. The affirmation one gives to a symbol or a Church cannot be the same as one gives to God. "Only a religion that includes in its own symbols this negativity toward itself has the power to become a world religion."[5]

Clearly, Tillich did not see the Roman Catholic Church of his day as having that power. In analyzing the religious situation of his day (1926), he acknowledged the attractiveness of Roman Catholicism, even for non-Catholics.[6] It was an appeal arising from its sacramentality. Tillich agreed with Ernst Troeltsch that the Catholic Church was the greatest sacramental institution in all of world history.[7] But its will to power had caused it to lose the vitality and receptiveness which had marked it until the late Middle Ages. The Roman Catholicism of Tillich's day was that of Vatican I, anti-modernist oaths, and the unremitting extension of papal power. It was his allergy not to sacraments but to unlimited authority and hubris that led Tillich to criticize Catholic claims as idolatry, a charge he would level at Lutheran orthodoxy and biblical fundamentalism as well.

Despite the fact that Protestants as well as Catholics could make absolute claims, Tillich linked what he had earlier called the "prophetic attitude" with Protestantism. In 1929 he described Protestantism as a "critical and creative principle," and reproved Counter-Reformation Catholicism for a deeper fault than its authoritarianism.[8] At the basis of its misuse of authority was its misconception of grace. Tillich elaborated the traditional Reformation criticism of the medieval category of created grace. Grace was a presence (*Gegenwart*), not an object (*Gegenstand*), he insisted, and Catholic theology erred in inferring the latter from the former. To objectify grace was to mistake it as something tangible and fixed. Grace became identified with the Church and entrusted to its administrators, so that any prophetic criticism of the Church's existential reality was rendered virtually impossible.

Here too, characteristically dialectical, Tillich went beyond the traditional controversies. Grace, he acknowledged, can be "intuitively perceived." But as a manifestation of transcendent reality, grace is incomprehensible, actual but not objective. Though not an object in itself, grace is in objects as their transcendent meaning. What he had earlier described as theonomy, Tillich here described as a "*gestalt* of grace," in which a finite reality comes to bear a meaning that unconditionally transcends it. Here too Tillich began to develop his concept of the participatory power of religious symbols. More than merely a pointer to the transcendent as something external to it, a *gestalt* of grace is the "Glory of God" becoming visible.

As the Second Vatican Council would do thirty-five years later, Tillich described the Church in sacramental terms, as a *gestalt* of grace. But to this Catholic affirmation he immediately added a Protestant no to any claims to being above criticism or history. One of the consequences of objectifying grace is to raise a form or bearer of grace above change. It renders impossible that what has become a form or bearer of grace can ever be surpassed. Essential change or the possibility of anything essentially new is denied in principle, and history is viewed as without decisive significance. If, on the contrary, grace is not objectified but viewed as realized in the world of changing historical forms, its transcendent meaning remains unchanged, but the forms in which it appears can and do change. The Catholic Church had not yet ceased its objectification of grace, but it was a step, Tillich was sure, Catholics would take. It was unavoidable.

For the same reasons, Tillich was critical of Protestant Churches. By attempting to restrict the dynamics of history and prophetic criticism, Protestant orthodoxy and biblical fundamentalism no less than Catholic claims to *jus divinum* were sinning against the unconditioned nature of grace. The Reformation Churches had rejected the Catholic notion of grace objectified in the sacraments and placed at the disposition of the hierarchy. The one form of grace that Protestantism preserved was Scripture. Despite their origins in prophetic criticism, the Protestant Churches likewise fixed the form of grace by not appreciating the "purely symbolic character of Scripture" and reducing it to pure doctrine.

Tillich saw the secularism of his day as breaking loose from its "old moorings" and offering the Churches a *kairos,* an opportunity and a challenge to recognize new forms of grace without surrender of prophetic criticism. The Protestant Churches would also have to go beyond their traditional forms, particularly if they were to avoid the peril of becoming secularized. Because "grace is the *prius* of criticism," so too is sacramentality or Catholic substance. The separation of the priestly and prophetic traditions in Western Christianity had led to the erosion within Protestant Churches of their sacramental foundations. Protestant criticism had led to the reduction of the sacraments to two, and in some Churches even these had lost their significance. Sacramentality or Catholic substance, however, was the one essential element of every religion and its decline was responsible, in Tillich's opinion, at least in part for the phenomenal growth of secularism in Protestant cultures.[9]

The System

By his own admission, Catholic substance, the concept of symbol as a medium of divine presence, was to be found throughout Tillich's system. "The center of my theological doctrine of knowledge is the concept of symbol," he wrote.[10] There is simply no way to speak of God except in symbols. All religions, even those that are non-theistic, require materialization in symbols, rituals, and doctrines. The unconditional can appear only in concrete, conditioned embodiment. Like everything else in the realm of the human spirit, revelation, religion, and faith depend on language, and their language is that of religious symbols.

One of Tillich's closest links with Roman Catholic theology was his theology of religious symbols. He expressly viewed it as within the tradition of Scholastic thinking regarding the analogy of being. But it put him at odds with both Bultmann and Barth. He agreed with Barth that analogy could not be a basis for natural theology. It was not a method for discovering truths about God. But analogy constituted the only form in which revelation could be expressed. For the same reason he took issue with Bultmann's attempt to demythologize the Scriptures by removing their mythic, symbolic character. Demythologizing the Scriptures, or any other religious statement, could only mean interpreting their symbols, not replacing them. It is the purpose and within the power of religious symbols to express precisely that which will not submit to any other kind of conceptualization.[11]

As readers of Tillich know well, religious symbols for him were more than representative signs. By participating in the power of what they represent, symbols can be stirring, elevating, and integrating, as in the case of the cross for Christians, or destructive and disintegrating, as in the case of the Nazi swastika. Symbols are rooted fast in the essence of the human spirit. Like music and painting they open up levels of reality that otherwise would remain hidden, unlock dimensions of the psyche that would otherwise remain untapped. In answer to the once commonly heard phrase, "only a symbol," he answered: "Nothing less than symbols and myths can bring to expression what concerns us ultimately."[12]

Criticism of Tillich's understanding of religious symbols has focused naturally enough on the question of their reality or truth, in epistemological terms on how it is possible to differentiate between true and false statements in religion if it is all a matter of symbols.[13] Tillich identified the truth of religious symbols with their adequacy and ultimacy. A religious symbol is adequate when it is able to communicate the power and spiritual presence of the divine, when it is able to evoke a genuine religious experience and move people to action. When it ceases to create such a response, the symbol is dead.

Religious symbols are born when a situation is ripe for them and they are able to produce a response in a group. But they die when that situation changes and they are no longer able to open up either the depth dimension of reality or the corresponding level of the human spirit. In illustration of this aspect of his theory, Tillich proposed the symbol of the Virgin Mary, which he regarded as having died for most Protestants.

Tillich's second criterion or test of the truth of religious symbols was their ultimacy. A religious symbol is ultimate when it communicates the divine presence without being raised to absolute validity and significance. In virtue of the Protestant principle, a symbol is true when it expresses not only the ultimate but its own lack of ultimacy.[14]

Tillich distinguished between religion in the broad sense of ultimate concern and religion in the narrow sense of communities, like the

Church, bound together by common religious symbols. Such groups are receivers and bearers of the symbols that mediate revelatory events. They become symbols of the revelatory events that brought them together in the first place and permit new generations of persons to enter into them and to be grasped by the same ultimate concern that grasped the first generation.

In virtue of the universal need for Catholic substance, religious communities constitute themselves through ritual symbols and interpret themselves through doctrinal symbols. They necessarily develop scriptures, dogmas, organization, and institutions. When it was in vogue to disparage all organized religion in the name of personal spirituality, Tillich dismissed the attacks as lacking serious thought. Though one could and should reject certain forms of organization within a religion, one could no more dispense with organization and institutions altogether than one could dispense with symbols. It is precisely a manifestation of our estranged, human condition that we need institutions within religion: sacred times and sacred places, temples and services, structures and authorities.

The fact that our human condition of existential estrangement renders organized religion necessary in no way absolves it from ambiguity. Language requires community, and only within religious communities can religious symbols, the language of religion, remain alive. It is the glory of religious communities that through their symbols they communicate an experience of the divine presence and ultimate meaning. But in receiving and communicating that experience, they also tend to distort it. Tillich shared Calvin's estimation of the human mind as a "perpetual manufacturer of idols." It is the shame of religious communities that they tend to identify their doctrines, rituals, and laws with the ultimate. They tend to see themselves as ultimate and scorn if not persecute those who refuse to be subject to them.

Tillich described this idolatrous tendency, present in all religion, as demonic. Early in his career he began to retrieve the concept of the demonic from biblical mythology, first describing it in terms of creative and destructive irrationality but then making it almost synonymous with idolatry. He reminded us that demons were not simply negations of the divine, that, although they distorted it, they participated in the power of the divine. To elevate that which points to the Unconditioned to being unconditioned itself, to identify the bearer of holiness with the Holy itself, is to render it demonic and as such destructive of the human spirit. Tillich regarded his rehabilitation of the demonic as among his most important and truly original contributions to theology.[15]

Having experienced the rise of Nazism in Germany, Tillich recognized that any national group or community was capable of demonic tendencies. Fascism was a demonic form of nationalism and communism a demonic form of socialism. But because they live by their symbols, religious communities are particularly prone to the demonic identification of their doctrines, rituals, and laws with the absolute, the Christian Church no less than any other. A religious community can be demonic in any of four ways: politically, by trying to destroy other communal structures; personally, by creating conflicts within individuals who do not accept its absolute claims; cognitively, by claiming absolute truth for its dogmas and suppressing other expressions of truth; and aesthetically, by suppressing authentic expressions of art and literature in the name of a religiously consecrated style.[16] As mentioned above, Tillich's favorite examples of demonic religion were Counter-Reformation Catholicism, the absolutes of Protestant orthodoxy, and biblical fundamentalism. The more than a quarter of a century since his death has provided many more examples that would certainly qualify for the attribution.

Given the centrality of Catholic substance in Tillich's fundamental theology, it comes as no surprise to see it appear throughout his system. "God" in the sense of *a* person and therefore *a* being, even though the Supreme Being, is a symbol for the "God beyond God," for the divine Absolute. Put paradoxically, "God is a symbol for God."[17] The God who is *a* person is a symbol for the God who is being itself, who is the power of being that transcends all beings. For Tillich as for Saint Thomas Aquinas, the divine absolute is beyond any categories, including that of being, and Tillich explicitly likened his celebrated description of God as the ground and abyss of being to the *esse ipsum* of the medieval Scholastics.[18]

By attributing the category of symbol to the concept of a Supreme Being, Tillich raised questions about his theism. By attributing the same category to Jesus as the Christ, he raised questions about his Christianity. Tillich radically reinterpreted the incarnation with the language of Catholic substance. Jesus could be called "the *Ursakrament* of Christianity."[19] Jesus "manifests" the coming together of the divine and human in New Being, the healing of estrangement. He is the central and for Tillich superior symbol and bearer of the divine because he not only embodied divine presence but sacrificed himself in order not to become an idol; if Tillich's Jesus is the fundamental symbol of the divine presence for Christians, the cross is the pre-eminent expression of the Protestant principle. If Christianity for Tillich has a superior truth among its symbols, it is the crucified Christ who as a medium of divine presence embodies both Catholic substance and the Protestant principle.[20]

Likewise the Church, by experiencing the divine presence in Jesus and accepting him as the Christ, embodies and mediates that presence. The Church "manifests" the invisible community of grace which Tillich called Spiritual Community. It "represents" the kingdom of God in history. It participates in the reality behind those symbols, even while transcended by it. Unlike the crucified Christ, however, it succumbs to the temptation of idolatry when it raises its scriptures, dogmas, rituals, or structures to the level of ultimacy.

For Christianity no less than any other religion, sacramental form is the one essential element or substance, and Tillich feared that the decrease of sacramental thinking and feeling in the Protestant Churches was endangering their very basis. A disappearance of sacramentalism or Catholic substance would lead to the disappearance of cult and ultimately to the dissolution of the Protestant Churches themselves. Given this concern and emphatic assertion that ritual symbols are utterly requisite for any religion, it is remarkable that Tillich wrote so little on sacraments in particular. What he did write makes it clear that he did not find any particular sacrament or sacraments essential to the Church, simply sacramentality or ritual symbolism in general.

Tillich defined sacrament along the broadest possible lines as any object or event in which the transcendent infinite is perceived as present to the finite. If this larger sense of sacrament is disregarded, the sacraments in the strict, narrower sense lose their meaning. Their holiness is representative of what is essentially possible in everything and every place. Sacraments, therefore, should not be limited to two or seven.[21]

Although in principle anything could become a sacramental bearer of the divine presence, Tillich saw certain elements like water, bread, wine, fire, and oil as having inherent, natural qualities that make them not only adequate to their symbolic function but irreplaceable. Words might appeal to our intellects and move our wills, but the sacramental grasps our unconscious as well as conscious being. The discovery of the unconscious by twentieth-century psychology permits us to realize anew the need to use the powers of nature to mediate the Spirit to the whole person. Neglecting this aspect of religion within Christianity can only lead to its being intellectualized or moralized.

Because nature is ambiguous, a purely natural sacrament is unacceptable for a Christian. Every sacramental reality within Christianity must be related to Jesus as the *Ursakrament* or fundamental symbol of Christianity. He is the source of all the sacraments in the Church, and no Christian sacrament can be understood apart from him. This does not mean that grace is bound to any particular finite form. Jesus did not come to give new ritual laws. For Tillich as for St. Paul, Jesus was the end of ritual law. It follows from the nature of the Church that it receive and mediate the divine presence and that it worship, but the same cannot be said for any particular sacrament or form of worship.

Tillich saw the concrete organization of the sacramental symbols as a matter of tradition. Tradition, not divine institution, constitutes the basis for any individual sacrament. The decisive question is whether they are able to mediate divine, spiritual presence. All sacramental acts must somehow refer to the historical and doctrinal symbols which have emerged within Christianity, but, within those parameters, the Church is free to appropriate new sacramental symbols, so long as they possess the power to mediate spiritual presence. If large numbers of Christians are no longer grasped by certain sacramental acts, no matter how ancient their tradition, one must ask if those acts have lost their sacramental power. No less than cognitive symbols, ritual symbols too can die.[22]

Tillich did not neglect to make recommendations to Protestant Churches. A renaissance of sacramental thinking was not beyond the range of possibility. The one thing needful was a change of the Protestant attitude toward sacramentality. The traditional opposition between word and sacrament was no longer tenable. Protestants could no longer limit their worship to the spoken or written word. The word of God is God's self-communication, and this can occur through actions, gestures, and forms as well as through sounds and syllables.[23]

Anticipating by four decades those who speak today of paradigm shifts in Christianity, Tillich wrote in 1948 of a transformation taking place in Western civilization, requiring a transformation in the Church. The Protestant era was coming to an end.[24] What was to be expected and prepared for was not a return to a Catholic era or the early Church but a "new form of Christianity" not yet named, uniting priestly and prophetic elements, sacramentality with self-critical openness to reform. In 1937 he called it "evangelical Catholicism."[25] In 1965, at what would be the last public expression of his thought, he called it the "Religion of the Concrete Spirit."

As it had so early and often before, the Catholic-Protestant dialectic appeared in Tillich's final lecture on "The Significance of the History of Religions for the Systematic Theologian."[26] The whole history of religion, he declared, was a struggle for the Religion of the Concrete Spirit. The experience of the Holy within the finite was the universal sacramental basis of all religion. Mysticism criticizes sacramental em-

bodiments of the Holy for their inadequacy; the prophetic element criticizes them when they deny justice in the name of holiness.

While all three elements are to be found in every religion, the predominance of one or another creates certain religious types. The Religion of the Concrete Spirit unites the elements into a synthesis. The
Religion of the Concrete Spirit cannot be identified with Christianity
or any other particular religion. Neither does it seek to supplant them
with a single, amalgamated world religion. Rather, it is the transcendent ideal or *telos* of all religion. More than only a futuristic expectation, however, it has appeared in fragmentary ways at various moments
in history, whenever demonic or secularist distortions of religion have
been overcome. Tillich believed his typology shed light on the otherwise seemingly chaotic history of religions.

Assessment

To venture a new Catholic assessment of Tillich poses the same problems for me as for the other essayists in this volume. Anything like
a single Catholic standard for measuring his thought simply does not
exist. Pluralism, even when suppressed as in Tillich's lifetime, survived
withal, and in the years since his death and the close of the Second
Vatican Council has become a salient hallmark of the Catholic Church.
If one judges Tillich with a gauge constructed at the Vatican's Congregation for the Doctrine of the Faith, he can be airily dismissed as
just another critical Protestant. If one selects a widely respected and
immensely influential theologian like Karl Rahner as representing contemporary Catholicism, the verdict is more nuanced and differentiating.

The similarities between Tillich and Rahner have been noted before
and provide too broad a subject to be explored here in any detail. Both
were profoundly influenced by their respective encounters with secularity. In an effort to overcome the dichotomy between orthodoxy and
the Enlightenment, they each attempted to speak to our century about
the sacred present in the profane and each assumed an anthropological starting-point to do so. They shared similar views on the Church
as a sacrament of universal grace. If Rahner did not share Tillich's pho-
bic attitude toward idolatry, his understanding of historicity as a universal attribute of human existence functioned in a manner comparable
to Tillich's Protestant principle. For Rahner, historicity conditions every
aspect of our being and therefore our thinking, our concepts and therefore our dogmas.

But pointing out how much similarity there is between Tillich and

Rahner or any other Catholic theologian, while interesting, would not be as worthwhile an enterprise, I believe, as essaying an assessment, however brief, of contemporary Catholicism from a Tillichian perspective. With his dialectical typology of Catholic substance and the Protestant principle, Tillich more than once analyzed the religious situation of his day, up to his last lecture on the history of religions. That history is surely no more chaotic than the condition of the Roman Catholic Church today.

Shortly after the Second Vatican Council there was reason to fear that the Catholic Church would fragment and fall prey to secularity.[27] Now at a greater distance, we see that secularity is as fragile for Catholics as for anyone else and that heteronomy and the demonic are still the more prevalent temptations confronting institutional Catholicism. Loyalty oaths, prohibitions of dissent, and the silencing of recalcitrant theologians are only some of the measures intended to restore a preconciliar Catholicism now recognized even by ordinary Catholics as blatantly authoritarian and fundamentalist.

It is fundamentalism, not idolatry or Tillich's concept of the demonic, that has come to describe the universally human phenomenon of raising absolute claims for historically conditioned realities. Once limited to characterize anti-modernist Protestants who rejected historical biblical criticism, the term has become broadened to embrace other analogous anti-modernist postures, religious and political. This expansion of the term represents, I believe, a victory for Tillich's insight that idolatry has more to do with attitudes toward authority than with icons. Image-abhorring Muslims, orthodox Jews, and Calvinist Christians can be just as idolatrous as any Catholic, and Catholic champions of papal power and dogmatic orthodoxy can be just as fundamentalist as any Bible-quoting televangelist. They all reject the impact of history upon the human.

It is not Catholic efforts to restore orthodoxy and authority that are striking, however, but the widespread continuing existence and growth of Catholic self-criticism. What Tillich called the prophetic or Protestant principle continues to thrive in the Catholic Church, more, I would submit, than in most other Churches. Throughout North America and Europe, organized groups of clergy, laity, and theologians actively protest a variety of church policies. Lack of fiscal accountability by bishops, the imposition of clerical celibacy, the systematic exclusion of women from positions of decision-making power, the appointment of ideologically conservative bishops estranged from the people they are meant to serve—these are only some of the issues that have provoked calls for reform.

Passive criticism in the Catholic Church is even more remarkable. Masses of Catholics from southern California to Italy and Poland vote for policies and political candidates contrary to the recommendations of their bishops. Despite all manner of recruiting and advertising efforts, seminary enrollment continues to decline steadily, portending massive shortages of priests in the near future. Catholic officialdom lays the blame on materialism and a moral decline in the West, but other western Churches do not experience comparable shortages. Similarly, in contrast to other Churches, there has been a dramatic drop in the financial support by U.S. Catholics of church structures and institutions.

There is perhaps no more stunning indication of a widespread albeit passive critical posture toward tradition in the Catholic Church than the virtual demise of auricular confession. Throughout much of the Catholic world, almost overnight, individual confession of sins to a priest seems to have lost its power as a form of sacramental penance. Tillich spoke of symbols dying. If that is true of confession for most Catholics in Western Europe and North America, the reason, of course, is the popular recourse to regular weekly reception of the Eucharist as a sacrament of reconciliation.

Catholics may reject the traditional form of confession and papal teaching on birth control, but they persist in their attachment to sacramental symbols, especially to the Eucharist. More than anything else, the glue of Catholic substance appears to be keeping critical Catholics within the Catholic Church and participating in the Eucharist. With relatively few exceptions, reform-minded Catholics have not gone over to mainline Protestant Churches. They remain despite their disagreements. In the United States as in Latin America, Catholics who do leave for other Churches tend to join fundamentalist groups which can provide the support of small communities, something that a clerical Church with a clergy shortage simply cannot afford.

The massive explosion of critical thinking in the Catholic Church can be attributed partly, of course, but not solely to the expectations generated by the Second Vatican Council, followed by disappointments caused by the birth control encyclical and subsequent restrictive measures by the Vatican. For educated elites, at least, application of the historical-critical method in theological studies has also had a relativizing impact. But even more widespread and liberating than a new historical consciousness, I believe, is the impact made by the shifting of metaphors with respect to grace.

Tillich criticized the objectification of grace within the Catholic Church as lying at the basis of Catholic authoritarianism: grace was some *thing* entrusted to the authorities and at their disposal. Pre-conciliar, Neo-Scholastic theology categorized sanctifying grace not as a substance but as a quality inhering in the soul, but popular Catholic preaching and religious education did reify it with metaphors like infusion. Tillich's criticism was not altogether off the mark. Even before the council, however, Catholic theologians writing on grace (Rahner, de Lubac, et al.) underscored the tradition of seeing the divine spirit itself as uncreated grace. Even more, biblical metaphors like covenant and personal acceptance have resulted in a quiet but critical change of categories. In preaching and religious education alike, grace has generally come to be described in relational terms. As a consequence, sacraments have ceased to be regarded as channels of reified grace and are now seen as personal and communitarian encounters. No longer privileged administrators of sacramental grace, priests have become presiders at communitarian worship and builders of Christian community. If pre-conciliar Catholics once saw the hierarchy as having grace at their disposal, that day is now over.

Writing from a Tillichian perspective such as this, Langdon Gilkey generously described the Catholic Church as perhaps the most viable form of modern Christianity.[28] His justification was the dogged loyalty and attachment of Catholics to the sacramental tradition and life of the Church conjoined with a critical consciousness. The validity of Tillich's dialectic continues to win converts among Catholics exposed to it. But even for those who are not, the experience of heteronomy in their Church, less subtle than ever, yields unintended critical reactions. The 1968 birth control encyclical resulted in more Catholics approving artificial contraception than before. Similarly, attempts to restrict critical thinking in the Catholic Church have done more to promote it than has any number of liberal theologians.

What conservatives may regard as virtual schism, Tillich would have seen as an unavoidable, *kairotic* tension in a Church holding on to Catholic substance while learning to embrace the Protestant principle. It should not be surprising that Roman Catholics can learn some truth about their Church from an outsider like Tillich. It is a commonplace that ours is a Church in transition, and Jesus said something about a seed dying before it can bring forth new life. If, as I believe, the abiding presence of the Protestant principle in the Catholic Church is something to celebrate, we have no one more than the institutional authorities to thank for it.

Notes

[1] Gustave Weigel, "Contemporaneous Protestantism and Paul Tillich," *Theological Studies* 11 (1950) 185–87.

[2] For an analysis of Tillich's ecclesiology, see Ronald Modras, *Paul Tillich's Theology of the Church: A Catholic Appraisal* (Detroit: Wayne State University, 1976).

[3] Wilhelm and Marion Pauck, *Paul Tillich: His Life and Thought* (New York: Harper and Row, 1976) 1:64–65.

[4] Paul Tillich, *The Protestant Era* (Chicago: University of Chicago, 1948) 47.

[5] Paul Tillich, *Political Expectations* (New York: Harper and Row, 1971) 58, 65, 73.

[6] Paul Tillich, *The Religious Situation* (New York: Meridian, 1956) 184.

[7] Paul Tillich, *A History of Christian Thought*, ed. Carl E. Braaten (New York: Harper and Row, 1968) 154.

[8] Tillich, *Political Expectations*, 10–39.

[9] Tillich, *The Protestant Era*, 94–112.

[10] Paul Tillich, "Reply to Interpretation and Criticism," in *The Theology of Paul Tillich*, eds. Charles W. Kegley and Robert W. Bretall (New York: Macmillan, 1952) 333.

[11] Paul Tillich, *Systematic Theology* (Chicago: University of Chicago, 1951–63) 3:128–41.

[12] Paul Tillich, *Gesammelte Werke*, ed. Renate Albrecht (Stuttgart: Evangelisches Verlagswerk, 1959–74) 8:148.

[13] The problems raised by the peculiarities of religious language have only begun to be acknowledged by the Catholic Church's teaching office. In its 1973 declaration, "Mysterium Ecclesiae," the Vatican's Congregation for the Doctrine of the Faith conceded that defined dogmas could be incomplete and historically conditioned, but not errors. Without denying the truth in defined dogmas, Karl Rahner pointed out appropriately that it is not clear where an imperfect, historically conditioned formulation ends and an error begins. Nor has the magisterium made clear just what constitutes an "error" in dogmatic statements. See Karl Rahner, "Mysterium Ecclesiae," in *Theological Investigations* (New York: Crossroad, 1981) 17:139–55.

[14] Paul Tillich, *Dynamics of Faith* (New York: Harper and Row, 1957) 96–97.

[15] See Werner Schüssler in Michel Despland, Jean-Claud Petit, and Jean Richard, *Religion et Culture* (Quebec: Laval University, 1987) 160. Also Pauck, *Paul Tillich* 1:108.

[16] Tillich, *Systematic Theology* 3:105–6.

[17] Tillich, *Dynamics of Faith*, 46.

[18] Tillich, *History of Christian Thought*, 189.

[19] Tillich, *Gesammelte Werke* 3:158; *Protestant Era*, 102, 109.

20 Tillich, *Systematic Theology* 1:136; *Dynamics of Faith,* 98; *Theology of Culture,* 67. See also the essay by John C. Dwyer in this volume.

21 Tillich, *Protestant Era,* 108, 111.

22 Tillich, *Systematic Theology* 3:123–24, 189.

23 Tillich, *Protestant Era,* 111–12, 218.

24 Ibid., xviii, 220. *Gesammelte Werke* 7:157–58.

25 Tillich, *Gesammelte Werke* 7:157.

26 Paul Tillich, *The Future of Religions,* ed. Jerald C. Brauer (New York: Harper and Row, 1966) 80–94.

27 Langdon Gilkey, *Catholicism Confronts Modernity, A Protestant View* (New York: Seabury, 1975).

28 Ibid., 15. See also *Gilkey on Tillich* (New York: Crossroad, 1990) 22.

'Catholic Substance' Revisited: Reversals of Expectations in Tillich's Doctrine of God*

Julia A. Lamm

In his afterword to the predecessor of this volume, Paul Tillich summarized his general impression of all the chapters: "A large part of the criticisms are an expression of the basic differences between the Roman Catholic and the Protestant understanding of Christianity."[1] To this I would add that not only the criticisms but also the commendations were rooted in the context of that fundamental division of Catholic and Protestant. This was a perfectly natural and valid response at that time. Historically, it reflected the enthusiastic yet still cautious attitude of the emerging ecumenical movement. Tillich was necessarily of immense importance to Catholic ecumenists because, as an eminent Protestant theologian, he expressed appreciation for the religious depth and ontological insight of Catholicism.[2] Theologically, many of his Catholic admirers perceived him as remaining undeniably Protestant in his preference for subjectivity, autonomy, and symbol (as opposed to objectivity, authority, and analogy).[3] This assumption of the fundamental division between Catholic and Protestant reflected Tillich's own distinction between what he called 'Protestant principle' and 'Catholic substance'. He argued that these need to be held together in dialectical tension; nevertheless, the tension remained, a tension between polar opposites. In labeling two key principles of his theology "Protestant" and "Catholic," he thus opened the possibility for genuine discussion and, at the very same time, ran the risk of further entrenching those presumed irreconcilable differences.

When it comes to Tillich's theology, the temptation for Catholic thought is to pursue that family of themes intended by the label 'Catho-

* I am grateful to my colleagues John F. Haught, William C. McFadden, S.J., and Alan C. Mitchell, S.J. for their critical readings of this paper.

lic substance': ontology, mysticism, immediate awareness, culture, etc. Indeed, it is inevitable that this approach be taken. When done responsibly, it has shown itself to be illuminating. It can also, however, be somewhat self-serving. As Catholics, we can revel in the value that Tillich recognizes in us, but we can also bristle with an edge of defensiveness when he seems to criticize us. A full and honest appraisal of Tillich's significance for Catholic thought must extend beyond a self-congratulatory focus on 'Catholic substance' and must view it as it was intended, in dialectical relation with 'Protestant principle'. Anything less would fail to meet what Tillich identifies as the main criterion of theology, namely "its ability to preserve the absolute tension between the conditional and the unconditional."[4]

This appraisal requires a threefold agenda: (1) exploring anew the full breadth of what is included under 'Catholic substance', even though what we discover may not fit comfortably with our own self-understanding; (2) understanding Tillich's 'Protestant principle' not as something foreign to Catholic thought and spirituality (thus to be at best tolerated) but as integral to it; (3) relinquishing the labels "Catholic" and "Protestant" and seeking new ways, ones more meaningful to our present situation, of expressing Tillich's very profound insight into two basic religious impulses. This last task I take to be a thoroughly Tillichian move. The symbolic power of the terms 'Catholic substance' and 'Protestant principle', however effective thirty years ago, no longer holds the same force.[5] Yet what Tillich intended by those terms remains significant and is better captured by the terms 'ontological commitment' and 'prophetic criticism', respectively.[6]

Agreeing wholeheartedly as I do with Tillich's claim that "theology is first of all doctrine of God,"[7] I shall focus my attention on that key doctrine. Thirty years ago there was a "should" attached to the significance of Tillich for Catholic thought. Catholic theologians "should" be intrigued by his doctrine of God for two primary reasons: its historical roots marked a retrieval of a vital strain of the Catholic tradition that had been relegated to the underside; its constructive claims offered exciting new possibilities for pursuing ontology in a self-consciously "modern" way. This "should" remains the case today, although the imperative is all the greater because so many leading Catholic theologians have been profoundly influenced by Tillich, not to mention the fact that his writings have become standard in undergraduate courses in Catholic theology departments. In order to understand ourselves, we must understand Tillich. This means that so many of the formerly familiar categories no longer hold. Thinkers are no longer to be interpreted in terms of religious denomination and the accompanying

stereotypes but in terms of various religious, theological, and philosophical impulses—impulses which can combine in unique and sometimes unpredictable ways. Boundaries are therefore much less clear,
but the new "plurality and ambiguity"[8] can open up other possible
ways of understanding God, thereby reminding Catholic thought that
it is not a monolithic thing and that it stands indebted to what it does
not necessarily recognize as its own.

Ontological Commitment

Examined in terms of the full breadth of what he intends by the term
'Catholic substance', Tillich's doctrine of God may not be as familiar
to or affirming of Catholic thought as it would first appear. What is
familiar is its Platonic undertones, even though the Platonic metaphysics is translated into a "dynamic ontology."[9] Two crucial elements,
however, are much less familiar, sometimes to the point of seeming
utterly foreign. First, although he does in fact retrieve the Augustinian-
Franciscan tradition, that retrieval is not direct but is necessarily filtered
through German Idealism and Romanticism; it is post-Kantian and
cannot be understood otherwise. Second, Tillich's retrieval of this
tradition includes more than formerly neglected parts of the Catholic
intellectual heritage (e.g., Bonaventure, Eckhart, Cusanus); indeed it
is expansive enough to include figures in a wider strain of the Judeo-
Christian tradition (e.g., Spinoza, Schleiermacher) whose systems of
thought are often considered to be antithetical to Catholic thought.
The common denominator is the underlying ontological commitment.
By 'ontological commitment' I mean the fundamental confidence in
the interrelatedness, comprehensibility, and final unity of the conditionally real because of its grounding in the unconditionally real.

Three characteristics in particular are usually culled from what Tillich means by 'Catholic substance' in order to illustrate the deep affinities it has with Catholic thought: a sacramental world view, the
immediate awareness of God, and a Trinitarian ontology. Since these
three points of affinity have been carefully and eloquently described
elsewhere,[10] I shall here offer a brief summary which assumes a basic
familiarity with the main components of Tillich's theology. I agree that
the affinities are profound, yet I want to make the next dialectical move
and respond to that yes with a no—or perhaps more accurately, with
a "yes, but."

One defining characteristic of Tillich's 'Catholic substance' is its
sacramental world view. Because the divine transcendence is defined in
terms of immanence, God is immediately present in and through the

finite. Everything finite, therefore, because it participates in the divine, has the potential to be a sacrament, a bearer of the holy. Theologically, this religious world view is articulated in terms of the metaphysical principles of exemplarism and expressionism for Bonaventure, the principle of analogy for Aquinas, and the principle of the coincidence of opposites for Nicholas of Cusa. For Tillich, who is especially attracted to Cusanus, it forms the basis for his theory of symbolism. Because there is an essential unity of subject and object in Being-itself, finite being incessantly points beyond itself to other finite realities and ultimately to the divine.[11]

This leads to a second characteristic, namely an emphasis on the *immediate awareness* of God. In virtually all his references to Bonaventure and the other early Franciscans, Tillich focuses on this issue: ''Behind their endeavors stood the mystical-Augustinian principle of the immediate awareness of 'being-itself'.''[12] This immediate awareness is the precondition for the possibility of any other form of knowledge. It is in fact this insight that Tillich takes as the departure point for his own ontological approach to God, what he calls the ''Augustinian solution.'' This approach begins with a turn to the subject as the ''locus of the coincidence of the finite and the infinite.''[13] For Augustine and the early Franciscans, knowledge of God is correlated with knowledge of self. Only by turning inward and penetrating beyond the cognitive to other modes of awareness that precede and inform reason (affections, habits, memories, values, desires, moods) can new dimensions of reality be opened up; only then can we be led further and further in our knowledge and love of God. For Tillich, too, awareness of God begins with an awareness of finitude, not through detached observation of the world but as experienced immediately and existentially, from the inside.

A third characteristic of 'Catholic substance' is the *ontology of love*[14] which undergirds Tillich's doctrine of God, and hence his whole theological system. This necessarily becomes expressed in Trinitarian symbols: God as the living God can only be conceptualized as dynamic *Trinity*; because all being participates immediately in Being-itself, it too is triadic in nature. To be living means to be in essential relation with self and with other. All being, all power, all life seeks to go out of itself and to return to itself, reuniting what has become estranged. Although his lack of references would suggest otherwise, some of Tillich's most interesting affinities with Bonaventure, Eckhart, and Cusanus are to be found in his reflections on the divine love and the Trinity. Unlike his Protestant predecessor Schleiermacher, whose ambivalence about the doctrine of the Trinity is reflected in the fact that it is not integrated into his system but for all practical purposes appended to it, Tillich gives it ontological priority.

As these three characteristics indicate, Tillich has good reason for labeling his basic ontological commitment 'Catholic substance', since he does draw heavily from various strains of the Catholic tradition. It would be a grave mistake, however, to presume that his sources are somehow limited to Catholic thought, since in fact his inspiration is drawn from a much broader tradition of which Catholicism is but one part. In order therefore to remain meaningful, 'Catholic substance' must be more broadly construed so as to reflect accurately Tillich's definition of it as "the concrete embodiment of the Spiritual Presence."[15] This means, for instance, that Catholic thought has much to learn from the oft-maligned or neglected Spinoza, whom Tillich regards as a central figure in the ontological tradition. In Spinoza, as in the Franciscans, is found the "all-pervading presence of the divine,"[16] an emphasis on immediate intuition, the mystical tendency of uniting knowledge and love as well as interpreting the self in terms of the One, and finally the conviction that all reality is interrelated and ultimately knowable. Of course, there are fundamental differences. The invitation is not to obscure these differences but to reconsider basic assumptions and to pursue fresh interpretations.

The more fundamental argument, however, is not that the periphery of 'Catholic substance' must be expanded so as to be more inclusive; it is, rather, that the ontological commitment must be made philosophically intelligible in a post-Kantian world. That Tillich's approach to the question of God is post-Kantian is evidenced by the fact that his own version of the Augustinian solution is what he calls a 'self-transcending realism'.[17] This 'self-transcending realism' has certain affinities with the 'mystical realism'[18] of the early Franciscans in that each is committed to *both* the conditionally real *and* the unconditionally real.[19] There is, however, a qualitative difference between these two forms of realism, a difference that becomes apparent when Tillich's 'self-transcending realism' is recognized as being irretractably rooted in German Idealism and Romanticism.[20] Insofar as this is true, his 'Catholic substance' introduces ambiguities for Catholic thought. First, Tillich's *dynamic ontology* is a development of the organic monism of Herder, Schelling, and Schleiermacher. While this dynamic ontology has certain affinities with the medieval sacramental world view, it also replaces it. Second, Tillich's *ontological awareness* (the 'ecstatic' or 'self-transcendent idea of God') is virtually identical to Schleiermacher's 'feeling of absolute dependence'. While this ontological awareness has certain affinities with the 'immediate awareness' of the

Franciscans, its closer ties to Schleiermacher suggest a rift from Catholic thought. Finally, Tillich's *Trinitarian ontology* introduces ambiguities for Catholic thought not only because it is influenced by Böhme and Schelling, but also because it addresses the dark and hidden aspect of the divine and because it rejects the dominant Trinitarian model in Latin Christianity.

Tillich interprets Kant's philosophy as an unremitting expression of the 'principle of distance'; translated religiously, it is an expression of the 'Protestant principle'. In his insistence that we are bound by our finitude and by the inability of our reason to break through that finitude to something infinite, Kant offers a profound analysis of the human condition.[21] Taken alone, however, it is inadequate in that it becomes yet another formulation of a mechanistic and dualistic world view. There emerges an unbreachable gap between subject and object, between phenomenon and noumenon. For Tillich, the sober realization that our knowledge is inescapably dependent on the structures of our experience, and that therefore one must always begin with an analysis of the subject, need not necessarily lead to the inability to explain "how knowledge can grasp reality and not only appearance."[22] What is needed is a viable ontology—a dynamic ontology—that does not fall subject to Kant's dismissal of metaphysics.[23]

Following Herder, Schelling, and Schleiermacher, Tillich goes beyond the critical philosophy of Kant by repositioning it in a non-dualistic world view. The inspiration here is Spinoza, but the result is neo-Spinozism—that is, Spinoza transformed through the philosophical and scientific conversations of late eighteenth-century Germany. For example, inspired by recent discoveries in chemistry and biology, Herder translated Spinoza's monism from a relatively static, structured universe to a dynamic system of organic powers.[24] Spinoza's "substance" [God] thus becomes described as the infinite "substantial force." One result of this fundamental shift is a different understanding of causality, relationality, and individuality. For Herder, everything is a presentation of power, the result of forces that combine and cohere in a certain place and time, yielding a unique microcosm of the whole. Accordingly, God is understood as the infinite and absolute force, the precondition and source of all finite forces. The transcendence of God is maintained, but it is radically redefined in terms of immanence. Finite being, understood in terms of force, is actively and continually dependent on God, not in some abstract or formal way, but immediately and existentially. These same themes appear in Tillich's dynamic ontology. Very briefly stated, although Tillich retains the terminology of 'being', for him 'being' is always interpreted as power, and consequently relations are to be understood as internal and essential, not as accidental;[25] although Tillich appeals to a classical formulation of God as Being-itself, for him God is always the living God, by which he means the *power* of Being-itself.

Tillich is attracted to the neo-Spinozist world view for many of the same reasons he is attracted to the sacramental world view of the medieval Franciscans. It is an aesthetic world view; it recognizes the essential unity of subject and object in their infinite ground; it describes transcendence in terms of immanence. The two world views, however, do not represent equally viable options for Tillich. Nor is it a matter of simply exchanging one metaphor for another. The dynamic ontology of Tillich, influenced by the organic monism of neo-Spinozism, represents a significantly "changed vision of reality."[26] This changed vision is illustrated by the fact that transcendence, immanence, and the relation between them are significantly re-conceptualized. In Tillich's dynamic ontology, spatial metaphors are replaced by metaphors of power, movement, relatedness, and intensity; hence 'level' (which suggests domination) becomes 'dimension', 'degree', or 'state'.[27] The divine transcendence becomes defined in terms of a relationship of freedom to the world; our own transcendence is our capacity, not to escape our situation of relatedness in the world, but to discover the ground of our freedom precisely through our immersion into that relatedness.[28] This stands in contrast to the sacramental world view of the medieval Franciscan tradition, which assumes a hierarchical and static view of reality that—because it contradicts modern science, reinforces anthropological dualisms, and encourages theological supranaturalism—Tillich insists is no longer acceptable. Because the medieval sacramental world view interprets transcendence spatially, its religious impulse is an ascetic one that seeks to leave behind the material world. It thus winds up negating its own defining characteristic—the mediated immediacy of the divine presence. Tillich reminds us, however, that there is no escaping the finite. There can be no relation to the unconditioned apart from our relation to conditioned, finite reality. The organic monism of Herder, Schelling, and Schleiermacher offers a more adequate vision of reality—more adequate scientifically, philosophically, and religiously.

Tillich's dynamic ontology is the presupposition of his 'ontological reason' (through which we know finite reality)[29] and 'ecstatic' or 'self-transcending reason' (the organ through which we "know" God). Here Tillich understands his own project to be the same as Schleiermacher's—a retrieval of the notion of immediate awareness, but as filtered necessarily through the principle of distance imposed by Kant. The two types of reason coincide: they cannot be separated, nor can they be identified. This is the key to Schleiermacher's and Tillich's response to Kant. In relation to finite existence the argument goes as follows. If subject and object are intrinsically related, if there is mutual participation, then reality can be 'grasped' and 'shaped'.[30] The emphasis in the expression 'to grasp' is on the objective side of reality and our relation of receptivity to it. Tillich, along with Schleiermacher, espouses a form of realism insofar as he, in no uncertain terms, rejects the attempt of idealism to derive object from subject. Yet it is not simply realism; that is, it is not a naïve realism that assumes reality *is* just as we perceive it to be. It is a 'higher realism' that, although confident that reality can be grasped, also realizes that grasping involves subjectivity; there is no grasping apart from shaping.[31] Our cognitive powers depend not only on the structure of the reality encountered but also on the structure of cognition itself and on how those two structures are related.[32] Hence the emphasis on *self* in Tillich's 'self-transcending realism': we must always begin our quest for understanding with a turn to the subject and an analysis of the structure of experience.

In relation to God, unlike in relation to the conditionally real, we experience utter and immediate receptivity. It is not we who grasp but we who are grasped, grasped absolutely, although always in and through our experience of mutual receptivity with finite existence. The utter receptivity we experience in relation to God is the precondition of the mutual receptivity we experience in relation to the rest of finite existence. The operative principle here is, once again, the coincidence of opposites. The absolute manifests itself always and only in the concrete. Our awareness of God is thus a mediated immediacy: it is the immediate, pre-reflective awareness of the power of Being-itself as the *prius* of the subject-object world; it is "not mediated by inferential processes," although it is mediated through the conditionally real. Ecstatic reason, in other words, does not occur in a discrete moment alongside other moments, because God, the 'Whence' of ecstatic reason, is not an object (or subject) alongside other objects. The immediate awareness of God is therefore not "objective," yet neither is it for that reason untrue or merely subjective.[33] Our whole person, not merely our cognitive functions, is grasped by the immediate presence of God. The impulse is to conceptualize this fundamental experience, to bring it to cognition; yet our conceptualizing is always bound to the finite structures of experience, and therefore all definite ideas of God are uncertain. The immediate existential awareness itself, however, is "unconditionally certain."[34]

With regard to our immediate awareness of God, therefore, Tillich is "thoroughly on the side of Schleiermacher."[35] Although the connection to Catholic thought remains, since Tillich virtually identifies Schleiermacher's 'feeling of absolute dependence' with the 'immediate awareness' of the early Franciscans,[36] it is rendered somewhat tenuous by the fact that he also shows a definite preference for Schleiermacher. The mystical realism of the medieval Franciscans, Tillich says, still sought to escape the finite and still hoped for union with God.[37] For theology in a post-Kantian world, however, not only *can* the unconditional be known through the conditional (as is the case with 'mystical realism'), but it *can only* be known through the finite (hence Schleiermacher's 'higher realism' and Tillich's 'self-transcending realism').[38] Schleiermacher is more acceptable both religiously, in that he maintains the principle of distance, and philosophically, in that he recognizes that we must begin with the self because we can never extricate ourselves from the finite structure of experience. This admittedly allows ambiguity, but if we try in arrogance or fear to deny what is existentially inescapable, we lose our openness to the depth of reason, and the result is heteronomous faith. In Schleiermacher, Tillich concludes, " 'Catholic substance' reappeared under the control of the 'Protestant principle'."[39]

The turn to the subject as the starting point of theology is certainly not foreign to Catholic thought, for it can be argued that just as Rahner's theology is a retrieval of Thomas Aquinas through Kant and Heidegger, so Tillich's is a retrieval of Augustine and Bonaventure through Kant and Schleiermacher. The dilemma for Catholic thought presents itself in the fact that the very issue that is supposed to mark the deepest affinity between it and Tillich's theology—namely, the immediate awareness of God—also aligns Tillich with Schleiermacher, who is often considered to be at odds with Catholicism. Because of Rahner, among others, Catholic theology has grown accustomed to integrating Kant into its system of thought; in the case of Tillich, however, the challenge is to integrate not just Kant but Schleiermacher's response to Kant. Schleiermacher, however, has too often been interpreted as a subjectivist and has been blamed (by Protestants and Catholics alike) for the complacency of liberal Protestant theology. Tillich himself thus becomes suspect of subjectivism. The options for Catholic thought are no longer to avoid this dilemma by assuming that the choice is between objectivism and subjectivism, and therefore by ignoring Tillich's indebtedness to Schleiermacher or rejecting him because of it. The challenge is rather to acknowledge the connections (between 'Catholic substance' and Schleiermacher's ontological commitment) and thus to be willing to reconsider the conventional interpretations; indeed, this has increasingly been the course taken in the past thirty years. Tillich's own recommendation is that "instead of making mutual accusations of objectivism and subjectivism, the Catholic-Protestant dialogue should center around the nature of that experience which I have called 'ultimate concern' or 'self-transcending reason' or 'Spiritual Presence'."[40]

The final point of comparison between Catholic thought and Tillich is the doctrine of the Trinity. Here, perhaps more than with any other current of thought, there seems to be an especially high correlation between the degree of affinity and the force of ambiguity. The Trinity for Tillich is not an afterthought, an appendage to Christology.[41] Not only is it at the heart of his ontology, but he also structures his *Systematic Theology* around it. Tillich's Trinitarian theology could be described as a substantial reinterpretation of the neo-Platonic *exitus* and *reditus* in terms of the coincidence of opposites and in ways that emphasize the dynamic aspect of the divine life. For all these reasons, there are deep affinities with the history of Catholic thought. Yet once again, while he begins with what (from the perspective of Catholicism) is familiar, he moves very quickly into what, if not exactly foreign, is much less familiar.

Like Bonaventure, and in contrast to Aquinas, Tillich's doctrine of the Trinity reaches back through the Pseudo-Dionysius to early Greek Trinitarian theology and thereby rejects the dominant course of Trinitarian thought in Latin Christianity. In his tracing of this backward-moving trajectory, Tillich reveals his preference for conceptualizing Being-itself in terms of power rather than through the substance-oriented symbols of the *personae* of Latin Christianity—symbols that are too static and anthropomorphic, that undermine the significance of internal relations, and that are especially vulnerable to becoming idols. His doctrine of the Trinity is, he thinks, closer to Augustine, who acknowledged "that the statements about the mutual relations of the *personae* are empty"[42] and who represented Latin Christianity before its Trinitarian imagination became too reified after the sixth century.

This backward-moving trajectory has influenced Tillich's Trinitarian thought in three ways. First, Augustine's psychological analogies provide a resource for Tillich in finding language for a dialectical model of the Trinity. For example, Augustine's analogy of the divine life in the relational terms of *amans, amatus, amor* leads Tillich to this description of the movement of the divine life: "Through the separation *within* himself God loves himself. And through separation *from* himself . . . God fulfils his love of himself—primarily because he loves that which is estranged from himself."[43] Second, the appeal to relation-symbolism rather than to substance-symbolism aids Tillich in emphasizing that, because of the fluidity of the imagery, the mind can never stay fixed on any one aspect of the divine but must constantly, in its desire to know and to love, move within the flow of the relations themselves. Third, Augustine's psychological analogies are reflected in Tillich's reluctance to understand the Trinity in terms of person-symbolism, which very easily passes over into gender-symbolism.[44] Tillich formulates his own Trinitarian thought in such a way as to reduce the "predominance of the male element in the symbolization of the divine."[45] It is interesting that on this point his criticism is directed mostly at Protestant orthodoxy and its discomfort, due to its focus on the father-image, in acknowledging that the symbol of God-as-ground points "to the mother-quality of giving birth, carrying, and embracing, and, at the same time, of calling back, resisting independence of the created, and swallowing it."[46] Here Tillich echoes a long and hallowed, albeit neglected, tradition that can be found in Hebrew Scripture, the New Testament, and medieval Catholicism.[47] Tillich does not recommend replacing one gendered metaphor with another; he means rather to point to the limitations of such concrete gendered metaphors and hence to the need to go beyond them.

Tillich's doctrine of the living God, which is necessarily expressed through the symbol of the Trinity, also carries forward that same trajectory he has traced backward through the Pseudo-Dionysius. While this forward-moving aspect of the trajectory retrieves neglected strands of Catholic thought, it also acts to challenge certain assumptions by "shaking the foundations" and extending Catholicism beyond itself. This forward-moving trajectory traces the voluntarist tradition, which rejects the priority given to intellect in the divine life and instead emphasizes the divine will as the more comprehensive term. Once again, we find Tillich rejecting a strand of the tradition that he identifies with Aquinas and Ockham.[48] After tracing this voluntarist tradition back to Augustine ("its first clear appearance"[49]), he carries it forward through a familiar course to the medieval Franciscans, a course that he now expands so as to include Duns Scotus as well as Bonaventure. He also extends the trajectory even further to incorporate the Renaissance humanists, Luther (that Augustinian monk), Böhme, the later Schelling, and eventually Nietzsche. This voluntarist strand, by focusing on the dynamics of will, "emphasized the openness of reality toward the future and . . . made a place for the contingent, the new, the unique, the irrepeatable"[50]—and, one might add, the unpredictable. While he insists that this is not a blind or irrational will, he at the same time thinks it necessary to find language for the dark and hidden side of God.

Tillich's doctrine of the Trinity provides an excellent example of how his doctrine of God is significant for Catholic thought with regard to both the historical task of theology, insofar as he retrieves essential but neglected parts of the tradition, and also the constructive task, insofar as he anticipates Catholic feminist theology in recognizing the danger of applying gendered metaphors to God. Moreover, Tillich's doctrine of God provides an excellent example of how 'Catholic substance' (or, the ontological commitment) must integrate the 'Protestant principle' (or, prophetic criticism), for his Trinitarian monotheism is really what he calls a 'dialectical realism' and is rooted in the *via negativa* of the Pseudo-Dionysius.

Prophetic Criticism

If 'Catholic substance' is not as familiar to Catholic thought as it would first appear, so 'Protestant principle' is not as alien. For what Tillich intends by the term 'Protestant principle' is an articulation of the apophatic tradition, which of course is integral to the history of Catholic thought. In his development of the apophatic strain of his doctrine of God, Tillich once again does a several-fold service for Catholic thought: he retrieves theological and religious undercurrents of the Catholic tradition; he reminds Catholicism of its tendency to dilute the demands of the divine transcendence; he offers other resources and new possibilities for reflection on the experience of the abysmal aspect of the divine. Tillich readily acknowledges the fact that the moment of protest in no way belongs exclusively to Protestantism, and indeed his doctrine of God, as it is developed under the rubric of 'prophetic criticism', defies any sharp distinction implied by his labels 'Catholic substance' and 'Protestant principle'. Religiously speaking, Tillich's 'Protestant principle' is a manifestation of the ancient prophetic tradition; theologically, it is a retrieval of the *via negativa* of the Pseudo-Dionysius; philosophically, it is an observation of the limits of human understanding.

If one follows this line of interpretation, it becomes apparent that the relation between what is Catholic and what Protestant in Tillich becomes very complex and fluid, moving through its own series of affirmations and negations and undermining any attempts at easy classification. The *via negativa* of the Pseudo-Dionysius, which is appropriated by Tillich, also lies at the foundation of Aquinas's analogical approach to language about God,[51] Bonaventure's anagogic mysticism,[52] and Cusanus's coincidence of opposites. For all these thinkers, while religious experience may be rooted in the immediate awareness of the divine presence, reflection on that experience requires the *via negativa*. Affirmations about God are possible because of the divine immanence; negations are required by the divine transcendence. Nevertheless, Tillich's adaptation of the *via negativa* does have a decidedly different emphasis from that of either Bonaventure or Aquinas. In emphasizing the "infinite gap between the finite and the infinite," he does not allow even the hint of an infinitely "continuous approximation."[53] According to Tillich, to say that God is the *ground* of all being (i.e., absolutely immanent) is also to say that God is the *abyss* of all being (i.e., absolutely transcendent).[54] His determination to maintain this tension and to remain true to the implications of God-as-abyss intensifies the negative moment of religious language. Because of the transcendental gap, every symbol, however true and however revealing, must be immediately "annihilated" in order to remain true.[55] Although attracted to the mystical realism of the Franciscan tradition and the learned ignorance of Cusanus, Tillich still suspects that their underlying goal was union with what is unapproachable. So, he tempers Bonaventure with Schleiermacher and Cusanus with Kant.[56] At first glance, this unrelenting proclamation of the principle of distance does seem to be a Protestant corrective to Catholic thought. Upon further examination, however, it reflects an adherence to the more radical demands of the *via negativa*; this could be said to bring Tillich as close to Eckhart as it does to Luther.[57]

Tillich clearly sees himself as, in part, standing in the theological heritage that can be traced through Augustine and the Greek Fathers to the Pseudo-Dionysius and Bonaventure. Yet on two points, despite his frequent references to the early Franciscans, Tillich's doctrine of God seems to find in the Pseudo-Dionysius resources that are not to be found in Bonaventure, whatever their similarities. First, because of his emphasis on the dialectic, the Pseudo-Dionysius is more easily transposed into a non-hierarchical world view than is Bonaventure. Second, because of his emphasis on negation, the Pseudo-Dionysius suggests a way to speak of the dark side of the symbolic universe.

It is precisely in his retrieval of the Dionysian dialectic, divorced from a neo-Platonic framework, that Tillich develops his own version of the *via negativa*. For the Pseudo-Dionysius, as for Bonaventure, it is through a series of affirmations and negations of the signs of God in creation that the soul may rise to different levels and hierarchies, from the material to the spiritual and eventually to the absolute. For the

Pseudo-Dionysius, the negative moment of the *via negativa* is not a simple negation;[58] rather, it is a dynamic movement of interpretation.[59] Rooted in the conviction that there is *"something* and not *nothing"*[60] and spurred by the hope for richer interpretations, the negation is not necessarily the abandonment of a symbol, but the abandonment of our interpretations. Understood in this way, it is not bound to a neo-Platonic metaphysics. The movement is not spatial ('upward') but is dialectical; it is a relentless dialectic from affirmation to negation to further affirmations, which in turn will lead to the most radical of negations and eventually to the ironic affirmation of surrendering all interpretations.[61] In some cases, the negation may lead to an acceptance of another symbol of the same type, or it may lead to a different kind of symbol; for example, the movement may be from the concrete/metaphorical to the more abstract/conceptual. In other cases, the negation may lead 'deeper into' the same symbol, revealing other connections and dimensions, while simultaneously opening up "levels of our interior reality."[62] In all cases, the dialectical process leads to "a change of mentality, a new attitude toward the unconditioned transcendent."[63]

Tillich therefore transposes this dialectical movement from its neo-Platonic moorings into his dynamic ontology. 'Self-transcending faith' occurs in the "infinite drive of the finite beyond itself,"[64] in the simultaneous realization that God is unapproachable and ungraspable ('beyond' the categories of finitude to which we are bound), and finally in the need to return to the self in a new state, integrating and reintegrating what has been learned. The emphasis here is on the shocking recognition that God is not only ground, God is also abyss. This shock cannot be diluted; it demands a continual protest against our tendencies to secure the 'self' against the 'transcendent'. The meaningfulness of all theological language thus rests in the degree to which it maintains this inescapable tension of the coincidence of opposites: God is absolutely near and absolutely far.[65] If this tension is lost, if we loiter in the purely affirmative mode of religious language, if there is any fixation, then we become idolators. From this protest arises Tillich's controversial claim that a truly religious act involves an atheistic moment—a denial of any affirmation we make of God, even the affirmation that "God exists."[66]

Tillich's articulation of the *via negativa* is more than a way to use language; it is demanded by ontology.[67] The dialectical process of our own thinking reflects the dialectical process in the divine life itself. The demand in dialectical language for radical negation stems not only from the nonbeing that belongs to finite existence but also ultimately from the nonbeing that belongs to God Godself.[68] However troubling a claim this may seem, it is required, Tillich argues, if theological language is to maintain its integrity.[69] Tillich addresses the 'presence' of non-being in God under two related concepts: God as Being-itself and God as the living God. If God is not some dead identity, then God cannot be understood as pure being; rather, as Being-itself God transcends both being and nonbeing by 'embracing' their polarity within God-self. Yet here the term 'Being-itself' does not convey the full force of the dynamic aspect of God, so Tillich complements it with the notion of 'the living God'. "Nonbeing," Tillich insists, "makes God a living God."[70] The language here, he admits, is "highly symbolic"[71] but no less true on that account. If nonbeing belongs to God, then nonbeing—darkness, fragmentation, destruction—is revelatory, and not just because it drives us toward being. Nonbeing is revelatory because it grabs us in a way that being, or even the dialectic between being and non-being, sometimes cannot. There is an odd sort of comfort in this, for even when the raging forces of the hidden unconscious overwhelm us—even then there is participation in the divine life.[72]

The demanding nature of Tillich's *via negativa*—its awareness of ground as also abyss, its insistence that nonbeing belongs to Being-itself—is an inherent part of his retrieval of both the voluntarist tradition and early Greek Trinitarian theology. It also marks a retrieval of the notion of the hidden God.[73] In Tillich's identifying God as both ground and abyss, he exposes an underlying tension throughout his thought. On the one hand, with Aquinas, Spinoza, and Rahner, he wants to stress the intrinsically rational structure of reality (*logos*) and the essential union of knowing and loving. The unknowability of God refers not to some ultimate irrationality but to the infinite knowability of God that (for Aquinas and Rahner) involves the surrendering of any claim to knowledge.[74] This is part of the ontological commitment: the final relatedness of all reality in God as its ground. On the other hand, with Böhme, the later Schelling, Nietzsche, and the existentialists, Tillich wants to take nonbeing seriously. This means allowing the possibility that the world is not a unified whole, that it is fragmented and therefore not in the end comprehensible; it means also that the dynamics entailed by nonbeing are potentially violent. The tension between these two basic attitudes is partly resolved through Tillich's discussion of the polarity of dynamics and form, but not entirely.[75]

The tension is intensified in Tillich's version of the 'hidden God', which expresses not the raw religious experience of the 'presence' of nonbeing in God but the more terrifying experience of God-as-abyss. This is not fully developed in Tillich, but he seems to present two ways of understanding this experience of "the holy as *tremendum.*"[76] In both cases, he employs the principle of the coincidence of opposites. There is, first of all, the coincidence of God as the ground and the abyss of all that is. To say that Being-itself has a "double characteristic" (creative and abysmal)[77] is to point to the *divine depth* which is "the basis of the Godhead, that which makes God God. It is the root of his majesty, the unapproachable intensity of his being."[78] The hiddenness or abysmal nature of God in this sense does not destroy, rather it infinitely exceeds, human reason; it does not rupture the union of the will to know and the will to love.

A subtly yet significantly different understanding of the hiddenness of God can be found in Tillich's elusive exposition of another coincidence of opposites, one that necessitates Trinitarian symbols. Tillich's description of the second Trinitarian principle, the *logos* that grounds the rational structure of being, suggests that the divine depth is more abysmal than creative: "Without the second principle the first principle would be chaos, burning fire, but it would not be the creative ground. Without the second principle God is demonic, is characterized by absolute seclusion, is the 'naked absolute' (Luther)."[79] Clearly something more is meant here than just the divine transcendence. In exposing the nerve of the radical sense of contingency, fragmentation, alienation, and arbitrariness, this second, demonic type of divine hiddenness undermines the final ontological unity of knowledge, love, freedom, and power. The imagery is not that of the excess of unfathomable depths but of obliteration; the experience is not that of freedom but of frozen terror.

With regard to the first understanding of the 'hidden God' (hiddenness experienced not as terror but as 'holy mystery'), interesting parallels between Tillich and Karl Rahner appear. These parallels reflect the introduction of the third motivating concern of 'Protestant principle', namely the demand of critical philosophy to observe the limits of reason. Tillich and Rahner share an 'ontological commitment'. Both begin with a turn to the subject, an examination of the conditions of our subjectivity, and a reflection on our transcendental orientation towards mystery.[80] Yet in that 'ontological commitment', precisely because it is post-Kantian, 'prophetic criticism' becomes a determining factor. Our language about God, while analogical, must not be mistaken as constitutive. For instance, God cannot be said to be "*the* infinite" or even simply "infinite" without those terms being significantly qualified (negated). According to Tillich, "Infinity is a directing concept, not a constituting concept. It directs the mind to experience its own unlimited potentialities, but it does not establish the existence of an infinite being."[81] Rahner makes the same point: "The infinite horizon, which is the term of transcendence and which opens us to unlimited possibilities . . . cannot itself be given a name"; we can call the term of transcendence "the infinite, but in doing this we have not given [it] a name, but have called it nameless."[82] Infinity is not a thing but a demand;[83] nothing can be posited about it, and it cannot be posited about God.

This convergence of the religious sense of the ineffability of God and the philosophical requirement of remaining within the limits of reason presents a third way of understanding the hidden God. Both Tillich and Rahner strive to find language to express the never-quite-thereness of the immediate, always already presence of God.[84] Since God is not an object, there is no 'there' at which to arrive, no 'there' which can be grasped; yet always there is the dynamic presence that beckons and commands, that offers 'new being'. Both Tillich and Rahner find the language of 'mystery' helpful in reflecting on the hidden quality of the divine revelation that does not obliterate human reason but at the same time cannot be dissolved into it; for Rahner, of course, 'mystery' is the dominant metaphor, but it is to be found in Tillich as well.[85] Both strive to find language that is neither so abstract as to be meaningless nor so concrete as to stunt our religious imaginations, and therefore both are wary of notions such as 'absolute being' and are more drawn to indefinite images such as 'ground', 'abyss', and 'horizon'. Rahner prefers 'horizon', since he thinks 'ground' and 'abyss' are "always fraught with images which go beyond what the word really wants to say."[86] Yet it is for that very reason that Tillich says those two terms must be held in dialectical tension, for then the mind is not allowed to rest on any one image; the dialectic between them thus maintains the sense of the terms (dynamic inexhaustibility) without letting them become too concrete. To say that God is abyss is to say that the horizon is empty—it has no specific content, it cannot be filled; it is not to say, however, that it is empty of meaning, only that it is the ground of all meaning. Both Tillich and Rahner turn to language that lures the mind beyond the fixity of the concrete to the *terminus a quo* and *terminus ad quem* of our freedom, our willing, and our love.[87] These parallels are further demonstration of the fact that it is under the rubric of 'Protestant principle' as well as 'Catholic substance' that Catholic thought finds itself at home in Tillich.

My purpose here has been to show how Tillich's profound insight into the dynamic tension between the two basic religious and theological impulses has had important implications for both the historical and the constructive tasks of theology, especially with regard to the doctrine of God. To this end, I have argued that Tillich's rubrics 'Catholic substance' and 'Protestant principle' are not what they first appear to be. Under the rubric of 'Catholic substance' Tillich begins with what, for Catholic thought, is familiar and moves to what is less familiar, sometimes even foreign. Tillich rightly recognizes his project to be a retrieval of the Augustinian-Franciscan tradition, but "retrieval" is not "adoption." What Tillich calls 'Catholic substance' is really a process of appropriations. If Catholic thought wants to appeal to Tillich's commendation of its 'substance', it must follow the course he himself took. This means that 'Catholic substance' must be more broadly construed and therefore that the label itself should be abandoned. The label was intended to capture the sense of the basic religious and theological impulse that arises out of the awareness of God's immanent presence; that impulse is characterized by a fundamental confidence that all reality is interrelated, comprehensible, and ultimately unified because of its participation in Being-itself. For that reason I have referred to it as the 'ontological commitment'.

Under the rubric of 'Protestant principle' the movement of Tillich's thought is even more complex. Again, for Catholic thought, it could be said that he begins with what seems foreign and incorporates the familiar. Yet the imagery involved is not so much of a one-directional movement as it is of an oscillation between the familiar and the unfamiliar, the eventual outcome being a reversal of expectations. Often, what appears to be alien to Catholic thought actually could find a home there, and what appears to be familiar can suddenly seem rather unsettling. The label 'Protestant principle' is therefore misleading and should be abandoned. The label was intended to capture the sense of the basic religious and theological impulse that arises out of the awareness of God's absolute transcendence. For that reason I have argued that a more adequate term for it is 'prophetic criticism'.

A dialectical tension between Catholic and Protestant remains, but it is not the controlling polarity. The main polarity is that between the 'ontological commitment' and 'prophetic criticism': both are necessary for the health and integrity of any religion; each manifests itself in Catholicism as well as Protestantism; under each there are other polarities that are operative. Because of the complexity and dynamics allowed by this model, formerly familiar categories break down, the old insularity is undone, and new possibilities emerge. Catholic thought remains indebted to Tillich.

Notes

[1] Paul Tillich, "Afterword," in *Paul Tillich in Catholic Thought*, eds. Thomas O'Meara, O.P., and Celestin D. Weisser, O.P. (Dubuque: The Priory Press, 1964) 301.

[2] Indeed, such appreciation should not be underestimated, especially since, as Langdon Gilkey points out, the Catholicism with which Tillich was most familiar was represented by the triumphalistic and rigidly dogmatic Church of the decades preceding Vatican II: "It is surprising, therefore, that Tillich's analysis of pre-Vatican II Catholicism was as positive as in fact it was—more positive than that of most liberal Catholics at present" (Gilkey, *Gilkey on Tillich* [New York: Crossroad, 1990] 20 n.11).

[3] See Tillich, "Afterword," 301.

[4] Paul Tillich, "Realism and Faith," in *Paul Tillich: Main Works*, vol. 4: *Writings in the Philosophy of Religion*, ed. John Clayton (Berlin and New York: De Gruyter—Evangelisches Verlagswerk GmbH, 1987) 353.

[5] "The truth of a symbol depends on its inner necessity for the symbol-creating consciousness" (Paul Tillich, "The Religious Symbol," in *Paul Tillich: Main Works*, 265).

[6] David Tracy's identification of the two "classical forms of religious expression" as *manifestation trajectory* and *proclamation trajectory* suggests the same distinction intended by Tillich's terms *Catholic substance* and *Protestant principle*. See Tracy, *The Analogical Imagination: Christian Theology and the Culture of Pluralism* (New York: Crossroad, 1981) 202ff.

[7] Paul Tillich, *Systematic Theology*, 3 vols. (Chicago: University of Chicago Press, 1951–63) 1:67.

[8] I take the phrase from the title of David Tracy's *Plurality and Ambiguity: Hermeneutics, Religion, Hope* (San Francisco: Harper and Row, 1987).

[9] See Tillich, *Systematic Theology*, 1:56.

[10] See especially Ewert H. Cousins, *Bonaventure and the Coincidence of Opposites* (Chicago: Franciscan Herald Press, 1978); John Dourley, "God, Life and the Trinity in the Theologies of Paul Tillich and St. Bonaventure," in *S. Bonaventura 1274–1974* (Rome: Collegio S. Bonaventura Grottaferrata, 1974) 4:271-82; Karl-Hermann Kandler, "Die Einheit von Endlichem und Unendlichem: Zum Verhältnis von Paul Tillich zu Nikolaus von Kues," *Kerygma und Dogma* 2 (April–June 1979) 106–22; Norbert Ernst, *Die Tiefe des Seins: Eine Untersuchung zum Ort der Analogia Entis im Denken P. Tillichs* (St. Ottilien: EOS Verlag, 1988).

[11] "The one reality which we encounter is experienced in different dimensions which point to one another. The finitude of the finite points to the infinity of the infinite. It goes beyond itself in order to return to itself in a new dimension. This is what self-transcendence means. In terms of immediate experience it is the encounter with the holy" (Tillich, *Systematic Theology* 2:8). Cf. Paul Tillich, "Religious

Symbols and Our Knowledge of God" in *Paul Tillich: Main Works*, 395–404; "The Meaning and Justification of Religious Symbols," in *Paul Tillich: Main Works*, 415–20; *Systematic Theology*, 1:278.

[12] Tillich, *Systematic Theology*, 1:41. Cf. Paul Tillich, "The Two Types of Philosophy of Religion," in *Paul Tillich: Main Works*, 290, 292; *Systematic Theology* 1:85; *Perspectives on 19th and 20th Century Protestant Theology*, ed. Carl E. Braatten (New York, Evanston, and London: Harper and Row, 1967) 193.

[13] Cousins, *Bonaventure*, 263.

[14] See Tillich, *Systematic Theology*, 1:279; *Love, Power and Justice* (New York: Oxford University Press, 1960) esp. 22, 24–34; "Biblical Religion and the Search for Ultimate Reality," in *Paul Tillich: Main Works*, 382.

[15] Tillich, *Systematic Theology*, 3:245.

[16] Ibid., 1:231.

[17] See Paul Tillich, "The Problem of Theological Method," in *Paul Tillich: Main Works*, 301; "Realism and Faith," 344, passim; *Systematic Theology*, 2:7, 8.

[18] This is not to be confused with the 'medieval realism' of the late Middle Ages that stood in opposition to nominalism. 'Mystical realism' represents a synthesis that, Tillich argues, was endangered by Aquinas and shattered by Ockham.

[19] Tillich considers his 'self-transcending realism', a precursor to which is 'mystical realism', as being a third alternative to what he deems to be two unacceptable positions. The first he calls *technical realism* (elsewhere he refers to it as 'supranaturalism', the 'Thomistic dissolution', or 'positivism'), which he thinks loses the unconditionally real. The second he calls *idealism* (elsewhere, 'naturalism'), which he thinks loses the conditionally real. (Although idealism and naturalism would seem to make strange partners, Tillich says that each is a form of monism in which there is a complete identity of the many in the One so that the many are eventually lost. Whereas naturalism deifies nature, idealism deifies consciousness.)

[20] Referring to Goethe, Herder, Schelling, and Schleiermacher, Tillich writes, "All these men were Kantians" (*Perspectives*, 74). Yet they had profound disagreements with Kant and often appealed to Spinoza as a corrective to Kant's critical philosophy. The result was a "synthesis of Spinoza and Kant" (ibid.). Tillich's 'self-transcending realism' is deeply indebted to this earlier synthesis.

[21] See Tillich, *Perspectives*, 66, 74; *Systematic Theology*, 1:82 n.7.

[22] Tillich, *Systematic Theology*, 1:95.

[23] See ibid., 1:20, 163.

[24] "If [Spinoza] had chosen the conception of force and activity, then everything would have been easier for him, and his system would have been much more clear and unified" (Johann Gottfried Herder, *God, Some Conversations* [1787], trans. and ed. Frederick H. Burkhardt [1940; reprint ed., Library of Liberal Arts, Indianapolis and New York: Bobbs-Merrill Co., 1963] 108). I focus my discussion of organic monism on Herder, but Schelling and Schleiermacher shared this basic world view,

even though the three thinkers would eventually come to varying views of the self and of the possibility for knowledge.

25 No longer can individual things be viewed as standing "alongside each other, looking at each other and at the whole of reality, trying to penetrate step by step from the periphery toward the center, but having no immediate approach to it, no direct participation" (Tillich, "Biblical Religion," 363).

26 Tillich, *Systematic Theology*, 3:15.

27 See ibid., 3:12–17. "Of course, if being is defined as 'object of thought' no matter what content it has, the idea of 'degrees of being' is senseless. But if being is 'power' the assertion of such degrees is natural, and it is a vital necessity for the mind to penetrate into the strata in which the real power of a thing reveals itself" (Tillich, "Realism and Faith," 345).

28 See Tillich, *Systematic Theology*, 1:263; 2:8–9.

29 "Ontological reason can be defined as the structure of the mind which enables it to grasp and to shape reality" (ibid., 1:75).

30 As Gilkey puts it, "As we have seen, however (and here Tillich goes beyond Kant), for Tillich the 'objective' structure of that world (of being) is known to us *directly* or *immediately* ('subjectively') through our participation in that structure as existing and self-aware examples of being" (*Gilkey on Tillich*, 87).

31 "In every act of reasonable reception an act of shaping is involved, and in every act of reasonable reaction an act of grasping is involved. We transform reality according to the way we see it, and we see reality according to the way we transform it. Grasping and shaping the world are interdependent" (Tillich, *Systematic Theology*, 1:76).

32 See Tillich, "Theological Method," 302.

33 See Tillich, "Afterword," 306.

34 Tillich, "Theological Method," 308.

35 Tillich, *Perspectives*, 91. Indeed, a careful comparison of Schleiermacher and Tillich will bear this out. It should also be noted that, in siding with Schleiermacher on this issue, Tillich departs from Schelling, for Schleiermacher's 'higher realism' and Tillich's 'self-transcending realism' are both meant, in part, to be correctives to Schelling's idealist system. I therefore disagree with the thesis that "Tillich was not a Christian and was instead a heretic in 'his attempt to interpret Christianity through Schelling'" (Randall E. Otto, "The Doctrine of God in the Theology of Paul Tillich," *Westminster Theological Journal* 52 [1990] 304).

36 "When [Schleiermacher] defined religion as the 'feeling of absolute dependence', 'feeling' meant the immediate awareness of something unconditional in the sense of the Augustinian-Franciscan tradition" (Tillich, *Systematic Theology*, 1:41).

37 It should be emphasized that Tillich did not dismiss mysticism because of that tendency; indeed, he defended it to Protestant theologians such as Ritschl and Barth who tried to "establish an absolute contrast between mysticism and faith" (Tillich, "Realism and Faith," 351; cf. 349).

[38] In his essay "Tillich's 'Two Types' and the Transcendental Method" (*Journal of Religion* 55/2 [1975]), John C. Robertson, Jr., makes a fundamental mistake in interpretation when he concludes that Tillich's appeal to the 'Augustinian solution' meant the acceptance of Augustine's and Bonaventure's notion of immediate awareness *in toto:* Tillich "overlooks . . . the *mediation* of the experience of God. . . . The self has only to turn within to apprehend immediately Being-Itself— unnuanced and, so to speak, all at once. I do not think that this direct form of introspection is an adequate account of the human cognition of anything" (203). This is precisely where Tillich departed from the medieval Franciscans, as is evident if one refers not only to the well-known essay "The Two Types of Philosophy of Religion" but also to "The Problem of Theological Method" and "Realism and Faith." Robertson's very thoughtful suggestion of a third alternative, an articulation of which he finds in Transcendental Thomism, is already developed by Tillich in terms of 'self-transcending realism'.

[39] Tillich, "Afterword," 303.

[40] Ibid.

[41] "The living God is always the trinitarian God, even before christology is possible, before the Christ has appeared. . . . [God] is not a dead oneness in himself, a dead identity, but he goes out and returns. This defines the process of life everywhere. If we apply this symbolically to God, we are involved in trinitarian thinking. . . . [T]he movement of the divine, going out and returning to himself— this is decisive if we speak of a living God" (Tillich, *Perspectives,* 112).

[42] Tillich, *Systematic Theology,* 3:290.

[43] Ibid., 1:282.

[44] Gregory of Nazianzus recognized this danger: "Or maybe you would consider our God to be a male, according to the same arguments, because he is called God and Father, and that deity is feminine, from the gender of the word, and Spirit neuter, because it has nothing to do with generation; but if you would be silly enough to say, with the old myths and fables, that God begot the Son by a marriage with his own will, we should be introduced to the hermaphrodite god of Marcion and Valentinus. . . ." (*The Theological Orations,* in *Christology of the Later Fathers,* vol. 3 of Library of Christian Classics [Philadelphia: The Westminster Press] 198).

[45] Tillich, *Systematic Theology,* 3:294.

[46] Ibid.

[47] See, for example, Phyllis Trible, *God and the Rhetoric of Sexuality* (Philadelphia: Fortress Press, 1978); Caroline Walker Bynum, *Jesus as Mother: Studies in the Spirituality of the High Middle Ages* (Berkeley, Los Angeles, London: University of California Press, 1982).

[48] The voluntarist tradition stands, he says, in opposition to, on the one hand, Aquinas's *actus purus* (see Tillich, *Systematic Theology,* 1:180, 246) and, on the other hand, Ockham's emphasis on the irrationality of the divine will (see Tillich, *Perspectives,* 194).

⁴⁹ Tillich, *Perspectives*, 193.

⁵⁰ Tillich, "Biblical Religion," 385.

⁵¹ See *Summa Theologica* 1.13. Note that Tillich does not reject the "classical doctrine of 'analogia entis' "; he only rejects "any attempt to use it in the way of rational construction" (Paul Tillich, "Symbol and Knowledge," in *Paul Tillich: Main Works*, 274; cf. *Systematic Theology*, 1:239–40). See Robert R. N. Ross, "The Non-existence of God: Tillich, Aquinas, and the Pseudo-Dionysius," *Harvard Theological Review* 68 (April 1975): 141–66.

⁵² "Let us, then, die / and enter into the darkness; / let us impose silence / upon our cares, our desires and our imaginings" (Bonaventure, *The Soul's Journey Into God*, in *Bonaventure*, trans. Ewert Cousins, The Classics of Western Spirituality [N.Y., Ramsey, Toronto: Paulist Press, 1978], 116).

⁵³ Tillich, "Realism and Faith," 351.

⁵⁴ "The ground of being is at the same time the abyss of any definite being; and conversely . . . the abyss of being which transcends all special beings is at the same time the creative ground of all forms of existence" (Tillich, "Symbol and Knowledge," 273; cf. *Systematic Theology*, 1:216).

⁵⁵ Paul Tillich, "The Religious Symbol," 264; cf. "Realism and Faith," 351–52.

⁵⁶ See Tillich, *Systematic Theology*, 1:82.

⁵⁷ An interesting argument could be made that Tillich's *via negativa* combines Luther and Eckhart: like Luther, he abandons the Platonism of the Pseudo-Dionysius and interprets the *via negativa* more in terms of the coincidence of opposites (e.g., Luther's early theology of the cross); like Eckhart (and in contrast to Aquinas), he emphasizes the apophatic side of the analogical imagination and relies on dialectical language to do so.

⁵⁸ "Now we should not conclude that the negations are simply the opposites of the affirmations" (Pseudo-Dionysius, *The Mystical Theology*, in *Pseudo-Dionysius: The Complete Works*, trans. Colm Luibheid, The Classics of Western Spirituality [New York and Mahwah: Paulist Press, 1987] 136).

⁵⁹ See Paul Rorem, "The Uplifting Spirituality of Pseudo-Dionysius," in *Christian Spirituality: Origins to the Twelfth Century*, eds. Bernard McGinn and John Meyendorff (New York: Crossroad, 1987) 132–51.

⁶⁰ Tillich, *Systematic Theology*, 1:110.

⁶¹ Speaking of the 'supreme Cause', the Pseudo-Dionysius writes: "It is not wisdom. It is neither one nor oneness, divinity nor goodness. Nor is it a spirit, in the sense in which we understand that term. . . . [I]t is also beyond every denial" (*The Mystical Theology*, 141).

⁶² Tillich, "Religious Symbols," 397.

⁶³ Tillich, "The Religious Symbol," 253–69.

⁶⁴ Tillich, *Systematic Theology* 1:191.

⁶⁵ See Tillich, "Realism and Faith," 352.

66 See Tillich, "The Religious Symbol," 264; "Symbol and Knowledge," 275; "Two Types," 297–98; "Realism and Faith," 355; *Systematic Theology* 1:237.

67 "Therefore, the very structure which makes negative judgments possible proves the ontological character of nonbeing"; "The mystery of nonbeing demands a dialectical approach" (Tillich, *Systematic Theology* 1:187). "But the dialectical method goes beyond ['yes' and 'no' and 'yes']. It presupposes that reality itself moves through 'yes' and 'no,' through positive, negative, and positive again. The dialectical method attempts to mirror the movement of reality" (ibid., 1:234).

68 According to Gilkey, "Rather, being and nonbeing are, I think, to be taken as Tillich's major polarity, not only in relation to the finite but even more in relation to God" (*Gilkey on Tillich*, 108).

69 "The nonbeing of negative theology means 'not being anything special,' being beyond every concrete predicate. This nonbeing embraces everything; it means being everything; it is being-itself. The dialectical question of nonbeing was and is a problem of affirmative theology. If God is called the living God, if he is the ground of the creative processes of life, if history has significance for him, if there is no negative principle in addition to him which could account for evil and sin, how can one avoid positing a dialectical negativity in God himself? Such questions have forced theologians to relate nonbeing dialectically to being-itself and consequently to God" (Tillich, *Systematic Theology*, 1:188–89).

70 Paul Tillich, *The Courage to Be* (New Haven and London: Yale University Press, 1952) 180.

71 Tillich, "Biblical Religion," 384.

72 "As Spirit [God] is as near to the creative darkness of the unconscious as he is to the critical light of cognitive reason" (Tillich, *Systematic Theology* 1:250; cf. 1:242, 279). See also Tillich's discussion of the experience of meaninglessness in *The Courage to Be*, 174–76.

73 A salient discussion of the notion of the hidden God can be found in B. A. Gerrish, " 'To the Unknown God': Luther and Calvin on the Hiddenness of God," chap. 8 in *The Old Protestantism and the New: Essays on the Reformation Heritage* (Chicago: University of Chicago Press, 1982) 131–49.

74 Rahner explains Aquinas on this point: "The incomprehensibility of God is given for Thomas in an *excedere*, . . . [which is] the ultimate and fundamental movement of the spirit and its activity (*intellectus agens*) toward the infinite being of God in his incomprehensibility, and this is the ground of all knowing" ("Thomas Aquinas on the Incomprehensibility of God," *Journal of Religion* 58 [1978], Supplement: S107–S125).

75 See Lewis S. Ford, "The Appropriation of Dynamics and Form for Tillich's God," *Harvard Theological Review* 68 (1975) 35–51. Ford argues that the tension between form and dynamics is not maintained and that Tillich winds up "identifying divine dynamics with the creative power of being" (35).

76 Tillich, *Systematic Theology*, 1:216.

77 "In calling it creative, we point to the fact that everything participates in the infinite power of being. In calling it abysmal, we point to the fact that everything participates in the power of being in a finite way, that all beings are infinitely transcended by their creative ground" (ibid. 1:237).

78 Ibid., 1:250.

79 Ibid., 1:251. The ultimate "grasps us when and where it will, for it is always also darkness, judgment, and death for us" (Tillich, "Realism and Faith," 354).

80 See Karl Rahner, *Foundations of Christian Faith: An Introduction to the Idea of Christianity*, trans. William V. Dych (New York: Crossroad, 1984).

81 Tillich, *Systematic Theology*, 1:190.

82 Rahner, *Foundations*, 61, 62.

83 See Tillich, *Systematic Theology*, 1:190.

84 "The non-symbolic element in all religious knowledge is the experience of the unconditioned as the boundary, ground, and abyss of everything conditioned. This experience is the boundary-experience of human reason and therefore expressible in negative rational terms. But the unconditioned is not God. God is the affirmative concept pointing beyond the boundary of the negative-rational terms and therefore itself a positive-symbolic term. The attempt of bad metaphysics to establish the idea of God in positive-rational terms is irrefutably rejected by Kant who follows here the predominant theological tradition" (Tillich, "The Religious Symbol," 273).

85 See, e.g., Tillich, *Systematic Theology*, 1:109–10, 157.

86 Rahner, *Foundations*, 60.

87 See ibid., 65.

The Implications of Tillich's Theology of the Cross for Catholic Theology

John C. Dwyer

Background

Liturgy, public worship, and the Eucharistic celebration are virtually convertible terms for Catholics, and anyone who is aware of this and who reflects on Paul's statement about Eucharist to his community at Corinth ("When you break this bread and pass this cup, you proclaim the death of the Lord until he comes"),[1] will find it strange that Catholic theology has never developed a theology of the Cross[2] with strong scriptural roots. It is not that Catholic thought has balked at connecting Eucharist with the death of the Lord; since the Council of Trent it has consistently asserted that "the sacrifice of the Mass is the same sacrifice as that of the Cross." But this way of speaking of the relationship of the Cross and the Mass, with its strong emphasis on the notion of sacrifice, virtually insured that theologies of the Cross which sprang up on Catholic turf would be based on speculation of the patristic and Scholastic periods and would lack a reputable scriptural pedigree.

A theology of the Cross that seeks authentic scriptural roots will find in the epistles of Paul[3] a privileged source. The Cross is at the very center of Paul's theological vision: he wants to "know only Jesus Christ, who is, and remains, the crucified one,"[4] and for him, "the Cross is . . . the wisdom and power of God."[5] But to take Paul's understanding of the Cross seriously means to turn definitively from the view of Eucharist as a sacrifice,[6] and from the satisfaction/reparation theory on which it rests. This theory, which has been dominant since Trent, originated with Anselm of Canterbury, and it passed into the theological tradition in the form which Thomas Aquinas gave it, after stripping it of some of its more crudely juridical elements. With its notion of a "god" who demands compensation for the insult offered by sin,[7] and who seems to have difficulty in balancing his justice and his mercy, this theory is arguably the most harmful ever to surface in the theological tradition. It has transformed God into a strange being whose demand for justice must be satisfied before he can, or will, show his mercy; as a consequence, it has led to the view of Mass or liturgy as a satisfactory sacrifice, offered by the priest, who functions precisely as a sacrificial minister. From the time this theory was first developed until the Second Vatican Council, it has made it difficult to see the Mass as the family meal of the Christian community, at which Jesus is present, precisely as one who, through suffering and death, brings God's acceptance and reconciliation to his followers.

This "satisfaction/reparation/compensation/atonement" theory of the Cross is not Pauline (although it has often been given a pseudo-Pauline pedigree), and it might seem strange that, in the absence of any real foundation in Paul's writings, it has assumed such a prominent position in dogmatic theology manuals and has been able to exercise such a destructive influence on liturgy and devotional life. However, the central theses of Paul's theology[8] virtually disappeared before the end of the first century and remained underground through most of the patristic period. Neither the Platonism of the Greek Fathers, nor the mixed Platonic and Aristotelian legacy that was exploited by the Scholastic theology of the Middle Ages, could provide the context necessary for understanding Paul. As a result, Catholic thought treated the doctrinal and theological tradition as a *de facto*, if not *de jure*, theological source more important than Scripture itself.[9]

The Contribution of Paul Tillich

More than any theologian of this century, Paul Tillich thought deeply about the meaning of the Cross. As with Paul of Tarsus, the Cross was at the very center of his theological vision, and like Paul, he strove to present his understanding of the Cross in language his contemporaries could understand. It is the contention of this article that he succeeded, and that his theology of the Cross is particularly relevant for Catholic reflection on the meaning of the death of the Lord, and is therefore of the greatest importance for understanding Eucharist and liturgy.

There are several factors which make Tillich an appropriate guide for Catholic theologians interested in fashioning a theology of the Cross that has a solid scriptural basis. First, as he himself put it, Tillich lived his life "on the boundary" between philosophy and theology. Unlike so many of his Protestant confrères, he had a positive view of the relationship between philosophy and theology, and was not in the slightest embarrassed at granting philosophy a role within the theological enterprise itself.[10] Second, his recognition that the Christian message implies a dialectical relationship between Catholic substance and the Protestant principle provides a fascinating counterpoint to the rediscovery of the Protestant principle at the Second Vatican Council.[11] Third, Tillich understands the psychological appeal of Anselm's satisfaction/reparation theory, but rejects the theory for very sound reasons. This is why Tillich can help Catholic reflection on liturgy and Eucharist break away from a concept of sacrifice which owes incomparably more to pre-Christian Germanic tribal law and Roman jurisprudence than it does to Scripture. Fourth, he understands Paul's theology of atonement[12] and presents Paul's authentic teaching in a conceptual framework that is intelligible to people of our day. Fifth, he deals explicitly with the question of how the Cross works and achieves its effect on each of us in our concrete situation of estrangement. And finally, Tillich's understanding of the Cross as the unique and defining element of Christian faith can put an end to something which is so common today, so "politically correct" and so theologically devastating: the relativizing of the claims of the Christian message, apparently out of the desire to avoid offense to those of other faiths (or of no faith at all!). For all of these reasons, Tillich's theology of the Cross raises questions and suggests approaches that are of great value to Catholic theology, above all in its reflection on Eucharist, the central act of Catholic worship.

Tillich's Theology of the Cross

Tillich's theological understanding of the Cross can be conveniently summarized under four headings: revelation, participation, acceptance, and the unique role of the Cross in effecting the first three.

The Cross Is God's Final Revelation

First, the Cross works, produces its effects on us, precisely because it is the final revelation. As *revelation*, it is not merely the communication of knowledge, the divulging of previously hidden information; it is an event which changes the structure, meaning, and aim of existence. When revelation on the Cross is called "final," this does not mean that it is the last in a temporal sequence. No reputable theology of revelation, least of all one developed by Paul Tillich, would see the death of Jesus in this light. The word "final" here means definitive, ultimate, unsurpassable, and a revelation can have this quality only when the medium, the bearer of revelation, exhausts himself in the revelatory act, or, as Tillich puts it, "denies himself without losing himself."

Tillich explains this somewhat cryptic phrase by pointing out that, since every revelation is conditioned by the medium in and through which it appears, our ultimate concern can be present only when the bearer of that revelation denies its own ultimacy. This can happen only in the personal life process of "one who is united with the ground of being and meaning without separation and disruption,"[13] and who, in the very act of resigning all claims to ultimacy, "becomes completely transparent to the mystery he reveals."[14] To define final revelation in this way means that, although "revelation" is a religious term, final revelation cannot be limited to the religious realm and it does not offer the satisfaction of our merely religious needs. Final revelation is rather the answer to our most basic human need: the need to escape from our situation of estrangement, of alienation, of separation from others, of the meaninglessness of so much in life, of inevitable despair, and of the destructiveness, the irrationality, the nihilism of violence, which human beings perpetrate every day and which lurks in the dark corners of the human heart.

Only the presence of the living God in our midst, in an alienated world, and with us in our alienation, can penetrate this darkness, can bring our estrangement to an end, and give us the reconciliation, re-union, creativity, meaning, and hope we need.[15] And this is precisely what revelation is and does; it is the presence of God in our midst, in the brokenness of the world, as one who is in our world and a part of it; and this is why the Cross is needed and why it has the power to transform human existence. Although various partial revelations are not without impact on us as we struggle with different aspects of our estrangement, only the *final* revelation can bring our estrangement to an end, and a revelation is final when the one who bears it (the medium of revelation) rejects all claims to ultimacy for himself, and is, in virtue of this, utterly transparent to God. Precisely this is what happens on the Cross.

Participation

The second part of Tillich's theology of the Cross, and the one which brings us to the heart of the matter, is his assertion that the Cross has the power to transform the structure, meaning, and aim of human life because it is there that God himself participates without reserve in human existence; it is there that he participates in our estrangement and alienation, suffering and death. These are the facts and the factors that mark our existence; because they mark the end toward which we are inexorably tending, they also mark every moment of life. But it is precisely here that God has chosen to be with us. The human condition is one of separation and alienation from God; but he has brought that separation and alienation to an end by entering into it, by taking it upon himself, by making it his own.

Jesus involves and implicates God, his Father, in all that he does, and it is in God's name that he moves into that domain which is commonly thought of as alien to God and as an inappropriate place for him to be. In Jesus, God lays claim to the whole world, to the world where grace abounds and to the world where sin still reigns, to the world of the devout and the world of the sinner. On the Cross, God takes the estrangement, the meaninglessness, and the despair of human existence into himself, and when he does this, they become "ways of God" and are stripped of their destructive power. God allows the human fate of suffering and death to overtake his Son, and in his Son he becomes vulnerable to the ultimate negativities of life. But when God takes death into himself, it means not the end of God but the end of death. It is not that the Cross trivializes death; there is nothing tentative about death, and in purely human terms it is the negation of all our hopes and dreams. But God is with Jesus when life turns against him and when all the props are gone. God is with Jesus when he encounters the ultimate negation of life, and as a result, death will never again be a sign of the absence of God and of our separation from him.

This is the great paradox of the Cross. We are estranged from God, and that estrangement and its destructive consequences are so much a fact of our existence that God himself cannot remove them without destroying us. But God is far from powerless, and Tillich finds the manifestation of that power in God's atoning activity which "must be understood as his participation in our estrangment and in its self-destructive consequences."[16] God reconciles us, not by pretending that we are not estranged or that we have not affirmed ourselves against him, but by being present to us as we exist and where we exist. Those aspects of our lives which separate us from God, and which therefore have destructive consequences, are not removed, not deprived of their ontological standing, but they are transformed.[17]

Because God, in Christ, has refused to be confined to the heavenly realm, but has taken his place in our midst, suffering remains real, but it is no longer a sign of our alienation from God or of his absence from our world; rather, it is a sign of his presence with us and for us. Once God, in his Son, has taken his place with us in the midst of pain and suffering, once he has participated in our existential estrangement in taking the world's suffering upon himself,[18] there will be no dark corner of human existence until the end of time which will be a sign of God's absence or which will confirm our alienation from him. The end of our rebellion against God, which we cannot achieve by any human efforts, and which God will not achieve by destroying us, he brings about by entering into the destructive structures of human existence, and suffering their consequences. The man on the Cross is the realization in history of the eternal message that nothing in heaven or on earth can separate us from the love of God.

Participation as Acceptance

The third part of Tillich's theology of the Cross is the affirmation that God's participation in the negativity of existence is an act of acceptance[19] and of love. Real love always expresses itself in sharing the concrete destiny of another, and in Jesus, God has participated without reserve in the human condition. In Jesus Christ, God's acceptance of us has reached into our lives in their totality and has touched us at the heights and depths of the human condition, because in him God has participated in the negativities of creaturely existence.[20] God's victory over the ambiguity of good and evil has appeared in a unique, definitive, and transforming way in Jesus.

God's acceptance is not some kind of bland tolerance: on the Cross he forgives us and claims us. On the Cross God offers his forgiveness, because when he participates in our estrangement and alienation, he makes it clear that he will not allow anything to separate us from him.[21] On the Cross God claims us totally, because sharing the destiny of another creates a zone of intimacy so intense and so deep that concern for the other can no longer be distinguished from concern for oneself. It is on the Cross of the Christ that God manifests and realizes the fact that he is eternally reconciled. Reconciliation is the absence of all barriers which separate God and human beings; it is the "nonseparation" of God and ourselves. But this situation can be brought about only by God's acceptance of us, and this acceptance becomes real precisely in God's participation in the negativities of existence.

Tillich uses the traditional term *agape* to describe the kind of acceptance and love that comes to expression on the Cross. *Agape* has certain qualities which raise it above the other forms of love and give it the power to unite with them, to judge them, and to transform them.[22]

Specifically, *agape* has three characteristics which are rooted in the innermost core of life itself: it is *receptive*, because it accepts the one who is loved unconditionally and without restriction; it is *paradoxical* because it holds on to this acceptance in spite of the estranged and alienated state of those who are loved; and it is *anticipatory*, because it awaits the restoration of the holiness, the greatness, and the dignity of the beloved through the very act of accepting him or her.

The Cross is the expression and the realization of this love. It is the source of the message "which is the very heart of Christianity and makes possible the courage to affirm faith in the Christ: namely that, in spite of all the forces of separation between God and man, this is overcome from the side of God."[23] It is on the Cross that the threefold structure of divine love manifests itself under the conditions of estranged existence, and, in the final analysis, it is only through the Cross that this loving acceptance can touch human life.

The Need for the Cross

For Tillich, the Cross is not simply one way in which God might participate in the human condition, it is essential: "Only by taking suffering and death upon himself could Jesus be the Christ, because only in this way could he participate completely in existence and conquer every force of estrangement which tried to dissolve his unity with God."[24] In terms of the traditional Anselmian "satisfaction theology," Tillich puts the problem clearly: "It is an astonishing abstraction when Anselm states that Jesus owed God active obedience, but not suffering and death—as if the unity between God and the Christ could have been maintained under the conditions of existential estrangement without the continuous acceptance of his suffering and having to die."[25]

Only the man on the Cross is the realization in history of the eternal message that nothing can separate us from the love of God.[26] Here Tillich is not simply alluding to the fact that suffering and death are part of the human situation which God accepts by participating in it; he is rather stating that there is something about the human condition that inevitably involves God in suffering and violent death, when he decides to participate without reserve in that condition. Suffering and death are accepted by Jesus, because this is the only way in which he can affirm his union with God and with us, and therefore the only way in which God can participate fully in existence.[27] In the world of estrangement and existential disruption, where our destiny of estrangement holds our freedom in bondage, it is only by radical rejection of the universal human tendency to elevate ourselves on the basis of our good works or achievements that Jesus himself can maintain his perfect unity with God.[28]

The Implications of Tillich's Theology
of the Cross for Catholic Theology

Tillich stated the essential elements of Paul's doctrine of the atonement in language which can be understood not only by theologians but by lay people in the twentieth century, and this is of the greatest importance for all Christians and for all the Churches. However, it is of particular importance for Catholics, for a number of reasons.[29] First (and the key to all the others), Anselm's satisfaction/reparation theology has played an incomparably more important role in Catholic theology and devotional life since the Reformation than it has in any of the Protestant Churches, and Tillich's restatement of Paul effectively destroys the foundations of that theology. Second, Catholic theology, and, above all, popular piety have suffered from a loss of the sense that Jesus Christ is the one mediator between God and human beings. Third and last, since medieval times and increasingly since the Council of Trent, the Mass has been interpreted as, in some way, the same action as the Cross, with the implication that it functions as a satisfactory sacrifice.[30]

Tillich's Theology of the Cross and Anselm's Satisfaction Theory

Tillich's view of Christ's suffering and death differs profoundly from traditional theories that see the Cross as an act of propitiation or satisfaction which Jesus offers to his Father to make atonement for sin. For Tillich, Jesus is not the one in and through whom human beings offer compensation and sacrifice to God for their sins and offenses (even though this would ultimately be at the divine initiative). Tillich criticizes, in the sharpest terms, doctrines of the atonement "according to which God is the one to be reconciled,"[31] and he points out that "the message of Christianity is that God, who is eternally reconciled, wants us to be reconciled with him."[32] Christ cannot be a mediator in the sense that God is dependent on him for his saving activity; Jesus, as the Christ, is rather the "place" where God identifies with human beings in their estrangement. It is here that God accepts the unacceptable and achieves a final victory over the ambiguity of good and evil.[33]

The authentically Pauline character of Tillich's doctrine of the atonement shows very clearly that Anselm's theory, either in its original form, or in the version of Thomas Aquinas, is not Pauline. As Tillich noted, "The first and all-decisive principle [of the atonement] is that the atoning processes are created by God and by God alone. This implies that God, in the removal of the guilt and punishment which stand between him and man, is not dependent on the Christ, but that the Christ, as the bearer of the New Being, mediates the reconciling act of God to man."[34] These lines are so reminiscent of Paul's words in 2 Corinthians 5:19 ("God was the one who, in and through Christ, reconciled the world to himself") that we might wonder how it was ever possible for satisfaction/reparation theories to develop in the first place, but Tillich may be right when he suggests that Anselm's theory, mistaken as it is, owes its strong psychological power to the fact that it allows us to take our guilt seriously while, at the same time, experiencing the removal of that guilt by the sacrifice of Christ. As Tillich pointed out, it was this which "kept the Anselmian doctrine alive in spite of its dated legalistic terminology and its quantitative measuring of sin and punishment."[35]

The Loss of Jesus as the One Mediator

Paul had affirmed that Jesus Christ is the one mediator between God and human beings, and, although it is true that the conciliar theology of the fourth and fifth centuries pushed Jesus so totally into the divine sphere that it was difficult for him to function as a mediator, it was, nevertheless, the Anselmian theology of satisfaction and reparation that completed the process. A god who must be placated and appeased, to whom we must make reparation and atonement, and whose ultimate relationship with us is determined by the juridical categories of satisfaction and compensation, is not a God to whom we can pray, to whom we can cry out in our pain, or to whom we can turn in faith and hope and love.

Christians inevitably turned from a god who demanded the payment of a debt of pain before he would forgive,[36] and they found the broken man on the Cross to be an incomparably more attractive figure—one who is with us in our pain and who shares our suffering. However, the problem is not merely one of distaste or dissatisfaction with a particular picture of God; Anselm's satisfaction theory made the mediator, Jesus, into one upon whom God (that is, the Father) is dependent for his saving activity, and into one whom God needs in order to be reconciled. But this "god" is no longer the real God; he is irrelevant to Christian faith, and, although Christians were probably not aware of what they were doing, they inevitably cast him aside so that Jesus could take his place.[37] But in so doing they rejected the deeply Trinitarian theology of the prayers of the old Roman liturgy (we pray *to* God, *through* the Son, *in* the Spirit) and called into question the unique distinctions of Father, Son, and Spirit. To put it succinctly, when Jesus is no longer the mediator, God is no longer God.

Tillich's Theology of the Cross and a Contemporary Statement of Pauline Eucharistic Theology

Tillich's theology of the Cross can make a major contribution to Catholic theology and life because it can put the understanding of that central act of worship, the Eucharistic celebration, on a solid Pauline foundation. In their zeal to reject the sometimes one-sided statements of the Reformers, the theologians at the Council of Trent came dangerously close to transforming the meal which Christians celebrate with their Lord, who is really present, into a repetition or re-enactment of what these theologians conceived of as the satisfactory sacrifice made by Jesus on the Cross.[38] During much of the Counter-Reformation, this was the theology that was taught in the seminaries and imparted in catechetical instruction; even more significantly, it stood behind the custom of collecting Mass stipends from those who wanted the liturgy celebrated in order to apply the satisfactory value of Jesus' death to friends and relatives, and thus lessen their sufferings in purgatory.

It is true that there is little evidence that most Catholics had this particular understanding of Jesus' death in mind when they went to Mass, but the very fact that this blend of sadism and juridicism was the official theological explanation of the Cross meant that Eucharist and liturgy would lose their link with the death of the Lord, and would become merely celebrations of his real presence or objective "means of grace," which result in the infusion of a share in divine life. But precisely this is the problem. Paul had said that, as often as we eat of the bread and pass the cup, we proclaim the death of the Lord until he comes, and he interpreted not only Eucharist, but faith and baptism as well, as events which deepen our share in the death of the Lord. Manifestly, a Eucharistic celebration that ignores this connection cannot be reconciled with Paul's teaching.[39]

Tillich's theology of the Cross is a valuable tool that can help us to rediscover the link between Eucharist and the Cross and to accept Paul's teaching without becoming involved in any of the problems created by the satisfaction theory. In other words, Tillich's principles of the atonement make it possible to rediscover Paul's understanding of Eucharist, to preach it, and to live it. They do this because they are, in essence, a contemporary restatement of Paul's theology. It will be interesting to indicate, even though briefly, some of the elements of an approach to the Eucharist which would draw on Paul's thought, as made accessible by Tillich's theology of the Cross.

The Eucharist as a Revelatory Event

Eucharist has often been reduced to a memorial (this has been characteristic of some American Protestant Churches), to a satisfactory act, or to a means of acquiring grace (both specifically Catholic problems), but it is more than any of these. Like the Cross, Eucharist is a *revelatory* act, and, as such, it does not merely point to the one revealed but involves and implicates him in the world. Jesus, as the Christ, is the one in whom God is really present; he is the bearer and medium of revelation; and the bread and wine are the signs which mediate Jesus' real presence, as one who is and who remains the crucified one.[40]

Because it is a revelatory event (more accurately, because it is ongoing revelation), Eucharist calls for a response (and, in fact, it will be a revelation for each of us only when that response is given; the purpose of revelation is not to *inform* but to *transform*, and it can do this only when it is received). When we ''proclaim the death of the Lord'' (Paul's description of the Eucharistic celebration) we do much more than merely tell or re-enact what he did. Paul is not interested in the past as past; he is interested in it only insofar as it is an element of the present situation. To proclaim the death of the Lord is to accept Eucharist as the same revelation as that of the Cross, and for this reason, Eucharist is a call to understand our lives and ourselves in a new way, to revise and reform our scale of values, to change our thinking about success and failure, about life and death, and to reject the pretensions to absoluteness of any merely human claim. Like the Cross, and because it is a proclamation of the word of the Cross, Eucharist is a call to accept God's definition of himself and of us which he made real on the Cross. Eucharist is a call to let the death of the Lord be an event which determines our existence today, an event which brings God himself into the fragility and brokenness of our lives and which assures us that our weakness and vulnerability, our inability to secure our own lives, will never again be a source of fear, anxiety, or despair. Finally, Eucharist is a call to accept freedom from the iron laws of fate and destiny, which have determined how we treat each other and which force us to act in such profoundly inhuman ways (''an eye for an eye and a tooth for a tooth . . .''). Only the man on the Cross, who took the worst the world could throw his way, and who forgave his enemies, can summon us and empower us to love our enemies.

The Final Revelation

Eucharist has the power to summon us, to call us to turn away from our false selves which are determined by the value systems of the world, ancient and modern, and to discover our true selves, because it makes the *final* revelation of the Cross present. Revelation is always an event in which God, the absolute and ultimate one, is present in our midst, but there have been many revelations, and all except one have been fragmentary, provisional, and partial. That one exception is the revelation on the Cross. Eucharist makes this final revelation present again, and it proclaims the presence of God with us in the midst of the alienation and estrangement which mar and mark the human condition. In Eucharist Jesus makes present again the God who does not look down on our pain from a great distance, but who takes our suffering into himself and endows it with saving power. As the crucified one, Jesus is present as one who renounced all claims to ultimacy, who "did not grasp at his unity with God, but accepted the lot of a slave,"[41] and, as a result, gave us the power to stop playing God, to stop trying to "be like gods," and to be our weak and vulnerable human selves, who rejoice in the presence of the real God "who calls into being the things that are not and raises the dead to life."[42] Eucharist is a call to accept the paradox of a God who is with us in the emptiness and negativity of life and who, as a result, has the power to transform that emptiness and negativity into a sign of his presence.

Eucharist as God's Participation in our Lives

Tillich's use of the concept of participation is an interesting way of speaking of what Paul and the Synoptics call *sôma*, usually translated as "body." Paul speaks of the Eucharistic bread as Jesus' *sôma*, his real self—that is, precisely as one who is really present and is in communion and communication with us, and through us with our world. Paul also says that Jesus' *sôma* is "for us"—an expression he uses to speak of the death of the Lord as the event through which God fashions a new relationship with us. What Paul affirms here is that Jesus is present in Eucharist as the one in whom God participates in the emptiness and negativity of life, as the one in whom God accepts us unconditionally, and as the one who, in virtue of this acceptance, lays claim to all we are and all we can be. Eucharist is not simply the celebration of the resurrection of Jesus or of the fact that he now lives; it is the celebration of the God who came into the "unwhole-ness" and the "unholiness" of the human situation and who came to stay. It is the celebration of the fact that, in Jesus, God has come to be with us, in our existence which ends inexorably in death, and that, as a result, death and the suffering which precedes it and prefigures it have lost their sting.

Eucharist is a celebration of the fact that God has participated in the negativities of life and, in so doing, has created a domain of shared existence in which he has united his destiny with our own. In doing this, God has claimed us totally, because to share the concrete destiny of another is to create the kind of intimacy in which his claim on us cannot be distinguished from the claim we make on ourselves. The paradox, of course, is that God's claim on us is pressed not for his benefit but for ours. His claim on us is his desire to love us with the same love with which he loves himself.

Eucharist as Our Response to Revelation

Eucharist can be thought of in two ways. It is, first of all, a summons, a call, a revelatory event which confronts us with the offer and the demand to interpret our lives in a new and different way. But when we take an active part in Eucharist it becomes our response to this offer and demand. It is the event in which we affirm our love of, and loyalty to, this incredibly wonderful God who has come to share in our estrangement, up to and including suffering and death. It is our statement of who we want to be and who we have the power to be, as a result of Christ's presence on the Cross. It is obvious that to celebrate Eucharist is to make an act of faith. But this faith should not be reduced to accepting the doctrine of transubstantiation, nor should we feel obliged to ponder the mysteries (which so preoccupied the authors of the Neo-Scholastic theology manuals) of how Jesus can multilocate (be at once in heaven and in hundreds of thousands of places on earth), or how he can be compressed into a tiny host (while not losing the all-important Aristotelian accident of quantity or extension!). Faith is not the acceptance of pseudo-mysteries, it is always the act of letting God define himself on his own terms; faith in Eucharist means the act of letting God define himself in Eucharist as he did on his son's Cross, of letting him accept, affirm, sustain, support, and love us unconditionally in the act of sharing in our concrete destiny of estrangement.

Such an approach to Eucharist is deeply rooted in Paul's theology of the Cross, and here Tillich's contribution is twofold: he has demonstrated the fallacies of Anselmian satisfaction theology while developing a contemporary statement of Paul's theology of the Cross, and, at the same time, he has made it possible to affirm the link between Eucharist and the Cross. Freed from the burden of the theology of satisfaction, we can experience, as often as we break the bread and pass the cup, God's unconditional acceptance of us, the sinners whom he wants to be with him. And finally, the celebration of Eucharist is the full expression of what it means to be a human being: to act as one who has received a great gift—the precise meaning of the Greek word *eucharisteîn*.

Conclusion

Christians may disagree today, as they did in New Testament times, about what the heart, the center, the sum and substance of the Christian message is; but for Paul (the first to write anything now preserved in the New Testament) and for Mark (the first to write a Gospel), there is no doubt that it is the Cross, as the event in which God reconciled the world to himself, which occupies center stage. No theologian in modern times has spoken more eloquently of the Cross than Paul Tillich, and no theologian has based himself more firmly on the theological vision of Paul of Tarsus.

What is at stake, of course, in the theology of the Cross, is nothing less than the identity of God and therefore the believability of God in a world where the percentage of our race which believes in the God of the Old Testament and the New seems to be in a process of irreversible decline. It used to be stated, by those who were convinced by Pius IX's somewhat oversimplified philosophy of history, that the movement away from the Church in the sixteenth century had led men and women away from Christ in the seventeenth and eighteenth centuries, and then away from God in the nineteenth. However, the resistance of so many highly intelligent men and women in the fields of philosophy and natural science to what they perceive as the Christian message suggests that the causes of modern atheism may lie elsewhere. What modern non-believers cannot accept is a "god" who competes with human beings and is an obstacle to human maturity[43] and progress, and a "god" who must be placated and who demands repayment in pain and suffering certainly does so compete. Such a god is not real and never was, and "believing" in such a god has nothing to do with Christian faith. Tillich's rejection of such a god may well represent his most enduring contribution to theology and to the Church.

Notes

[1] 1 Cor 11:23-26.

[2] The term "theology of the Cross" has different meanings. Here it is used in a general sense to refer to an understanding of how the suffering and death of Jesus work, and of how they effect our salvation.

[3] Mark also sees the Cross as central, but he does not develop a theological *theory* to go with this view; he is important for any theology of the Cross precisely because he links Paul's emphasis on the Cross with the historical Jesus.

[4] 1 Cor 2:2.

[5] 1 Cor 1:24.

[6] At least in the ordinary sense of the word as "something offered to God to render him favorable to us."

[7] Or restoration of his external glory, in its Thomistic form.

[8] Specifically, Paul's understanding of *dikaiosyne* (commonly mistranslated as "righteousness" or "justice"), faith, and the Cross.

[9] This unfortunate tendency was virtually canonized by Pius XII in his encyclical *Humani Generis*, in which he announced that it was the task of the Catholic theologian to show that the latest teaching of the *magisterium* was already contained in Scripture, with the same meaning and the same sense. See *Humani Generis* (NCWC Edition, Washington, 1951) paragraph 21, lines 2–5.

[10] For a variety of reasons, Catholic thinkers have usually been more comfortable than Protestants in using philosophy as a tool for understanding the faith. However, Catholic thought has sometimes failed to recognize the danger of granting too much autonomy to the speculative logos, and Tillich's principle of correlation is a valuable corrective. In addition, his penetrating analysis of the cultural situation of his day and his insistence that theology engage in that dialogue in every period insures that his theology of the Cross will not remain in the realm of airy speculation.

[11] Constitution on Divine Revelation, ch. 2, paragraph 10. It is no exaggeration to find in this text an affirmation of the Protestant principle. For the first time since the Reformation, official Catholic teaching accepted the role of Scripture as a critical norm, called to judge the Church itself.

[12] *Atonement* is, admittedly, a dangerous word. Its etymology is impeccable (reconciliation through reunion of the estranged), but it has come to be virtually a synonym of *reparation*, and, to this extent, is unusable.

[13] Paul Tillich, *Systematic Theology*. Vol. 1 (Chicago: University of Chicago Press, 1951) 133.

[14] Ibid.

[15] We cannot be ultimately concerned about an event which takes place in a transcendent "other" world; for Tillich, a God "up there" who remains there cannot really accept us "down here," because such an acceptance would leave the negativity, the shadow side of human existence, untouched.

[16] Paul Tillich, *Systematic Theology*. Vol. 2 (Chicago: University of Chicago Press, 1957) 174.

[17] Tillich's appropriation and adaptation of the classical "Logos" Christology demonstrates the real power of participation. The Logos, the divine principle of self-manifestation (or God himself, as one who, from all eternity, intends to reveal himself exhaustively in a human being), "reveals the mystery and reunites the estranged, by appearing as a historical reality in a personal life" (*Systematic Theology*, 2:112).

[18] Tillich, *Systematic Theology*, 2:175.

[19] "Acceptance" is Tillich's translation of a word commonly translated as "justification." He notes that "justification" is a biblical term, and as such, it cannot be rejected by the Churches, but it is a word which has lost all meaning for a number of people, and it should be replaced in teaching and preaching by "acceptance," a word which also describes the act by which God unites us with himself, but in terms which are more suggestive of our actual experience of the need for this union (*Systematic Theology*. Vol. 3 [Chicago: University of Chicago Press] 225). This acceptance is God's reconciling act, which brings about a radical change in the human situation—in fact it brings about a transformation, a state in which all the forces of separation between God and human beings are overcome. Reconciliation "is not caused or conditioned by the Christ, for the first and all-deciding principle of the atonement is that God, in removing the guilt and the punishment which stand between him and man, is not dependent on the Christ, but that the Christ, as the bearer of the New Being, mediates, the reconciling act of God to man."

[20] Tillich, *Systematic Theology*, 1:270.

[21] This is the point of the great text of Rom 8:35-39.

[22] Note this use of the word *judge*—it is the same word Tillich uses in speaking of the Cross as final revelation.

[23] Paul Tillich, *The Dynamics of Faith* (New York: Harper and Row, 1958) 104.

[24] Tillich, *Systematic Theology*, 2:123.

[25] Ibid., 2:124.

[26] Rom 8:35-39.

[27] "Only by taking suffering and death upon himself could Jesus be the Christ, because only in this way could he participate completely in existence and conquer every force of estrangement which tried to dissolve his unity with God" (*Systematic Theology*, 2:123).

[28] Paul Tillich, *Christianity and the Encounter of the World Religions* (New York: Columbia University Press, 1923) 181–82.

[29] Limitations of space make it inevitable that this section will merely indicate some of the directions in which theological reflection might move in applying a genuinely Pauline theology of the Cross to a number of different problems.

[30] The word *sacrifice* itself has been contaminated, to some degree, by the satisfaction theory, and this is particularly the case when it is implied that Jesus offers himself as a sacrificial gift to God, to compensate for the insult offered to God by sin. Even worse is the implication that Jesus on the Cross is the one that *we* offer to God, to compensate for our sins, with the inevitable image of Jesus being crucified again at every celebration of the Mass. It is interesting to note that the term "sacrifice of the Mass" is used much less often today than it was before the Second Vatican Council; given the implications of the term, this is probably a good thing. If it were possible to go back to Augustine's usage, there would be no problems; he had defined *sacrifice* in *De civitate Dei* 10.6 as that which tends to unite us with God.

[31] Tillich, *Systematic Theology*, 2:169.

[32] Ibid., 2:169–70.

[33] Tillich, *Systematic Theology*, 3:226.

[34] Ibid., 2:173–74.

[35] Ibid., 2:173.

[36] They did this despite the psychological appeal of the satisfaction theory.

[37] Although, in such a scenario, Jesus is no longer the mediator, the need for a mediator remains, and a horde of new contestants inevitably rush in to fill the vacuum. The notion of the saint as the man or woman who has lived the life of faith in an exemplary way has a real, though indirect, New Testament foundation, but the notion of the saint as the mediator (now, very often, as one who brings our petitions to Jesus), although prevalent in much popular Catholic piety, has no basis in the New Testament.

[38] This satisfaction theology caused many problems; it led to the multiplication of private Masses, to the frequent offering of Masses for the dead (to spare them suffering in purgatory) and to the establishment of foundations which insured that Masses would be celebrated in perpetuity for the souls of those rich enough to finance such endeavors. Although these practices were already centuries-old by the time of Trent, it was that council which articulated the theological theory which was used to justify them. (Precisely because this theory was presupposed by the bishops at Trent, it may be doubted that they expressly taught it.)

[39] In the years since the Second Vatican Council, the Church, perhaps without entirely realizing it, has moved away from this association of liturgy and Eucharist with Anselm's satisfaction theology (the liturgical reforms which were authorized by the council and which came into effect in the years immediately following it had important effects here; of the four different Eucharistic prayers or "canons" authorized, only one, the translation of the Roman Canon, makes much use of

sacrificial terminology), but this approach risks making the liturgy into a family celebration without any clear connection with the Cross, and it has left many Catholics without any real insight into what they should be doing when they take part in the Eucharistic celebration.

[40] 1 Cor 2:2.

[41] Phil 2:7.

[42] Rom 4:17.

[43] See, for example, Merleau-Ponty, "Faith and Good Faith," *Sense and Nonsense*, trans. Hubert L. Dreyfus and Patricia Allen Dreyfus (Evanston, Ill.: Northwestern University Press, 1964) 172–81, in which he criticizes the "internal and external God" of Christianity.

Tillich's Understanding of Symbols and Roman Catholic Sacramental Theology

Kenan B. Osborne, O.F.M.

Introduction

The Roman Catholic fascination with the thought of Paul Tillich has proven to be exceptionally long-lasting. From 1950 to 1980 this fascination became quite intense. Since then, the intensity has to some degree declined, but the same fascination lingers on in quieter and subtler ways. Perhaps this Roman Catholic interest has been fostered by Tillich's own fascination with philosophy.[1] Perhaps it stems from Tillich's unabashed enthusiasm for and concentration on the symbolic.[2] Whatever the reason or combination of reasons, Tillich remains, even as we come to the end of the second millennium and move into the third millennium, a contemporary theologian with deep Lutheran rootage and with amazingly strong Roman Catholic appeal.

In the area of sacramental theology, Tillich's appeal is both understandable and mystifying. One can justifiably understand the Catholic interest in Tillich's writings, since he spent so much effort in elucidating his analysis of the symbolic, and each and every sacrament, theoretically and liturgically, thrives on symbolism. Nonetheless, one might at the same time be mystified, since Tillich himself wrote only in passing ways on specific sacraments, such as baptism and Eucharist,[3] and he even tended to move beyond a narrow view of the sacramental field, common to both Lutheran and Roman Catholic Churches, into the quite cosmic view of pan-sacramentalism.[4]

There is no need in the following pages to rewrite, even in a summary form, the excellent studies on the Roman Catholic evaluation of Tillich's sacramental insights.[5] Such an endeavor would result in a mere cataloguing of various authors and of their respective theological evaluations on the theme. Rather, the following few pages will attempt to move the contemporary quieter and more subtle dialogue between Roman Catholic sacramental thought and Tillich into a deeper dimension, i.e., beyond the analytic elements of the symbolic *per se* into Tillich's foundational positions regarding the very *raison d'etre* of the symbolic, drawing together Tillich's insights into the primordial rootage of the symbolic, on the one hand, and on the other, the insights of Roman Catholic sacramental theology, at least in its post-Vatican II environment, on the primordiality of sacramental thought. Some of these observations derive specifically from the reply of Tillich himself to the several articles gathered together in the volume, *Paul Tillich in Catholic Thought*, published in 1964.[6] In this volume, certain Roman Catholic theologians raised serious objections to Tillich's basic stance towards various aspects of theology. On his part, Tillich responded to the three basic criticisms these Catholic authors had developed: namely, subjectivity rather than objectivity; autonomy rather than church authority; symbol rather than analogy. However, Tillich went on to pursue the issues into even more fundamental layers of theological thought: namely, into the very meaning of the term "God" and of Christology.

It is important to note that it is precisely the God-question and the Jesus-question that are key in today's post-Vatican II Roman Catholic theology. Accordingly, it is primarily this interfacing—Tillich's theology and Roman Catholic sacramental theology as it expresses the reality of God and the reality of Jesus—which the following pages will pursue. One additional theme, however, will also be raised, even though this was not a part of the response by Tillich to the Roman Catholic authors in the volume just mentioned. It is the theme of faith, which Tillich continually brought into the discourse on religious symbol, but which, as we shall see, Roman Catholic and Lutheran authors, with their differing understandings of faith, rarely, if ever, confront.

Inevitably, then, the following pages will touch on some of the foundational Lutheran positions of Tillich's thought as regards sacramental theology. These Lutheran positions, however, only stress more fundamental Christian positions found in the Word of God itself, and their recall raises once again both a positive and negative critique on any sacramental theology, Roman Catholic or Lutheran, that attempts to emphasize structure over spirit.[7] In this regard, J. Pelikan, in his volume *Spirit Versus Structure: Luther and the Institutions of the Church*, wrote in a telling way:

> The institutions of the medieval Christendom were in trouble, and everyone knew it. Intended as windows through which men might catch a glimpse of the Eternal they had become opaque, so that the faithful looked at them rather than through them. The structures of the Church were supposed to act as vehicles for the spirit—both for

the Spirit of God and for the spirit of man. . . . Instead what he [man] found was a distortion of faith.[8]

At the time of the Reformation, it was not sacramental theology *per se* that formed the areas of contention. Rather, the sacraments, especially baptism, Eucharist, and order, were, in these sixteenth-century confrontations, the *foci* in and through which far deeper issues appeared. These sacramental issues were indeed the *foci* of distortion to which Pelikan refers. Both sacramental theology and sacramental liturgy, within the centuries of Christian tradition, can move and, at times, have indeed moved into a narcissistic embrace with their own structural, symbolic beauty, preventing the major emphasis from resting on the deeper beauty of that which is symbolized itself. In sacramental or symbolic theology and liturgy, it is not the symbolic itself that should rivet one's attention of mind and heart, but the symbolized, and more specifically, that which is ultimately symbolized, that which is at the heart of the *mysterium fascinosum et tremendum*. Pursuing Pelikan's metaphor, one could state the case as follows: a Christian must see through the stained-glass sacramental window, beautiful as this window might be, even if this can take place only in a dim and partial way, and never arrest one's gaze at the sacramental window itself. Through the glass darkly a Christian strives to see the ultimate mystery, which draws and awes at one and the same time.

The Status of Current Roman Catholic Sacramental Theology

Before we consider Tillich's relationship to Roman Catholic sacramental theology in this post-Vatican II period, it seems necessary to reflect briefly on the status of current Roman Catholic sacramental theology. Vatican II did not cause the current unrest in sacramental theology, but it certainly provided a catalyst for the coalescing of many issues within Catholicism which have contributed to the current situation.

It is not only fair but unabashedly honest to say that current Roman Catholic sacramental theology and its liturgical practice is a somewhat splintered reality. Since 1900 various factors have caused a veritable "revolution" within Roman Catholic sacramental thinking.[9] The major factors in this reconstruction include: the scholarly research into the history of sacraments which began to develop around 1900; the appearance of the theological view that the Church itself is a basic sacrament, a view which was officially adopted in the documents of Vatican II; the theological acceptance of Jesus, in his humanity, as the primordial or original sacrament; the entrance of phenomenology and proc-ess modes of thinking into an arena dominated by Neo-Thomism; the ecumenical movement with its major rewriting of both sacramental thought and practice; and the unabated influence of three imposing forms of liberation theology: namely, the Latin American forms, the African American forms, and the several feminist forms, each of them with their emphases on the social dimension of sacramental thought and practice. All of these issues have caused a deep "shaking of the sacramental foundations" within the Roman Catholic sacramental world.

As a result of this rather revolutionary sacramental thinking, there is, in the final decade of the twentieth century, considerable stress. There are basically some inner-Roman-Catholic-Church pressures that urge these newer understandings of sacramental life and thought, and simultaneously there are other inner-Roman-Catholic-Church pressures that urge a return, in some degree at least, to pre-Vatican II positions. The following examples are recounted merely as indicative of these tensions.

Jesus as Primordial Sacrament

The view of Jesus, in his humanity, as the most fundamental and basic sacrament, remains quixotic. After the initial writings of Semmel-roth, Rahner, and Schillebeeckx, together with various lesser theo-logians who continued their insights into Jesus as primordial sacrament, Roman Catholic Christology has, by and large, returned to issues which had been central to the field throughout this century: namely, the lengthy Protestant and Catholic discussion on the meaning of the resur-rection; the ongoing discussion on the relationship of Jesus to the vari-ous strands of co-terminous Jewish religious thought; the Christologies of liberation, mentioned above; and the more biblical and less dog-matic forms of Christology.[10] In many ways, such Christological studies ought to supplant any current discourse on Jesus as primordial sacra-ment, since these investigations will ultimately better qualify "which" Jesus might serve as primordial sacrament. It is one thing to name Jesus in his humanity as the primordial sacrament; but it is quite another thing to specify the theological image of Jesus in his humanity, which then serves as the primordial sacrament. A theological portrait which does not do justice to the meaning of resurrection, to the Jewishness of Jesus, to the biblical picture of Jesus, or to the social dimension of Jesus will not and ought not be considered the primordial sacrament.

Church as Basic Sacrament

Although the documents of Vatican II spoke of the Church itself as a "basic sacrament," there are many Roman Catholic leadership people, both administrative and theological, who give only lip service to this position. The Church, for these leadership people, remains a sacrament only in an analogous way, with the primary analogue, however, still embedded in the seven-fold sacramental system.[11] For such authors, the Church is a basic sacrament, but only in a derivative manner. Such a view of analogy, however, does not do justice to the magisterial statements that present the Church itself as the basic sacrament. That the Church is the basic sacrament means that the Church is the basic analogue, the primary analogue, in the sense that the very meaning of the individual sacraments depends for their very essence on the constitutive sacramental nature of the Church. It is the Church as basic sacrament which makes baptism, Eucharist, etc. sacraments; it is not baptism, Eucharist, etc., which make the Church a sacrament. The basic sacramentalism of the Church itself—the Church therefore as a sacrament of Jesus—places the discussion of Tillich's understanding of symbol on a different plane, and until the inner conflicts of Roman Catholic thought are resolved, it is difficult to utilize Tillich's insights, without seeming to favor one or the other side of the Catholic inner-church struggle.[12]

Baptism and Confirmation

Roman Catholics, in their discussions and in their liturgies of the sacrament of baptism, have been continually confronted in the last decade of the twentieth century by a concerted effort on the part of high church leadership to acknowledge that baptism, in its dimension as an entry into the Church, means no more and no less than an entry into the only true Church, i.e., the Roman Catholic Church. Cardinal Joseph Tomko, for instance, when addressing the Asian Bishops' Conference in Bandung, Indonesia (July 1990), chastized those movements which made the "kingdom," not the Church, the focal point of evangelization. In such a venture, he said, "the consequences are simply devastating. The scope of evangelization is reduced and distorted; the necessity of faith in Jesus Christ, of baptism and the Church, are put in doubt."[13] In the context of his address, the reference to baptism/Church means faith in the Roman Catholic Church; for Tomko evangelization means conversion to the Roman Catholic Church. Tomko's interpretation is part and parcel of the effort of the Congregation for the Doctrine of the Faith to discredit any current theological interpretation that maintains that the statement in *Lumen Gentium*, "Haec ecclesia, in hoc mundo ut societas constituta et ordinata, subsistit in ecclesia catholica" (8b), involved an openness by Vatican II of true ecclesiality to any other Church except the Roman Catholic Church. All other Churches, in this interpretation, have at best "elements" of Church, but cannot be considered the true Church.[14]

This same approach is seen in the official response to the Lima Document, *Baptism, Eucharist, and Ministry,* formulated by the Secretariat for Promoting Christian Unity and the Congregation for the Doctrine of the Faith. In their response, the authors did not say that the Roman Catholic Church leadership could "accept" the document, *BEM;* rather, these authors indicated those areas in which *BEM* agrees with the Roman Catholic position, as well as those areas which fall short of Roman Catholic thought.[15] Over and over again, the issue is turned from baptism itself to ecclesiology, and rightfully in many ways, since without a solid ecclesiological base the sacraments of baptism, Eucharist, and order will not find their full meaning. Little effort, however, is made by the authors to base these sacraments in Christology. The document notes that the Catholic Church is unable "presently to engage in general eucharistic sharing. For in our view we cannot share in eucharist unless we share fully in that [individual ecclesial community's] faith."[16] Nonetheless, a series of documents from the Vatican has established guidelines for the reception of the Eucharist in nonuniate Orthodox Churches by Roman Catholics and *vice versa,* and for the reception by Protestants in Roman Catholic Eucharist. In these cases, acceptance of a given Church's baptismal faith, either that of the Roman Catholic or that of one of the Orthodox Churches, is not at all required. In these "individual" cases, Protestants do not have to accept the Roman Catholic understanding of the papacy nor the Roman Catholic approach to apostolic succession. Orthodox Christians, for their part, do not have to accept the papacy, nor is there any change required as regards their belief in episcopacy. In all of this, there are "mixed signals" on baptism-Eucharist, which stem from official documents of the Roman Church.

In Roman Catholic thought, confirmation, for the most part, remains a rudderless ship, dominated from diocese to diocese by the changing and ephemeral winds of the "age-of-confirmation" question, not by deeper questions of its sacramentality. Such a situation perdures in spite of important contributions by scholars on the history of confirmation and its relationship to baptism, and on the relationship of confirmation to a theology of the Holy Spirit.[17] With this in mind, one must realize how difficult it is to relate Tillich's thought to contemporary Roman Catholic theologies on confirmation.

Eucharist

Roman Catholic Eucharistic theology and liturgical practice evidences a multiple dyslexia: one reads in official documents of the Roman Church about the real presence of Jesus in a multi-dimensional way, only to be faced with an opposite reading of the real presence within the consecrated bread and wine.[18] One reads of ecumenical agreements on Eucharistic theology, only to be faced with an opposite reading on the minister of Eucharist.[19] One reads that the primary and first-priority celebration of Sunday by a Christian community can only be the Eucharist, only to be faced, on turning the page, to find an opposite reading of priorities, namely the priority of an exclusively male and celibate priesthood.[20] Instead of opening the discussion on the basis of a strongly worded priority of Sunday Eucharist, to the evidently secondary issues of a married clergy or of the ordination of women, these official documents maintain a contrary priority, based on the masculinity and celibacy of priesthood over their own stated priority, that only the Eucharistic celebration is both the first and the proper Sunday celebration by a Catholic-Christian community. When one turns the page, the actual reading moves in an opposite direction: namely, communion services in the absence of a priest. With all of this in mind, one must carefully interface Tillich's theological thinking with current Roman Catholic Eucharist theologies.

Priesthood

As regards current discussion on the sacrament of order, the theological disarray, which has arisen in an attempt to interpret statements in Vatican II on the priesthood of all believers and on the sharing of all baptized and Eucharistic Christians in the *tria munera* of Jesus, has by and large displaced the ecumenical discussions on priesthood, with an internal struggle over the role of the lay person within the structures of the Roman Catholic Church.[21] Once again, one sees how gingerly one must face the prospect of uniting Tillich's theological insights into current Roman Catholic theology on church ministry.

Marriage

The recent volume on *The Marital Sacrament* by T. Mackin pinpoints the current fundamental discussion on marriage within Roman Catholic thought, which has less to do with its sacramentality, but more with the jurisdictional issues involved in marriage. Mackin takes to task the official stance of ecclesiastical leadership on such jurisdictional claims.[22] Mackin's volume is merely indicative of the ferment within Roman

Catholic discussion and practice on the issue of marriage and the sacramentality of marriage. Such an awareness of this ferment is clearly necessary as a prerequisite for any discussion of Tillich's thought and current Roman Catholic sacramental thinking.

Similar conflicting signals could be mentioned with regard to the sacraments of reconciliation and anointing of the sick. Let the above suffice to indicate that the current arena of Roman Catholic sacramental theology is not at all of one piece. Indeed, there are internal struggles, which in many ways dissipate sacramental energies both in theory and in liturgical practice. On the other hand, it must be said that the "revolutionary" issues which have entered into the theological discourse have played an energizing role as well. I have highlighted only the negative factors above with but one intent: to indicate that a relationship of Tillich's thought to current Roman Catholic sacramental thinking must be done with considerable circumspection, and in many ways such an enterprise today is far more complicated than one finds in the studies regarding Tillich and Catholic thought, which were formulated in the 1950–1970 period. Since that period, Roman Catholic sacramental thought has changed, not in any uniform way, but in ways which involve deeper divisions of sacramental thought than previously was the case.

Tillich's Understanding of Symbol

Following the lead of Nörenberg, I want to preface my analysis of Tillich's understanding of symbol with some theological issues of which Tillich himself, time and again, reminds his readers. He says very clearly that there are basic ultimate objects that govern any and all theology, including the theology of symbols and the theology of sacraments. Moreover, there are criteria which adjudicate any and all theology, including the symbolic and sacramental. These ultimate objects and basic criteria cannot be placed to one side, if one intends to enter into Tillich's approach to the symbolic. Rather, these are the dimensions which undergird all that he says about the symbolic, and about which Tillich himself is ultimately concerned, as he himself treats each and every preliminary symbolic concern.

In a work which Tillich himself rewrote at least three times, *Dimensionen, Schichten und die Einheit des Seins*, he tried to come to grips with the foundational area of symbolic thought: "We know that real representative symbols, prevalent in history, art, and religion, cannot be arbitrarily substituted by other symbols. They have come out of a particular encounter with reality and are living only as long as the experience is alive."[23]

In this essay, Tillich speaks warmly of the fifteenth-century cardinal, Nicholas of Cusa: "He seeks to understand the infinity of the infinite and realizes that the infinite would cease to be infinite if the finite would stand next to it as a distinct limiting area."[24] Nicholas' *coincidentia oppositorum* means that there is a presence of the infinite in every finite being, and that every finite being is present in the infinite. In a way similar to that of Luther, Tillich sees that Nicholas understood that God is present in every grain of sand: the center of divine infinity is present in every point of the periphery, in every finite being. With this immanent/transcendent view in mind, Tillich indicates that one does not approach the infinite God through a structuring of hierarchical layers (*Schichten*); rather, one begins to see the infinite God in the dimensions of each and every being. Symbolic existence, and especially religious symbolic existence, is ultimately not hierarchically structured. According to Tillich symbolic existence is dimensionally interfaced, i.e., each dimension of finite being, whether in the center of some structure or at the periphery, is open to the dimension of infinity or at least is ontologically able to be so. It is on this basis that Tillich is able to speak of a pan-sacramentalism, which does not mean that all entities are religious symbols, but only that any and every entity could be a religious symbol. Tillich is quite aware that religious symbols need the acceptance of a human community, not merely of an individual, in order that they be considered and experienced as living symbols.

When one transfers this way of thinking into a specific form of symbolic thought and practice, namely, sacramental theology and sacramental liturgy, one concludes: hierarchical structure is not the *controlling factor* either for a theological understanding of the sacrament or for the liturgical praying of the sacrament. Rather, the *controlling factor* is the dimensional interfacing of each and every aspect and being of sacramental theology and sacramental liturgy with the presence of the ultimate, the infinite.[25] This does not mean, however, that hierarchical structure should be summarily abolished; on the contrary, it means that hierarchical structure itself stands under the judgment of the same ultimate theological objects and the same ultimate criteria which undergird each and every aspect of the theological elements of the Christian life. Hierarchy itself shares in the symbolic fabric of the religious dimension of life, and consequently hierarchy shares in both the advantages of the symbolic and the temptation of the symbolic to be demonic. Tillich's preference for the metaphor of dimension rather than the metaphor of structure seems to be closer to the symbolic and the sacramental theology one finds in Roman Catholic, post-Vatican II theology and liturgy, namely the view that the Church, i.e., the total people of God, is the basic sacrament, and that Jesus in his humanity is the primordial sacrament. In this approach the humanity of Jesus primordially, and the people of God fundamentally are the constitutive reasons why hierarchy within the Jesus-community can be sacramental. It is not sacramental hierarchy which is the basis for a sacramental Church; it is a sacramental Church which is the basis for a sacramental hierarchy. It is precisely this position which is at the basis of the phrase: the Church is a fundamental sacrament. However, the Church is only Church because of a deeper reason: Jesus in his humanity is the primordial sacrament, which allows the Jesus-community itself, the people of God, to become a sacrament in its own dimension.[26]

Symbol and God as ''ultimate concern''

The most important aspect of Tillich's thought that bears on the issue of the Christian sacraments is, consequently, his insistence on God as ''ultimate concern.'' Long before one begins to speak about a sacrament or a symbol in relationship to God, Tillich emphasizes the issue of *ultimacy* within our human concern about God, and even more profoundly the *ultimacy* of the object of that concern itself, who is God for us. ''The object of theology is what concerns us ultimately. Only those objects are theological which deal with their object in so far as it can become a matter of ultimate concern for us.''[27]

Tillich makes more precise his understanding of God as ultimate concern: ''Our ultimate concern is that which determines our being or not-being. Only those statements are theological which deal with their object insofar as it can become a matter of being or not-being for us.''[28]

To begin a discussion on sacramental theology within Tillich's approach and not to begin with his theology of ultimacy, i.e., God, would be to forget how deeply Lutheran Tillich's approach to all theology truly is. The key and deepest issue that Luther had raised against the Roman approach to sacraments at the time of the Reformation can be stated as follows: sacraments cannot manipulate God. In such a sentence, the emphasis does not fall on the sacrament itself, but rather on God, or more accurately on the absolute freedom of God. Such an emphasis was not new to Luther, for one finds this concern about the absolute freedom of God in an immediate tradition of high and late Scholastic theology, in John Duns Scotus, William of Ockham, and

Gabriel Biel. Biel, in a very direct way, influenced the thought of Luther, and Luther's shadow is on every page of Tillich's writings.

Let us consider more carefully the first of Tillich's statements cited above: the object of theology is what concerns us ultimately. Since sacraments or religious symbols are signs of God's action, the formal criteria of Tillich's systematic theology stands at the very threshold of any approach to sacramental theology within a Tillichian framework. Preliminary concerns are indeed related to the ultimate concern, and as a consequence are also related to the theological enterprise. This occurs whenever preliminary concerns become the media of ultimacy, i.e., a vehicle which points beyond itself.[29] At times, however, these preliminary concerns can be elevated to a position of pseudo-ultimacy, and when this happens, for instance, in liturgical worship or in Bible worship, the preliminary becomes demonic, and the result is a warped legalistic or magical sacramentalism, or a warped biblical fundamentalism.

In his quest for ultimate concern, Tillich is doing no more than pursuing the first commandment: God alone is ultimate and every idolatry is the elevation of something preliminary into a pseudo-ultimacy.[30] Perhaps in this first formal criterion we hear only the "thou shalt not" of the first commandment. It is his second, formal but co-relative criterion, which presents the positive side.

The second formal criterion answers in a general way the question: what does concern us ultimately and unconditionally? The answer Tillich gives is this: as far as our human life is concerned, our ultimate concern is that which affects our being or our nonbeing.[31] Through this second formal criterion, the issue Tillich poses for us is not a choice between two different ways of being. Rather, we are confronted by only one way of being, to which we must answer: "Ja oder Nein." Beyond this one way of being is absolute nonbeing. Nonbeing, in this context, is not *me on* but *ouk on.*[32] The boundary Tillich describes is not a boundary between one form of being and another form of being, and therefore a passage from being in one way to not being in that same way. Rather, the passage is from being at all to not being at all. It is this ontological/non-ontological boundary that Tillich time and time again addressed: a *Grenz-situation*, in which being itself is at stake.[33]

In the dimension of the theologically symbolic, these norms, as far as Tillich's thought is concerned, play a foundational role, and the rootage of this approach of Tillich can be traced back to the diverse reformations of the sixteenth century, and from these reformations back to the word of God itself. The more closely religious symbolism leads us to that which is of ultimate concern, the more validly religious it is and the more authentically symbolic it is. The more religious symbolism presents us with something only of preliminary concern, the more demonic it is and the more inauthentically symbolic it is. Though not using the precise language which Tillich employs, the Reformation theologians of the sixteenth century expressed serious hesitation with the Roman approach to sacraments, which tended to raise good works, priestly power, and papal control—all of which are only preliminary concerns—to the level of ultimate concerns. Luther's *Babylonian Captivity*, with all of its harsh and unsettling language, centered on this critique of the then commonly-portrayed view of Roman Catholic sacramental theology, and the ferocity of Luther's language should not dissuade one from perceiving the accuracy of his critique.[34]

Pre-Vatican II Roman Catholic sacramental theology almost univocally centered on the valid matter and form, the validity of the minister, and the intentionality of the recipient. All of these are preliminary concerns. In comparison, the manuals of theology offered fewer pages on God's action in the sacramental event. These various theological textbooks concentrated far more on what humans did, and what they did in a "valid" way, *so that* God's action could take place in the sacraments. Human actions became, to some degree, pseudo-ultimate, in the sense that good works, i.e., the proper using of matter, the proper speaking of *formulae*, the proper intentionality of both minister and recipient, became conditions for grace, i.e., God's own free action. In post-Vatican II sacramental theology, there is, as we have seen above, an inner-church struggle, with some leadership people, both ecclesiastical and theological, emphasizing these same preliminary concerns: matter, form, intentionality, proper ministry, and these precisely as conditions for the effectiveness of grace. On the other hand, there are some who make the action of the Church-community, i.e., the people of God, actions which condition the free giving of God's grace. For them, the sacramental celebration is a celebration of community, not the celebration of ultimacy. Only when Roman Catholic sacramental theology and liturgical practice celebrate what God is doing more insistently and consistently than what Church or hierarchy or recipient are doing will Roman Catholic theology become transparently sacramental. Such a *desideratum* or goal indicates the value of Tillich's entire approach to religious symbol, when it interfaces with Roman Catholic sacramental theology and liturgical practice. Tillich's theology challenges Roman Catholic sacramental theory and worship to come to grips with ultimate concern.

Tillich's Theology and the Issue of Faith

Key to Tillich's approach to sacramental and symbolic theology is the constitutive relationship of sacrament and faith: "There is no sacramental object apart from faith which grasps him because he has been grasped by it. Apart from the faith-sacrament correlation, no sacrament exists."[35] A Roman Catholic might read this statement and immediately affirm such a correlation. However, a major complication lies behind these words. The Roman Catholic understanding of "faith" and the Lutheran understanding of "faith" do not coincide. For the Roman Catholic, the understanding of faith, at least in the way it developed from Augustine, through the period of high Scholasticism, and reached the Council of Trent and the post-Tridentine theology, was this: faith alone is a condition or a precondition for true justification or sanctification. *Fides caritate informata* became the standard approach to faith, which one finds in all the above-mentioned sources. Charity is equivalent or quasi-equivalent to sanctifying grace, so that one can indeed have faith, but without charity (sanctifying grace) such an "uninformed faith" will neither sanctify nor justify. Only with the "infusion of sanctifying grace" can faith become justifying. Seripando, the general of the Augustinians, who played a major role at the Council of Trent, wrote on the margin of a draft-document, given him by the secretarial staff of Trent: "What do I hear? All that we read in the Scriptures about justification by faith is to be understood of the disposition?" Does the New Testament's use of the term "faith" mean the same as *fides caritate informata?* or does it simply mean *fides?*[36]

During and since the Council of Trent the discussions between Roman Catholics and Lutherans, even those which have taken place in our own century, have never addressed the differences in this understanding of faith. Vorgrimler writes: "As regards the theologically central question of Luther—the question of faith—Trent . . . did not address it."[37]

Just as the objects and criteria of all theology are foundational for any approach of Tillich's thought to current Roman Catholic sacramental theology, so, too, is the issue of faith. Tillich, as a profound Lutheran scholar, uses the term "faith" in ways which Roman Catholics do not, and *vice versa*. The term "faith" for Tillich involves the total acceptance of that which concerns one ultimately, and an acceptance which sees in such an ultimate concern a matter of being and non-being. Is this a *fides fiducialis?* Indeed it is. It is the entrusting of one's total finite being into infinite being. But it is more than this as well. In fact, more basically, it is God's work: "Faith, formally or generally defined, is the state of being grasped by that toward which self-transcendence aspires, the ultimate in being and meaning. In a short formula, one can say that faith is the state of being grasped by an ultimate concern."[38]

Tillich readily admits that at times "faith becomes religion in the churches—ambiguous, disintegrating, destructive, tragic, and demonic. But at the same time, there is a power of resistance against the manifold distortions of faith—the divine Spirit and its embodiment, the Spiritual Community."[39] Symbolic and sacramental theology and liturgy become undistorted to the degree that they allow the ultimate to grasp those involved within the symbolic and sacramental event.

Concluding Remarks

Tillich, in his "Afterword: Appreciation and Reply" to the volume on *Paul Tillich in Catholic Thought,* initially summarized the negative critiques under the three categories previously cited: his subjectivity over against the Catholic authors' objectivity; his autonomy over against their position on church authority; his use of symbol over against their understanding of analogy. Thirty years later Catholic thought on the sacraments has been deeply touched by phenomenology, particularly through Rahner's use of Heidegger's thought, and Schillebeeckx's incorporation of phenomenology and the results of his discussions with the monks of Taize. Clearly, the analysis of *Dasein* in Heidegger is not an analysis of a totally "objective being." It is an analysis of *Sein,* but only within a structure that we know, the *Dasein.* What *Sein* might be beyond that analysis remains conjectural at best. In the phenomenological writings of Maurice Merleau-Ponty, we find again a subjectivist trend, but one which, as in the works of Heidegger, cannot be avoided. The phenomenology of perception is a perception *only* from the standpoint of human perception. There is no perception *sub specie aeternitatis.* The stress on objectivity, which the Catholic authors had stated so categorically, is a stress with many presuppositions of its own, which these same authors did not sufficiently analyze. Tillich rightly noted his disagreement, and his disagreement was based on the inability of finite nature to have "objective" knowledge of all being, and above all an "objective" finite knowledge of infinite being.

When the argument of church authority was broached, Tillich again stated a very Lutheran and Protestant position, namely, that the Word of God stands over and against any and all words of human beings. He did this not in any neo-orthodox or Barthian way; rather, he spoke about the autonomy of the subject, who is filled theonomously with the Spirit of God. Interestingly enough, one finds in the documents of Vatican II the clear indication that the *Light of the World* is Jesus alone, and that the Church, including Church leadership, is thereby relativized. Only when the Church and Church leadership reflect Jesus are they truly Church [*Lumen gentium*]. Interestingly enough, one finds in these same documents the inviolability of the human conscience, in which the Spirit of God speaks to a person, and into which no other voice will and can penetrate [*Gaudium et spes*]. One also finds in these same documents the position that Scripture confronts everyone in the Church with an accountability: all are under the Word of God, Church authority included [*Verbum Dei*].

As regards the discussion on analogy and symbol, Tillich rightly indicated that the *analogia entis* of Thomas Aquinas, and the two forms, namely the analogy of attribution and the analogy of proper proportionality, are but one strand of Scholastic teaching, and not by any means the only Catholic strand. There is, he noted, the Augustinian-Franciscan school, which Bonaventure and to some degree Scotus represent and to which Tillich felt great kinship. This latter form is not based on *analogia entis*, nor on such structures as attribution and proper proportionality. In other words, the gauge against which Tillich was criticized is itself open to serious criticism, for the gauge is Thomistic, and there are other quite acceptable gauges within the Scholastic tradition which critique the Thomistic gauge. In Roman Catholic thought, sacraments, in particular, do not have to be studied either through a system of *analogia entis*, or through the structures of an analogy of attribution and of proper proportionality. If, in Roman Catholicism, the teaching of *analogia entis* is but one way of approaching symbol and sacrament, why is Tillich's approach to symbol and sacrament unacceptable?

These three conflicting positions, however, are preliminary to Tillich's main concerns, and the first issue for deeper discussion is the doctrine of God, the ground of being and the ultimate concern, which was mentioned above. Tillich's theology even today critiques contemporary, post-Vatican II sacramental theology with the question of God. What God, and what kind of God, does the Roman Catholic Church celebrate in sacramental liturgy? What God and what kind of God appears in the sacramental theological literature of current Roman Catholic scholars? If the God which one finds, either in liturgy or in theory, is not a God of ultimate concern, then there is a major question as to the very validity of either the sacramental liturgy or the sacramental theory.

Second, God must be understood as a gift of spiritual presence to each and every being, above all to each and every human person. God's presence is not the "essence of all things," but God's presence is indeed in all things in a theonomous way. All things, therefore, *ex natura sua* could be symbols. In the area of religious symbols, a community, not merely a single individual, needs to find such symbols as opening to the ultimate. This is, of course, an ambiguous and often difficult task, but such ambiguity and difficulty is not and cannot be erased by some heteronomous authority, even church authority, since church authority itself is symbolic, or, as the documents of Vatican II teach, it is Jesus who is *Lumen gentium*, not the Church and not church hierarchy, even at its highest level. The Church and church hierarchy at all levels are called on to reflect the true *Lumen gentium*, Jesus. Whenever the Church and church hierarchy do this, they are truly ecclesial. Whenever the Church and church hierarchy do not do this, they share in what Tillich calls the demonic. Christology, not ecclesiology, is fundamental, as the documents of Vatican II clearly specify.

Third, although Tillich does not mention this in the "Afterword," there is the basic question of faith which he does mention often in other writings. Without faith there are no sacraments, but what is faith? In so many of his writings, Tillich again and again raised the issue of the meaning of faith. Time and time again, the Lutheran-Catholic dialogue has failed to center its discussions on the meaning of faith. Until this task is forthrightly done, the issues separating Tillich's thought and the mainline of Roman Catholic thought will remain at odds.

Finally, one could say that Jesus is the primordial sacrament, in Tillich's view, only when Jesus, in his humanity, is the primordial sacrament of the ultimate, that which confronts us human beings as being or nonbeing. Until current Christology reaches some conclusion regarding the integral role and meaning of the resurrection, the Jewishness of Jesus, the more biblical and less dogmatic understanding of Jesus, and the social consequences of the Jesus-event, Jesus, as the primordial sacrament, will undoubtedly not be a sign of ultimate concern. However, once Jesus truly becomes in Roman Catholic sacramental theory and liturgy the primordial sacrament, then the Church and the sacramental liturgies themselves will indeed be experienced as symbols of ultimacy. Jesus, for the Christian communities, remains the key, or as Tillich wrote: "The Logos doctrine of the identity of the absolutely concrete with the absolutely universal is not one theological doctrine among others; it is the only possible foundation of a Christian theology which claims to be *the* theology."[40] "Wherever the assertion that Jesus is the Christ is maintained, there is the Christian message;

wherever this assertion is denied, the Christian message is not affirmed."[41] These assertions are basic to the way in which Tillich's thought interfaces with Roman Catholic sacramental theology: when Roman Catholic sacraments assert that Jesus is the Christ, then these sacraments are indeed true Christian sacraments.

In all of the above, Tillich continually calls on all sacramental Churches, including the Roman Catholic and the Lutheran, to focus on the ultimate concern, and find in the ultimate concern the most fundamental criterion for any and all evaluation of both sacramental thought and sacramental *praxis*.

Notes

[1] On the Roman Catholic interest in Tillich, cf. esp. G. Weigel, "The Theological Significance of Paul Tillich," in *Paul Tillich in Catholic Thought* (Dubuque: The Priory Press, 1962) 3–24; T. O'Meara, "Tillich and the Catholic Substance," in *The Thought of Paul Tillich*, eds. J. L. Adams, W. Pauck, and R. L. Shinn (San Francisco: Harper and Row, 1985) 290–306; R. Modras, *Paul Tillich's Theology of the Church: A Catholic Appraisal* (Detroit: Wayne State University Press, 1976) esp. 163–73; B. Reymond, "La Réception de Tillich et de ses oeuvres dans les pays d'expression française," in *Religion et Culture: Colloque du Centenaire Paul Tillich* (Paris: Editions du Cerf, 1987) 31–45, esp. "La lecture catholique de Tillich," 34–38. Reymond notes that among French authors, Catholic writing on Tillich is almost totally post-Vatican II, with the one exception of G. Tavard, "Le Principe protestant el le système théologique de Paul Tillich," *Revue des sciences philosophiques et théologiques* (1962) 224–54. Reymond lists several important French Roman Catholic authors who contributed substantial works on Tillich: Jean Rieunaud, Marc Michel, Jean-Claude Petit, Fernand Chapey. However, he notes that the French interest in Tillich was primarily focused on the philosophical issues and did not seem to move beyond those issues. For the North American scene, however, Reymond notes: "Surtout si l'on tient compte de l'audience persistante de Tillich en Amérique du Nord, et de son influence considérable plus profonde qu'elle ne fut jamais en Europe en général, et parmi les francophones en particulier" (p. 38). This article was published in 1987 and provides us with an overview of Tillich's post-Vatican II influence on Roman Catholic scholarship, among French authors in particular, but with an indirect reference to North American authors as well.

[2] Tillich's interest in symbol is already evident in some of his earliest writings: *Religionsphilosophie der Kultur* (Berlin: Reuther and Reichard 1919) and *Das System der Wissenschaften nach Gegenständen und Methoden* (Göttingen: Vandenhoeck and Ruprecht, 1923). He developed his ideas on symbol in more explicit ways in such later writings as: "Das religiöse Symbol," *Blätter für deutsche Philosophie*, 1 (1928) 277–91; "Religiöse Symbol," *Religiöse Verwirklichung* (Berlin: Furche Verlag, 1930);

"Existential Analyses and Religious Symbols," in *Contemporary Problems in Religion* (Detroit: Wayne University Press, 1956) 35–55, ed. H. A. Baselius. The theme of symbol remains a constant in almost all of his major works, particularly in his *Systematic Theology*. Klaus-Dieter Nörenberg has analyzed Tillich's approach to symbol in *Analogia Imaginis: Der Symbolbegriff in der Theologie Paul Tillichs* (Gütersloh: Gerd Mohn, 1966), see especially chapters 4, 5, and 6 (76–128). It is important to note that Nörenberg only approaches Tillich's understanding of symbol after he has established in the second chapter Tillich's preconditions for symbolic thought and expression, namely within the framework of the fundamental criteria for all theology. Cf. also Jocelyn Dunphy, *Paul Tillich et le symbole religieux* (Paris: J.-P. Delarge, Éditions Universitaires, 1977); A. Rössler, "Das Symbolverständnis Paul Tillichs in seiner Bedeutung für die kirchliche Praxis," in *Die Bedeutung Paul Tillichs für die kirchliche Praxis*, ed. W. Schmidt (Stuttgart: Evangelisches Verlagswerk, 1976) 53–77; G. F. McLean, "Symbol and Analogy: Tillich and Thomas," in *Paul Tillich in Catholic Thought*, 145–83.

³ Cf. Tillich, "Natur und Sakrament," *Religiöse Verwirchlikung* (1928) revised to some extent in Paul Tillich, *Gesammelte Werke*, ed. Renate Albrecht (Stuttgart: Evangelisches Verlagswerk, 1959–75) 7:105–23; *The Protestant Era* (Chicago: University of Chicago Press, 1948) esp. the introductory chapter; *Systematic Theology* 3 vols. (Chicago: University of Chicago Press, 1951–63) 3:120–24, 217–20.

⁴ Cf. Tillich, "Natur und Sakrament," 110. Cf. also R. C. Crossman, *Paul Tillich: A Comprehensive Bibliography and Keyword Index of Primary and Secondary Writings in English* (London: The Scarecrow Press, 1983), who lists only two references to the word *sacrament* in his cross-referencing of Tillich's own writings and writings on Tillich [until 1983].

⁵ Cf. L. J. Putnam, "Tillich on the Sacraments," *Theology and Life* 8 (1965) 2, 108–16; Modras, *Tillich's Theology of the Church*, 107–12, 194–99, 253–56.

⁶ Cf. Tillich, "An Afterword: Appreciation and Reply," in *Paul Tillich in Catholic Thought*, 301–11.

⁷ Tillich himself wrote in "Die protestantische Ära," *Gesammelte Werke* 7:23: "Der protestantische Protest hat zu Recht die magischen Elemente im katholischen Sakramentalismus zerstört, aber er hat zu Unrecht die sakramentale Grundlage des Christentums bis an den Rand des Verschwindens gebracht, und damit die religiöse Grundlage des Prinzips selber."

⁸ J. Pelikan, *Spirit versus Structure: Luther and the Institutions of the Church* (New York: Harper and Row, 1968) 5.

⁹ Cf. K. Osborne, *Sacramental Theology* (New York: Paulist, 1988) 1–17.

¹⁰ In Roman Catholic and Protestant Christology today the focus has been on the meaning of the resurrection of Jesus, cf. G. Ghiberti, who lists 1,510 scholarly books, monographs, and articles in the major European languages on the resurrection of Jesus written between 1920 and 1973, *Resurrexit: Actes du symposium international sur la Résurrection de Jésus*, ed. E. Dhanis (Rome: Libreria Editrice Vaticana, 1974) 643–745; on the issue of the Jewishness of Jesus, cf. E. P. Sanders, *Jesus and Judaism* (Philadelphia: Fortress, 1985); J. Charlesworth, *Jesus within Juda-*

ism (New York: Doubleday, 1988); J. Meier, *A Marginal Jew: Rethinking the Historical Jesus* (New York: Doubleday, 1991); D. Crossan, *The Historical Jesus: The Life of a Mediterranean Jewish Peasant* (San Francisco: Harper, 1991); on a Roman Catholic biblical, rather than a dogmatic approach to Jesus, cf. E. Schillebeeckx, *Jesus* (New York: Seabury, 1979); and on the social dimension of Christology, cf. J. Sobrino, *Christology at the Crossroads* (New York: Orbis, 1978), and L. Boff, *Jesus Christ Liberator* (New York: Orbis, 1978).

¹¹ O. Semmelroth, "Die Kirche als Sakrament des Heils," *Mysterium Salutis* (Einsiedeln: Benziger, 1972) 4/1:320, speaks unclearly on this issue of analogy; the same can be said of R. Schulte, "Die Einzelsakramente als Ausgliederung des Wurzelsakramentes," ibid., 46–63; cf. Osborne, *Sacramental Theology*, 86–97.

¹² Cf. H. Döring, "Die sakramentale Struktur der Kirche in katholischer Sicht," in *Die Sakramentalität der Kirche in der ökumenischen Diskussion* (Paderborn: Bonifatius Verlag, 1983) 20–125; G. Gaßmann, "Kirche als Sakrament, Zeichen und Werkzeug," ibid., 171–201.

¹³ Cf. the text in *Origins* 20 (1991) 46, 753–54. Tomko is the prefect of the Roman Congregation for the Evangelization of Peoples, and as such spoke at Bandung in an official Vatican capacity.

¹⁴ Cf. F. A. Sullivan, "The Significance of the Vatican II Declaration that the Church of Christ 'Subsists in' the Roman Catholic Church," *Vatican II Assessment and Perspectives* (New York: Paulist, 1989) 2:272–87. A view opposing Sullivan can be found in G. Ghirlanda, "Universal Church, Particular Church, and Local Church at the Second Vatican Council and in the New Code of Canon Law," ibid., 233–71, esp. 240–41.

¹⁵ An English translation of the text is found in *Churches Respond to BEM*, ed. M. Thurian (Geneva: World Council of Churches, 1988) 6:1–40.

¹⁶ Ibid., 25.

¹⁷ On the issue of confirmation cf. A. Kavanagh, *Confirmation: Origins and Reform* (New York: Pueblo, 1988); K. McDonnell and G. Montague, *Christian Initiation and Baptism in the Holy Spirit* (Collegeville, Minn.: Liturgical Press, 1991); S. Regli, "Firmsakrament und christliche Entfaltung," *Mysterium Salutis* 5:297–347; N. Mitchell, "Dissolution of the Rite of Christian Initiation," *Made Not Born* (Notre Dame: University of Notre Dame Press, 1976) 50–82.

¹⁸ For a summation of this situation cf. Osborne, *The Christian Sacraments of Initiation* (New York: Paulist, 1987) 205–9.

¹⁹ Cf. the official Roman Catholic response to *BEM*, in *Churches Respond to BEM*, 28–36. In this response, the fundamental argument of the Catholic respondents is a view of apostolic succession, based on the transmission of "power" from the apostles themselves to the "bishops." The data from the earliest church documents, however, do not provide a basis for such a "clear" interpretation. Only around 200 A.D. does this "apostolic succession of bishops" view begin to solidify. Nor can "ordination" be posited as a ritual of such transmission from the beginning of the post-resurrection Jesus-community. Prior to 200 any and every reconstruction of the data as to the way in which church leaders were installed remains highly

conjectural. From 200 onward an ordination form of such installation began to become commonplace, but even at that earlier period of time the stated purpose of such ordination rituals to the order of episkopos, presbyter, and deacon do not correspond to later stated purposes of similar ordination rituals.

20 Cf. Congregation for Divine Worship, *Directory for Sunday Celebrations in the Absence of a Priest* (Vatican City, 1988) esp. nos. 8–17 for the insistence on the priority of Sunday Eucharist. From n. 18 on, the alternate and secondary priority is a Eucharistic service by a deacon or a non-ordained person. The NCCB response, *Gathered in Steadfast Faith* (Washington, D.C.: USCC, 1991) briefly mentions the need for "creative solutions" (no. 3) but nos. 10–17 merely repeat the priority emphasis of the Vatican document. The issues of a married clergy or of the ordination of women are not mentioned as lesser priorities.

21 I have dealt at length with this discussion in *Ministry: Lay Ministry in the Roman Catholic Church. Its History and Theology* (New York: Paulist Press, 1993) 527–564.

22 Cf. T. Mackin, *Marriage as a Sacrament* (New York: Paulist, 1989).

23 Cf. Tillich, "Dimensions, Levels and the Unity of Life," *Kenyon Alumni Bulletin* 17 (1959); a revised edition is found in "Dimensionen, Schichten und die Einheit des Seins," *Neue Deutsche Hefte*, vol. 71 (1961); and the text in *Gesammelte Werke*, 4:118–29 also differs from neither of the above. Citation is from this latter version, 118–19.

24 Ibid., 119.

25 Tillich deliberately avoids such substantives as "*the* Ultimate," "*the* unconditioned," "*the* universal," "*the* infinite." Even the Hegelian "The Absolute" is not acceptable to Tillich. Rather Tillich speaks more often of ultimate, unconditional, total concern. Cf. K. Osborne, *New Being: A Study on the Relationship between Conditioned and Unconditioned Being according to Paul Tillich* (The Hague: M. Nijhoff, 1969) 25ff., 76–82.

26 Cf. Tillich, "Natur und Sakrament," 121: "Das Heilige is allgegenwärtig insoweit, als der Seinsgrund nicht weit von jedem Seienden ist; das Heilige ist dämonisiert wegen der Trennung des unendlichen Seinsgrundes von jeder endlichen Wirklichkeit. Und schließlich ist das Heilige manifest in seiner Macht, das Dämonische zu überwinden an gesonderten Orten, letzlich an *einem* Ort, in Jesus als dem Christus."

27 Tillich, *Systematic Theology*, 1:12; cf. Osborne, *New Being*, 25.

28 Tillich, *Systematic Theology*, 1:14. Cf. Osborne, *New Being*, 25.

29 Tillich, "Das religiöse Symbol," 88–90, presents four characteristics of religious symbol: "Uneigentlichkeit," "Anschaulichkeit," "Selbstmächtigkeit," and "Anerkanntheit." Cf. also Nörenberg, *Analogia Imaginis*, 83–112.

30 Tillich began to make this principle central to his thought quite early on. In *Protestantisches Prinzip und proletarische Situation* (1931), he relates this principle to the social order; he continues in this vein in 1933 with the lengthy work, *Die sozialistische Entscheidung*. Cf. also *Das Dämonische* and almost all the articles in vol. 7 of *Gesammelte Werke*.

³¹ Cf. J. L. Adams, *Paul Tillich's Philosophy of Culture, Science and Religion* (New York: Harper and Row, 1965) 36–38; cf. Tillich, *Systematic Theology*, 1:14; cf. also Osborne, *New Being*, 27.

³² Cf. Tillich, *Systematic Theology*, 1:188.

³³ Cf. Tillich, "Das Religiöse als kritisches Prinzip: Die protestantische Verkündigung und der Mensch der Gegenwart," in *Religiöse Verwirklichung*, 31; reprinted in *Gesammelte Werke*, vol. 7; cf. ibid., 74: "Die menschliche Grenzsituation ist da erreicht, wo die menschliche Möglichkeit schlechthin zu Ende, die menschliche Existenz unter eine unbedingte Bedrohung gestellt ist." A few paragraphs later he writes, *Gesammelte Werke*, 7:75: "Denn die Grenzsituation des Menschen ist gerade darum möglich, weil er nicht eins ist mit seiner vitalen Existenz"; in *Religiöse Verwirklchung*, the text reads: ". . . mit seinem unmittelbaren Dasein." The change from *unmittelbares Dasein* to *vitale Existenz* indicates a development in Tillich's thought.

³⁴ The accuracy of Luther's critique can be seen in two decrees from the Council of Trent, namely, the decree on the Mass as a sacrifice, which upheld the full efficacy of the sacrifice of the cross, with no additional expiatory efficacy from a so-called "sacrifice" of or by the Church; and the decree on justification, which essentially endorsed the position of Luther on the issue of grace and good works, namely, that grace is an absolutely free gift of God, and that any human work, i.e., satisfaction, cannot be construed as efficaciously causing this free gift of God.

³⁵ Tillich, "Natur und Sakrament," 120.

³⁶ Cf. Osborne, *Reconciliation and Justification* (New York: Paulist, 1990) 190ff. for the details and implications of this comment by Seripando.

³⁷ Cf. H. Vorgrimler, "Der Kampf des Christen mit der Sünde," *Mysterium Salutis* 5:429–30.

³⁸ Tillich, *Systematic Theology*, 3:130; cf. this entire section, 129–38; also ibid., 173–77; also Tillich, *Dynamics of Faith* (New York: Harper and Row, 1957).

³⁹ Tillich, *Systematic Theology*, 3:173.

⁴⁰ Ibid., 1:17.

⁴¹ Ibid., 2:97.

History, Symbolism, and Eternal Life: Tillich's Contribution to Catholic Eschatology

Raymond F. Bulman

Eschatology is presently undergoing something of a revival in Catholic theology. This renewal, however, is very recent, having its origins at the time of Vatican Council II. If we look at the longer historical picture, this comeback is still in its infancy, leaving much work to be done. The current attempts to update eschatology reveal a significant tension with the teachings of the past. In this sense, despite some very promising new developments and retrievals of past doctrine, California theologian Joseph Colombo can find justification for claiming that "eschatology . . . has fallen on hard times."[1]

Despite its long neglect and general state of petrification, the numbers and quality of recent studies do give some reason for hope in a genuine renewal. Dermot Lane, who is obviously more optimistic than Colombo in this respect, has been able to point to some significant "stirrings in eschatology."[2]

All Christian eschatology concerns itself with the object of Christian hope, which is traditionally put in a futuristic mode as the "last things." While "individual eschatology" deals especially with the traditional topics of death, judgment, heaven, and hell, "general eschatology" concentrates on the collective destiny of the human community and of the world as a whole, focusing on the general resurrection of the body and the coming of God's kingdom. One of the major problems facing Catholic eschatology today is that "in the course of the history of theology these two aspects of eschatology have tended to become detached."[3]

The split between individual and general eschatology was part of a long process whereby a number of dualisms crept into medieval eschatology. Present and future hope were so sharply distinguished that the doctrine of parousia slipped into the shadows. The destiny of body and soul were sharply differentiated, so that immortality of the soul eclipsed the teachings on individual and general resurrection. Within this context the doctrine of purgatory as a separate place of punishment came into prominence by the twelfth century. These major medieval emphases, supported by a well-defined Scholastic metaphysics, continued to dominate Catholic thought up until the time of Vatican Council II.

The biblical and liturgical renewal which accompanied Vatican II, the growing awareness and sensitivity to the secular critique of Christian beliefs concerning the afterlife, a developing dialogue with modern science and the anxieties raised by the possibility of nuclear holocaust, all contributed to the recognition that a new framework was necessary for doing eschatology today. The ecumenical movement which emerged from Vatican II also had a revitalizing effect on Catholic eschatology. Protestant theology, for its part, had been undergoing something of an "eschatological renaissance" throughout much of this century. With the pioneering work of Johannes Weiss (1892) and the subsequent contributions of Albert Schweitzer and Karl Barth, eschatology returned to a central position in Protestant thought. It was Barth, for example, who wrote that "Christianity that is not entirely and altogether eschatological has entirely nothing to do with Christ."[4]

More recently the works of Wolfhart Pannenberg and of Jürgen Moltmann have had a profound impact on both Protestant and Catholic theology—effectively bringing eschatology to the forefront of theological concern. The eschatological teachings of Vatican II are certainly not systematized, but they nevertheless reflect a very definite vision of Christian hope—one that is steeped furthermore in biblical imagery and determined by scriptural themes. This biblical emphasis has had the effect of further bridging the gap separating Protestant and Catholic formulations of eschatology. The ensuing engagement with Protestant thought as well as the steady advances in Catholic biblical scholarship have proven very helpful to the Catholic study of eschatology. One major result has been the realization that eschatology "must permeate the whole of theology and should not be left as a single tract coming at the end."[5]

Protestant theologian Paul Tillich (d. 1965) has had an enormous influence on Catholic as well as Protestant theology. His eschatological doctrine, however, has to a great extent been neglected, primarily because of the misconception that Tillich's mature work had an exclusively inner-psychological thrust with little concern for the future eschaton or its impact on the present political situation. I have tried elsewhere to show not only that this view is quite mistaken, but that

Tillich's late work offers a rich and coherent eschatology with much to contribute to the current Catholic discussions and controversies.[6]

Tillich's eschatology originated in a profoundly political context during the German Weimar Republic. It developed out of a keen sense of living in a special moment of history—a *kairos* situation—"in which the eternal breaks into the temporal, and the temporal is prepared to receive it."[7] Tillich's early eschatology was a response to the call of religious socialism for a greater religious responsibility for the historical situation.[8] It was unmistakably revolutionary in tone. Yet even in this period of intense political involvement, he staunchly resisted any materialistic or utopian reduction of the Christian hope, on the grounds that history itself has no meaning apart from the eternal.[9] While Tillich's theology of his American period reflected a totally different context—a non-kairic time of waiting or what he also called a "sacred void"—his late eschatological writings never lose continuity with their historical, prophetic, and revolutionary roots, even as they probe the more inward-looking concerns of anxiety and meaninglessness that were so characteristic of the Cold War setting following World War II.[10] Indeed, the final formulations of Tillich's eschatology incorporate his earlier political concerns into a broader, more systematic picture. Early Catholic attempts to appreciate Tillich's eschatology were often hampered by a somewhat narrow Scholastic mind-set, which made it impossible to understand Tillich in his own terms.[11] Since that time, however, a whole series of developments has occurred in Catholic theology, which makes the time ripe for a new look at Tillich's thought in this important area of systematic theology. I hope to show that this second look is well worth the effort.

New Directions in Catholic Eschatology

In describing some of the developments in Catholic eschatology since Vatican II, Dermot Lane has identified a number of clearly discernible shifts in priorities. These include a new emphasis on (1) unity, (2) holism, (3) Christological grounding, and (4) historical reference.[12] Further exploration of the literature points to some specific issues that have also emerged as major concerns in Catholic eschatological reflection. Among these, the problem of hermeneutics, the question of the universality of salvation, and the interpretation of the "intermediate state" stand out. In this section I will examine the major shifts and in the following section I will explore the special issues. In both instances, I will try to determine how dialogue with Tillich's thought might serve to advance Catholic eschatology.

A Unitary Eschatology

When Lane writes of a unitary or unified eschatology, he is talking about the principle of *solidarity* whereby humanity is related to the rest of God's creation. In such a model for eschatology the destiny of the individual is tied to the destiny of humanity and the destiny of humanity is tied to the destiny of the cosmos. The unitary model is fully grounded in the biblical image of a "new heaven and new earth"—the establishment of a new creation. Vatican II had already provided the basis for this shift by providing a unifying vision of Christian destiny, which combined an earthly and a heavenly perspective in one sweep. *Lumen Gentium*, for example, describes the "restoration of all things" as a time when "the human race as well as the entire world, which is intimately related to man [the human being] and achieves its purpose through him, will be perfectly re-established in Christ."[13]

Zachary Hayes contrasts this new "christological-communitarian" model with the pre-Vatican II individualistic one, which he claims clearly left the impression that "the joy of heaven is totally unrelated to the world."[14] The new unitary emphasis in Catholic eschatology is deftly summarized by Cardinal Ratzinger when he depicts the new life of resurrection as being "ordered to the transformation of all life, to a future wholeness for man [the human being] and for the world."[15]

While Catholic theologians continue to develop this unitary vision of the future in a variety of ways, few have provided a coherent, systematic foundation for this vision. For this we might well want to look once again at the theology of Paul Tillich. Tillich's theology is ontologically based—a feature which ought not to be strange to the Catholic tradition. The guiding ontological principle of interpretation for his eschatology is Schelling's concept of "universal essentialization,"[16] by which he meant the conquest of the negativities of the finite through the power of the Infinite. It entails a movement of being "from essence through existential estrangement to essentialization."[17] Tillich understands essentialization to be the philosophical correlate to the Pauline doctrine of the *pleroma:* "the ultimate fulfillment of everything in God."[18] He argues, in this vein, that "eternal blessedness" must be attributed to all beings, because all participate in the Divine Life. Similarly, in his introduction to the eschatological section of the *Systematic Theology*, Tillich prepares his readers for a theology which will not only explore the meaning of human history, but will "strive to understand the historical dimension in all realms of life, and finally, to relate human history to the 'history of the universe.' "[19]

The controlling biblical symbol of Tillich's eschatology is the "kingdom of God." The power of this essentially political symbol requires the rejection of all purely individualistic interpretations of eternal life. "Eternal Life is identical with the kingdom of God in its fulfillment."[20] The conquest of life's ambiguities which it implies must include the polar elements of individualization and participation; the destiny of the individual cannot be separated "from the destiny of the whole race and of being in all its manifestations."[21] Tillich's eschatology is political as well as transcendent, social as well as individual and cosmic as well as historical. It contains a grand unitary vision, firmly grounded in biblical faith and coherently articulated through a consistent ontology.

A Holistic Fulfillment

The second shift in Catholic eschatology noted by Lane is the emphasis on the holistic nature of ultimate human fulfillment. This shift consists essentially in a "renewed anthropology," which insists that the divine call is to the *whole person,* body as well as spirit. Vatican II made this point quite emphatically in the document *Gaudium et spes.* Relying on the authority of St. Paul, the document claimed that through the Holy Spirit, "the pledge of our inheritance (Eph 1:14), the whole man [person] is renewed from within, even to the achievement of the redemption of the body" (Rom 8:23).[22] This change of focus, however, has created a serious challenge for Catholic theology. Since the Middle Ages Catholic thought on the last things has been closely tied to a metaphysical doctrine of the soul. At least at the popular level, the goal of God's redemptive work is too often depicted as that of "saving souls." Even official Catholic teaching finds it difficult to view salvation in terms other than the immortality of the soul.

This is evident in the 1979 "Letter on Certain Questions concerning Eschatology" issued by the Sacred Congregation for the Doctrine of the Faith. Informed as it is by modern biblical studies, today's Sacred Congregation could not but stress the resurrection as the central symbol of Christian hope, emphasizing that this resurrection-hope refers to the whole person (*totum hominem*). Yet, almost as if nervous about its own affirmation, the Letter immediately makes a strong claim about the survival and subsistence of "a certain spiritual element" after death, and further asserts that the traditional word "soul" (*anima*) must be retained as a "necessary verbal instrument for sustaining the faith of Christians."[23]

The Vatican Letter was greatly influenced by an earlier in-depth study on eschatology (1977) by Joseph Cardinal Ratzinger, who was soon to become prefect of the same Congregation. In his very thorough and

highly nuanced work, Ratzinger frankly recognizes some of the problems and confusions connected with the term "soul" and strives to
show that the term is not inherently dualistic, despite some popular
abuses to the contrary.[24] He nevertheless finds it necessary to spend
fifty-seven pages trying to explain and defend the concept of the "immortality of the soul."[25] The cardinal, I believe, might have saved himself this astute, but perhaps futile effort by exploring the possibility
of an alternate term to defend the basic Catholic belief in "an element
that abides."[26] The term *spirit* (or "spiritual dimension") comes to mind
here—a term that had been carefully elaborated by Paul Tillich as a
corrective to the misleading and distorting connotations so often attached to the term *soul*.

Many leading Catholic theologians of recent vintage take pains to
avoid the term *soul*. Richard McBrien, for example, prefers to talk of
"the transcendental dimension of human existence."[27] Karl Rahner,
Hans Urs von Balthasar, and Monika Hellwig regularly prefer the word
spirit to *soul*, especially when referring to questions of the human
future.[28] Nevertheless, the cardinal prefect's understanding probably
will have the greater impact on official Church teaching, as well as on
parish preaching.

Tillich, for his part, is totally unambiguous on the subject. While
defending the legitimate use of the term *soul* in biblical, liturgical, or
poetic language, he nevertheless insists that "it has lost its usefulness
for a strict theological understanding of man [the human being], his
spirit and its relation to the Divine Spirit." He claims that the term
spirit, which he understands as "the unity of power and meaning,"
is the best "substitute for the lost concept of 'soul,' transcending the
traditional term in range, in structure, and especially in dynamics."[29]
For Tillich *spirit* is a dimension of material life which is distinctively
human, but is found in all other dimensions of life, at least in potential form. It is in the dimension of spirit that self-awareness is actualized under the right conditions.[30] He refers to this situation as "the
multi-dimensional unity of life."[31] From the psychological perspective,
Tillich always stressed what he called human centeredness, so that,
for example, the subject of faith is neither the intellect, the will, nor
the emotions, but the centered self or "personal center," which includes all the elements of personal life within it.[32] This is another way
of talking about the spirit or the "spiritual core."

Tillich strongly opposed the continued theological use of the traditional term *soul* in that it was so often interpreted literally, rather than
symbolically, and when so understood, tended to evoke a dualistic
understanding of human destiny which is "incompatible with the sym-

bol 'resurrection of the body' ''[33]—the central Christian eschatological theme. In short, Tillich's teaching on the spirit supports the Catholic insistence on a "spiritual element" which "survives and subsists after death,"[34] while at the same time avoiding any angelistic view of final human destiny.

A Christologically Grounded Eschatology

Both biblical renewal and liturgical reform have encouraged Catholic systematicians to firmly anchor eschatology in Christological doctrine. Dermot Lane captures the spirit of this endeavor when he writes that "the Crucified and Risen Christ represents the shape of the Eschaton to come and this Eschaton is already present in the Christian Community as a seed in the process of creative transformation."[35] Lane appeals to Paul's teaching on the inauguration of a "new creation" in the death and resurrection of Jesus as the basis for his Christologically based eschatology.[36] We find the same strong Christological focus in the eschatology of Cardinal Ratzinger, who draws attention to the prayer life of the early Church to illustrate that hope in the parousia was inextricably tied to faith in the resurrection of Jesus.[37] Vatican Council II had already prepared the way for this development by linking eschatology to the paschal mystery of Christ, on the grounds that the goal of this mystery is nothing other than "the new life of resurrection" itself.[38]

At first blush, it might appear that Tillich's eschatology has little to offer on this score. The early German political eschatology initially lacked a strong Christological point of reference and no commentator has ever identified liturgical thinking as a major feature of Tillich's thought. The *kairos* of the early eschatology was understood as a general breakthrough of the divine into the historical and political process. It had scant explicit linkage to the Christ event. Jean Richard has pointed out, however, that radical Christological developments occurred in Tillich's thought during this period, ending with the understanding of Jesus as the unique, great *kairos*, which finds its ongoing historical realization in each particular *kairos*.[39] By the time of his mature Christology (*Systematic Theology*, 2) in 1957, Tillich was able to show important connections between the doctrine of Christ and the major eschatological symbols.[40] The organizing theme of his Christology is the manifestation of the New Being in Jesus the Christ. Christ is to be understood as the "Lord of History" in that the whole historical process is also moving toward fulfillment in the New Being. The eschatological symbols all throw further light on the meaning of this basic

Christological theme. The symbol of the second coming, for example, "excludes the expectation of a superior manifestation of a New Being" and corroborates the resurrection of Jesus Christ as the central Christian symbol.[41] We would not expect to find the liturgical framework in Tillich's eschatology that we find in so many post-Vatican II Catholic theologians, but he does at least recognize in principle the richness and power of eschatological liturgical symbols for the life of the Church.[42] The Christological basis of the eschatology, on the other hand, is explicit and offers a fruitful resource for Catholic thought.

Responsibility For History

European political theology and Latin American liberation theology have both contributed to a more this-worldly, political understanding of eschatology in the Catholic Church. These influential movements have effectively forced Catholic theology to take history far more seriously than it has in the past. "To hope in Christ," writes Gustavo Gutierrez, "is at the same time to believe in the adventure of history, which opens infinite vistas to the love and action of the Christian."[43] Zachary Hayes expresses the same basic conviction when he argues that the Christian vision of the future must entail a consummation which includes both God and "the fruit of history"—otherwise we end up denying "any meaning to the whole of creation and its history."[44] Monika Hellwig stresses the importance of continuity between the history of the world and the eschaton.[45] This new turn in eschatology demands a greater "responsibility for all that happens in the history of the world," and is rooted in the eschatology of Vatican II, which insisted that "the expectation of a new earth must not weaken but rather stimulate our concern for cultivating this one."[46]

By the same token, official church teaching has strongly resisted a strictly inner-historical or utopian interpretation of Christian hope. This is evident in the Vatican condemnation of those forms of liberation theology which might confuse the Christian vision of the kingdom with materialistic categories drawn from Marx's philosophy of history.[47] Nicholas Lash tried to strike the balance when he wrote that the Church must serve as "the sacrament, in this world, of God's kingdom," while at the same time resisting the temptation of "identifying God's kingdom with any past, present or future state of affairs in this world."[48] Fortunately, this new Catholic emphasis on relating the eschaton to history has also been able to avoid the fundamentalist pitfall of trying to pin down eschatological events to specific times and places by way of prophetic speculation. Catholic theology stands ready to read the "signs of the times," but will not get trapped into predicting "the signs of the end."[49]

Tillich's eschatology is particularly strong in developing the relationship between the historical and the transcendent meaning of the eschaton. The core issue in eschatology, for Tillich, is always the *present* relation of the temporal to the eternal, however future-sounding the symbolism might be.[50] Time is not discontinuous with eternity: "Time not only mirrors eternity; it contributes to Eternal Life in each of its moments."[51] We stand at "every moment in the face of the eternal."[52] Tillich's well-known concept of the "Eternal Now"—a reappropriation and update of Johannine theology of Eternal Life—serves to overcome the false dichotomy between a this-worldly and an other-worldly eschatology. In the Tillichian scheme, the eschatological vision is necessarily both inner-historical and transcendent, because the human being "belongs both to the order of temporality and eternity."[53]

The specifically historical side of the "Eternal Now" is expressed in Tillich's concept of the *kairos*. *Kairos* is a biblical term, borrowed from St. Paul, for whom it meant the fulfillment of time, the unique event in history—the manifestation of God in Jesus Christ. Tillich employed it in a broader, more secular sense to cover any special, historical, revelatory moment. It served him as a useful tool for a theological interpretation of important political and social movements, such as Marxist Socialism and Nationalist Socialism in Germany.

Kairos was not only an analytic tool for Tillich, but also served him as a powerful prophetic symbol, because it brings the notion of divine judgment to the present historical moment. It carries with it a demand for decision as well as a sense of expectation. As an historical anticipation of the coming kingdom of God, the *kairos* serves as a reminder that an awareness of the final aim of history provides passion and power for the struggle against demonization of the historical process.[54] In recent years, Tillich's notion of *kairos* has functioned world-wide as a galvanizing symbol for the pursuit of social justice.[55] In short, a *kairos* awareness makes the future hope responsible to history. It provides an answer to the Catholic dilemma of undertaking a serious, prophetic reading of "the signs of the times," while at the same time avoiding the fundamentalist temptation to turn Christian hope into an oracular speculation about the end of the world.

Symbolism and Universality of Salvation: Key Issues Today

In the course of the struggle to make these general shifts in eschatological reflection, Catholic theology has encountered several new, thorny problems and difficult challenges. Foremost among these are the recognition of the symbolic and metaphorical nature of eschatological statements, the question of the universality of the Christian hope for salvation, and the problem of the intermediate state.

The Hermeneutics of Symbolic Language

Dermot Lane has recently written that eschatology is "heavily dependent on the non-literal import of images."[56] In his now famous essay, "The Hermeneutics of Eschatological Assertions," Karl Rahner has established the now standard Catholic principle for the interpretation of eschatological symbols, to wit, that all eschatological statements are to be understood as transpositions "into the future of something which a Christian person experiences in grace as his present."[57] Cardinal Ratzinger clearly concurs with the Rahnerian principle when he describes eschatological statements as "extrapolations" from Christian life in the present. The cardinal is quick to add, however, that while these extrapolations point to the reality of eternal life, they fall far short of revealing its inner essence, inasmuch as the object of our eschatological hope "lies completely outside the scope of our experience."[58] Hence the absolute necessity of symbolic, figurative, or analogical language to express or allude to a reality that defies the capacity of literal, direct language.

On the other hand, ambiguity belongs to the very nature of symbolic language—a fact which ought to remind theologians of the need for modesty and reserve when discussing the eschatological future. The Congregation for the Doctrine of the Faith fully recognizes this need in its assertion that "neither scripture nor theology provides sufficient light for the proper picture of life after death."[59] It is not surprising, then, that a number of Catholic theologians are currently calling for a more nuanced and discriminating understanding of symbol and metaphor in the study of eschatology.[60]

Now if there is any area of Tillich's thought that eschatologists ought not neglect, it is his interpretation of religious symbols. Few theologians have explored this issue with an originality, detail, or breadth comparable to that of Tillich's. In fact, throughout his long career, Tillich staunchly defended the symbolic nature of *all* theological language.

But with eschatology, he believed, the issue of symbolism took on a very special urgency, for, as he put it, ''all images of eternal life are symbols and not statements about empirical objects or happenings.'' Furthermore, with these symbols, what is at stake is nothing less than the ''very question of human existence itself.''[61]

Like Rahner, Tillich required that all eschatological symbolism be rooted in what he termed ''immediately existential experiences.''[62] The symbol of ''eternal death,'' for instance, derives from the present, inner experience of the threat of the loss of meaning in one's life.[63] The image of the ''last judgment'' is based on the experience of the exposure of evil as evil in our lives, when it would try to disguise itself as something positive. In every moment, Tillich claimed, we can experience the power of the eternal as a ''burning fire'' which consumes all ''that which pretends to be positive but is not.''[64]

Yet despite the symbolic nature of eschatological language, theology still has the task of analyzing and conceptualizing the meaning of these symbols. Tillich recognized the difficulty of this task, especially inasmuch as the theological language of eschatology often seems to lie on the border between concept and symbol. Tillich's own notion of ''essentialization'' (borrowed from Schelling) is itself a good case in point. While ''essentialization'' is used to conceptualize and clarify traditional biblical symbols, at times it takes on a certain symbolic value of its own. Its conceptual capacity is seen, for example, in its role of mediation between the idea of the ''threat of Eternal Death'' and that of the relativity of human finitude. But ''essentialization'' also serves as a powerful symbol, suggesting both the sense of despair at wasting one's potentialities forever as well as the experience of ecstasy at ''the elevation of the positive within existence (even in the most unfulfilled life) into eternity.''[65] Aware of this twofold function of the term, Tillich describes it as a ''conceptual symbol.''[66] This paradoxical phrase is consistent with Tillich's theoretical position that religious terms can sometimes function both as signs and symbols.[67]

Only in recent years, as Catholic eschatology has continued to make great strides in breaking from its ''physicalist'' past, have Catholic theologians really had to come to grips with the hermeneutics of eschatological symbols. There might very well be much to learn in this regard from Tillich's highly developed and nuanced doctrine of the religious symbol.

The Universality of Salvation

Both biblical scholarship and the secular critique of Christian eschatology have reawakened a great deal of theological interest in the ancient question of the "restitution of all things." Origen's doctrine of *apokatastasis panton* has found a renewed vitality—albeit in modified form—in post-Vatican II eschatology.

Following the lead of Karl Rahner, Catholic theology, for the most part, agrees on a certain asymmetry between the eschatology of loss and of salvation. In Rahner's words, the two eschatologies are "not on the same plane."[68] The two ways—one to salvation, the other to perdition—are not parallel. While the Church has never insisted that anyone, in fact, will definitively and totally reject God through serious sin, "the doctrine that the world and the history of the world as a whole will *in fact* enter into eternal life with God"[69] is central to the gospel message. Hans Urs von Balthasar pushes the issue even further by drawing attention to the total solidarity of Christ with sinners, even in their very rejection of God. This is what he refers to as the "mystery of Holy Saturday." While maintaining that human freedom can theoretically reject God forever, von Balthasar claims that the "unimaginable depth of God's love and fidelity—made manifest in the descent into hell—makes it improbable that "human freedom can remain perpetually closed to the divine love."[70] The richness and substantiveness of these new Catholic variations on universalism notwithstanding, the Catholic magisterium tenaciously continues to insist that "there will be eternal punishment for the sinner, who will be deprived of the sight of God, and that this punishment will have a repercussion on the whole being of the sinner."[71]

Most Catholic theologians take great pains to avoid trivializing the seriousness of human freedom or the ultimate threat to happiness entailed in the symbol of "eternal damnation." They reject, however, the view that hell is a punishment which God inflicts upon the sinner, and see it rather as a "self-chosen state of alienation" or "isolation" from God.[72] Paul Tillich's eschatology effectively defends the seriousness of the threat of eternal loss and understands "hell" as a symbol of existential decision.[73] In Tillich's own words, the drama of human life includes "the threat that one's whole existence in time will be judged as a failure."[74] On the other hand, his understanding of human finitude and the "unity of everything in divine love" make it impossible for him to accept the symbol of hell as "an everlasting state of pain."[75] Tillich's understanding of "essentialization"—his ontological framework for eschatology—is that it occurs in degrees. This he finds incompatible with the absoluteness of judgments found in the symbols of "hell" or "eternal death."[76] His middle ground position might not resolve all the difficulties of the thorny problem of universalism vs. the eternity of hell, and it very likely stands in need of further elaboration and updating, but despite these cautions, it certainly merits an important place in the discussion.

The Intermediate State

Besides the questions of religious symbolism and eschatological universalism, another area of Catholic concern to which Tillich's thought may well contribute is that of the interim or intermediate state, i.e., the state of the individual person from the time of death to the final judgment and general resurrection. In recent years two questions in particular have arisen in this connection: the possibility of resurrection at the very moment of death and a rethinking of the meaning of purgatory.

The first issue has caused a heated discussion in Catholic theological circles, with official authority insisting that the idea of resurrection at the moment of death fails to do justice to the full corporeal nature of Christian hope.[77] Despite this high-level opposition, however, Catholic theologians are disinclined to simply abandon the theory in that "it firmly places the resurrection at the center of christian life and living."[78] Tillich had previously dealt with the same issue in *Systematic Theology* 3, where he specifically defends the idea of the resurrection at the moment of death by an appeal to the Pauline idea of the "Spiritual body."[79] His adaptation of the Pauline theme to the current issue deserves Catholic theological attention, for it preserves the centrality of the resurrection symbol, while avoiding the most obvious pitfalls to which the magisterium objects.

As regards the doctrine of purgatory, Catholic theology, as well as official teaching, is trying to preserve the central, core meaning of the doctrine, namely, "the possibility of a purification of the elect before they see God,"[80] while stripping the doctrine of all its superstitious and distorted trappings. Despite the fact that Tillich came from the Reformation tradition, he was able to see an important element of truth in the doctrine of purgatory, namely, "a powerful expression of belief in the unity of individual and universal destiny in Eternal Life,"[81] which he saw reflected in the liturgical practice of prayers for the dead. Combined with his idea of essentialization by degrees, Tillich, the Protestant theologian, thus offers several key ingredients for a successful retrieval of the doctrine of purgatory.

Conclusion

I have purposely skimmed over the last two examples of points of contact between Tillich's thought and Catholic eschatology, as I intended only to indicate some worthwhile areas of further exploration. My main purpose throughout the article, however, has been to relate Tillich's eschatology to the main shifts in Catholic thought that have occurred since Vatican Council II. These have been identified as unity, holism, Christological grounding, and historical responsibility. In addition, I have examined two major problems that have emerged in Catholic theology as a result of the new questions involved in these shifts—namely, the hermeneutic of religious symbolism and the universality of the Christian hope for salvation.

I believe it has become apparent that Tillich's interests interface closely with the main Catholic concerns in eschatology and, at least in some key areas, offer significant contributions to the current discussions. His most important contributions, it seems clear, are his notion of *kairos*, as a vehicle for relating transcendent hope to current political concerns, and his doctrine of religious symbolism, which provides an important hermeneutic tool for avoiding superstitions and ungrounded fantasy in reinterpreting the ancient eschatological symbols. Tillich's approach to the problem of universalism vis-à-vis the reality of the threat of "eternal damnation" further shows the unusual depth and balance of his thought—a combination which certainly merits serious attention by Catholic theologians.

Of course, Tillich's theology does not have all the answers, and Catholic systematicians will, no doubt, want to be more explicit about the Christological foundations and, certainly, will have to put far greater emphasis on the liturgical context of eschatological beliefs than Tillich was wont to do. In using Tillich, they might also consider updating some of his formulations through a closer interaction with the natural sciences. A growing number of Catholic theologians have already moved in this direction by supplementing more traditional accounts of eschatology with a "new story" attuned to the insights of modern science, "and especially to recent developments in the field of astronomy."[82] Tillich himself used Schelling's ontology and depth psychology in addition to strains of existentialist philosophy to transpose the Christian gospel into modern thought categories. This synthesis continues to have great value, and should not be replaced, but rather supplemented by insights drawn from the natural sciences.

In terms of the larger picture, however, I think it is safe to say that the biblical authenticity, the ontological consistency, and the dialectical balance of Tillich's eschatological vision recommend it highly as a resource for contemporary Catholic reflection.

Notes

[1] Joseph Colombo, "Eschatology Past and Present: A Review Essay," *Living Light* 25 (March 1985) 266.

[2] Dermot Lane, "Stirrings in Eschatology," *Furrow* 40 (October 1989) 577–85.

[3] Dermot Lane, "Eschatology," *The New Dictionary of Theology*, eds. Joseph A. Komonchak, Mary Collins, and Dermot A. Lane (Wilmington, Del.: Michael Glazier, 1987) 329.

[4] Karl Barth, *Epistle to the Romans* (London: Oxford University Press, 1933) 314. Cited by Lane, "Eschatology," 329.

[5] Lane, "Eschatology," 338.

[6] See my argument in "Tillich's Eschatology of the Late American Period (1945–1965)," *New Creation or Eternal Now: Neue Schöpfung oder Ewiges Jetzt,* ed. Gert Hummel (Berlin and New York: Walter de Gruyter, 1991) 137–52.

[7] Paul Tillich, *The Protestant Era*, trans. James L. Adams (Chicago, Ill.: The University of Chicago Press, 1948) xix.

[8] Jean Richard, "The Roots of Tillich's Eschatology in his Religious-Socialist Philosophy of History," *New Creation or Eternal Now*, 31.

[9] Paul Tillich, "Symbols of Eternal Life," *Harvard Divinity Bulletin* 26 (April 1962) 1.

[10] Bulman, "Tillich's Eschatology of the Late American Period," 139.

[11] A good example is the work of Carl J. Armbruster, S.J., *The Vision of Paul Tillich* (New York: Sheed and Ward, 1967), whose uneasiness with Tillich's symbolic approach to eschatology is clearly rooted in the "realism" of his Scholastic ontology.

[12] The recent stress in Catholic theology on clearly linking eschatological doctrine to the mystery of Christ justifies my addition of "Christological grounding" to Lane's original list of three "significant shifts" in eschatology. See Lane's own statement that the first principle of eschatology "affirms that the person of Christ is the norm and foundation of eschatology" ("Eschatology," 341).

[13] *Lumen gentium*, 48.

[14] Zachary Hayes, O.F.M., *Visions of a Future* (Wilmington, Del.: Michael Glazier, 1989) 199.

[15] Joseph Ratzinger, *Eschatology: Death and Eternal Life*, trans. Michael Waldstein (Washington, D.C.: The Catholic University of America Press, 1988) 119. This is an English translation of *Eschatologie: Tod und ewiges Leben* (Regensburg: Friedrich Pustet Verlag, 1977).

[16] Paul Tillich, *Systematic Theology*, 3 vols. (New York: Harper and Row, 1963) 3:408; see also 400.

[17] Ibid., 3:421.

[18] Ibid. See also Bulman, "Tillich's Eschatology of the Late American Period," 145.

[19] Tillich, *Systematic Theology,* 3:405, 297–98.

[20] Ibid., 3:401. See also 3:359, where Tillich describes the kingdom of God as "a kingdom not only of men; it involves the fulfillment of life under all dimensions. This agrees with the multidimensional unity of life; fulfillment under one dimension implies fulfillment in all dimensions."

[21] Ibid., 3:409.

[22] *Gaudium et spes,* 22.

[23] Congregation for the Doctrine of the Faith, "Letter on Certain Questions concerning Eschatology," (Vatican City, 1979) no. 3.

[24] Ratzinger, *Eschatology,* 148. See also 13–14.

[25] Ibid., 104–61.

[26] Ibid., 148.

[27] Richard P. McBrien, *Catholicism* (Minneapolis: Winston Press, 1980) 1:135, 148.

[28] See, for example, Karl Rahner, *Foundations of Christian Faith,* trans. William V. Dych (New York: Crossroad, 1985) 434; Medard Kehl and Werner Loser, eds., *The von Balthasar Reader* (New York: Crossroad, 1982) 90–92; and Monika Hellwig, "Eschatology," *Systematic Theology: Roman Catholic Perspectives,* eds. Francis Schüssler Fiorenza and John Galvin (Minneapolis: Fortress Press, 1991) 2:356.

[29] Tillich, *Systematic Theology,* 3:24.

[30] Ibid., 3:20–21.

[31] Ibid., 3:11–30.

[32] Paul Tillich, *Dynamics of Faith* (New York: Harper and Row, 1957) 4–8.

[33] Tillich, *Systematic Theology,* 3:410.

[34] "Letter on Certain Questions," no. 3.

[35] Lane, "Stirrings," 583.

[36] Lane, "Eschatology," 332.

[37] Ratzinger, *Eschatology,* 7.

[38] *Gaudium et spes,* 22. See Dermot A. Lane, *Christ at the Centre: Selected Issues in Christology* (Mahwah, N.J.: Paulist Press, 1990) 115.

[39] Richard, "The Roots of Tillich's Eschatology," 40.

[40] Tillich, *Systematic Theology,* 2:161ff.

[41] Ibid., 2:163–64.

[42] See, e.g., ibid., 3:375–76; also Paul Tillich, "Religious Symbols and Our Knowledge of God," in F. Forrester Church, ed., *The Essential Tillich* (New York: Macmillan Publishing Co., 1987) 46.

[43] Gustavo Gutierrez, *A Theology of Liberation,* trans. Sr. Caridad Inda and John Eagleson (Maryknoll, N.Y.: Orbis Books, 1973) 238–39.

[44] Hayes, *Visions of a Future,* 202.

[45] Hellwig, "Eschatology," 363.

[46] *Gaudium et spes,* 39.

[47] Congregation for the Doctrine of the Faith, "Instruction on Certain Aspects of the 'Theology of Liberation' " (Vatican City, August 6, 1984).

[48] Nicholas Lash, "Theologies at the Service of a Common Tradition," *Concilium* 171 (January 1984) 77.

[49] Rudolf Schnackenburg, *Christ: Present & Future,* trans. Edward Quinn (Philadelphia: Fortress Press, 1978) 35–36. See also Ratzinger, *Eschatology,* 195.

[50] Tillich, *Systematic Theology,* 3:298-99.

[51] Ibid., 3:420.

[52] Ibid., 3:395.

[53] Tillich, "Symbols of Eternal Life," 1.

[54] ST 3, 376. For Tillich's emphasis on the "inner-historical-political" significance of the symbol "Kingdom of God," see ST 3, 356–61, and for his understanding of the role of particular historical "kairoi" for furthering the power of the kingdom, see ST 3, 369–74.

[55] See Robert McAfee Brown, ed., *Kairos: Three Prophetic Challenges to the Church* (Grand Rapids, Mich.: William B. Eerdmans Publishing Co., 1990). The "kairos" documents in this collection represent the "prophetic witness" of South African, Central American, and Asian Christian communities.

[56] Lane, *Christ at the Centre,* 126.

[57] Rahner, *Foundations,* 433.

[58] Ratzinger, *Eschatology,* 161.

[59] "Letter on Certain Questions Concerning Eschatology," no. 7.

[60] See, e.g., Lane, *Christ at the Centre,* 126; Colombo, "Eschatology Past and Present," 273.

[61] Tillich, "Symbols of Eternal Life," 3–4, 9.

[62] Ibid., 3.

[63] Ibid., 9.

[64] Tillich, *Systematic Theology,* 3:399.

[65] Ibid., 3:407.

[66] Ibid.

[67] Tillich, "Religious Symbols and Our Knowledge of God," 46.

[68] Karl Rahner, "The Hermeneutics of Eschatological Assertions," *Theological Investigations,* trans. K. Smith (Baltimore: Helicon Press, 1966) 4:338.

[69] Rahner, *Foundations,* 444.

[70] John R. Sachs, S.J., "Current Eschatology: Universal Salvation and the Problem of Hell," *Theological Studies* 52 (1991) 246. Sachs discusses von Balthasar's "Holy Saturday" doctrine: 244–46.

[71] "Letter on Certain Questions concerning Eschatology," no. 7.

72 Sachs, ''Current Eschatology,'' 235. See Ratzinger, *Eschatology*, 217–18.

73 Tillich, *Systematic Theology*, 3:406.

74 Paul Tillich, *The Eternal Now* (New York: Charles Scribner's Sons, 1956) 124.

75 Tillich, *Systematic Theology*, 3:408.

76 Ibid., 3:406–7

77 Hayes, *Visions of a Future*, 164; Ratzinger, *Eschatology*, 252.

78 Lane, *Christ at the Centre*, 125.

79 Tillich, *Systematic Theology*, 3:412.

80 ''Letter on Certain Questions,'' no. 7.

81 Tillich, *Systematic Theology*, 3:418.

82 Bulman, ''Tillich's Eschatology of the Late American Period,'' 151. See Lane's ''new cosmic story,'' *Christ at the Centre*, 148–50; Charles R. Meyer, *Religious Belief in a Scientific Age*, (Chicago: The Thomas More Press, 1983), esp. chap. 7, ''The Last Things.''

The Kingdom of God as Utopia

George H. Tavard

The Methodological Problem

Toward the end of the introduction to *Systematic Theology*, Paul Tillich briefly announces that, following the "epistemological part" and the three central parts of the system—"Being and God," "Existence and Christ," "Life and the Spirit"—there will be a fifth part: "Finally, life has a dimension which is called 'history.' And it is helpful to separate the material dealing with the historical aspect of life from the part dealing with life generally. This corresponds to the fact that the symbol 'Kingdom of God' is independent of the trinitarian structure which determines the central parts" (1:67).[1]

Tillich at this point considers history to be a dimension of life. Because of this, the symbol, kingdom of God, must have a special connection with the previous symbols, Spiritual Presence and Divine Spirit, which are, in the system, the theological correlates of life. But Divine Spirit, as explained in part 4 of *Systematic Theology*, makes no sense outside of a Trinitarian conception of God. It is therefore very strange that in the same passage Tillich should also affirm the non-Trinitarian character of history and of its correlate, the kingdom of God.

This affirmation raises several problems. First, it seems illogical that a dimension of life should be independent of the Trinitarian structure in which life properly fits, and that as a consequence it should be excluded from life's correlation with the Divine Spirit and with the Spirit's impact upon human life in the Spiritual Presence. Second, this exclusion raises a problem of consistency. Tillich has justified the construction of an epistemological part (part 1) as "necessary," given the methodological importance of the epistemological question, while the separation of part 5 from part 4 is only justified as "helpful." A few lines below, however, a certain correspondence of parts 1 and 5 is suggested. Part 1 must open the system, since it deals with a presupposition of all subsequent parts, the revelation. In turn, part 5 must close the system. Why? Tillich is reticent here. He says only "for obvious reasons" (1:68) that are not otherwise spelled out. Third, there is a theological problem in that the kingdom of God, a pervading symbol of the New Testament that is deeply rooted in the Old, becomes independent of the three persons whom the Christian faith identifies with God. The theological principle of such a disconnection, should there be one, ought to be carefully explained.

Given the lengthy analysis of the method of correlation that is presented as the key to the proposed system, I take it that Tillich was aware of the oddity of the reasoning by which he introduced the separation of "life" and "history" in the structure of the system. Why he did not explain it more satisfactorily is, at this point, a moot question.

The analysis of part 4 brings Tillich to posit in human life a "quest for unambiguous life" (3:107). Such a quest has been expressed "in the ambiguous form of religion"—meaning here the Jewish and Christian religious traditions—with the help of three symbols: Spirit of God, kingdom of God, and Eternal Life; Spirit of God or Spiritual Presence "will guide our discussion in the fourth part of the system" (3:108). That is, the analysis of life will lead us to formulate the question of unambiguous life, and by the same token to grasp the answer: this will be Spiritual Presence, the experience of the divine Spirit in the creaturely realm. Spiritual Presence draws its "symbolic material" from the contrast between the Divine Spirit and the human spirit; kingdom of God finds its material in the historical dimension of life, and Eternal Life in "the categorical structure of finitude" (3:109), with these two serving as horizon for the Spiritual Presence. It is evidently too early for the full meaning of these symbols to emerge at this juncture. Tillich simply names their transcendental counterpoint: Spiritual Presence refers to the Divine Spirit, kingdom of God to "the ultimate fulfillment toward which history runs," Eternal Life to the conquest of the "ambiguities of life beyond history."

Given these three symbols of unambiguous life, two logical courses were available to the author of *Systematic Theology*. The simpler one was to treat the three symbols together, the last two being subsumed under the symbol Spiritual Presence or Divine Spirit. More awkwardly, the three could be examined separately in what would have been parts 4, 5, and 6 of the system. Here, however, an additional oddity has crept in. Part 5 (the kingdom of God) follows part 4 (the Divine Spirit), but the symbol Eternal Life is subsumed under it: kingdom of God is studied "within history" (part 5, section 2, pp. 362–93), while Eternal Life becomes equivalent to "the End of History" or "the Kingdom of God as the End of History" (part 5, section 3, pp. 394–423). Since these are the last pages of *Systematic Theology*, the entire system ends on what seems to be an improperly explained structural defect. This was in fact foreseen from the start by Tillich: it fits the contents of the Introduction. But the explanation that is provided is hardly satisfactory, and the question remains: why did Paul Tillich, whose project was to follow a carefully drawn philosophico-theological methodology, and who, when occasion called for it, could be utterly logical and unbendingly rational, accept a methodological flaw at the end of the system?

The Place of Eschatology in the Tradition

The introduction to part 5 does little to lift the veil. It calls the fifth part "an extension of the fourth, separated from it for traditional and practical reasons" (3:297). The practical reasons are not listed. But in "the theological tradition," we are informed, "the questions of the relations of revelation to reason and of the Kingdom of God to history have always received a comparatively independent and extensive treatment" (3:298). The parallel between parts 1 and 5 is still operative, but the separation of parts 4 and 5 is also justified by an appeal to tradition. But why, one may wonder, should a theological tradition be followed at this point simply because it exists? And one may ask about the weight of such a tradition.

In the first place, the tradition of the older Church was quite different. In the Nicene Creed, the kingdom of Christ, including the last judgment, belongs in the second article: "He will come in glory to judge the living and the dead, and his kingdom will have no end." This was directed against the heretics who distinguished the kingdom of Christ from the kingdom of God (the Father): Christ loses his kingship when he surrenders his kingdom to God at the end of the present world. But the kingdom of Christ, the fruit of his dying and rising, is already the kingdom of the Father since it is entirely the Creator's work. Furthermore, at the end of the creed "the life of the world to come" is introduced by the third article, on the Spirit: the saints belong to the kingdom by virtue of faith and grace, appropriated to the Holy Spirit. Thus God's kingdom was essentially Trinitarian.[2]

In the second place, this credal structure was not followed in the Scholastic tradition. After the *Sentences* of Peter Lombard (c. 1150), the commentators normally ended their fourth book with discussions relating to heaven and hell. From the commentaries this locus of eschatological questions passed into other theological treatises. Bonaventure's short *summa*, *Breviloquium*, closed with the consideration of the last judgment, its final chapter entitled, "The glory of Paradise" (7.7). If

Thomas Aquinas did not himself finish the *Summa theologica*, his Dominican colleagues who composed the Supplement to the *Summa* also concluded with questions on hell and damnation (q. 99). This was also in keeping with the ending of the *Summa contra gentes*, 4:97: "The state of the world after the judgment." And it fitted loosely the Neo-Platonic structure of descent and ascent that Aquinas had chosen for the *Summa*.

In the third place, however, the Scholastic tradition was broken at the Reformation. Philip Melanchthon did mention "Condemnation" and "Blessedness" at the end of a list of traditional theological topics; yet his *Loci communes* (1521) concluded with "On Magistrates" (chap. 29) and "On Offense" (chap. 30), and did not include any teaching on the eschaton. Jean Calvin's *Institutes of the Christian Religion* (final edition, 1559) ended with a study of the Church, the sacraments and, finally, civil government (4.20); eschatology was located at the end of the third book, after the doctrine of predestination (3.25: "The final resurrection"). Likewise, in the early Anglican tradition, the *Laws of ecclesiastical polity* of Richard Hooker (1597) did not discuss the kingdom of God, and concluded on practical questions relating to the life and obligations of ministers (5.81); but they were by no means a systematic treatise.

In the nineteenth century, the great Protestant theologian, Friedrich Schleiermacher, did place eschatology next to last, under the general title, "the Consummation of the Church" (*The Christian Faith*, 2nd ed., 1830, §157–59), but this was followed by a section on "the divine attributes which relate to Redemption" (§164–68) and by an appendix on the doctrine of the Trinity (§170–72).[3]

Undoubtedly, Paul Tillich generally shows deep appreciation for the great classics of the Scholastic era. Yet this scarcely explains his departure from the general Protestant tradition regarding the place of eschatology in his theological system.

The Symbol of the Kingdom

Whatever the weight of tradition, Tillich adduces another argument for his problematical choice. There is "a more theoretical reason for dealing separately with the ambiguities of history and the symbols which answer the questions implied in them. It is the embracing character of the historical dimension and the equally embracing character of the symbol 'Kingdom of God' that give particular significance to the discussion of history. The historical quality of life is potentially present under all its dimensions . . ." (3:298). This theoretical reason derives from the need to distinguish between three aspects of history: "history in its full and proper sense, i.e., human history"; the "historical dimension in all realms of life"; and the "history of the universe." All this should be related theologically "to the symbol of the Kingdom of God, both in its inner-historical and in its transhistorical sense." Inner-historically, the symbol kingdom of God "reaches back to the symbol 'Spiritual Presence'," while transhistorically it "goes over into the symbol 'Eternal Life'," which is concerned with eschatology and "the doctrine of the 'last things'." The inner-historical is tied to the origin of all, to creation; the transcendental relates to the future, the end, the final purpose of history.

This explanation, however, does not clarify whether the theoretical reason is simply that, with its three aspects, history becomes too vast to be treated as a dimension of life, although it is one; or that, with its backward and forward orientations, the kingdom of God embraces the origin and the end, and is then infinitely more than either "the consciousness of presence or the expectation of the coming" that are implicit in the experience of life (3:391).

In the first case, the fulfillment of history follows the model of a horizontal unfolding that is necessarily pregnant with demonic possibilities: "Demonic consequences result from absolutizing the fragmentary fulfillment of the aim of history within history" (3:390). The image of a "third stage," deriving from Joachim of Fiore, which Tillich mentions briefly, evokes a well-known distortion of the Trinitarian model.

In the second case, what is emphasized is "the vertical line of salvation over against the horizontal line of historical activity" (3:391). Tillich, however, does not endorse either of these accents in their exclusiveness, and he seems to hesitate between two reasons for the separate existence of part 5. Thus, no adequate justification is given within the system why part 5 (The Kingdom of God) should exist at all: its topic belongs to the fuller consideration of what is located in part 4 (The Divine Spirit). Or, granted that part 5 will exist, there is no reason, other than practical, why it should not be followed by a short part 6 (Eternal Life). Yet Tillich's hesitation, one may presume, is not accidental. And in this case the reason will be found outside the system. At the heart of part 5, in fact, Tillich gives a broad hint as to where it will be found.

The main divisions of part 5 are "History and the Quest for the Kingdom of God," "The Kingdom of God within History," and "The Kingdom of God as the End of History." Given the method of correlation that has determined the structure of *Systematic Theology*, the heart of each part lies at the junction of the question that has been posed with the answer that will be given. To the philosophical question that explicitly or implicitly emerges from Tillich's existential analysis of the human situation, there corresponds a theological answer which is connected with the revelation of Jesus as the Christ, the New Being under the conditions of existence. In part 5, the heart of the system lies in the emerging correlation between the ambiguities of life (in the first division) and the kingdom of God. This emerging correlation is the topic of the section entitled: "Interpretations of history and the quest for the Kingdom of God" (3:348). At this point, Tillich has just surveyed three kinds of "positive but inadequate answers to the question of the meaning of history" (3:352).

The first is the belief in a necessary progress of humanity through science and civilization. Such a belief prevailed in the philosophy of the nineteenth century under the influence of Hegel in Germany and Auguste Comte in France.

The second is utopianism: "the utopian interpretation of history" (3:354) believes that it will be possible to reach a stage within history at which the ambiguities of life will be abolished. Such a view is ultimately tied to the perspective of a "third stage" or age of humankind as envisioned in the Trinitarian unfolding of history according to Joachim of Fiore. Present in the utopias of the Renaissance, these notions have flourished in "the many forms of secular utopianism in the modern period and have given incentive to revolutionary movements up to the present day."[4]

The third is a "transcendental" type of interpretation, which is "implicit in the eschatological mood of the New Testament and the early church up to Augustine. It was brought to its radical form in orthodox Lutheranism" (3:355). This view totally separates the kingdom of God and the kingdoms of this world: "Historical action . . . cannot be purged from the ambiguities of power, internally or externally. There is no relation between the justice of the Kingdom of God and the justice of power structures." This transcendental interpretation of history has a paradoxical situation. For on the one hand, it is implicit in the New Testament and it is theologically necessary as "a counterbalance to the danger of secular as well as religious utopianism." Yet on the other hand, it "falls short of an adequate interpretation of history." For it isolates the individual "from the historical group and the universe"; it allows for a Manichean opposition of creation and salvation; and it interprets the kingdom of God "as a static supernatural order into which individuals enter after their death—instead of understanding the symbol, with the biblical writers, as a dynamic power on earth for the coming of which we pray in the Lord's prayer and which, according to biblical thought, is struggling with the demonic forces which are powerful in churches as well as empires'' (3:356).

A Fourth Way: Religious Socialism

It is curious that to the transcendental interpretation Tillich opposes Thomas Muenzer's judgment "that the masses have no time and thought left for a spiritual life, a judgment that was repeated by religious socialists in their analysis of the sociological and psychological situation of the proletariat in the industrial cities of the late nineteenth and early twentieth centuries." Correct as this judgment may be, it not only contradicts one aspect of the New Testament and Martin Luther's two-kingdom theory, it also seems irrelevant to the eschatological expectation of the kingdom of God. It has to do rather with whether the symbol, kingdom of God, can be properly applied to even the best of human societies on earth, either civil or ecclesial. The erroneous, radically Pelagian, application of the symbol of the divine kingdom to some future historical society was precisely the reason why Tillich criticized utopianism.

Admittedly, Tillich sees a difference between utopianism and his rejection of "transcendentalism." This difference lies in his view of the contribution of religious socialism to the Christian concept of society. It is precisely Tillich's claim on behalf of religious socialism that introduces the link between question and answer: "It was the dissatisfaction with the progressivistic, utopian, and transcendental interpretations of history (and the rejection of the non-historical types) that induced the Religious Socialists of the early 1920s to try a solution which avoids their inadequacies and is based on biblical prophetism. This attempt was made in terms of a reinterpretation of the symbol of the Kingdom of God" (3:356).

Kairos

The last pages of *Systematic Theology* refer again to religious socialism, in connection with Tillich's adaptation and use of the Greek notion of *kairos*: "This term was frequently used since we introduced it into theological and philosophical discussion in connection with the religious socialist movement in Germany after the First World War" (3:369). I take it that "we" in this quotation refers to Tillich himself. There, it seems, in Tillich's involvement in religious socialism, lies the key to the very existence of part 5 and, by the same token, to the doctrine on the kingdom of God and the eschatology of *Systematic Theology*.

Kairos, in the singular and the plural, is explained at length. In the New Testament the word, translated as "fulfillment of time," designates "the point at which history, in terms of a concrete situation, had matured to the point of being able to receive the breakthrough of the central manifestation of the Kingdom of God." As chosen in the context of the religious socialist movement it connoted several ideas: the "self-transcending dynamics of history"; the feeling that "a moment of history had appeared which was pregnant with a new understanding of the meaning of history and life"; the qualitative as distinct from the quantitative dimension of time, called chronos; the nearness of the Kingdom of God; and "the moment of maturity in a particular religious and cultural development" (3:370).

In this last meaning, however, the perception of a *kairos* is ambiguous. At all times indeed the kingdom of God is present in history, but it is rarely experienced in its "history-shaking power" (3:372). A certain spiritual maturity is necessary to its discernment. And maturity results from education by the law. But the law nurtures the capacity to resist as well as to accept the kingdom of God. A *kairos* is therefore not simply given. Rather is it seen in a "vision" that can be "demonically distorted" and erroneous (3:371). The only *kairos* that Tillich regards as free from all distortion is "the Cross of the Christ" as "the absolute criterion." In the historical moment of religious socialism, the *kairos* that had been perceived was distorted by Adolf Hitler and the National Socialist Party.

Readers of Paul Tillich know of course that the notion of *kairos* recurs frequently in his works. It is featured in *The Protestant Era* in texts that were written in 1922 and 1929 besides more recent texts composed after the Second World War. A philosophical essay, entitled "Kairos," relates the term to the Tillichian dialectic of autonomy and theonomy: "Autonomy is the dynamic principle of history. Theonomy . . . is the substance and meaning of history," while heteronomy is the legalistic distortion of theonomy.[5] "There are moments, as I myself have emphasized on different occasions, in which 'kairos,' the right time, is united with 'logos,' the 'eternal truth,' and in which the fate of philosophy is decided for a special period."[6] An undated essay, unpublished before *The Protestant Era* (1948), explains the term with the help of Aristotle, who defines it as "the good in the category of time," and relates it to *telos* (fulfillment), *parousia* (presence), *ktizein* (founding), *logos* (word, reason), *aletheia* (truth), and *ecclesia* (assembly, church).[7]

At the Oxford Conference on Life and Work (1937), Tillich identified "the *kairos* of the present moment" in the light of three "demonic forces of the present day," namely, autonomous capitalism, nationalism, and dictatorial tyranny.[8] The kairos in question was, within the Church, "the preparation of a historical existence of her own after the self-destruction of the present structure of historical existence," or, more simply, after the fall of capitalism, nationalism, and dictatorship. Outside the Church, that is, "in the action of the church outside her own borders," it meant fighting for "the unity of the human race," for socialism as expressing "the demand for justice in the situation of disintegrating capitalism," and asserting "the finite character and yet the dignity of every human being."

In Tillich's more recent writings, the notion of *kairos* is operative in his published sermons even when it is not named: it designates the moment when the faithful are grasped by the full meaning of the Cross of Jesus Christ. This personal meaning is not absent from *Systematic Theology*, yet it is the world-historical meaning that predominates: "*Kairoi* are rare and the great *kairos* is unique, but together they determine the dynamics of history in its self-transcendence" (3:372). This notion is at the kernel of Tillich's understanding of the impact of the kingdom of God on human history.

Tillich's Socialism

Paul Tillich's involvement in religious socialism is of major importance for his interpretation of the kingdom of God and for his doctrine of eschatology. He constantly refers to the movement. Indeed there was such a movement in post-World War I Germany, especially in Berlin. One of its more theoretical and philosophical participants was Tillich himself. The movement was tied to, though not identical with, the political orientation of the mutually hostile political parties of the Second International (Socialist, which existed in two versions, the Social Democratic Party and, more to the left, the Independent Socialist Party, which Tillich preferred) and the Third International (Communist). It was forced to disappear when its members were expelled, imprisoned, or silenced under the assault of Nazism. Yet one may wonder if religious socialism in Berlin ever amounted, otherwise than in Tillich's mind, to the theological breakthrough that he never ceased to claim for it.[9] It is also a matter of fact that, although it did publish a periodical, religious socialism never counted more than a handful of adepts.[10]

The very notion of *kairos* that stands at the center of Tillich's religious socialism has its origin in the psychological and spiritual evolution of Tillich during the First World War. Believing, in the tradition of Prussian militarism, that Kaiser Wilhelm II was wielding the lance of Christian civilization against the corrupt democracies of the West, Tillich had joined the chaplain corps of the German army with enthusiasm. But when, at the first battle of the Marne (September 1914), the German assault was stopped on the way to Paris in what he experienced as an unexpected blood bath, Tillich quickly became disenchanted. He began to see the conflict from the standpoint of the soldiers in the mud and muck of battle. "A night attack came," he was to say much later, "and all night long I moved among the wounded and the dying as they were brought in—many of them my close friends. All that horrible, long night I walked along the rows of dying men, and much of my German classical philosophy broke down that night."[11] This first-hand experience with disaster not only shattered his "belief that man could master cognitively the essence of his being, the belief in the identity of essence and existence. . . ." It also confirmed and reinforced Tillich's previous vague doubts about the social values he had inherited from the bourgeois bureaucracy and the Lutheranism of East Prussia. But while these doubts had formerly made him turn toward the group of "artists, actors, journalists and writers" that he called "Bohemia,"[12] he now veered toward the first victims of the misery of war, the proletarian masses. The confrontation with the collective evil of war became symbolic of all oppressions of the working classes.

To use Tillich's language in *Systematic Theology*, the experience of World War I, the defeat of the German armies, the fall of the empire, and the ensuing social chaos functioned as a "revelatory situation" (1:127). The war and its misery constituted a revelatory event. What Tillich learned from it, not immediately, but by subsequent reflection, was that the times in which he was living presented humanity with a unique *kairos*. They were special times, pregnant with revelatory meaning.

The Critique of Socialism

Light is thrown on this meaning by the small volume that Paul Tillich published in 1933, just before the elections that gave a majority to the National Socialists and made Hitler Chancellor of the Reich: *The Socialist Decision*.[13] Politically, the timing of this book was disastrous, but it at least points to the author's great personal courage. In this volume Tillich not only espouses the socialist cause in terms of practical politics. Above all he uses the Marxist analysis of society and its expectations for the future as steps toward a religious reconstruction of society. As he had explained at length in his volume of 1926, *The Religious Situ-*

ation,[14] the religious dimension of a given period is hidden and active in its culture rather than expressed in the Churches. The culture of the new period pointed to the demise of the bourgeois mind, the deterioration of the capitalist way of life, and the awakening of the proletariat. All this was then interpreted as the wave of the future, the emergence of a new creation of society.

Indeed, in *The Socialist Decision* as in *Systematic Theology,* Tillich rejected the absolutism of the Marxist claims and their total subordination of everything human to the purpose of proletarian dictatorship for the sake of a future classless society. This he saw as a secular form of the Joachimite myth of the "third age" of the world, the reign of the Holy Spirit. In Tillich's theology of culture every effort for humanity, like every dimension of culture, remains under the judgment of the Cross. Where the self-critical principle is absent, as in the Marxist prediction of the withering away of the state, the hope of humanity degenerates in a visionary utopianism whose promises are bound to remain frustrated. In another vocabulary, the Protestant principle must be at work in the reorganization of society: "The Protestant principle is the judge of every religious and cultural reality. . . ."[15] Bringing this principle to bear on the revolutionary struggle of the proletariat was in Tillich's mind, precisely, the meaning and the task of religious socialism.

At the same time, however, Tillich's application of this critical principle to the communism of the Soviet Union remained remarkably uncritical. Shortly after coming to America Tillich compared the totalitarian states of Hitler's Germany and of Stalin's USSR. He was strangely ambivalent about the latter. Although he recognized that the Stalinist regime was more universally oppressive than that of Hitler, Tillich saw the critical principle at work in Soviet communism to an extent that remained unequalled everywhere else:

> In Russia the totalitarian state has been more effectively realized than even in Germany. Economic life, culture and education are all equally subject to state centralization. The motivating force behind the subordination, however, is not the state but the individual and the full development of his collectivistic activities. . . . The totalitarian character of the Soviet state, therefore, is to be understood on the one hand as a bulwark against the penetration of bourgeois capitalist elements, and on the other hand as the education of an entire continent in communistic enlightenment. Every step forward in this educational process means essentially a strengthening of the critical anti-authoritarian and anti-totalitarian forces among the people. Thus the more successful it is in the realization of its goal the closer the totalitarian state

comes to digging its own grave. This corresponds precisely to the theories of Marx and Lenin on the state.[16]

In 1992, now that the oppressed peoples of Eastern Europe have thrown off the yoke of proletarian dictatorship and collectivism—because of the non-realization of their goal—and the people of the Soviet Union are eager to restore some form of capitalist freedom, it is easy to see how badly, in 1934, Tillich was misreading the signs of the times.

How was this appalling misreading possible? As I see it, the distinction that Tillich makes between utopianism, transcendentalism, and religious socialism is inadequate. Utopianism pursues an unattainable goal; transcendentalism finds no ultimate purpose on earth other than the preparation of individual souls for heaven; but socialism, "so far as its substance is concerned, is prophetic."[17] It is "prophetism on the soil of an autonomous, self-sufficient world." Should socialism make only "moralistic demands," it would "create utopias" and degenerate into utopianism. In order to escape being another form of utopianism it must be based, Tillich believes, not on morality but on expectation, and more precisely on a type of expectation that is both prophetic and rational. "Prophetic expectation is transcendent; rational expectation is immanent."[18] What will be produced by human effort is already immanent in human nature. What is given above human effort is transcendent. The problem is of course to keep transcendence and immanence together. The socialism of Paul Tillich sets transcendence within immanence: "The transcendent is in fact immanent. It appears to be totally immanent: equality, freedom, the satisfying of human needs, etc. But when one examines the content of socialism's final expectation more closely, one finds that it presupposes a radical transformation of human nature, and in the last instance—since human nature constantly grows out of nature as such—a transformation of nature and its laws."[19]

At this point, however, the difference between the Tillichian perspective and that of any pursuer of utopias is vanishing. What is described is, precisely, a utopia: the transformation of nature and laws certainly cannot derive from the struggle for a new society! The transcendent cannot be created in human history by the immanent.

In the great battles of 1914, Paul Tillich was caught in a revelatory situation that shook his world and shattered his horizon. Reflecting upon this in the light of Marxism in *The Socialist Decision,* he believed that the crisis of modern society and, as being part of it, the "inner conflict" of socialism, result from a clash between two lines. On the one hand is the line of "whence," of the past, the roots, "the myth of origin," "the mythical powers of origin." These powers are experienced in "political romanticism" through the very Germanic symbols of the blood (race), the soil, and the group, that is itself led and symbolized by its *Führer*.[20] Nazism embodied the myth of origin to the point of reducing the eschatological nisus to the millennial prospect of a Third Reich that would last in a *pax germanica* of a thousand years. Indeed, Tillich held that no system of government can succeed unless it taps the wealth of the roots by which humanity as a whole and its own people in particular are nurtured.

On the other hand Tillich also wanted the myth of origin to be balanced by the teleological perspective, by the drive to the future. How can the weight of the past be properly joined to the urge towards "whither," to the "principle of hope," the "fundamental openness of life," the prophetic expectation, the demand for justice that can only come true in the future since it was not fulfilled in the past and is not yet realized in the present?

The inner conflict of socialism is sparked by the clash of these two lines, and the entire argumentation of *The Socialist Decision* strove to show that there lurks within socialism a "socialist principle" which has the capacity to do justice to both "origin and goal." When therefore Tillich concludes with the hopeful assertion: "Only expectation can triumph over the death now threatening Western civilization through the resurgence of the myth of origin. And expectation is the symbol of socialism,"[21] it is not difficult to see that the "socialist principle" is a more secular form of the Protestant principle. It is the protest against the past and the present in the name of the future, against the exclusive polarity of immanence in the name of self-transcendence, against empirical self in the name of essential self, against death in the name of resurrection.

Theological Transformation

Systematic Theology, I believe, makes no mention of the socialist principle, and the Protestant principle, prominent in many shorter writings, is not heavily stressed. Yet this is not to say that they have been forgotten. Undoubtedly, once he had emigrated to the United States, Tillich did not try to insert a religious dimension into the concepts and practices of the socialist organizations that existed on American soil. Given the differences in the situation of artists in America and in Europe, he was led to abandon his familiarity with "Bohemia," although he continued to write occasionally on matters of art and aesthetics.[22] As a German immigrant faced with the polarities of the Democratic and the Republican parties, which shared in slightly different ways the bourgeois mind and capitalist principles, he also had to give up his direct involvement in politics and his public advocacy of socialism with a religious face. Indeed, in a sympathetic history of *Christian Socialism*, John Cort wonders how much of Tillich's socialist convictions remained when, in 1963, at the Waldorf-Astoria, he "was the principal speaker at Henry Luce's gala party in celebration of the fortieth anniversary of *Time* magazine."[23]

Paul Tillich in America lived more and more like a bourgeois in the upper circles of high-caliber seminaries and universities. Yet I believe that he did not abandon the principles that had nurtured his life. His lot was, for many years, that of an exile. "I have always," he wrote in 1936, "felt so thoroughly German that I could not dwell on the fact at length. Conditions of birth and destiny cannot really be questioned."[24] Exiles dream what they no longer live. What he could not live because of his new environment and could not forget without betraying his experience of the past and his personal myth of origin, he now transformed and transcended. Already in Germany the socialist principle had metamorphosed into the Protestant principle. The momentary kairos of the battle of the Marne had become an embodiment of the permanent *kairos* of the Cross of Christ in its revelatory power. In America, through the long theological reflection that culminated in *Systematic Theology*, the Protestant principle metamorphosed into the universal prophetic principle of the kingdom of God. Like the religious socialist utopia, which has first to prepare and then finally to transform society, human nature, and even the laws of nature, the kingdom of God "has an inner-historical and a transhistorical side" (3:357). It is successively propaedeutic and transforming.

Now, however, the perspective is theological. The symbol of the kingdom of God has, for most Christians, lost some of its strength—partly because of the "sacramental emphasis of the two Catholic churches" (that is, Orthodox and Roman), and partly as a result of "its use (and partial secularization) by the social gospel movement and some forms of religious socialism." Even so, the symbol of the kingdom of God remains indispensable: ". . . Jesus started with the message of the 'Kingdom of God at hand' and . . . Christianity prays for its coming in every Lord's Prayer" (3:357). But the inner and the futuristic dimensions of the kingdom express much more than two essential aspects of the struggle for a just society: "In the former quality it is manifest through the Spiritual Presence; in the latter it is identical with Eternal Life."

If a utopia is a state of humanity that is expected yet cannot be realized on earth, then the kingdom of God is still more a utopia than the socialist expectation.[25] The perfect socialist society is far distant from us, but "the socialist society is infinitely distant from the Kingdom of God."[26] The three polarities of being—integration, creativity, transcendence—and the corresponding three functions of life are to be transformed by the "end of history and the final conquest of the ambiguities of life" (3:401). The "ambiguities of historical self-integration, self-creativity, and self-transcendence" are to vanish in the plenitude of unambiguous self-integration, self-creativity, and self-transcendence. The kingdom of God is Paul Tillich's ultimate version of the religious socialist utopia.

For this reason part 5 was needed: not for the structure of *Systematic Theology*, but for Tillich himself. Because Tillich had to save and transform his past, the socialist expectation now evoked the kingdom of God, which then became as much of a utopia as the establishment of a just society along socialist lines. And this is why a part 6 was unnecessary: the symbol of Eternal Life is entirely given in the statement, "God is eternal" (3:420); being "subjected neither to the temporal process nor with it to the structure of finitude," it is not related to the socialist expectation and to the ephemeral religious socialism of the 1920s in Berlin.

Conclusion

I see three lessons that can be learned from the present investigation.

First, coherence is a requirement of a theological system. A basic coherence undoubtedly underlies the central parts of *Systematic Theology*.[27] Yet, as I see it, this coherence is undermined by a defective horizon analysis in the third volume. This flaw points to the inherent difficulty of composing a system of theology today. We now witness a renewed search for a Catholic system[28] in the spirit of Vatican II; and this is a welcome change from the numerous "theologies of . . ."[29] that have been published since the council. But, as Tillich's example shows, it is extremely difficult to sustain systematic coherence over a long period of thinking and writing. The coherence of a systematic project may well originate in a moment of insight. But it then needs to stretch out and be sustained over a long period of research, reflection, and writing. Meanwhile, the author's life and mind may well take turns that will break the original coherence of the project.

Second, Paul Tillich's perspective was nurtured by his perception of a *kairos* in the years that followed the First World War in Germany.

But is it today's *kairos?* Tillich did not live to see the coming year 2000 raised to the level of an eschatological symbol. This is happening in several ways and forms. Indeed, this symbolic year is repeatedly mentioned in the works of John Paul II: ''In the time leading up to the third Millennium after Christ, while 'the Spirit and the bride say to the Lord Jesus: Come!', this prayer of theirs if filled, as always, with an eschatological significance, which is also destined to give fullness of meaning to the celebration of the great Jubilee. . . . *this prayer is directed towards a precise moment of history* which highlights the 'fullness of time' marked by the year 2000.''[30] Undoubtedly, Tillich's conception of time holds that a *kairos* is attached precisely to a particular moment. It would not rule out that the year 2000 may have a special *kairos*. But though a *kairos* may well be hoped for, it cannot be predicted; it is simply given.

Third, the overall lesson of Tillich's system is not that Catholic or Christian imagination should abstain from discovering new symbols of the eschaton. It is that no symbol may be absolutized. However hallowed by tradition or elicited from the signs of the times, no symbol is adequate to the ultimate fulfillment of God's promises. Whether one resonates better to the symbol of the kingdom, or of Eternal Life, or of the Year 2000, or of Omega Point, or of the Yin and the Yang, or of New Age, all images fall and all concrete expectations collapse before ''the ambiguities of self-transcendence [that] are caused by the tension'' between expectation and history (3:390). One should above all beware of confusing human achievements—technical, economic, political, social, or personal—with the sounds, faintly heard from a distance, of the New Jerusalem.

I have tried to show that the reason for this is found in Tillich's own life and especially in the ''shaking of the foundations'' that he experienced in the First World War and in his ensuing commitment to the otherwise little-known movement of religious socialism. The kingdom of God is other than the Spiritual Presence, since it is Tillich's projection of utopian hopes in a perfect socialist society. This makes part 5, I believe, the weakest in the three volumes of *Systematic Theology*. But it at least shows that the making of the system was not as abstract and theoretical as it often seems to diligent readers. Part 5 of *Systematic Theology* may not tell us much about the heavenly kingdom and how to relate to it in prayer and hope. Yet it does teach a lesson that is badly needed in the glow of the Gulf War: for those who are aware of the meaning of the Cross of Christ, the revelatory power of military defeat may well be greater than that of victory.

Notes

[1] The references in my text will all be to volume and page of Paul Tillich, *Systematic Theology*, 3 vols. (Chicago: University of Chicago Press, 1951-63). Other references will be in endnotes, one being valid until another is given.

[2] It is on purpose that I use the expression "kingdom of God," designating the extensive domain of authority, rather than the currently fashionable "reign of God," designating the kind of moral authority that is exercised. The Greek *basileia* and the Latin *regnum* include both meanings. Once these different connotations are separated, kingdom remains richer than reign.

[3] More recent theologians vary. John Macquarrie's *Principles of Christian Theology* (1966) locates "Christianity and the World" at the end (chap. 20) of the third part, "Applied Theology," while "the Last Things" come at the end (chap. 15) of the second part, "Symbolic Theology." Gordon Kaufman concludes his *Systematic Theology: A Historicist Perspective* (1968) on the *triplex munus* of Christ, "Prophet, Priest, and King" (part 4, chap. 33), the doctrine of the eschaton being in part 2, after the doctrines of creation and providence. Geoffrey Wainwright, however, does put "life through death" and "the divine kingdom" in the conclusion of his *Doxology, The Praise of God in Worship, Doctrine and Life, A Systematic Theology* (1980).

[4] The passage of Joachimism from the religious to the political sphere has been illustrated by Henri de Lubac, *La postérité spirituelle de Joachim de Flore*, 2 vol. (Paris: Lethielleux, 1979 and 1981).

[5] 1922: Paul Tillich, *The Protestant Era* (Chicago: University of Chicago Press, 1966) 46.

[6] 1929: Ibid., 13: Inaugural address at the University of Frankfurt.

[7] Ibid., 27-31.

[8] Paul Tillich, "The Kingdom of God and History," in *Theology of Peace*, ed. Ronald H. Stone, (Louisville: Westminster-John Knox Press, 1990) 25-56.

[9] See the account of Religious Socialism in Germany in John C. Cort, *Christian Socialism. An Informal History* (Maryknoll, N.Y.: Orbis Books, 1988) 213-21. In this story Tillich appears as an esoteric speculative figure with little practical impact. On religious socialism see the references in note 25, and also Eduard Heimann, *Tillich's Doctrine of Religious Socialism*, in Charles W. Kegley and Robert W. Bretall, eds., *The Theology of Paul Tillich* (New York: Macmillan, 1952); John R. Stumme, introduction to the American edition of *The Socialist Decision* (San Francisco: Harper and Row, 1977); Wilhelm and Marion Pauck, *Paul Tillich, His Life and Thought* (New York: Harper and Row, 1976) 1:67-79.

[10] *Blätter für Religiösen Sozialismus* began to appear at Easter 1920; it became *Neue Blätter für den Sozialismus* in January 1930; it ended in 1933.

[11] As quoted in *Time* magazine, March 16, 1959, p. 47.

[12] Paul Tillich, *On the Boundary*, 1966, 21-24.

[13] Paul Tillich, *Die Sozialistische Entscheidung* (Potsdam: Alfred Protte, 1933).

[14] Originally, Paul Tillich, *Die Religiöse Lage der Gegenwart* (Berlin: Ullstein, 1926).

[15] Tillich, *The Protestant Era*, 163; this is taken from chap. 14, the original form of which was published in 1931. See "Protestantism as a Critical and Creative Principle," in *Political Expectation* (Macon: Mercer University Press, 1981) 10–39.

[16] Paul Tillich, "The Totalitarian State and the Claims of the Church," in *Social Research*, vol. 1 (Nov. 1934) 413. In a milder form, similar claims were made in "The Protestant Principle and the Proletarian Situation" (chap. 11 in *The Protestant Era*, originally a pamphlet published in 1931).

[17] Tillich, *The Socialist Decision*, 101.

[18] Ibid., 110.

[19] Ibid., 111.

[20] See the analysis in ibid., 13–44.

[21] Ibid., 162.

[22] As in the essay "Protestantism and Artistic Style," in Paul Tillich, *Theology of Culture* (New York: Oxford University Press, 1972) 68–75.

[23] Cort, *Christian Socialism*, 219.

[24] Tillich, *On the Boundary*, 93–94; this volume is a reprint of the first part of *The Interpretation of History*, 1936.

[25] On the importance of utopian expectation in the political thought of Tillich, see the essays collected by James Luther Adams under the title, *Political Expectation*, notably, "Religious Socialism" (1930), "Basic Principles of Religious Socialism" (1923), "The Political Meaning of Utopia" (1951) (p. 40–57, 58–88, 125–80).

[26] Tillich, *On the Boundary*, 79.

[27] I have recognized this coherence in my *Paul Tillich and the Christian Message* (New York: Scribners, 1962) and in my contributions to Thomas A. O'Meara and Celestin D. Weisser, eds., *Paul Tillich in Catholic Thought* (chap. 4: "The Protestant Principle and the Theological System of Paul Tillich," 85–96; and chap. 12: "Christ as the Answer to Existential Anguish," 224–36) (Dubuque, Iowa: The Priory Press, 1964).

[28] As in Frans Jozef van Beeck, *God Encountered. A Contemporary Catholic Systematic Theology*, vol. 1: "Understanding the Christian Faith" (San Francisco: Harper and Row, 1989). Three volumes are projected and will be published by The Liturgical Press.

[29] The theologies of liberation are the best known; but there are also theologies "of hope," "of the laity," "of Religions," "of Paganism". . . .

[30] *Encyclical Letter 'Dominum et vivificantem,'* n. 66, (Vatican City: Vatican Polyglot Press, 1986, 135–136) (underlining in the text). Many other instances can be given.

The Socialist Tillich and Liberation Theology

Jean Richard

In a new Catholic assessment of Paul Tillich, the relation of his thought to liberation theology deserves a special consideration since the movement has been one of the main issues in Catholic theology for the last two decades. This is not to say that liberation theology is found in an exclusively Catholic stream of thought; in fact, the ecumenical dimension of the movement is widely acknowledged today.[1] Nevertheless, a few specific Catholic features remain: (1) it is connected with Vatican II through Medellin (1968); (2) the locus of its first proponents was Latin America; and (3) above all, nowhere more than in the Catholic Church has liberation theology precipitated so much criticism and tension.[2] The present paper purports to be part of that struggle and hopes to be more than a mere comparison between two pieces of theological literature. With the help of the socialist German Tillich, it aims at getting more deeply into liberation concerns, to see the real issues beyond superficial opposites.

Let us see first the relevance of Tillich to the present situation. Not only do we find in his socialist writings thoughts and categories that should prove to be of great use to liberation theology, but there is also a striking similarity between the struggle of religious socialism in the first decades of this century and the struggle of liberation theology today. Leonhard Ragaz (1868–1945), the founder of religious socialism, might be considered as a liberation theologian *avant la lettre*.[3] And after 1919, Tillich followed in Ragaz's footsteps, deepening the idea of socialism and coining new concepts within the Berlin *kairos* Circle.

The similarity of the situations is well-stated by Jacques Ellul when he writes that a proletariat appears wherever industrialization spreads out, so that the Third World will necessarily undergo a tremendous increase of the proletariat.[4] I would like, however, to bring out here an important nuance. A strong proletariat appeared in the West at the time of wild capitalism. Nowadays it has been tamed in our countries, but the same unrestrained capitalism is still in force on an international scale in Third World countries with the same devastating effects on the new proletariat. Here we find a very concrete link between both situations, which accounts for the similarity evident between the Christian answer afforded by religious socialism and by liberation theology.

The present theme, "Tillich and liberation theology," has been more than once tackled by Tillich scholars.[5] Here I will limit myself to the socialist German Tillich, more especially to the socialist Tillich of the Berlin period (1919–24), who became the leader of an intensive socialist reflection inside the *kairos* Circle, centered around the *Blätter für religiösen Sozialismus*.[6] I will also concentrate on three specific topics wherein Tillich's religious socialism casts penetrating light on crucial issues in liberation theology: the relationship between Christianity and socialism; the relationship between divine salvation and human liberation; and the religious significance of the proletarian masses.

Christianity and Socialism

The presupposition of the whole paper is that liberation theology is moved by a profound socialist inspiration. This is easily felt by anyone who has even a little acquaintance with the socialist spirit. But it is not easy to demonstrate; liberation theologians themselves are understandably very cautious on this point because today the word "socialism" has fallen into disrepute. In Roman Catholic orthodoxy, it now is equal to "real socialism," which refers to the late totalitarian Communist states. So, surprisingly enough, the best and shortest way to arrive at a clear expression of Marxist socialist inspiration is via the detour through the 1984 Instruction of the Congregation for the Doctrine of the Faith on the theology of liberation. From the outset, the charge is clear and precise: liberation theologians, in the social analysis of their situation, make use of concepts borrowed from various currents of Marxist thought, "in an effort to learn more precisely what are the causes of the slavery they want to end," but in so doing they necessarily adhere also to the Marxist ideology itself "which is incompatible with Christian faith and the ethical requirements which flow from it."[7]

For liberation theology, the entrance door to socialism is certainly Marxist social analysis. And this is also the first complaint of the Roman Instruction. An adequate social analysis requires "total openness to the reality to be described." But this is impossible if one adheres to a particular method and viewpoint. And that is so much the case with

Marxism, since all data received from observation and analysis are brought together in a global vision of reality: "The ideological principles come prior to the study of the social reality and are presupposed in it."[8] This is quite true, and the intimate connection between Marxist analysis and Marxist ideology is thus well-stated. But should it be otherwise? Yes, according to the naïve epistemology of the Roman congregation: the true scientific observer should get rid of all ideological presupposition to look at reality as it is.

Liberation theologians seem to be here more critical when they acknowledge the necessary ideological presupposition, or "social theory," behind any concrete method of analysis—hence, the ethical criteria which unite with the scientific criteria in the choice of an adequate method. There are basically two orientations. The *functionalist* tendency presupposes order, harmony, or equilibrium; consequently it will analyze society as a form of organic whole. The *dialectical* tendency, on the contrary, conceives of the world as a place of conflict, tension, and struggle; so it analyzes society as a complex, contradictory whole. The theologian who acknowledges the sin of the world, and who makes an option for the liberation of the poor, will quite naturally assume the dialectical Marxist social theory as being congenial with the prophetic spirit of the gospel.[9]

The Roman congregation sees things the other way around. The Marxist concept of "class struggle" opposes the universality of the Christian love of neighbor.[10] Its immediate consequence is the idea of a "revolutionary struggle" which necessarily implies violence: "To the violence which constitutes the relationship of the domination of the rich over the poor, there corresponds the counterviolence of the revolution, by means of which this domination will be reversed."[11] And such a revolution achieved by violent means leads by itself to a totalitarian regime.[12] Thus, the shift is completed from Marxism to Leninism. Bolshevism should be considered as the revelation of the essence of Marxism: "Atheism and the denial of the human person, liberty, and rights are at the core of Marxist theory."[13]

The Marxist idea of "class struggle" also suffers consequences in the conception of the Church: "The conclusion is drawn that the class struggle thus understood divides the church itself, and that in light of this struggle even ecclesial realities must be judged."[14] For instance, "it is disputed that the participation of Christians who belong to opposing classes at the same eucharistic table still makes any sense."[15] Moreover, the sacrosanct hierarchy, "and especially the Roman magisterium are thus discredited in advance as belonging to the class of the oppressors. Their theology is a theology of class."[16] Doubtless, here is to be found the main fault, the original sin of liberation theology, since "one of the conditions for necessary theological correction is giving proper value to the social teaching of the church."[17]

However, here also one might see otherwise. One might think that the main fault of the social teaching of the Catholic Church, beginning in the encyclical *Rerum Novarum* (1891), is precisely its anti-socialist bias. After a century, nothing has changed on this point, and the recent encyclical *Centesimus Annus* (1991) still objects to any reconciliation between Marxism and Christianity. Now, here is precisely the point where Tillich can help us. In the years after the First World War, as a socialist he met the same objections from his Church. But at that time in Germany, Marxist socialism had not yet fallen into disrepute; rather, it was blossoming into a new democratic regime, the Weimar Republic. Tillich openly behaved as a socialist, and he answered directly the charges of the Church by showing the intimate relationship between Christianity and socialism.

Indeed, from the beginning, Tillich had to confront Church opposition. On May 16, 1919, he was called by the president of the Lutheran Consistory of the Province of Brandenburg to report on his address to the rally of the Independent Social Democrats.[18] The report to President D. Steinhauser, signed by Paul Tillich and Richard Wegener, is now available in two versions, the second of which bears more clearly the stamp of Tillich.[19] According to the authors, it restates substantially the content of the address, which dealt with the relationship between Christianity and socialism.

The main objection of the Lutheran Church was the same as the Roman Catholic: it bore upon the materialist-atheistic ideology of Marxist socialism. Here Tillich first states the original meaning of the Marxist idea; then he proceeds to a criticism of incidental features that are not essential to socialism, and which are no more than remnants of the past. What is at stake here is the Marxist conception of history, which should be called economic rather than materialist. In itself, it does not imply the negation of spiritual or religious life. It states only a causal link between the economic foundation and the spiritual construction of culture, which is proving to be a very fruitful methodological insight for all human sciences. Here we have exactly what liberation theologians refer to as the Marxist social analysis. Of course, the economic interpretation of history often meets with real atheistic metaphysical materialism in Marxist literature. But this is not an essential feature; it is a legacy of the bourgeois culture which alters rather than enhances the true prophetic spirit of socialism.[20]

Let us turn now to the ethical objection, the class struggle. The Roman congregation holds that the Marxist concept of "class struggle" opposes the universality of Christian love. Tillich for his part argues exactly the other way around. The ethics of Christian love denounces a social order grounded on the basis of economic egoism, which aims at profit as an ultimate goal. That means the struggle of all against all, and leads finally to the class struggle. Religious socialism does not instigate but rather exposes class struggle as a direct sequel of capitalist economy. Tillich here explicitly states that the Christian love-ethics finally challenges the principle of class struggle and brings about the suppression of social classes.[21]

In another article of the same period, he expresses more precisely the complex relationship of religious socialism to class struggle: "Religious socialism must affirm the class struggle, not absolutely but according to the conditions of historical reality. The class struggle is a defense against an injustice. . . . The class struggle is itself, however, exactly like competition, an expression of the demonic character of capitalist economy."[22] Thus class struggle is at the same time affirmed and denounced by religious socialism. The solution of the dilemma is to be found in two articles of the Frankfurt period. Class struggle flows directly from the essence of capitalism; it is grounded in the natural laws of liberal economy. It is a structural reality of capitalism, and it has nothing to do with personal ethical values like the hatred of classes. To claim a socialism (or a liberation theology) without class struggle is to play the game of capitalism and to betray the real situation of the proletariat. Therefore, one cannot stand for or against class struggle, since it is an ineluctable demonic reality. However, through the class struggle the proletariat aims at what it is deprived of, that is the meaning of life. Thus, it is a fight against the destructive power of the demonic and for the kingdom of God.[23] In other words, the proletarian class struggle is always at the same time a fight to overcome the system which, by its very structure, produces the class struggle. Hence the ambivalence of the proletarian struggle: it is a struggle for life *in* the system, and at the same time a fight *beyond* the system to break the necessity of such a struggle of all against all for one's own life.[24]

These are Tillich's general considerations on Christianity and socialism. He comes finally to the more concrete question of the relationship between the Church and the socialist movement. He then addresses the Church with a highly paradoxical demand, almost impossible to realize: it should take a positive attitude toward socialism, but, on the other hand, it should not try to bring the workers back to itself, since it is actually a creation of the bourgeois society, which remains foreign to the spirit of the socialist workers.[25] In the revised edition of his report to the consistorium, he goes further in the matter. Representatives of the Church who stand on socialist ground should not be prevented from entering the socialist movement. In the same way, no one should be turned aside from leadership in the Church because of his socialist ideas. Of course, this will create conflict within the Church, but, contrary to the sect, the Church can withstand such tension. Thus, the Christian socialist movement will have a positive effect upon the Church. Otherwise, the Church will have no right to be called "Church of the people" (*Volkskirche*).[26]

Here we find another parallel to liberation theology, which also has been accused of creating a separate "popular Church" with its base community movement.[27] One is amazed at the similar phenomenon of the proliferation of the *Volkskirchen* in Germany after the Revolution of 1918.[28] In 1919 Tillich reported on a book about the Church in the new political order. One of the co-authors, Dibelius, dealt explicitly with the new features of the Church after the revolution, like the board and the ministry of the popular Churches. He stressed especially the achievement of the Alliance of the Popular Church which had gathered half a million members in but three months.[29] Moreover, Tillich himself, in December 1918, participated in the foundation of the New Church Alliance, which supported the new republic and a farsighted socialism.[30]

However, Tillich did not participate for very long in the New Church Alliance. He was more concerned with the theoretical side of the debate between Christianity and socialism and especially with the elaboration of the idea of socialism, since the lack of understanding in this respect was more manifest. In his subsequent endeavours of reconciliation, he proceeded from the idea of socialism to the Christian faith. The methodological—and epistemological—aspect of this process is noteworthy. It seems to me quite different and yet complementary with regard to liberation theology. Clodovis Boff has summarized its methodology with the phrases "socio-analytic mediation" and "hermeneutic mediation." First, the situation is analyzed objectively by means of the social sciences; the theologian then proceeds to the interpretation of the Scriptures; finally, both processes are correlated in the theology of the political.[31] In his preface to the recent French edition of his dissertation, Boff acknowledges, however, a few shortcomings, especially the concrete commitment to the poor and the oppressed—a factor which has not been emphasized enough as the root of all liberation theology. Such a *praxis* of social transformation in solidarity with the oppressed is now stated as an epistemological condition for liberation theology. Yet, the connection within the whole methodological process is still not apparent.[32]

This comes through more clearly in Tillich when he proceeds to "the religious and philosophical elaboration of socialism."[33] Socialism here is explicitly identified with the workers' movement—one might say as well with the movement of the poor.[34] Now Tillich states first that such an elaboration cannot be considered as a purely objective scientific observation, without interest or involvement. On the contrary, it is a consideration that comes from the reality itself (*aus der Sache*). It is the acknowledgment of the reality, the conceptual expression of the self-consciousness of the people at a particular time. Such a consideration is also normative, stating what should be, asserting a goal. It is a science of socialism which has the power to transform socialism. This is therefore, above all, more than a positive or a dogmatic consideration of socialism. If one does not want to call this kind of reflection science, certainly one will not deny it the name of philosophy.[35]

A few years later in Frankfurt, Tillich applied the same consideration to Marxism. The true reality of Marxism is the fact that the proletariat has become self-conscious, that out of a complete loss of meaning it has become filled with a powerful consciousness of its worth. So, Marxism has created a special type of human being, the being of the masses. This is the true content of the Marxist idea, an idea which was born from the situation of its time, and which therefore had the power to transform its time. Now one has to recover and give proper expression to this essential Marxist idea beyond the conceptual form it has received in the Marxist doctrine or dialectics, which in many important points is a betrayal of the original idea. In the background of the Marxist dialectics, there is indeed a religious consciousness of the future. Such an awareness is truly faith. It is the belief that one is fighting for a kingdom coming with the necessity of fate, endowed with a divine power overcoming all obstacles. Thus, Marxism has created an eschatological community which shares the conviction of the coming victory. Tillich says finally that the religious dimension of Marxism—expressed in a non-religious language—consists precisely of the two elements of any religious thought: the responsibility of action (or *praxis*) and the faith and belief that what one is fighting for will necessarily come.[36]

This comment on the religious meaning of Marxism constitutes, I believe, the best summary of the 1923 article on religious socialism.[37] From the very outset, Tillich emphasizes the prophetic character of socialism, which he defines as the higher synthesis of the sacramental attitude, centered on the sacredness of what is given, and the autonomous attitude, directed toward the rational form of truth and justice: "It is the unity and the higher form of both of the former tendencies. The demand of the holy that should be arises upon the ground of the holy that is given."[38] Hence, the religious goal of socialism, which is conceived of as theonomy: "Theonomy is a condition in which the spiritual and social forms are filled with the import of the Unconditional." In biblical terms, this is the meaning of the kingdom of God: "God is all in all."[39]

The struggle of religious socialism is the struggle for the kingdom of God, the struggle for a theonomous attitude toward the world, toward society, toward each other. In the cognitive sphere, it tries to overcome a purely external, objective approach to reality and to recover the internal import and meaning of things.[40] In the same way, in the practical sphere of industrial economy, religious socialism fights to overcome the purely external relationship whereby things are deprived of their intrinsic power and become pure economic instruments. This is the radical perversion of capitalist ownership that has no limits and leads directly to the struggle of all against all and ultimately to the class struggle.[41] The religious understanding of socialism gives birth finally to a spiritual community which is not without analogy to a base community movement: "The consciousness of the Kairos in the sense of an emerging theonomy creates a community of those who are filled with the same import and who strive for the same goal."[42] However, such a community is not a Church (or ecclesial community), since it remains on the soil of critical secular autonomy. Neither is it identical with political socialism, since it joins no political party. Yet Tillich still calls it "socialism" "because it has adopted the anti-demonic socialist criticism historically and substantially, and because it supports the political struggle of socialism as far as it intends to break the domination of political and social demonries." He adds that the socialist criticism should revolve also on political socialism itself.[43]

This is enough to see how Tillich elaborates the idea of Marxist socialism and also to realize how his thinking might help us to understand what is going on between Roman and liberation theology. Liberation theologians are satisfied with Marxist social analysis, and they seem to dismiss everything else as irrelevant. But in so doing, they miss the religious core of socialism, its prophetic inspiration, or what Tillich calls the Marxist socialist "idea." Thus, the Roman congregation is correct when it sees much more in liberation theology: it is a new hermeneutic, a socialist and Marxist interpretation of the Christian message. For

Roman theology, this amounts to a total perversion of the gospel, since any interpretation appears to be reduction and corruption—the only authentic reading of the Bible being the dogmatic. Tillich's religious and philosophical elaboration constitutes here a direct answer, showing the prophetic and Christian roots of the socialist idea, giving a Christian interpretation of Marxism. Of course, once more Roman theology would not be satisfied with such an interpretation since for it the only true Marxism remains the dogmatic. Thus, the meaning of the statement of John Paul II in *Centesimus Annus* (no. 26) becomes clear. One should read: "There is no possible conciliation between dogmatic Marxism and dogmatic Christianity."

Salvation and Liberation

Let us turn now to one of the main issues of liberation theology: the theological significance of the liberation of the poor, and its relationship to the salvation from sin in Jesus Christ. This is the first complaint of the 1984 Instruction of the Roman congregation. Liberation is first of all "liberation from the radical slavery of sin." It aims at "the freedom of the children of God, which is the gift of grace." Other kinds of liberation are mere consequences, since the many different kinds of slavery—cultural, economic, social, political—derive ultimately from sin. Liberation theologians, however, are charged with inverting the true order of priority: "Faced with the urgency of certain problems, some are tempted to emphasize, unilaterally, the liberation from servitude of an earthly and temporal kind. They do so in such a way that they seem to put liberation from sin in second place, and so fail to give it the primary importance it is due."[44] One has to note here the Pauline background of Roman theology: "Christ, our liberator, has freed us from sin and from the slavery to the law and to the flesh, which is the mark of the condition of sinful humankind."[45] Thus, sin, the root of all evils, is conceived of as a strictly personal act, as an interference in the relation of the human heart with God: "New Testament revelation teaches us that sin is the greatest evil, since it strikes humankind in the heart of its personality." Therefore, one should not speak of "social sin," but of the "social effects" of sin.[46]

The Roman congregation charges liberation theologians with a reductionist reading of the Bible: the essence of salvation is reduced to the economic and political struggle for human justice and freedom.[47] The real issue appears finally to be the distinction between history of salvation and profane history. For non-dualist liberation theology, there is only one human history: "Thus there is a tendency to identify the kingdom of God and its growth with the human liberation movement and to make history itself the subject of its own development, as a process of the self-redemption of humankind by means of the class struggle."[48] In its "full presentation of Christianity," the Roman congregation emphasizes those essential aspects which tend to be eliminated by liberation theology: "the transcendence and gratuity of liberation in Jesus Christ, true God and true man; the sovereignty of grace; and the true nature of the means of salvation, especially of the church and the sacraments."[49]

Two years later, in 1986, the same congregation issued another Instruction "On Christian freedom and liberation," which is but a theological elaboration of the main lines already stated in the previous document. The main features are resumed and fully developed. First, liberation from sin by the redemption of Christ: "Through his cross and resurrection, Christ has brought about our redemption, which is liberation in the strongest sense of the word, for it has freed us from the most radical evil—namely, sin and the power of death."[50] Such a radical evil is still conceived of in a purely personal and intimate way: "For the sin which is at the root of an unjust situation is, in a true and immediate sense, a voluntary act which has its source in the freedom of individuals. Only in a derived and secondary sense is it applicable to structures."[51] Freedom from sin is then spoken of in a strikingly Pauline-Lutheran fashion, as justification by grace through faith: "The heart of the Christian experience of freedom is in justification by the grace received through faith and the church's sacraments. This grace frees us from sin and places us in communion with God."[52] Finally, once again the Roman document lays stress on "the distinction between the supernatural order of salvation and the temporal order of human life."[53] It laments the false ideology that misleads the worker movement, ignoring "the transcendental vocation of the human person," and attributing to humankind "a purely earthly destiny."[54]

This second Instruction of the Roman congregation aims at presenting a model of true liberation theology. It is certainly orthodox theology. But it is not liberation theology at all. The difference is striking in many points. For instance, Christ has chosen on earth a state of poverty and deprivation, not to identify himself with the poor, but "in order to show in what consists the true wealth which ought to be sought, that of communion of life with God. He taught detachment from earthly riches so that we might desire the riches of heaven."[55] Still more surprising, the Vatican Instruction presents a striking similarity with Schubert Ogden's essay *Faith and Freedom*.[56] Ogden also wants to offer an alternative model of liberation theology, grounded on the

Pauline principle of justification by faith. One may even find in his book the same two main features: the shift from the concept of liberation to the concept of freedom, and the shift from the notion of liberation (emancipation) to the notion of salvation (redemption). Ogden's essay constitutes, I think, a still better achievement of what the Roman congregation wanted to do. But its liberation theology is no better. One has said that Ogden is a countermodel of "how not to do a theology of liberation."[57] This applies *a fortiori* to the Roman Instruction.

From the beginning, liberation theologians themselves have had a clearly defined position against all kinds of dualism and supranaturalism. Gustavo Gutiérrez includes a special chapter on the topic, "Liberation and Salvation," in his seminal book, *A Theology of Liberation*. He notes first the endeavor of Vatican II, in *Gaudium et spes*, to overcome the dualistic approach to the natural and supernatural orders. However, the outcome is not completely satisfying since it results in some kind of juxtaposition: "The final text is limited to two general affirmations: there is a close relationship between temporal progress and the growth of the Kingdom, but these two processes are distinct."[58] The human work is conceived of as the transformation of nature, and thus as the continuation of creation. The perspective is different within liberation theology. There, attention is directed above all to the negative results of technological progress—a historical situation of misery, of despoliation, and of exploitation of human beings.[59] Such a situation appears as intrinsically unjust and sinful; therefore, any liberating action against oppressive and unjust social structures is at the same time a salvific action inspired with liberating grace: "Sin appears, therefore, as the fundamental alienation, the root of a situation of injustice and exploitation. It cannot be encountered in itself, but only in concrete instances, in particular alienations."[60] We might comment that the unjust situation is not only a consequence or effect of sin, which might be located somewhere else, for instance, in the privacy of the human heart; it is the concrete manifestation or realization of sin which otherwise would be reduced to pure abstraction. We may then conclude with Gutiérrez: "The historical, political liberating event *is* the growth of the Kingdom and *is* a salvific event, but it is not *the* coming of the Kingdom, not *all* of salvation. It is the historical realization of the Kingdom and, therefore, it also proclaims its fullness."[61]

Clodovis Boff, in his dissertation, examines the same question and thesis from another perspective, that of epistemology. There is only one reality, which, however, is open to different readings or interpretations: "Thus, for example, the sociological situation in Latin America is susceptible of a sociological interpretation, in terms of 'dependency,' and of a theological interpretation, in terms of 'sin.' "[62] It is the same with the terms "society/kingdom" and "liberation/salvation." When the social analysis reads "dependency" and "emancipation," the theological interpretation, in the awareness of faith, will offer a more profound, an absolute meaning: "In its own historical body . . . liberation will be seen to be charged with an *objective* salvific signification of grace or sin."[63]

There are not two realities (political liberation and divine salvation), but two approaches (political and theological) to the same reality. This is the reason why Boff eliminates the model of the Chalcedonian dialectic: "union without confusion, distinction without separation."[64] It presupposes a duality, two realities, two orders, natural and supernatural, to be connected as closely as possible. In the Chalcedonian dogma, we get at the fundamental issue. The whole theory of the supernatural is, indeed, grounded in the dogma of the two natures of Christ. If this is to be understood as two levels of reality, divine and human, the same duality will appear also in each of us, since we share in the divine filiation of Christ. Finally, the history of salvation will revolve on the higher level of divine filiation, as distinct from the mere human concerns of political and social liberations. This is a real theological problem, one which has not been resolved in Boff's epistemological study.

We know that Tillich opposed supranaturalism from the beginning, with his 1915 *Habilitationsschrift* on the concept of the supernatural before Schleiermacher. The question of the relation between Christianity and socialism constitutes for him another aspect of the same problem. At the core of their opposition lies, indeed, the question of immanence: Christianity is commonly seen as oriented toward the beyond, while socialism is concerned with the things of this world. But this is a false dichotomy that Tillich wants to overcome. There are not two worlds, the heavenly and the earthly. There is but one reality, and the only way to perceive the absolute is through and in the relative things of this world. The religious experience of the Unconditional does not mean the affirmation of the holy world of heaven, along with the negation of this finite and sinful world. Rather it is a yes and a no to all things and values of our world. In this way, one overcomes the opposition between a beyond that is absolute and perfect, and a "here-below" that is relative and defective. For Tillich this is a direct consequence of the Protestant principle of justification through faith alone, according to which the same personality and reality is both absolute and relative, eternal and temporal, perfect and defective. Therefore, one should no longer refer to the principle of justification as an argument on behalf of supranaturalism.[65]

This, however, does not lead to immanentism, or naturalism. There are, indeed, two different ways to relate to this world. One can deal with science, morality, economy, politics, in a purely profane way, seeking only profit or pleasure. Or, one can see in each of those realms a manifestation of life and spirit that inspires holy fear and respect. Such a religious inspiration is still alive in the socialist movement, although it has been profaned by many of its leaders. This should be the function of Christianity on behalf of socialism: the sanctification of cultural life in all its fields, the living experience of the Unconditional in everything conditioned and finite, in the totality of the real.[66]

Here we come to the critical issue: the transformation of the world and its relationship to redemption and to the kingdom of God. According to the supranaturalist conception, redemption comes directly from on high. Since our world is definitively perverted and lost, salvation is expected from the replacement of this painful world by a better one. But such an ideal and absolute world is, in fact, illusory. A real world is necessarily a world of tension between being and value, between what is and what should be. Only in this tension lies the space for real freedom. The same is true for the kingdom of God. It is real inasmuch as it comes into this world and out of this world by the immanent structuring and transformation of the world. This is the true meaning of the Christian affirmation: the kingdom of God coming into the world.[67]

But here again, the opposition to supranaturalism should not result in naturalism. The structuring of the world is the work of technical reason which plans the means best suited to the end. But for a true transformation of the world, something else is needed: meaning and ultimate end, value of the personality, revelation of the spirit, and creative thought. All this comes from beyond pure technical reason, from a depth which escapes the grasp of reason; in religious terms, all that belongs to the realm of grace, which is opened by the attitude of faith. So, the will to transform the world has to be grounded in faith as the experience of the Unconditional. When this happens, the structuring of the world is really identical with the coming of the kingdom of God.[68] Here is, once more, the ultimate goal of religious socialism: *theonomy*, as "a condition in which the spiritual and social forms are filled with the import of the Unconditional."[69]

Mention has been made previously of the "structuring" (*Gestaltung*) of the world. The negative aspect of the social situation—calling for a transformation into a better world, or for a liberation—has not yet been emphasized. During the Berlin period, Tillich expressed the social contradiction in terms of the demonic. Theonomy, as the goal of religious socialism, "stands in opposition to the predominance of the demonic." Therefore, "the conflict of religious socialism is directed against sacramental and natural demonries."[70] In the Frankfurt period, however, the philosophy of existence prevailed, so that the negativity of life was expressed in terms of sin. More particularly, "the problematic concept of 'original sin' denotes an original self-contradiction in human existence, coincident with human history itself."[71] Moreover, the notion of sin emphasizes human freedom and responsibility at the root of the contradictions of existence.

Let us see now how this radical conception of sin applies to the social order. Tillich is very clear on this point: "In the proletarian situation the perversion of man's nature shows its reality in the social realm." He goes on to say: "This assertion can be theologically denied only by those who conceive of the relation between God and the world as exclusively a relation between God and the soul." Tillich, on the contrary, holds that "the perversion of human existence is real in social, just as strongly as in individual, distortions and with even more primitive force; and collective guilt is just as real and perceptible as individual guilt; neither can be separated from the other."[72]

No doubt Tillich's conception here is the opposite of the Roman theology. Sin is not first a personal individual failure which then has negative consequences in the social order. Sin is still more radical. It has to be conceived of first as original sin, that is, as the radical contradiction of human existence and as the universal distortion of human history. Now, this radical contradiction is manifest in social alienation as well as (and even more clearly than) in personal perversion. In other words, "the universally human reveals itself in the proletarian situation." Thus, the Christian theologian has to learn from the socialist claims that "there are situations in which the perversion of man's essential nature is manifest primarily as a *social* perversion and as a *social* guilt." Conversely, the socialist may learn from Christianity that "the proletarian situation, far from being merely a historical accident, represents a distortion of essential human nature and a demonic splitting-up of humanity in general."[73] With Tillich, we have to acknowledge this radical recognition of sin as a specific achievement of Protestantism. Liberation theologians might certainly learn from him in the theological elaboration of the notion of "structural sin." Moreover, the question of social or structural sin is of great significance for liberation theology, since there is an immediate relation between sin and salvation. If the proletarian situation is in itself a sinful situation (not only a consequence of sin), one must conclude that liberation from that situation is also in itself salvation (not only a consequence or result of salvation).

Tillich reaches the same conclusion through his own negative way, that is, moving forward in his polemic against dualism. A direct consequence of the dualist conception of heaven and earth, of the supernatural and the natural, is indeed the dualism of soul and body, or of spirit and life, since "body is to be understood here as representing the whole vital sphere." Against such a dualism Tillich stresses the biblical idea of the unity of spirit and body, according to which the divine judgment, revealing the sin of the human person, bears upon the whole of human existence "in the same way upon the spiritual as upon the physical existence of man." Therefore, the contradictions in social and economic life are expressions of the sinful distortion of existence as much as the contradictions in the psychological or affective life of the individual. This is what has been revealed by the proletarian situation: "The distorted character of the vital existence of millions and millions of proletarians in city and country is too obvious to need much description. It is worse in some nations than in others and in some sections of a country than in others. It is at its worst in periods of unemployment, and intolerable—leading to mass explosions—in times of protracted mass unemployment." Tillich concludes that in confronting such a situation, a doctrine of salvation that is concerned with the soul only, or primarily, is itself unmasked as irrelevant and ideological: "The proletarian situation confirms the biblical doctrine; for in this situation there is a unity of both bodily and spiritual distortions of man's true nature, in the face of which every attempt to save the soul and leave the body to perdition must appear to be frivolous."[74]

The Masses of the Poor

This leads us to our last exploration, the philosophical and religious meaning of the painful reality at the core of all socialist and liberation thought: the proletarian masses, the masses of the poor. The previous two points converge on this third. For Tillich, Marxist socialist thinking is on the whole but the conceptual expression of the self-consciousness of the proletarian masses. It creates a community of all those who are conscious of the *kairos*, the emerging theonomy. This is the new eschatological community, the community of salvation, which constitutes a challenge to the Church, since it fulfills in itself the gospel for which the Church stands; nonetheless, it is outside the Church, on the soil of autonomous secular culture.

The last line of thought we studied was the 1931 article on "The Protestant Principle and the Proletarian Situation." There Tillich uses the Marxist term "proletariat." His definition is strictly socio-economic: "The proletarian situation is to be understood as the situation of that class within the capitalist system, its members being exclusively dependent upon the free sale of their physical ability to work, and its social destiny being wholly dependent upon the turn of the market."[75] Subsequently, we saw that in the same article Tillich insists on the contradictions inherent in such a situation, which he conceives of as the vivid expression of the distortion of human nature. The importance he places on the unity of the human being's body-spirit whole is such that, for him, the contradictions within physical vital existence constitute an alienation of human life in its totality. Thus, the conquest of such an alienation is not only liberation from economic oppression, it is truly salvation from sin.

We shall now turn to another analysis elaborated ten years earlier with different tools, namely, philosophy of the spirit and theology of culture, rather than economic analysis and theology of existence. Yet the same thesis is stated in a more complete and powerful way with the relevance of many themes to liberation theology being no less obvious. The essay, entitled *Mass und Geist*, was published in 1922 out of three previous articles (1920–22). In the preface, Tillich states the significance of the work. His reflections are not merely objective and uninvolved, sociological or philosophical. On the contrary, the main idea was born of the contemporary situation. The significance of the World War of 1914 and the German Revolution of 1918 impressed Tillich and his friends with ineluctable power. Moreover, the book's fundamental idea comes from a true religious feeling for the obscure depths of the life of the mass, with its misery, its formlessness, but also its creative power. Nevertheless, the ensuing reflections are not mere feelings, but rather concepts elaborated in an intensive philosophical work.[76] The affirmation of an idea that stems from a period's critical situation, from a *kairos*, is already present, as is the proposal of a religious and philosophical elaboration of that seminal idea. However, this is not yet the idea of socialism, but rather the idea of the masses, which is all the more fundamental, since it is the root and core of the socialist idea itself.

Attention should be first called to the word "mass." In his 1931 article on the proletarian situation, Tillich notes the difference between the "masses" and the "poor." Both are defined by a condition of physical and psychic misery. However, whereas in the first instance need and misery are "characteristic of a whole sociologically homogeneous mass," the misery of the poor is "a case of exception."[77] The poor as such is a singular case; the masses, a collective phenomenon. The phrase "masses of the poor" then expresses exactly what liberation theologians are talking about. It is more universal than the "proletariat," which indicates one concrete manifestation of the masses. As a first approximation, it is still more adequate than the "class of the poor," since it stresses the mere quantitative aspect of the phenomenon, without form or structure.

The specific point of view of Tillich in this writing, peculiar to his theology of culture, is apparent here. He does not conduct an economic analysis of the physical needs and oppression (dependence) of the masses, but rather a philosophical and religious analysis of their cultural (or "spiritual") alienation. Of course, economic misery is presupposed. But Tillich emphasizes the lack of cultural formation, the formlessness of the masses. The unity of physical and spiritual alienation is then manifest from the outset, as is consequently the unity of socio-economic liberation and spiritual salvation.

Alienation is characterized in a few words: "the masses stand under the malediction of unpersonality."[78] Once again there is a direct link with liberation theologians who call the poor of the Third World "non-persons." Tillich, however, digs deeper in the analysis of the condition of non-personality. In humankind, personality is achieved through the actualization of the spirit, of the rational form, out of the immediacy of natural existence. Specific human individuality is personal individuality, which is characterized by autonomy, creativity, and subjectivity. Thus, "the opposite of personal-individual actualization is the reprobation of stagnation in the masses."[79] Tillich proposes the following general definition: "In the historical sense of the word, the masses comprises the classes, races, circles and conditions of life whose common fate it is to be excluded from an individual, spiritual [or cultural] formation."[80] Another, consecutive, feature of the masses is objectification, that is, alienation from any creative subjectivity. The masses are mere object with regard to those who are endowed with subjective-active power: an object of economic domination, political manipulation, educational planning, and social welfare.[81]

One might think that the solution would be educational training of the masses, so that everyone might enjoy the cultural achievement which is now the prerogative of the elite. This, however, would be a misleading interpretation of the situation, a wrong solution, equivalent to developmentalism in the Third World. The roots of the problem are much deeper. The material and spiritual misery of the masses is but the symptom of a sickness that strikes the whole social body: "The masses occur when the creative spiritual principle of a society is dissolved, when its immediate validity, its natural formative power is lost."[82]

This brings to mind the main Tillichian criticism of secular autonomous culture. It is a culture which is purely rational and formal, concerned only with forms and laws specific to each realm of rationality. As such, however, it relies only on its own rationality, becoming void of *Gehalt*, of the spiritual substance which fills, animates, and inspires all forms of rationality. In the same way, when highly cultivated individuals critically oppose their own foundation, when they reject the spiritual substance on which they live, the time of their dissolution has arrived.[83]

The elite, while losing their spiritual substance, also become separated from the masses, dealing with these in a solely objective and objectifying way. This is the result of a "technical spirit," which is the spirit of bourgeois society. It supposes a consciousness separated from things which are no more than objects and means to an end. In this way, the same bourgeois, technical spirit "has produced the masses as an object and means to an end for a chosen few."[84]

Thus, the elite and the masses unite in a common deficiency. Both are void of spiritual substance (*Gehalt*): the elite, because they have cultivated only rational forms; the masses, because they have been objectified, deprived of its soul, life, and creativity. At this zero-point of deconstruction, a new construction may start again, established on a new foundation, namely a new spiritual substance filling both people and the individual personality: "Thus, all questions converge on a single answer: humanity must be regenerated from the depth of a new *Gehalt*, in which the opposition of masses and personality is overcome. But a new *Gehalt* is a matter of grace and destiny."[85]

The religious side of the analysis becomes evident here. The correlation of questions and answers appears as the correlation of liberation and salvation. Both are united as form and substance (*Gehalt*). Liberation occurs in the various realms of culture, where the masses are alienated under the pressure of a rational, objectifying elite. Still there will be no liberation if the elite are only superseded by the masses. Rather the solution must be a new *Gehalt* which overcomes the split between the masses and the elite. Such a new *Gehalt* "is a matter of destiny, something that cannot be produced, something that may at most be heartily desired and for which one can only make oneself free."[86]

This means that the new spiritual *Gehalt* which must regenerate the world will come as a revelation and will be received with an attitude of faith. In other words, salvation will come as grace. Here Tillich refers explicitly to the Pauline-Lutheran principle of justification: "The religious principle itself opens the way to a solution: it is the fundamental paradox which was fought for at the time of Reformation under the banner of justification . . . and which can nowadays be understood as the breakthrough of the unconditional *Gehalt* through the determination of each form."[87] The Protestant principle of justification by grace is interpreted here using the central idea of the theology of culture: the appearance of a new theonomy due to the breakthrough of the unconditional import (*Gehalt*) in the various forms of culture.

However, Tillich brings his socialist theology one step further towards concretion. The chosen people of God, the place of the revelation of the new *Gehalt*, are the masses rather than the cultivated, spiritual elite. The former's religious meaning is stated thus: "God and the masses: this means the revelation of the holy, of the Unconditional-Real through the masses."[88] This is not sheer paradox. There is in the Unconditional an element or moment which can only be manifested through the masses. It is the substantial-transrational *Gehalt*, which breaks all forms, whose infinity cannot find expression elsewhere than in the inexhaustible potentiality of the masses, deprived, as it is, of any definite form. Tillich concludes: "The masses are holy; indeed, they are the revelation of the creative infinity of the Unconditional-Real . . . perceived through the category of quantity."[89] Thus, in spite of the pharisaic judgment of the elite, which speaks of *massa perditionis*, under the paradox of the Unconditional, the masses remain a *massa sancta*.[90] There is clearly an allusion here to the paradox of the justification of the sinner, which then receives a collective application: the masses as such are declared holy in the judgment of God, in spite of the unacceptability of this judgment in human eyes.

This also has consequences for the conception of the salvation of the world. If the masses are where the new *Gehalt* is revealed, they become *ipso facto* the bearer of the destiny and salvation of the whole world. According to Tillich this prophetic sign of the times is apparent in the expressionist painting of the first two decades of this century: "A torpid something weighs on the [expressionist] masses, a metaphysical lack of redemption and longing for redemption. For that reason, they are sometimes approximated to animals, then again elevated beyond humanity to ecstatically visionary heights." The masses are portrayed here as objects of damnation and salvation. They are damned inasmuch as they are reduced to mechanical masses through objectification; they are saved and bearers of salvation inasmuch as they become a dynamic people, that is, inasmuch as they become the authors (or subjects) of their own liberation through the grace they have received: "The masses are subjects, entirely subjects; the leader, the redeemer is missing, and one feels that he cannot come from above. He must be born from the depth of the masses' longing." Indeed, the masses cannot be mere "objects" of salvation. That would mean infinite damnation, since their woe consists precisely in a reduction to the state of objects. Therefore, the savior of the masses must be identified with the masses, and the sufferings of Christ are to be interpreted accordingly: "The Christian symbols, which find application again, are just that—only symbols. They remain strange, unless they are reinterpreted as symbols of the suffering of the masses, in which the redeemed and redeemer must be one if there is genuinely to be redemption."[91] Thus, Christ is the leader of the masses, not as an extraordinary spiritual or divine personality, but rather as a being profoundly united with the masses in their dark and mute consciousness. In this way he may be also the prophet of the masses, insofar as he can reveal through the word the obscure principle, the divine *Gehalt* which lies in the midst of the masses.[92]

In this identification of Christ with the masses, Tillich's similarity with liberation theology is still more evident. The following points are particularly noteworthy. First, both the socialist Tillich and liberation theologians start from below, from the masses of the poor. Second, the humble are the people of God, the heirs of his kingdom: "The kingdom of God is conveyed through the masses which are the bearers of destiny."[93] Third, Christ the Savior has identified himself with the masses, so that the saved and the savior become one. Fourth, the sole aim of liberation theology, as well as of religious socialism, is the full actualization among the masses of the "idea" of salvation, which is already there by the grace of God.

However, there are also important differences, the main one being, no doubt, the Tillichian philosophical and religious analysis of the masses. Indeed, Tillich's philosophy of religion and theology of culture are absent from liberation theology; this difference is not just a matter of fact. A deliberate exclusion of philosophical mediation may be recorded in current liberation theology: as C. Boff says, "I have reason for refusing any primacy to philosophical mediation: it is speculative, or at least it has a tendency to be speculative. I opt to establish a relationship with empirical, positive analyses rather than with philosophical speculations, because I am afraid that, in the sociohistorical conjuncture that is currently ours, especially in the Third World, philosophy would inevitably end in a mystification of the reality of the oppressed masses, and more than likely a devastating mystification."[94]

Such a straightforward, candid statement calls for a few short comments. First, is Tillich's socialist philosophy equivalent to a philosophical speculation, ending in a mystification of reality? Second, would not a socialist-religious philosophy help liberation theology to integrate socio-analytic and biblical-hermeneutic mediation? Both analyses now seem extrinsically superimposed one on the other. Third, would not a more profound philosophical reflection help liberation theologians clarify their relationship with Marxist socialism? To say that one borrows Marxist social analysis while remaining unaffected by Marxist ideology is a pragmatic answer which convinces no one. Fourth, the risk of negating any use of philosophy is to practice *de facto* a crypto-philosophy. As a matter of fact, the above quotation from Boff is a clear example of naïve positivist philosophy, which is moreover contrary to the real spirit of liberation theology. Clearly, all liberation theology is not only an account of the misery of the masses, it is also a strong protest against such a situation. But where does this protest come from? Only from the Bible?

Let us turn now to the other partner in the debate, Roman theology. It is for us a privilege to have, in the two Roman Instructions of 1984 and 1986, such a clear and precise expression of the official position of the Roman magisterium. Tillich and Wegener could not rely on such a statement when they had to report to the Consistory of their Church in 1919. Earlier in this paper, I laid stress on these documents, because the significance of liberation theology within the Catholic Church cannot be given a valid assessment outside of this tension with Roman theology.

In the context of this debate, it is obvious that Tillich would have undoubtedly sided with liberation theology against Roman theology. In other words, one might say that the Roman congregation's objections against liberation theology apply as well to the socialist Tillich. Let us consider but a few examples relevant to our last topic, the masses of the poor. First, according to the Roman congregation, the "denial of the human person" is not the consequence of a technical bourgeois society, but of Marxist atheist theory.[95] Second, liberation theologians, like Tillich, "go on to a disastrous confusion between the poor of Scripture and the proletariat of Marx," and to a no less tragic confusion between the "church of the people," the "church of the oppressed" and the "church of the class."[96] Third, the Roman congregation laments the "unjust inequalities in the opportunity of culture, which is the specific mode of a truly human existence," and affirms "the necessity of promoting and spreading education, to which every individual has an inalienable right." But it makes no criticism of the bourgeois culture which is thus to be communicated.[97]

What is the meaning of such a theological debate? How is the tension between Roman and liberation theology to be interpreted? The temptation of the easy answer of class struggle should be resisted: Roman theology would simply be class theology, bourgeois theology. Such an answer would be, I think, unfair and superficial. Of course, the Roman institution, like any other, is not immune to the temptation of siding with the rich and the powerful. But this is not the main issue here.

The first Tillich is closer to the mark, I think, when he makes a distinction between "theology of culture" (*Kulturtheologie*) and "theology of the church" (*Kirchentheologie*).[98] I would define the theology of the Church as "institutional theology," that is, a theology which comes from the institutional Church and which finally tends toward the Church, so as to support the institution. In this theology, the religious truth (the truth about God, about Christ, and finally about the Church) has pre-eminence over social truth (the truth about the poor), and the latter is to be judged according to the former. In socialist and liberation theology the order of the relationship is inversed. The truth of the poor becomes the criterion for every other truth, the standpoint from which all ideology can be judged. Thus, the *praxis* of faith toward the poor may challenge the institutional doctrine of faith. An easy test may be made with the symbol "kingdom of God." Church theology proposes the Church itself as the concrete actualization of the kingdom of God on earth. On the other hand, liberation theology stresses the words of the gospel, according to which the kingdom is given to the poor. Finally, the powerful of this world might think that they are themselves the bearers of the kingdom, since they care and work for the common weal. Here we have the famous tripartite division of the first *Kairos* Document: state theology, Church theology, prophetic theology.[99]

Given what has been said here, the distinction and tension between Catholicism and Protestantism is no longer as relevant. Even the Tillichian distinction Catholic substance/Protestant principle is of no avail. What matters now is the New Substance, the New *Gehalt*, the New Being. It is the kingdom of God which comes to the masses of the poor, and which challenges both the Catholic and Protestant institutions.

Notes

[1] This is especially conspicuous in the book by Priscilla Pope-Levison, a United Methodist, interfacing with the following liberation theologians: six Roman Catholics (L. Boff, S. Galilea, G. Gutiérrez, O. Romero, J. L. Segundo, J. Sobrino) and four Protestants (M. Arias, E. Castro, O. Costas, J. M. Bonino). *Evangelization from a Liberation Perspective* (New York: Peter Lang, 1991).

[2] Cf. Arthur F. McGovern, *Liberation Theology and Its Critics. Toward an Assessment* (Maryknoll, N.Y.: Orbis Books, 1989).

[3] Cf. John C. Cort, *Christian Socialism. An Informal History* (Maryknoll, N.Y.: Orbis Books, 1988) 201-7.

[4] Jacques Ellul, *Changer de révolution. L'inéluctable prolétariat* (Paris: Seuil, 1982) 197.

[5] One may find a record of the main studies in Ronald H. Stone, "Paulus and Gustavo: Religious Socialism and Liberation Theology," *Laval théologique et philosophique* 44 (1988) 156 n.1.

[6] The German socialist writings of Tillich are now gathered and translated into French in the second volume of the French Tillich collection: *Christianisme et socialisme. Les écrits socialistes allemands (1919-1931)* (Paris: Cerf; Genève: Labor et Fides; Québec, Presses de l'Université Laval: 1992). Out of the thirty-one essays collected in this volume, twelve belong to the Berlin period.

[7] Congregation for the Doctrine of the Faith, "Instruction on Certain Aspects of the Theology of Liberation" (August 1984), in *Liberation Theology: A Documentary History*, ed. A. T. Hennelly, (Maryknoll, N.Y.: Orbis Books, 1990) 393-94.

[8] Ibid., 401-3.

[9] Clodovis Boff, *Theology and Praxis. Epistemological Foundations* (Maryknoll, N.Y.: Orbis Books, 1987) 57-58.

[10] "Instruction on the Theology of Liberation," 405-6.

[11] Ibid., 403-4.

[12] Ibid., 410.

[13] Ibid., 402.

[14] Ibid., 405.

[15] Ibid., 406.

[16] Ibid., 407.

[17] Ibid., 411.

[18] Cf. Ronald H. Stone, *Paul Tillich's Radical Social Thought* (Atlanta, Ga.: John Knox Press, 1980) 41-42.

[19] Paul Tillich, "Christentum und Sozialismus. Bericht an das Konsistorium der Mark Brandenburg" (1919), in *Gesammelte Werke*, ed. Renate Albrecht (Stuttgart: Evangelisches Verlagswerk, 1959-75) 13:154-60; "Der Sozialismus als Kirchenfrage" (1919), in *Gesammelte Werke* 2:13-20.

[20] Tillich, "Christentum und Sozialismus," 157–58; "Der Sozialismus" 16–17.

[21] Tillich, "Christentum und Sozialismus," 156; "Der Sozialismus" 14–15.

[22] Paul Tillich, "Basic Principles of Religious Socialism" (1923), in *Political Expectation*, ed. James Luther Adams (New York: Harper and Row, 1971) 78.

[23] Paul Tillich, "Klassenkampf und religiöser Sozialismus" (1930), in *Gesammelte Werke* 2:185–86.

[24] Paul Tillich, *Protestantisches Prinzip und Proletarische Situation* (Bonn: Cohen, 1931); cf. English version of 1948, in *The Protestant Era* (Chicago: University of Chicago Press, 1957) 169.

[25] Tillich, "Christentum und Sozialismus," 159–60; "Der Sozialismus," 19.

[26] Tillich, "Der Sozialismus," 19–20.

[27] McGovern, *Liberation Theology and Its Critics*, 59–60.

[28] Kurt Kaiser mentions the *Badische Volkskirchenbund*, the *Bund evangelischer Sozialisten*, the *Bund sozialistischer Kirchenfreunde*, the *Bund Neue Kirche*, the *Volkskirchenbund evangelischer Sozialisten* (*Materialen über den Religiösen Sozialismus in Deutschland aus der Zeit von 1918–1933*, Dissertation Universität Basel, pp. 18–19).

[29] Paul Tillich, "Revolution und Kirche. Zum gleichnamigen Buch verschiedener Autoren," (1919), in *Gesammelte Werke* 12:196.

[30] Stone, *Paul Tillich's Radical Social Thought*, 40–41.

[31] Boff, *Theology and Praxis*, (Maryknoll, N.Y.: Orbis Books, 1987).

[32] Clodovis Boff, *Théorie et pratique. La méthode des théologies de la libération* (Paris: Cerf, 1990) i–iv.

[33] This is the title of the lecture he gave in Barchem at the Conference of the religious socialists (July 1924): "Die religiöse und philosophische Weiterbildung des Sozialismus," in *Gesammelte Werke* 2:121–31.

[34] It is noteworthy that in *Rerum Novarum*, Leo XIII himself identifies the workers with the poor and the employers with the rich.

[35] Tillich, "Die religiöse und philosophische Weiterbildung des Sozialismus," 121.

[36] Tillich, "Klassenkampf und religiöser Sozialismus," 186–87.

[37] Tillich, "Basic Principles of Religious Socialism," 58–88.

[38] Ibid., 60.

[39] Ibid., 62.

[40] Ibid., 69–72.

[41] Ibid., 74–79.

[42] Ibid., 87.

[43] Ibid., 87–88.

[44] "Instruction on the Theology of Liberation," 393.

[45] Ibid., 397.

[46] Ibid., 398.

[47] Ibid., 400.

[48] Ibid., 405.

[49] Ibid., 411.

[50] Congregation for the Doctrine of the Faith, "Instruction on Christian Freedom" (March 1986), in *Liberation Theology. A Documentary History*, 462.

[51] Ibid., 485.

[52] Ibid., 476.

[53] Ibid., 487.

[54] Ibid., 465.

[55] Ibid., 482.

[56] Schubert M. Ogden, *Faith and Freedom. Toward a Theology of Liberation*, revised and enlarged edition (Nashville, Tenn.: Abingdon Press, 1989; first edition: 1979).

[57] Anselm Kyougsuk Min, "How Not to Do a Theology of Liberation. A Critique of Schubert Ogden," *Journal of the American Academy of Religion* 57 (1989) 83–102.

[58] Gustavo Gutiérrez, *A Theology of Liberation. History, Politics and Salvation*, revised edition (Maryknoll, N.Y.: Orbis Books, 1988) 98–99.

[59] Ibid., 101–2.

[60] Ibid., 103.

[61] Ibid., 104.

[62] Boff, *Theology and Praxis*, 84 (according to the French edition; a line has been dropped in the English translation).

[63] Ibid., 87–88.

[64] Ibid., 86.

[65] Paul Tillich, "Christentum und Sozialismus I" (1919), in *Gesammelte Werke* 2:26–27.

[66] Ibid., 27.

[67] Ibid., 25–26.

[68] Ibid., 26.

[69] Tillich, "Basic Principles of Religious Socialism" (1923) 62.

[70] Ibid., 66–69.

[71] Tillich, "The Protestant Principle and the Proletarian Situation," 165.

[72] Ibid., 166.

[73] Ibid.

[74] Ibid., 166–67.

[75] Ibid., 164.

[76] Paul Tillich, "Mass und Geist" (1922), in *Gesammelte Werke* 2:35.

77 Tillich, "The Protestant Principle and the Proletarian Situation," 170; quotations here are according to the original German version: *Protestantisches Prinzip und Proletarische Situation*, 17–18. — Similar remark by the liberation theologians Clodovis Boff and George V. Pixley, *The Bible, the Church, and the Poor* (Maryknoll, N.Y.: Orbis Books, 1989) p. 2: "Taking the poor as a collective phenomenon in this way, the first view to discount is the empirical or common perception of the poor as individuals, as particular cases."

78 Tillich, "Mass und Geist," 50.

79 Ibid., 72.

80 Ibid., 59.

81 Ibid., 61.

82 Ibid., 60.

83 Ibid.

84 Ibid., 51.

85 Ibid., 56.

86 Ibid., 50.

87 Ibid., 72.

88 Ibid., 71.

89 Ibid., 71–72.

90 Ibid., 77.

91 Ibid., 39–40; English translation by Robert P. Scharlemann, in Paul Tillich, *On Art and Architecture*, ed. John and Jane Dillenberger (New York: Crossroad, 1987) 63–64.

92 Tillich, "Mass und Geist," 62.

93 Ibid., 77.

94 Boff, *Theology and Praxis*, 7.

95 "Instruction on the Theology of Liberation," 402.

96 Ibid., 406.

97 "Instruction on Christian Freedom and Liberation," 490.

98 Paul Tillich, "On the Idea of a Theology of Culture" (1919), in *What is Religion?* ed. James Luther Adams (New York: Harper and Row, 1969) 175–81 (*Gesammelte Werke* 9:27–31).

99 Paul Tillich, "The Kairos Document. Challenge to the Church. A Theological Comment on the Political Crisis in South Africa," in *Kairos. Three Prophetic Challenges to the Church*, ed. Robert McAfee Brown (Grand Rapids, Mich.: W. B. Eerdmans, 1990) 29–60.

Paul Tillich and the Feminist Critique of Roman Catholic Theology

Mary Ann Stenger

Roman Catholic feminists have challenged the patriarchy in traditional theology and in religious and social structures as idolatrous and unjust. Rooted in these critiques of patriarchy, feminists are developing new theologies of liberation. As a Roman Catholic feminist, I ask: What use can feminist theology have for the thought of Paul Tillich, a male theologian who himself was rooted in patriarchy? Historically, Tillich's thought has been applied by some feminists in critiquing patriarchy and in formulating new theological approaches.[1] In this essay, I will first explore the relevance of Tillich's ideas to feminist critiques of idolatry and injustice and then suggest ways in which his thought is relevant to constructing feminist theology.

Feminist Critiques of Idolatry and Injustice

Critique of Idolatrous Symbols

In arguing that the pervasive patriarchal character of theological language and church structures is idolatrous, several Roman Catholic feminist theologians have used Tillich's critique of idolatry. For example, in her early critiques of the Roman Catholic Church, theologian Mary Daly calls for using the Protestant principle as a protest against false securities[2] and names idolatry as the primary evil to be eradicated from the Church.[3] Going beyond idolatry toward the really ultimate is a major purpose of her highly influential book *Beyond God the Father.*[4]

Like the early Daly, feminist theologian Anne Carr sees Tillich's critique of idolatry as a resource for feminist theology.[5] Carr uses Tillich's theory of religious symbols because it takes account of both positive and negative interpretations of symbols, both the element of participation in unconditioned reality and the conditioned nature of the symbol itself.[6] Applying Tillich's approach to feminist issues, Carr argues: ''In criticizing the functions of the symbols of God and Christ, feminist theology exposes the idolatry that occurs when preliminary or conditional concerns are elevated to unconditional significance; something finite (maleness) is lifted to the level of the infinite.''[7]

Although these women theologians use elements of Tillich's theology to critique the extensive patriarchy in theology and the Church, further analysis of Tillich's treatment of idolatry can open up additional significant issues for feminist theology. First, in Tillich's analysis, the possibility of idolatry is connected to the paradoxical structure of religious symbols. This paradoxical element is significant not only in criticizing existing idolatrous symbols but also as a criterion for avoiding idolatry in new symbols. Second, Tillich connects idolatry with destructive consequences for individuals in the form of existential disappointment and injustice.

For Tillich, any reality can function as a religious symbol or medium of revelation because all reality is rooted in the ground of being (1:118).[8] But the reality that manifests ultimacy is not itself ultimate. Therein lies the paradox, that the reality or the symbol is at the same time finite and bearing the infinite. In idolatry that paradox is broken, with the loss of recognition of the finite quality of the symbol. The symbol itself comes to be identified with the ultimate itself. Ideally, religious symbols negate themselves, moving the focus from the finitude of the symbol to the ultimacy it expresses. But if identification of the ultimate and the finite symbol occurs, there is no negation, but rather a focus on the finite aspect. Maintaining both the paradox and the element of negation can be used as a criterion for avoiding idolatry.[9]

When this analysis is used in the critique of patriarchy, the tendency to absolutize the maleness of symbols for God or Christ breaks the paradox and is rejected as idolatrous. This critique can also be applied to some feminist efforts to absolutize femaleness and assert the superiority of women over men. Mary Daly has recognized the tendency of some feminists to be idolatrous about certain political objectives, but she argues that openness to the future and to that which is really ultimate will protect against idolatry.[10] In my view, Daly does not always keep this openness in some of her later statements in *Gyn/Ecology*[11] and *Pure Lust*,[12] as she elevates woman's experience of becoming to an absolute status. That flaw does not immediately lead to rejecting the symbols she offers but rather calls for interpretations which keep the paradoxical structure. As with symbols rooted in male experience, symbols rooted in female experience can be authentic expressions of experiences of ultimacy, but they need to be continually relativized in relation to ultimacy itself. It is this "guardian standpoint"[13] of ultimacy which allows for and demands ongoing critique of religious symbols.

Such continuing criticism of traditional religious symbols is often rejected as threatening to the sacred elements of traditional theology. But that rejection is rooted in the failure to distinguish the finite expressions of ultimacy and ultimacy itself. Human formulations about God, Christ, and the Church are just that—human and finite. Critiques of idolatry are aimed at penetrating human formulations to recover the divine depth that the symbols were trying to convey.

Destructive Consequences of Idolatry:
Existential Disappointment and Injustice

Idolatry can have destructive consequences for an individual's faith experience. When a person is ultimately concerned about a finite object or ideology (often expressed in symbols), that person's commitment involves the risk of giving of oneself to that ultimate concern. What the person wants from that commitment is a sense of unity between the person and the center of faith, a connection to the ultimate power. But if that center is seen as ultimate in itself rather than the medium of ultimacy, then the person has committed to a finite center, subject to limits which we do not expect of something worthy of ultimate commitment. If the person recognizes the limits, his or her life is disrupted by loss of the center and deep existential disappointment.[14] An example of such limits would be the extent to which patriarchy permeates the symbolism in traditional Roman Catholic theologies and liturgies. Many women find themselves deeply disillusioned by such patriarchy, causing some to withdraw painfully from their Church and others to continue to be involved in spite of their loss of meaning.

Idolatrous identification also can lead to injustice. "Justice is the criterion which judges idolatrous holiness" (1:216). Tillich defines justice as "that side of love which affirms the independent right of object and subject within the love relation" (1:282). In *Love, Power, and Justice*,[15] Tillich asserts that structures of justice should fit the needs of people, treat all people as equal persons with inner freedom, and offer political and cultural self-determination. When religious symbols are made into idols, there are social and cultural effects which violate these principles of justice.

The identification of something finite as holy gives absolute power to that finite symbol, object, person, or movement. Those people who are associated with that sacred center take on the holiness and absoluteness also. It is clearly implied that other finite beings who are not intimately connected with that sacred center are profane and inferior. Using the authority of such sacred power, social and religious structures are established which delineate who has more of this sacred power and who is left outside of it. Unjust structures and the treatment of others as inferior become divinely legitimated; idolatry leads to a violation of the principles of justice.

When maleness is seen as a necessary element of religious symbols for God and Christ, it is not surprising to find women excluded from social, political, and religious power structures. Maleness (a quality of finite being) has been absolutized, creating an idol and legitimating injustice toward females. The Roman Catholic position on the ordination of women, as set forward in the 1977 Vatican "Declaration on the Question of the Admission of Women to the Ministerial Priesthood," offers an example of such idolatry and injustice. Although the document tries to argue that exclusion of women from the priesthood does not mean the superiority of males over females, such an argument ignores the absolutization of the male principle and the real injustice engendered by such idolatry.[16] Such a doctrine does not fit the needs of people in our current situation, violates the full personhood of women, denies equality, and limits their liberty within the institution of the Roman Catholic Church.

Critiques of patriarchy are threatening because the idolatry is tied up with social-political structures. Those who benefit from the idolatry are likely to defend traditional symbols and structures. They do not experience the injustice and are threatened by the possibility of their own existential disappointment if their objects of ultimate concern are revealed to be less than infinite. Thus, we have an ongoing tension in the Roman Catholic Church between those who call for more just church structures and more adequate religious symbols and those who want to hang on to the theological and social-political security of traditional symbols and structures.

Dominating Power vs. Empowerment

Implicit in this discussion of justice and injustice is the issue of power. In general use and in Christian theology, the concept of power contains an ambiguity: power as dominating and power as empowering. Women and other oppressed groups have been victims of dominating power used to keep them subordinate and often backed up with claims of divine power. An important element of the feminist critique of traditional theology has been the rejection of images and structures of dominating power and the affirmation of empowerment in symbolizing God and in positing new social and religious structures. Traditional hierarchical structures have been seen as unjust because they left women and other minorities with little or no public power. The extent to which patriarchal hierarchy (husband, wife, children, servants/ slaves) has continued to influence our social structures today is an example of such injustice.

Tillich's discussion of hierarchy is not helpful to feminist critiques of dominating power. He continued to defend hierarchy as a necessary or natural social structure even in egalitarian groups.[17] While Tillich is correct that groups do center power in leaders, it is also true that leaders can empower rather than dominate the members of the group. Decision-making and political, social power can be shared. Feminist theologies have emphasized the mutual power relations of friendship rather than hierarchy.[18] Such a model takes seriously each individual human person as a whole self, capable of self-determination and mutual interaction with others. This model of mutuality fits Tillich's own criteria for structures of justice better than the hierarchy which he supports.

Part of the process of women's affirmation of themselves as full human persons switches the image of power from being dominated to being empowered. For those who experience the process as spiritual, the image of God also changes from overpowering to empowering. Tillich's understanding of the power of being participating in all being and empowering all forms of courage can be useful. (This point will be discussed more fully later.)

What we see in these critiques of patriarchy is that Tillich's critique of idolatry and his analysis of justice can be helpful. But we also recognize that Tillich's patriarchal approach prevented him from seeing the implications of his analysis for male-female power in theology or in society, a task engaged in by feminist students of his theology.

Constructive Efforts in Feminist Theology

The Role of Female Experiences in Theology

A basic root of feminist theology is women's experience. Although traditional theology claimed to be universal, it often left women invisible except where sexual roles and procreation were discussed. The patriarchal language of theology and church liturgies (man, men, he, brothers, sons) is an example of such invisibility.[19] The power structures of Church and society which give final decision-making to men leave women out. Women who have experienced a new sense of themselves as full persons with autonomy yearn to have that experience integrated with their spiritual life, their church life, and their work for liberation of all oppressed peoples. Theology as well as the structures of Church and society need to include women's experiences while avoiding past stereotypes.

The American Roman Catholic bishops attempted to take account of women's experiences in the early drafts of their pastoral on women's concerns, but any final draft and vote will be produced by men, once again setting forward what the proper stance and roles of women in the Roman Catholic Church can be. The early process of listening to women is replaced in the end by a process of men deciding about women.

Because of their own sense of having been left out of past writings about women, feminist writers emphasize women's experiences. Wary of earlier claims of "universality" which ignored women, these thinkers are sensitive to the diversity of women's experiences and do not claim a universality for their own approaches.[20] Instead, they speak of setting forward their own perspectives and call on other women to do the same. Yet there has been general agreement on women's experiences of patriarchy and sexism and the injustice of structures that contribute to such experiences.[21] Based on these experiences, the best of feminist theology works to project images that do not subordinate any group but rather serve to liberate all people.

Tillich certainly acknowledged the important role of experience in developing theology (1:40–46). Experience is not only important as a source of theological reflection but also as the connector to, and practical verifier of, theology. The norms of theology should be rooted in the present situation, and one test of their adequacy is the ability to affirm and express people's religious experiences.[22]

While Tillich sees his theology speaking to universal human experience in his own time, that "universality" prevents his theology from being a liberation theology. His categories serve more to analyze the present situation than to criticize and transform it. But when his categories are brought into a particular context of oppression, such as contemporary women's experiences, they can be used as part of a liberating effort.

It was such an effort that engaged Daly in *Beyond God the Father*. To a great extent she followed Tillich's method of correlation because it called for analyzing the human situation as central to interpreting and constructing theological answers.[23] She also reinterprets many of Tillich's ontological and theological ideas: God as power of being, the experience of the power of being over nonbeing, courage as revelatory, and the New Being as a healing power overcoming alienation and self-estrangement.[24] Yet Daly argues that Tillich's theology cannot be fully liberating because he does not discuss the "relevance of God-language to the struggle against demonic power structures,"[25] such as sexual oppression.

Unlike many other theological writings of the mid-twentieth century, Tillich's theology used terms which were not immediately patriarchal. Their abstract nature transcended gender, making them more palatable to budding feminists. Daly has found Tillich's concepts useful also because of their dynamic quality and their existential roots. For example, she uses the concept of God as the power of being, emphasizes its dynamic dimension by also calling God "Verb," and connects it to the existential experience of dealing with threats of nonbeing. An example of Daly's reinterpretation of Tillich is her treatment of the forms of nonbeing. While Tillich specifies the threats of nonbeing as fate and death, guilt and condemnation, and doubt and meaninglessness,[26] Daly focuses on women dealing with threats of nonbeing from demonic power relationships and patriarchal structures. Participating in God the Verb who destroys forms and offers transforming power enables women to take positive steps beyond patriarchy.[27]

Given the extensive use of Tillich's terms in *Beyond God the Father* and the broad impact of that work on religious feminists, one might expect other feminist theologians to appropriate some of Tillich's terms. That does not happen, in part because some writers stress the patriarchy hidden in abstract concepts.[28] Daly also criticizes Tillich in her later works, *Gyn/Ecology* and *Pure Lust,* but she does argue that Tillich's work "is worth studying and criticizing by those who would embark upon the adventure of dis-covering Elemental philosophy (provided, of course, that we employ his writings only as springboards for our own original analysis)."[29]

Religious Symbols

To the extent that abstract concepts are suspected of latent patriarchy, some feminists have been exploring more concrete images as symbols and metaphors. They do not aim at the universality of abstract concepts, but they do hope that others will respond positively to such images. Most feminists intentionally focus on symbols from women's experiences that have been ignored in traditional theology.

It is interesting to note that Tillich recognized the lack of female symbolism in Protestant theology, particularly its rejection of the image of the Virgin Mary (3:293). He did not expect the image of the Virgin

Mary to be reinstated in Protestant circles, but he asked "whether there are elements in genuine Protestant symbolism which transcend the alternative male-female and which are capable of being developed over against a one-sided male-determined symbolism" (3:293). His suggestion was to recognize female qualities in the "ground of being." The symbolic aspects of "the ground of being" point to "the mother-quality of giving birth, carrying, and embracing, and, at the same time, of calling back, resisting independence of the created, and swallowing it" (3:294). Some might object to this description of female symbolism as stereotyping females, but some feminist theologians have also suggested imaging God with the qualities of mother.[30]

It is significant that Tillich was concerned to develop language which reduces male dominance and transcends the alternative male-female in symbols of the divine (3:294). Yet as Daly asserts, he did not recognize the connection between male-dominated symbolism and actual oppression of females. While Tillich did want balance, he did not call the pervasive male symbolism idolatrous, an application which could have pointed to the injustice of patriarchal imagery.

Similarly, feminists also have to be careful in assuming that use of female symbolism will be tied to a better power situation for women. A study of female symbolism in diverse cultures and faith traditions will destroy that assumption. One can have strong goddess imagery (such as in Hindu goddesses or in the Sun-Goddess of Japan) and still maintain a strongly patriarchal society and oppressive structures for women. Roman Catholic feminist Rosemary Radford Ruether cites Tillich's critique of the Protestant rejection of the image of the Virgin Mary, but then points out that "it is churches with a high Mariology which are most negative to women. It is the Protestant churches without Mariology which ordain women. . . . Mariology, as it is used by the clergy, seems antithetical to the liberation of women."[31] Recognition of the importance of female symbolism by itself does not challenge patriarchal structures of Church or society. The key issue, once again, is the use and abuse of power. What is needed is theological language for a new spirituality which emphasizes empowerment rather than dominating power and mutuality rather than hierarchy.

New Spirituality

Because the issue of power is tied to reformulating theological and spiritual language, some critics might argue that feminist theologians derive their theological answers from the human situation rather than from revelation. But most feminists would not quarrel with Tillich's method of correlation where the theological answers to life's questions must "be 'spoken' *to* human existence from beyond it," not derived from the analysis of human existence itself (1:64). Feminist thinkers would respond to their critics that they have indeed encountered new spiritual meaning, that the sacred is being experienced and acknowledged in new modes.

For several feminist theologians, the new spirituality emphasizes the interconnectedness of all beings, humans with humans and non-humans, rooted in an underlying divine unity. The interconnectedness is not just mystically experienced but also leads one to political efforts to eradicate sexism, racism, and classism.[32] Carr describes feminist spirituality as keeping the feminist critique of patriarchy and affirming feminist sisterhood but also as envisioning "noncompetitive, nonhierarchical, nondominating modes of relationship among all human beings and in relation to nature."[33] In *New Woman, New Earth*, Ruether calls for a "prophetic vision to shape a new world on earth," a vision that includes interiority but also a strong sense of reciprocal interdependence with all humanity and the earth.[34] Theologian Madonna Kolbenschlag describes the new spirituality as a spirituality of passion with a mission of solidarity.[35] The passion is a passion for life, which includes all aspects of life (physical, sexual, emotional, religious, social, political) and all of life (human and non-human), and includes resistance to traditional structures as well as creative imagination to envisage new structures of solidarity.[36] Although Daly definitely sees her work as post-Christian, she tries to express the spirituality of feminist women. In *Beyond God the Father*, she speaks of "sisterhood as cosmic covenant," a relationship and a process which re-names the cosmos, involves charismatic gifts of healing and prophecy, builds non-hierarchical, non-dogmatic community, and embraces the earth as part of the sisterhood.[37]

These efforts to express a new spirituality are directed toward other feminists who are in the process of transforming their whole selves to full human persons independent of patriarchal structures. The focus is the liberation of women, but the struggle for liberation is extended to all dominated beings, human and non-human. Liberation and its spirituality are not limited to women but can be seen as gifts of transforming power to the whole Church.[38]

Part of the power of these liberating efforts comes from the sense of newness many women experience in their spiritual self-development. Even when we turn to past sources, whether biblical or theological, we read them with "new eyes" and capture new insights. Sometimes these insights reveal patriarchy to be criticized; at other times we find empowering images or concepts. But the key of acceptance is the ability of those concepts and images to broaden empowerment to all humans and to help us create more just social structures and models of interdependence with our whole world (social and natural).

Feminist Appropriation of Tillich's Major Symbols

Tillich's theology on its own terms cannot provide the liberating spirituality envisioned by feminist theologians. But reinterpretations and applications of aspects of his theology can be part of a theological base for the new spirituality. For this purpose, three of his non-gendered theological concepts will be explored here: power of being, New Being, and Spiritual Presence. Although these terms are abstract, the application of the symbol is more concrete and potentially liberating.

The dynamic and immanent qualities of symbolizing God as power of being are very helpful to a feminist spirituality. Daly emphasizes the dynamic quality by imaging God as Verb, but I think it is important to maintain the focus on "power." Many women reject patriarchal power as overpowering and dominating others. Yet these same women feel themselves to be empowered in a new way and experience that empowerment as spiritual and not just social. God as the power of being participating in the struggles of life, as the root of our courage to face threats of nonbeing,[39] can express that experience of ongoing empowerment to meet and resist injustices. That power is experienced in the midst of life, as part of life, and yet it is greater and deeper than an individual's human power. In *The Courage to Be*, Tillich speaks of the power of being as the God above the God of theism, "the God who appears when God has disappeared in the anxiety of doubt."[40] For the feminist, the anxiety of doubt may be experienced, but more central is an anxiety that Tillich did not name individually—the anxiety of injustice and oppression.[41] The courage to face this anxiety is also rooted in the God who appears when ordinary human power has been squelched and oppressed—a spiritual power of being which empowers people to continue their efforts for justice.

The symbol of the power of being can also image the underlying unity of all beings, working well with the feminist emphasis on the interconnectedness of reality. Everything that is participates in the power of being and yet "the power of being is the power of everything that is, insofar as it *is*" 1:231). The power of being, then, is the root of our unity with all of reality, from the earth to God. What Tillich does not develop adequately is a more horizontal image of the interactive nature of the power of being.[42] For Tillich, ''the power of being must transcend every being that participates in it'' (1:231). But we also experience and can be empowered through other beings, both human and non-human. The experience of the power of being is not always a direct or more vertical experience of the ground of being or the God above God. How we treat other people, nature, and objects and how we are treated by them involves dynamics of power, and these experiences often mediate the spiritual, ultimate power of being.

Tillich's symbol of the New Being as saving, reconciling power can express the exciting, new energy which comes out of the feminist experience of overcoming self-estrangement and alienation. Daly broadens Tillich's term from its focus on Jesus as the Christ to describe women as the bearers of New Being as they struggle for justice in the midst of patriarchy.[43] At one point, Tillich hints at a broader application of the term than Daly's focus on women, suggesting that the universe is ''open for possible divine manifestations in other areas or periods of being'' (2:96). But if one takes seriously the feminist interest in a spirituality of interconnectedness, then the symbol of the New Being can be reinterpreted to speak of moments of reconciliation between people or between people and non-human beings. Certainly, Christians will see Jesus as the Christ as the one who best embodies that reconciling power, but other faith traditions and other religious approaches may name another.

Perhaps the least developed and yet potentially the most effective of Tillich's symbols for feminism is ''Spiritual Presence.'' It is the symbol which unites elements of meaning from the symbols of the power of being and the New Being.[44] Spiritual Presence expresses the experience of ecstatic moments when the normal ambiguity of life, the mixture of positive and negative (essential and existential), is transcended. Such moments involve the empowerment of the power of being and the reconciliation of the New Being, but Spiritual Presence expresses the underlying unity of such moments, the experience of transcendence or depth which momentarily eliminates the divisions between being and the limitations of life. People can experience Spiritual Presence through anyone or anything. Tillich connects the symbol of Spiritual Presence, with its implications of immanence and ongoing process, to people's experiences of faith, love, unity with others, and aesthetic, cognitive, or moral theonomy. The mystical quality or element of participation and unity connecting individuals and all dimensions of life with Spiritual Presence has great potential for grounding a spirituality of interconnectedness. Given the current interest in ecology, it would be helpful to add the dimension of nature to Tillich's discussion. It is important that Tillich continues to see Spiritual Presence as a guard against demonic power or idolatry or heteronomy. When ultimacy is connected with ordinary life, it is all too easy to absolutize the ordinary.

As feminists develop the symbol of Spiritual Presence, they will want to emphasize more fully than Tillich its implications for individual self-realization, interdependence and community, the struggle for justice for all peoples, and our ecological unity. Spiritual Presence can empower us through a kind of mystical participation which momentarily releases us from the ambiguities and anxieties of life. But that Spiritual Presence can also give us the courage to build community, to make others aware of our interdependence, to work for justice in the Church and in our global society, and to balance our relationship with the earth. That courage stems from the interpenetration and ongoing process of Spiritual Presence in all of reality and in all dimensions of life. Tillich's description of ecstatic moments of unambiguous life fit well with the moments of truth, beauty, justice, unity, etc. which we all experience in life. His recognition of the multi-dimensional unity of life and his rejection of a hierarchy of levels of life (such as spirit over matter) can be expanded by feminists who are working for new theological models of mutuality. Future development of feminist spirituality can be enhanced by critically developing the symbolism of Spiritual Presence.

Conclusion

Paul Tillich's theology has been and still can be a significant resource for feminist Roman Catholic theology, not only in its critique of traditional, patriarchal Roman Catholic theology, but also in the development of new theological approaches which seek to empower all humans and express the interdependence of all creation. Tillich and his theology lived under patriarchy and although his thought was "new" for his time, it still retained elements of that old patriarchal structure. But as we search for "new" spiritual depths which can empower us in the struggle for justice and harmony, we must build on the insights of the "old" and move beyond them to new modes of expression which address our current situation. This is not just a matter of "cleaning up" patriarchal language but producing other language which can continue to express the Spiritual Presence, the participation of the Eternal in our lives. Feminists must critically build upon the insights in earlier theologies while directing their theologies to present and future possibilities.

In *The Shaking of the Foundations,* Tillich expressed the relation of the old and the new to the experience of the power of the Eternal: "Its saving power is the power of the Eternal within it. It is new, really new, in the degree to which it is beyond old and new, in the degree to which it is eternal. And it remains new so long as the eternal power of the Eternal is manifest within it, so long as the light of the Eternal shines through it. For that power may become weaker; that light may become darker; and that which was truly a new thing may become old itself."[45] As always, we stand under ambiguity and the critique of idolatry, tools Tillich gives us, tools that can be applied to patriarchal theology (including Tillich's) and eventually also to our own new theological efforts.

Notes

[1] In *New Catholic Women* (San Francisco: Harper and Row, 1986), Mary Jo Weaver describes Roman Catholic feminist theology as "to some extent indebted to the profound insights of Paul Tillich" (146). Weaver especially notes Tillich's influence on Mary Daly (153-54) and Anne Carr (157).

[2] Mary Daly, "Return of the Protestant Principle," *Commonweal* 90 (June 6, 1969) 338.

[3] Mary Daly, "If You Could Make One Change in the Church, What Would It Be?" *Commonweal* 92 (May 1, 1970) 161.

[4] Mary Daly, *Beyond God the Father* (Boston: Beacon Press, 1973) 6: "For my purpose is to show that the women's revolution, insofar as it is true to its own essential dynamics, is an ontological, spiritual revolution, pointing beyond the idolatries of sexist society and sparking creative action in and toward transcendence."

[5] Anne Carr, *Transforming Grace* (San Fancisco: Harper and Row, 1988) 101-2.

[6] Carr, *Transforming Grace,* 101-2, 140, 167.

[7] Ibid., 102.

[8] Reference to Paul Tillich, *Systematic Theology,* 3 vols. (Chicago: University of Chicago Press, 1951-63) will be indicated by (volume number: page number).

[9] For a more detailed analysis of paradox as a criterion of religious symbols, see Mary Ann Stenger, "The Significance of Paradox for Theological Verification: Difficulties and Possibilities," *International Journal for Philosophy of Religion,* 14 (1983) 171-82.

[10] Daly, *Beyond God the Father,* 29.

[11] Mary Daly, *Gyn/Ecology* (Boston: Beacon Press, 1978). Daly describes the movement beyond patriarchy as one in which women dis-cover Life and participate in Paradise (6-7).

12 Mary Daly, *Pure Lust* (Boston: Beacon Press, 1984). Daly focuses on women's feminist experiences which reveal and participate in ultimate Be-ing (374).

13 Tillich discusses the "guardian standpoint" in "Kairos und Logos," *Gesammelte Werke* 4 (Stuttgart: Evangelisches Verlagswerk, 1961) 74.

14 Paul Tillich, *Dynamics of Faith* (New York: Harper and Row, 1957) 12.

15 Paul Tillich, *Love, Power, and Justice* (New York: Oxford University Press, 1960) 57–62.

16 This application of Tillich's critique of idolatry to gender and justice is discussed in greater detail in Mary Ann Stenger, "Male Over Female or Female Over Male: A Critique of Idolatry," *Soundings* 69 (Winter, 1986) 464–78.

17 Tillich, *Love, Power, and Justice*, 44–45, 94.

18 For example, see Sallie McFague, *Models of God* (Philadelphia: Fortress Press, 1987) chapter 6; Carr, *Transforming Grace*, 143–51; and Carter Heyward, *The Redemption of God: A Theology of Mutual Relation* (Lanham, Md.: University Press of America, 1982) 149–78.

19 Rita Burns, "Breaking the Grand Silence: A Diocesan Practice," *Women in the Church*, ed. Madonna Kolbenschlag (Washington: The Pastoral Press, 1987) 1:183.

20 Carr, *Transforming Grace*, 118.

21 Ibid., 118, 123.

22 For a fuller discussion of Tillich's theory of theological norms, see Mary Ann Stenger, "Paul Tillich's Theory of Theological Norms and the Problems of Relativism and Subjectivism," *The Journal of Religion* 62 (October, 1982) 359–75.

23 Anne Carr also recognizes the importance of this correlation for feminist theology (*Transforming Grace*, 117).

24 Mary Daly's use and reinterpretation of Tillich's concepts is analyzed more fully in my discussion in "A Critical Analysis of the Influence of Paul Tillich on Mary Daly's Feminist Theology," *Encounter* 43 (Summer 1982) 219–38.

25 Daly, *Beyond God the Father*, 21.

26 Paul Tillich, *The Courage to Be* (New Haven: Yale University Press, 1952).

27 Daly, *Beyond God the Father*, 43.

28 See for example, Rosemary Radford Ruether's discussion in *Sexism and God-Talk: Toward a Feminist Theology* (Boston: Beacon Press, 1983) 67. Ruether argues that "abstractions often conceal androcentric assumptions and prevent the shattering of the male monopoly on God-language."

29 Daly, *Pure Lust*, 29.

30 McFague, *Models of God*, 97–123.

31 Rosemary Radford Ruether, *New Woman, New Earth* (New York: The Seabury Press, 1975) 37.

32 Carr, *Transforming Grace*, 209.

33 Ibid., 207.

[34] Ruether, *New Woman, New Earth*, 211.

[35] Madonna Kolbenschlag, "Spirituality: Finding Our True Home," *Women in the Church*, 1:198.

[36] Ibid., 206–11.

[37] Daly, *Beyond God the Father*, chapter 6.

[38] See Carr, *Transforming Grace*, 214.

[39] Tillich, *The Courage to Be*, 178–81.

[40] Ibid., 190.

[41] Franklin Sherman made this suggestion of a fourth anxiety of injustice and oppression in a discussion of *The Courage to Be* for the North American Paul Tillich Society, meeting in Anaheim, California, November, 1985.

[42] Tillich does analyze the ontological unity of love and power in *Love, Power, and Justice*, 48–53. He speaks of every self as a power structure (53) and emphasizes that love involves reunion of those who are separated (pp. 48–49). He also speaks of love being united with power to destroy what is against love. But he speaks of the necessity of compulsory power rather than the radiating power of love which empowers individuals.

[43] Daly, *Beyond God the Father*, 72.

[44] This unity is not surprising when one contemplates the structure of Tillich's system. The power of being as one symbol of being-itself is the theological answer to the questions implied in essential being; the New Being is the theological answer to the questions implied in existential being. But life involves a mixture of essential and existential elements, giving us ambiguity (*ST* 3:12, 32). Spiritual Presence is the theological answer to the questions arising from the ambiguities of life.

[45] Paul Tillich, "Behold, I Am Doing a New Thing," *The Shaking of the Foundations* (New York: Charles Scribner's Sons, 1948) 185–86.

Tillich's Method of Correlation and the Concerns of African Theologians

Anthony A. Akinwale, O.P.

The aim of this essay is to examine Paul Tillich's method of correlation and the project of African theology with a view to showing their common preoccupation.[1] In striving to achieve this objective, I bear in mind that historically, culturally, politically, and geographically, there are crucial distinctions to be recognized if one is to understand what constitutes African-ness. In spite of fundamental similarities, the African continent is not a monolithic entity. To ignore this fact is to commit the fallacy of invalid generalization. Any attempt to address an issue from the African perspective, therefore, raises a number of questions that cannot be dismissed with a wave of the hand. Perhaps the most formidable of these questions is to explain, from the temporal and spatial point of view, what is meant by "Africa." From the point of view of time, does one speak of precolonial, colonial, or post-colonial Africa? In other words, does one speak of Africa before or after her contact with the Western world, or is one using a conception of Africa that synthesizes all the traits of these historical periods? From the point of view of space, one is besieged by a large number of tribes, veritable nations, each having its culture, its mode of apprehending the universe and the place of the human being within it. One could also speak of maghrebian Africa, subsaharan Africa, or southern Africa. Which of these sections could be chosen in order to obtain a sufficiently representative view?

The questions that have just been raised impose some limits on this essay. Failure to respect these limits might cast serious doubts on its intellectual honesty. In order to respond to the demand of intellectual honesty, it is necessary to state *ab initio* that this essay does not pretend to offer "the African contribution" but "the contribution of an African theologian to a new appraisal of Paul Tillich in Catholic thought."

Tillich's Method of Correlation

From the beginning of his magisterial work, *Systematic Theology*, Paul Tillich stated that there must be a link between the Christian message and the situation in which it is proclaimed. According to him, "A theological system is supposed to satisfy two basic needs: the statement of the truth of the Christian message and the interpretation of this truth for every new generation. Theology moves back and forth between two poles, the eternal truth of its foundation and the temporal situation in which the eternal truth must be received."[2] As far as Tillich was concerned, few theological systems have been able to strike a balance by meeting these two fundamental needs. While some sacrifice the truth of the Christian message, others do not take into consideration the situation in which the message is preached, and some others combine the two defects. Not wanting to compromise its eternal truth, the theological systems that ignore the situation in which the message is proclaimed fail to distinguish between the content of this message and its anterior formulation. By absolutizing some concepts or some traditional solutions and imposing them on a new situation, they mistake the eternal truth of the message with a temporal expression of this truth.

According to Tillich, the failure to balance the two demands is evident in European theological orthodoxy, known in America as fundamentalism, and in "kerygmatic" theology. The combination of fundamentalism with an antitheological attitude gives rise to a situation where the "theological truths of yesterday" are taken as immutable, and contradictory with the "theological truths of today and tomorrow." The failure of fundamentalism to come to grips with the present situation is traceable not to the fact that it speaks "from beyond every situation" but from the fact that it speaks "from a situation of the past." Fundamentalism "elevates something finite and transitory to infinite and eternal validity." The kerygmatic theology of Barth and his disciples, in an attempt to avoid the error of fundamentalism, overemphasized the immutable character of the message (*kerygma*) to the detriment of the exigencies of the changing situation.[3]

For Tillich, the "situation" is not "the psychological or sociological state in which individuals or groups live" but "the scientific, artistic, economic, political and ethical forms in which their interpretation of existence is expressed" in every period of history. By implication, if theology is not to fall into the error of a kerygmatic theology that ignores the situation, there must be a courageous collaboration of theology with the diverse forms of culture which serve as vehicles for the interpretation of human existence. Kerygmatic theology must have apologetic theology as a companion on the road that leads to the intelligent appropriation and assimilation of the truth of the Christian message.

This criterion of collaboration inspired Tillich's project of a theology of culture at the end of the First World War. The Tillich who resumed his theological enterprise just after the First World War saw "a deep gap between the cultural revolution and the religious tradition in eastern and central Europe."[4] The socialist movements, whose influence was increasing, not only fought the different forms of injustice of the era but saw the Church as collaborating in this injustice. Here is a description of this dichotomy between religion and culture according to Tillich.

> The Lutheran and the Roman and Greek Catholic churches rejected the cultural and—with some exceptions on the part of Roman Catholicism—the political revolutions. They rejected them as the rebellious expression of a secular autonomy. The revolutionary movements, on the other hand, repudiated the churches as the expression of a transcendent heteronomy. It was obvious to those of us who had spiritual ties with both sides that this situation was intolerable and, in the long run, disastrous for religion as well as for culture. We believed that it was possible to close the gap, partly by creating movements such as religious socialism, partly by a fresh interpretation of the mutual immanence of religion and culture with each other.[5]

The dichotomy between culture and religion inspired the project of a theology of culture, a synthesis of religion and culture, of heteronomy and autonomy in a theonomous culture. It was to be an "answering theology" addressing the questions posed by the situation. By way of summary, these questions could be thus formulated: "Can the Christian message be adapted to the modern mind without losing its essential and unique character?"[6] This question has been described by Marc Michel as "the only veritable question for theology; it [the question] unavoidably implies the fundamental tension between identity and significance which, beyond simple and illusory repetition, fixes for theology its stakes and its destiny."[7] To this question, says Michel, the traditional "theological superstructures" could not provide an adequate response.[8]

Tillich defined the goal of his method of correlation as the explanation of the contents of the Christian faith through the mutual interdependence between existential questions and theological answers in the elaboration of an apologetic theology. There is a correlation of correspondence between religious symbols and what they symbolize, a logical correlation between concepts that describe human realities and those which describe divine realities, and a real correlation between the ultimate concern of the human being and the one by whom he/she is concerned in an ultimate way, that is, God. The third type of correlation describes the divine-human relationship. In this correlation God responds to the questions posed by the human being under the impact of the divine response. Theology has to formulate the questions implied in human existence and furnish the answers implied by divine self-manifestation. The divine-human relationship is a revelatory event in which we find answers. But the answers make no sense unless they are in correlation with questions that touch the totality of human existence.

Before showing how Tillich's method of correlation can be in dialogue with African theology, we must acknowledge some of the objections raised against the method. Karl Barth and his school have pointed out that the relationship between questions and answers in the method raises a formidable problem. By making philosophical questions his point of departure, Tillich appears to have given priority to the questions over the answers. He has analyzed the human situation without any reference to Christ, thus ending up with an anthropology without Christology, an analysis of the human situation without the Cross. This has led Alexander McKelway to ask: ''Can any analysis of the ambiguities of life say more about man's estrangement from the ground of his being than the Cross?''[9] For Carl Armbruster, the human situation is not the only source of existential interrogations. The presence of divine revelation is also a source of questions for human beings who are not just interrogators of the Word of God but also its listeners. This Word is not just an answer but also ''a fulfillment, a transformation, an elevation and a gratuitous intervention.'' Consequently,

> Man stands before revelation not simply to play the quizmaster; he stands before it as before the sun, to be cheered and warmed and inspired. In the transfiguration episode all that Peter could utter was, ''Lord, it is well that we are here!'' (Mt 17:4, *RSV*). Man does more than question; he also exclaims in cries of marvel, of wonder, of awe. Tillich's method of correlation directs a constant stream of question marks at the Christian revelation, but they should be balanced by a few exclamation points.[10]

Kenneth Hamilton forcefully argues that Tillich has constructed a theological system that is incompatible with the gospel and alien to ''historical Christianity.'' In fundamental opposition to Kierkegaard,

Tillich has brought the Word of God before the tribunal of his self-sufficient philosophical system to answer charges. The Word of God is "in the position of a prisoner in the power of an inquisitor." The Christian *pistis* has been subjugated to a *gnosis*.[11]

These criticisms and many others center on the place of the Word of God in Paul Tillich's system. They could be summed up in this question: given Paul Tillich's opinion of the kerygmatic theology of Karl Barth, what is the status of the Word of God in the method of correlation? Does he accord it primacy? Are the system and the gospel compatible? Tillich's Barthian critics would have us believe that the Word of God is the junior partner in the method of correlation. Since it is the junior partner, Hamilton contends, Tillich's system is incompatible with the gospel. It is a distortion of the Christian message.

On the other hand, Jean Richard's study of the evolution of the thought of Paul Tillich vis-à-vis the relationship between philosophy and theology has pointed out that Tillich accepts the primacy of the Word of God. According to Richard, in spite of Tillich's opposition to the kerygmatic theology of Karl Barth, he agreed with the latter's fundamental intuition, with its emphasis on the absolute transcendence of God. And in the question-answer dialectic of the interrelation between divine revelation and the human mind, the final word belongs to the Word of God.[12]

I shall respond to the criticisms directed at Tillich by adding that while the primacy of the Word may not be clear in Tillich he always put his faith in the Word made flesh. The method of correlation could be seen as a practical implication and a methodological application of the doctrine of the Word made flesh. In Tillich's system, the Word of God enters the human situation, a situation full of ambiguities, without losing its glory, its authority, or its power. This is what he calls the "living reciprocity" of the interpersonal relationship which dynamically characterizes the divine-human relationship portrayed in the Bible. Hamilton's contention that the Christian has to choose between the gospel and the system could be turned around. My response to Hamilton's criticism in particular is that the method of correlation is not a case of "the system or the gospel" but one of "the gospel in the system."[13] The Word of God can take partial historical expression in a philosophical system. The system does not represent a subjugation of *pistis* to *gnosis*. It is rather a theology which, in its dialogue with the modern mind, begins with *gnosis* in order to arrive at *pistis*.[14]

But it is not correct to say that Tillich has resolved all the questions. In spite of my belief that the method of correlating philosophical questions and theological answers is not in itself a subjugation of the Word of God to a philosophical system, I recognize the persistence of the difficulty of explaining the relationship between questions and answers in Tillich's version of the method of correlation. Perhaps one explanation for this persistent difficulty is the fact that the relationship between the human and the divine remains a perennial problem for Christology. If Tillich had resolved the problem he would have resolved the Christological problem, and indeed all theological problems, once and for all.

The Project of African Theologians

The difficulties I acknowledged at the beginning of this essay render the expression "African theology" highly problematic. They help to buttress the contention of Ngindu Mushete that " 'African theology' is an enormous subject that obviously cannot be treated in any detailed way in a few short pages."[15] From the historical point of view, the expression does not refer to the works of St. Augustine of Hippo, even though history testifies to his African origin. From the cultural point of view, it does not necessarily refer to a scientific study of the body/bodies of beliefs in the religions of traditional African societies. Rather, in the parlance of today's African theologians, the expression refers to attempts by contemporary Africans—regardless of their places of origin, or ethnic or cultural affiliations—to understand the Christian message in the situation in which they live.

The linguistic, ethnic, and cultural diversity of the continent has made some wonder if it would not be more appropriate to speak of "African theologies" than "African theology." But the succinct description of the project of African theology contained in the final communiqué of the 1977 Pan-African Conference of Third World Theologians emphasizes the common concerns of African theologians or "African theologies":

> We believe that African theology must be understood in the context of African life and culture and the creative attempt of African peoples to shape a new future that is different from the colonial past and the neo-colonial present. The African situation requires a new theological methodology that is different from the approaches of the dominant theologies of the West. African theology must reject, therefore, the prefabricated ideas of North Atlantic theology by defining itself according to the struggles of the people in their resistance against the structures of domination. Our task as theologians is to create a theology that arises from and is accountable to African people.[16]

In other words, the concerns of African theologians transcend the linguistic and cultural diversity that characterizes the continent. This is a significant landmark in the history of the theological enterprise on the African continent. By tracing the history of this enterprise, Ngindu was able to identify three major currents of theology on the African continent, namely, missionary theology, critical African theology, and "black theology" of South Africa.[17]

According to Ngindu, the nature of missionary theology is determined by the aim and goal of mission work. In this regard there are three principal schools of thought. The first seeks "the salvation of souls" or "the conversion of the infidel," the second seeks "the establishing or implanting of the church," while the third aims at "giving birth to a native church and helping it to grow properly . . . helping it to assume its proper role and responsibility in communion with Christ and all other local churches."[18] Ngindu locates the origin of the theology of the conversion of infidels in the missiological school of Münster. Its proponents, such as T. Ohm and K. Muller, argued that the goal of missionary activity was the conversion and christianization of peoples. This theology, which was founded on a dualistic anthropology, failed to distinguish between the universal revelation and its historical and particular expression in Judeo-Christian religious tradition, could not conceive salvation outside what had been imagined as the Church's "fixed boundaries," and, consequently, was incapable of any positive appreciation of the culture and the religious traditions of African peoples. In its zealous pursuit of the objectives of the missionary enterprise, these traditions were erroneously considered to be wholly and entirely "pagan" and diabolic.

While the theology of conversion of infidels was willing to acknowledge that the peoples in the missions had cultures, even though it branded these cultures pagan and "saw the souls of black people living in darkness and the shadow of death," the theology of implantation sought to establish the Church in the lands of peoples thought to be without culture or civilization. In the words of Ngindu, "On the clean slate, or the slate wiped clean, of people without culture or civilization, missionaries were to establish the church as it had been known historically in the West. Its personnel, its methods, and its works were to be copies of the western church."[19] It was a case of what H. Maurier describes as "implanting the Roman church, its doctrine, its liturgy, its discipline, its organization, and its outlook."[20] Therefore, to have to choose between the theology of conversion and the theology of implantation is to have to choose between a theology that devalues African culture and a theology that denies African culture. Ngindu perceives varying shades of the theology of implantation in the periodical *Eglise Vivante* of J. Bruls and J. Frisque published in Louvain, and in the *Revue Nouvelle de Science Missionaire* of J. Beckman and W. Bühlmann.

The third school of thought in missionary theology is the theology of the local Church of Vatican II.[21] Without giving an elaboration of this theology, Ngindu simply mentions in passing that the Second Vatican Council, while speaking of the propagation of the faith and the establishment of the Church, does not take a negative stand towards the cultures of the peoples of the mission territories. But a closer examination of this theology reveals a positive appreciation of the role of these cultures in the propagation of the Christian message. *Lumen Gentium*, the Dogmatic Constitution on the Church, takes the lead by emphasizing the unity and diversity of the Church. The Church is the new people of God to which all are called to belong. She remains "one and only one." At the same time, she "is to be spread throughout the whole world." In other words, "All the faithful scattered throughout the world are in communion with each other in the Holy Spirit so that 'he who dwells in Rome knows those in most distant parts to be his members' (*qui Romae sedet, Indos scit membrum suum esse*)." The Church that is thus presented is a communion of local Churches.[22]

Ad gentes, the Decree on the Church's Missionary Activity, would later follow the lead provided by *Lumen Gentium* by asserting that a local Church is born when, among other things, the assembly of the faithful is "rooted in the social life of the people and to some extent conformed to its culture." In the communion of local Churches which Vatican II presents, there can be no room for any negative attitude towards the cultures of the peoples who make up the young Churches. On the contrary, the young Churches "borrow from the customs, traditions, wisdom, teaching, arts and sciences of their people everything which could be used to praise the glory of the Creator, manifest the grace of the saviour, or contribute to the right ordering of Christian life."[23]

Having described the three schools of thought in missionary theology, Ngindu goes on to examine African theology.[24] The origin of this theology is usually traced to the year 1956 when a group of African theologians published the collective work *Des prêtres noirs s'interrogent*.[25] The authors were reacting to the failure of missionary theology to take into account Africa's culture, religion, and civilization.[26] The publication of the work gave birth to the theology of adaptation.[27] But Ngindu distinguishes a second stage whose theology he describes as "critical African theology."[28]

An African theologian whose life and work embody the theology of adaptation is the Zairean Vincent Mulago. The aim of Mulago and his school was to give an African expression to Christianity. Christianity will be given an African expression when its doctrines and practices are adapted to the culture of Africans.[29] The Christian message must be presented to Africans in their own terms and according to the categories provided by their culture. This presupposes that there are beliefs, rites, symbols, gestures, and institutions in the religions of traditional African societies which are compatible with Christianity and which, consequently, are "stepping stones" to Christianity. Ngindu examines the merits and demerits of this school. As far as its merits are concerned, the theology of adaptation has driven home the fact that the gospel message needs to become flesh not just in European culture but also in other cultures, specifically in African culture. In addition, the theology of adaptation has largely influenced the "Africanization" of Christianity in the areas of personnel, catechesis, and the liturgy. However, "the major defect of this theology of adaptation has been its *concordism*. It tends to equate Christian revelation with the systems of thought in which it has found historical expression." In other words, this theology does not identify and isolate the European expression of Christianity before seeking to adapt it. It has led to what Hurbon has called "a process of nativizing the Roman church."[30]

Consciousness of the defect of the theology of adaptation has led to the emergence of the so-called "critical African theology."[31] According to Ngindu, the proponents of this theology have two major preoccupations: "to establish closer contact with the major sources of revelation: the Bible and tradition," and "to open up wholly to the African milieu and its problems," that is, to the questions raised by the present situation of the African society. In pursuance of the first objective, a number of valuable works have been published in the areas of fundamental, historical, and biblical theology.[32] And in pursuance of the second objective, Ngindu observes that much attention is given to the theology of the local Church, the theology of the laity, and the theology of non-Christian religions in the theological study weeks of the Catholic Faculty of Theology in Kinshasa, the periodicals published on the continent such as *AFER, Cahiers des Religions Africaines, Revue Africaine de Théologie,* and the writings of scholars like John Mbiti,[33] L. Mpongo,[34] and Bimwenyi Kweshi,[35] to mention but a few.

Black theology, the third major current of theology in Africa identified by Ngindu, originated from North America through the pioneering efforts of A. Cleage and James Cone.[36] This theology seeks to offer a Christian response to the problem of racism of which African-

Americans have been victims. It found its way to South Africa in the seventies.[37]

It is pertinent to note that Ngindu's article is, to a great extent, a description of the theological activity of the Zairean school of African theology. While it is true that this school has been at the forefront of the quest for African theology, its brand of theology has been the object of very strong criticism by a Cameroonian Dominican, Eloi Messi Metogo.[38] I have already mentioned that one of the questions raised by the expression "African theology" is that of knowing which Africa one is talking about. Eloi Messi begins his work by raising the same question in a rather brutal fashion. In his opinion, since the publication of *Des prêtres noirs s'interrogent*, which marked the beginning of African theology in 1956, a lot has been said about the incarnation of Christianity in African culture. But African theological discourse has been bedeviled by a double misconception centering on the notion of African culture and on the notion of Christianity. This raises two questions: "Which Africa? Which Christianity?"[39] These, in Eloi Messi's opinion, are two questions that African theologians have failed to address. Instead, the basis of their discourse has been an anthropology mediated by the négritude movement.

Produced in the colonial situation, a situation in which anything African was denigrated, négritude set out to affirm the "anteriority of African civilization" by digging into the past and searching for African cultural values which would correspond to the cultural values of the West, thus leading to the recognition of the humanity of the African hitherto considered to be uncivilized. This implies using Western culture as the criterion of African culture. However, says Eloi Messi, "In itself, the thesis of the anteriority of African civilisations does not effect any change in the present situations of blacks. . . . The knowledge of our past creativity does not serve any purpose if it does not empower us to regain historical initiative here and now."[40] Négritude is an ethnophilosophy, that is, it collects the various customs, practices, myths, and beliefs otherwise collected and studied by ethnology, and presents them according to the categories of Western philosophy. The paradox of négritude becomes evident when one becomes aware of the fact that the ethnological studies that gave rise to it had been undertaken by Europeans and not Africans. Therefore, négritude has been created by the colonialists themselves under the pretext of promoting the values of African culture and in order to distract Africans from the reality of their colonial situation. "The Africanism of Africans was born of the Africanism of non-Africans."[41]

The legacy of this pretentious promotion of African culture has been "an erroneous and static vision of culture." African culture is misunderstood as something given once and for all. In the words of Eloi Messi: "Instead of a historical effectuation of the self, by the self and for the self, the latter [culture] appears to be the exhumation and the preservation of an eternal identity of the black, a supra-historic identity that cannot be assigned any place. By thus isolating her from living history, Africa is handed over to eternal colonisation without decline."[42] This ethnophilosophy has begotten a sterile, monotonous, and ineffective theological discourse produced by "concordist comparatism" (*comparatisme concordist*). Just as négritude tries to show that there is a correspondence between the values of African culture and those of Western culture, the theology it inspires tries to project the categories of biblical revelation and Christian theology into the traditional religions of Africa.[43] It is a "cultural" and "apolitical" theology. It is cultural because it is based exclusively on the values of traditional Africa expressed in her cosmogony, folklore, divination, proverbs, etc. It is apolitical because it is out of touch with the political and economic problems confronting Africa today.[44]

But the problem was not just the misunderstanding of what constitutes or should constitute African culture. There was also the misconception of Christianity. Like Ngindu, Eloi Messi points out that the Christianity whose incarnation was sought by African theology was the missionary Christianity "received from a tradition of Counter-Reform and the anti-modernist struggle."[45] However, unlike Ngindu, Eloi Messi insists that African theology has not evolved from the polemics of adaptation "to critical irenics." While Ngindu sees Bimwenyi Kweshi's *Discours théologique négro-africain* as a typical textbook of critical African theology, Eloi Messi contends that the latter simply follows the footsteps of ethnophilosophy by projecting the categories of Western philosophy into African culture. In other words, Bimwenyi Kweshi has studied the various customs, practices, myths, and beliefs of traditional African societies (ethnology), presented them according to the categories of Western philosophy (ethnophilosophy), and based his theological discourse (ethnotheology) on this ethnophilosophy. Bimwenyi Kweshi's declared intention was to lay the foundations for black African theological discourse according to the imperatives of African culture and the Christian message. However, there are indications that his work ended up as a "cultural" and "apolitical" theology. Bimwenyi's thesis therefore prolongs the attempt of the theology of adaptation "to acclimatise and tropicalise" a missionary Christianity imported from Europe.[46]

Eloi Messi sees the need for African theology to change its understanding of African tradition and its way of relating with it. This does
not imply the abolition or negation of the past but an end to what Mar-
cien Towa calls "the dictatorship of the past." African tradition must
be understood as the product of many transformations, an evolution
guided by creative liberty. Eboussi Boulaga defines this tradition as
"a given being-together (*être-ensemble*) and a factual having-in-common
(*avoir-en-commun*) which calls for a common destiny through the mediation of a rational and reasonable acting-in-common (*agir-en-commun*)."[47]
The given being-together is the coming together of loose ethnic groups
brought about by colonialism. What these loose ethnic groups have
in common is in fact a privation. It was their material inferiority and
their scientific and technological underdevelopment that rendered them
colonisable. And it is through the creative liberty of their common
action that an end will be put to this privation.[48]

T. Tshibangu, a leading figure in the Zairean school, in an apparently hasty manner, has dismissed the fundamental thesis of Eloi
Messi's book as unacceptable.[49] But I am of the opinion that its author
has raised serious questions of methodology in African theology which
should not be ignored. Since giving this book the attention it deserves
demands another essay, I shall only attempt a brief response here.

Eloi Messi's unwillingness to acknowledge with Ngindu Mushete
that African theology has evolved from adaptation to "critical irenics"
raises a problem concerning his bibliography. One observes that, with
the exception of Bimwenyi Kweshi's *Discours théologique négro-africain*,
the works of theologians that Ngindu classifies as belonging to the
genre of critical African theology are conspicuously absent from his
footnotes and bibliography. Eloi Messi was so fascinated and preoccupied by Bimwenyi's monumental thesis of seven hundred pages
that he did not pay attention to the writings of Tshibangu, Ntedika,
Atal, or Monsengwo, to mention but a few.[50] One cannot but wonder
if the failure to acknowledge these authors is not indicative of an out-
dated bibliography of African theology.

However, granted that Ngindu was right when he asserted that African theology has moved to the stage of "critical irenics," the fact remains that with the exception of Archbishop Bakole wa Ilunga,[51] the
Zairean school has maintained an almost deafening silence on the social, political, and economic issues confronting Zaire as a nation in particular and the African continent in general. Or how does one explain
the curious co-existence of such a prolific school of theology with
Africa's most brutal and most fraudulent dictatorship?[52] Little wonder then that the ingenuity of the Zairean school has produced the

Zairean Rite of the Mass, a liturgical masterpiece by any standard, while the people who celebrate this beautiful liturgy go back to their misery after the celebration with no access to the basic things needed for a decent standard of living. With this in mind, I can only submit that Eloi Messi's categorization of the négritude-inspired African theology as cultural and apolitical is dead on target.

Eloi Messi is of the opinion that scientific and technological development are prerequisites for spiritual and cultural autonomy.[53] But if one were to believe Cees Hamelink, the ability of a people to relate with its environment, which is manifested in scientific and technological creativity, is destroyed when its cultural autonomy is destroyed.[54] And even though Eloi Messi has made a good case for a new conception of African tradition, we must not pretend that the traditions of precolonial Africa are dead and forgotten. They may be dead and forgotten in urban Africa but they are not so in rural Africa. There is a certain measure of reciprocal relationship between the two "Africas." The historian Joseph Ki-Zerbo was right when he wrote: "The Africa of yesterday is still a given fact today. She is neither gone, nor, as some say, overtaken. There are courts of African traditional chiefs in which five or five hundred year-old rituals are repeated. There are probably sacrificial formulas which have not been changed for a millenary."[55] Ki-Zerbo advocates a new African civilization in which the Africa of yesterday and the Africa of today will be synthesized. Such a civilization avoids the "museographic complex" which is a "sterile diversion towards the past," as well as the "technocratic diversion" towards science without conscience. This new African civilization should be a modern version of Africanness and an African version of modernity.[56] It will provide a much-needed anthropological basis for a truly critical African theology; by this, I mean an African theology which will be a correlation between the Christian message and the new African civilization.

Points of Convergence[57]

African theology is a quest for correlation between the Christian message and the African situation, between the Christian faith and African culture. This culture is to be conceived as neither a sterile diversion to the past, nor a science without conscience. Rather, it is to be a way of conceiving and being in the universe issuing from a dynamic, critical, and creative dialogue that takes place in the African *geist*, that is, the dialogue between the Africa of yesterday and the Africa of today.

This dialogue leads to a new interpretation of existence and the long-awaited genuine emancipation of the African. With this in mind, and using two expressions of Paul Tillich, one might describe African theology as a "theology of African culture" and an "answering theology." Can the African become a Christian without becoming alienated from his or her culture? Can the Christian message become flesh in the African situation without losing what Marc Michel calls its "essential and unique character"? These and related questions, which are similar to the questions Paul Tillich sought to answer, are the questions that confront an African theologian today. To answer them, critical African theology seeks to respect the double imperative of fidelity to the Christian message and consciousness of the African situation in which it is being proclaimed.

Eloi Messi insisted that this demands a good grounding in the knowledge of the history of Christianity, her doctrines and her institutions on the one hand, and on the other hand, not just an ethnological knowledge of Africa (the African theology of adaptation limited itself to this type of knowledge), but also a sociological knowledge of the continent.[58] The African theologian, like every theologian, endeavors to know the content of the Christian message through assiduous study of fundamental, historical, and biblical theology. This has to be coupled with a knowledge of the African situation, that is, of the continent's politics, economy, and history and the psychology of her peoples in order to make an analysis of traditional and contemporary African societies.

An analysis of the African situation raises a number of existential interrogations which, in its endeavor to be sensitive to the African situation, African theology has to contend with. I have already referred to the question whether for the African being Christian is not in dichotomy with being African. To transcribe this question in the historical existence of the African is to raise the question of the correlation between the history of the African continent and the kingdom of God. The African continent has confronted and continues to confront difficult moments in her history. Africa has known slavery and colonialism and continues to live through their traumatic consequences. The thorny question of the correlation between the history of Africa and the kingdom of God is raised by the existence of bloodthirsty dictators who are products of the ambiguity of empire of the Cold War era, and by the social, political, and economic problems created by their corrupt regimes. This question, which Tillich did not neglect, is a major concern of African theology. For the African Christian belongs to two communities (Tillich would speak of two history-bearing groups) and bears the marks of humiliation and royalty. To be an African Christian is to belong to a race whose history is one of repeated humiliation. It is also to belong to a religious community founded by the proclamation of the good news of the kingdom of God, a priestly people, a royal people.

In his analysis of history Tillich speaks of the ambiguities of historical self-integration, historical self-creativity, historical self-transcendence, and the individual in history.[59] History has a goal because a historic event is the result of human intentions acting as decisive but non-exclusive factors. Other historical factors may be institutions and natural conditions. Whatever these factors may be, an event is historic only to the extent to which it is attached to intentional acts. "Processes in which no purpose is intended are not historical."[60] However, it is because the ultimate aim of history always remains to be achieved that we speak of ambiguities. The ambiguities of history are therefore explained in the following terms: "History, while running ahead toward its ultimate aim, continuously actualizes limited aims, and in so doing it both achieves and defeats its ultimate aim."[61] I am of the opinion that Paul Tillich's analysis of history in terms of ambiguities could be useful in a critical reading of African history. I shall first give a brief description of these ambiguities and their expressions in the history of Africa, and then I shall point out what I consider to be an unresolved issue in Tillich's correlation of history and the kingdom of God.

In the greatness of political existence and in the life process of self-integration, the human person struggles to achieve universality and totality in a history-bearing group. Though laudable, this struggle for universality and totality implies the ambiguities of empire and centralization in the history of the Church and in the history of secular movements. Empires originate not only from the will to exercise economic and political power but also from the vocational self-interpretation of a historical group. The vocational self-interpretation of a group is what the group considers to be its goal in history and the force of the desire to construct an empire is increased by the justification provided by this vocational self-interpretation. Thus the Romans sought to build the Holy Roman Empire under the central authority of the Roman law, the English understood their vocational consciousness as the submission of all peoples to a Christian humanism under the central authority of the British Empire, the French sought the intellectual and cultural leadership of the world, while the Americans pursued the ideals of democracy and liberty. Tillich saw dangers in the emergence of empires inspired by conflicting vocational self-interpretations as was the case between what he called "the American Empire" and "the Russian Empire."[62] But that was not the only problem. Within empires themselves there is the possibility of internal centralization degenerating into a dictatorship.[63] One may now ask: how do the ambiguities of empire translate themselves in the history of Africa?

In the nineteenth century, not long after the era of the trans-Atlantic slave trade, a number of European powers interpreted their vocational consciousness as a civilizing mission. To accomplish this mission, the "primitive" tribes of Africa and the "New World" had to be colonized, and these colonized nations became parts of the vast empires of Britain, Belgium, France, Germany, Portugal, and Spain. In an attempt to resolve the conflict that ensued among the colonial powers over which parts and how much of Africa to colonize, the map of Africa was redrawn at the Berlin Conference of 1878 separating Africans of the same tribe from each other and forcing many groups without linguistic affinities to live within common boundaries without prior consultation. A graphic description of what transpired is given in a recent book by Thomas Pakenham:

> The Scramble for Africa bewildered everyone, from the humblest African peasant to the master statesmen of the age, Lord Salisbury and Prince Bismarck. . . . Suddenly, in half a generation, the Scramble gave Europe virtually the whole continent: including thirty new colonies and protectorates, 10 million square miles of new territory and 110 million dazed new subjects, acquired by one method or another. Africa was sliced up like a cake, the pieces swallowed by five rival nations—Germany, Italy, Portugal, France and Britain (with Spain taking some scraps)—and Britain and France were at each other's throats. At the centre, exploiting the rivalry, stood one enigmatic individual and self-styled philanthropist, controlling the heart of the continent: Leopold II, King of the Belgians.[64]

The life of the African was governed from centers of power located in London, Brussels, Paris, Berlin, Lisbon, and Madrid.

In the twentieth century, the African struggles for independence raised the hopes of her peoples. It offered them promises of change. But their history since the "independence" of the 1960s is a history of change of promises.[65] Today's African political leaders, with few exceptions, embody the ambiguities of the history of the continent. Most of them were mercenaries of the Cold War. Through them the African continent has been recolonized, and through them the African peoples' aspirations to emancipation have been betrayed. It should be mentioned in passing that the missionary enterprise and the colonization of Africa happened simultaneously. While Africa was being colonized she was also being christianized.[66]

The ambiguities of historical self-creativity and historical self-transcendence have a common expression in the conflict between the old and the new in history. Following the example of Hegel, who affirmed that the old is contained in the new as that which is negated and preserved at the same time, Tillich puts forward the opinion that there is no pure novelty. This is an ambiguity underlying the conflict of generations in arts, philosophy, and in politics between the progressives and the conservatives, between the forces of revolution and the forces of reaction. "In this conflict partisans of the old become hardened and bitter, and partisans of the new frustrated and empty."[67] While the elements of revolution and reaction are parts of historical creativity, the problem is to reconcile the two elements in order to attain a historical creativity liberated from all ambiguity, from a destruction in the name of creation.

The conflict between the old and the new attains a destructive level when the two parties to the conflict elevate themselves to ultimate status by absolutizing the particular period of history they represent. As Tillich says, "From the point of view of historical dynamics, this is the conflict between different groups which claim to represent the aim of history either in terms of its actual or in terms of its anticipated fulfillment."[68] The conflict between the old and the new finds an expression in the conflict between the proponents of the "Africa of yesterday" and those of the "Africa of today," between those who have what Joseph Ki-Zerbo describes as the museographic complex and those who have the technocratic complex. I have already tried to show how this conflict influences theology in Africa.

Lastly, in describing the ambiguities of the individual in history, Tillich remarks that the individual receives his or her life from the history-bearing group and cannot fail to participate in history. The risk that arises from this is that the individual could be subordinated to the political group. This situation can arise not only in totalitarian systems but also in democratic systems in spite of their option for liberty: "The techniques of representation drastically reduce the participation of the individual, sometimes even to the vanishing point in mass societies with an all-powerful party bureaucracy. A majority can be produced and maintained by methods which deprive a large number of individuals of political influence altogether and for an indefinite time."[69]

Examples of this subordination of the individual to the political group abound in the many totalitarian states of the African continent. The individual must conform to the establishment in the one-party state. All opposition is systematically eliminated. And since opposition is a necessary ingredient for development, the existence of these one-party

states and military dictatorships has brought over two decades of un-
mitigated disaster on the African continent.

For Paul Tillich, the symbol "kingdom of God" responds to the problem of the interpretation of history because the kingdom of God is the
triumph over historical ambiguities. It already manifests itself in history,
though in fragmentary ways. God as the power of being is the source
of all the power of a particular being. Therefore, power by its nature
is essentially divine. In divine life, whose creative self-manifestation
is the divine kingdom, the ambiguities of power underlying the construction of empire and the centralization of power in a historical group
are conquered by unambiguous life. Consequently, the kingdom of
God triumphantly but in a fragmentary way manifests itself in historical existence in attitudes and in institutions which resist the destructive implications of power. But the kingdom of God is not to be
mistaken for democracy even though a democracy could be an instance
of the triumph of God in history. "Insofar as democratisation of political attitudes and institutions serves to resist the destructive implications of power, it is a manifestation of the Kingdom of God in
history. But it would be completely wrong to identify democratic institutions with the Kingdom of God in history."[70]

The conquest of the ambiguities of historical self-creativity assumes
the form of the reconciliation of the forces of revolution and the forces
of tradition in the negation of the destructive consequences of conflict.
When this conquest is accomplished, traditionalists adopt a fundamentally positive attitude towards revolution while revolutionaries adopt
a fundamentally positive attitude towards tradition. And the extent
to which democratic institutions succeed in reconciling tradition and
revolution is the extent to which they manifest the triumph of the kingdom of God in history. The victory of the kingdom of God over the
ambiguities of historical self-transcendence is the negation of the
demonic consequences of the absolutization of a fragmentary accomplishment of the end of history. It is also the negation of a certain utopianism which refuses to recognize the fragmentary accomplishment of
the end of history. The ambiguities of historical self-transcendence originate from the conflict between the "already" and the "not yet" of the
kingdom of God. The kingdom is the affirmation of what is already
accomplished and what is yet to be accomplished, between experience
and expectation. The individual who is thrown into history has to participate in history. This participation demands a sacrifice. But the kingdom of God is victorious over the ambiguities of the individual in
history where this sacrifice is assumed in a reflective way. The aim
for which I sacrifice myself in history must merit the sacrifice. If it does

not, my participation in history will be deprived of meaning.

Tillich's theology of correlation between history and the kingdom of God leaves us with an unresolved issue. An analysis of being in the historical dimension reveals the ambiguities of history, and the kingdom of God is the triumphant conquest of these ambiguities. In this respect, Tillich speaks of the fragmentary manifestation of the kingdom in history (Spiritual Presence), and of the unambiguous and non-fragmentary victory of the kingdom of God at the end of history (Eternal Life). At the end of history, the positive content of history is elevated into eternity to the exclusion of the negative. Eternal life is described as "the positive content of history, liberated from its negative distortions and fulfilled in its potentialities."[71] This is a point where Tillich's eschatology, in spite of its elegant language, leaves even his greatest admirers with crucial but unanswered questions. The transition from estranged existence to essentialization therefore remains a puzzle coming at the end of an otherwise monumental work like the *Systematic Theology*. By what means and when, one may ask, will the elevation and liberation of the positive content of history into eternity take place? This, I believe, brings us back to the problem of the relationship between time and eternity in God, a question with which the great St. Augustine of Hippo wrestled. Trying to describe the correlation between African history and the kingdom of God is like trying to describe the relationship between time and eternity. It is a question of the relationship between that which is eternal (the kingdom of God), and that which is temporal (the history of the African continent).

To explain the relationship between time and eternity, Tillich proposed the diagram of a curve "which comes from above, moves down as well as ahead, reaches the deepest point which is the *nunc existentiale*, the 'existential now,' and returns in an analogous way to that from which it came, going ahead as well as going up."[72] But the question raised by this diagram is, what role does Christ play in this eschatology? It is therefore pertinent to note that Tillich, who set out to construct an alternative to traditional theology in a language intelligible to the modern mind, ended up leaving unsolved two related questions that have troubled the theology he tried to replace: the Christological question of the relationship between the human and the divine (which, as I have already mentioned, manifests itself in the difficulty of explaining the relationship between philosophical questions and theological answers in the method of correlation) and the eschatological question of the "when" and the "how" of the transition from the fragmentary manifestation of the kingdom of God to its unambiguous and non-fragmentary manifestation.

It is easier to make a case for Tillich's recognition of the primacy of the Word of God than to make a case for his resolution of these two questions. And, as Carl Armbruster rightly observes, by not making a connection between the Christology and the eschatology implicit in the identification of Jesus the Christ as the New Being appeared in history, what Tillich has left unsolved, or partially unsolved, is "the question of the historical dimension of soteriology."[73] Consequently, while one may find his analysis of the ambiguities of history useful in reading African history, it must be borne in mind that the problem of the historical dimension of soteriology, which is the problem to be tackled by any African theologian who is concerned with giving a theological interpretation of the history of the African continent, is not sufficiently addressed in Tillich's theological system. It is this quest for correlation between salvation, on the one hand, and African historical experience of oppression and humiliation, of poverty in the midst of abundant human and natural resources, on the other hand, which makes the concern of the African theologian look like searching for God amidst the ruins of a blessed but battered continent.

Conclusion

My aim in this essay has not been to advocate that the African theologian must be Tillich's disciple. Rather, I have attempted to show that Tillich's theology, through the method of correlation, coincides with and expresses the concerns of African theology. This assertion is derived from the fact that the quest for the correlation of the Christian message and the situation in which it is proclaimed is at the heart of the two theologies. To illustrate the concerns of African theologians I have devoted a lot of attention to the divergent views of Ngindu Mushete and Eloi Messi Metogo. But even in these divergent views one is still able to discern a convergence of opinion among African theologians. The difference between the theology of adaptation and critical African theology lies in their divergence of opinion on two notions of crucial importance: African culture and Christianity. This divergence and the different methodologies it might inspire do not negate the fact that the quest for correlation is common to both currents of African theology. To acknowledge this quest for correlation is to acknowledge that Tillich's method of correlation coincides with and expresses the concerns of African theologians.

Tillich's theology of history attempts to answer a question that African theologians cannot avoid: does God intervene in the African continent's history of slavery, colonialism, political dictatorship, huge debt, and their consequences? I have therefore used Tillich's analysis of historical ambiguities to read the history of the African continent. In doing this, I agree with the opinion of Carl Armbruster that there is no explicit connection between Tillich's Christology and his eschatology. This, I have suggested, leaves the issue of the historical dimension of salvation begging for more attention. Perhaps this absence of an explicit connection is traceable to the problems raised by Tillich's reinterpretation of Christology. But exploring Tillich's Christology is beyond the scope of this essay.

In maintaining Armbruster's stance, I bear in mind a possible counter-argument: that Tillich's doctrine of *kairos* expresses the correlation between eternity and the "fragmentary manifestations of the kingdom of God in history."[74] It could be argued that when Tillich speaks of *kairos*, he means the breaking of the divine into history at the fullness of time.[75] It is the center of history, the opportune time when religion and culture attain their maturity in order to be able to receive the manifestation of the kingdom of God. The experience of the *kairos* is not just an experience that is had once and for all but one that repeats itself in the history of the Churches. Hence, Tillich distinguishes between the experience of the "great *kairos*" and that of the "relative *kairoi*." The "great *kairos*" repeats itself in the "relative *kairoi*." It is the source and criterion of the "relative *kairoi*": "every moment which claims to be spiritual must be tested, and the criterion is the 'great *kairos*.' " Every historical moment is to be submitted to the judgment of the "great *kairos*,"[76] which is the apparition in history of Jesus as the Christ. To say that the apparition of Christ in history is the central manifestation of the kingdom of God in history is to affirm that in this apparition, humanity witnesses an event that is criterion and source of the apparition of salvation in history.[77] However, the question here is not whether or not the doctrine of *kairos* provides a link between Christology and eschatology in the theology of Paul Tillich. The question is: how strong is the link?

It is my contention that when one takes into account the following points it might be possible to arrive at the conclusion that the bridge linking Christology with eschatology in Paul Tillich's theology is in need of greater fortification. First, it is to be borne in mind that Tillich's eschatology is an eschatology in two parts. In the first part he speaks of the fragmentary manifestation of the kingdom of God "in history" (Spiritual Presence), and in the second part he speaks of the unambiguous manifestation of the kingdom "above history" (Eternal Life).

Second, while there is an explicit treatment of the doctrine of *kairos* in Tillich's study of the kingdom of God "in history," the same cannot be said of his study of the kingdom of God "above history." Tillich does not say that the "great *kairos*"—the manifestation of Jesus as the Christ—is the end of history. Rather, it is the center of history. The "great *kairos*" is within history, in the midst of history's ambiguities. The Gospels seem to buttress this fact by showing that even Jesus, in whom the *kairos* manifests itself, had to confront the ambiguities of life. He taught his disciples to pray for the coming of the kingdom while he was with them. Since the "great *kairos*" is fulfilled time within history, one may perhaps contend that there is no problem relating it to time. But eternal life is outside history. What then is the relationship between the "great *kairos*" and eternal life—the unambiguous manifestation of the kingdom—in Paul Tillich's eschatology?

Third, in the *kairos*, Christ enters into history. But when it comes to what happens "above history" in eternal life, there is no mention of Christ. Armbruster made a very pertinent observation when he said Tillich's discussion of the resurrection makes no mention of the relationship between our resurrection and Christ's resurrection.[78] In fact, in the whole of the second part of his eschatology, which is devoted to the study of the end of history or eternal life, Tillich mentions the name "Christ" only twice.[79] Where does Christ stand in Paul Tillich's eternal life? It might be possible to fit Christ and the *kairos* in, but that would still leave open the question whether or not there is an explicit link between Christology and eschatology in the *Systematic Theology.*

All along I have been attempting to show the relationship between Paul Tillich's theology and the project of African theologians in general. Since this essay is meant to contribute to a Catholic assessment of Tillich there is need to give it greater focus by relating his theology to the work of African Catholic theologians. However, I would like to refrain from using the expression "African Catholic theology" because until now much of what has been written in the area of African theology has been written in an ecumenical setting. The fundamental quest for correlation in African theology is not unique to African Catholic theologians. It is a concern that cuts across denominational lines.[80]

Robert Schreiter has rightly pointed out that one of the fruits of the Second Vatican Council is the acknowledgement by official Roman Catholic teaching of the relation between the gospel message and the social and cultural contexts in which it is preached.[81] In this regard, the Decree on the Church's Missionary Activity, *Ad gentes divinitus,* provides us with a means of relating Paul Tillich to the project of African Catholic theologians. Tillich was convinced that the correlation of the Christian message and the situation in which it is preached is an imperative to which every theological system must respond. The attempt to respond to this imperative animated African theology when a group of African priests got together in 1956 to publish *Des prêtres noirs s'interrogent*. This attempt received the official endorsement of Roman Catholicism with the publication of the decree *Ad gentes* on December 7, 1965, the eve of the closure of the Second Vatican Council, and barely two months after the death of Paul Tillich.

In *Ad gentes*, the Roman Catholic Church recognizes that she has been sent by Christ to reveal the love of God to all peoples. She also recognizes the need to be sensitive to the situation in which this message of love is to be communicated. According to *Ad gentes*: "If the Church is to be in a position to offer all men the mystery of salvation and the life brought by God, then it must implant itself among all these groups [the groups of people to whom the Church has been sent to communicate God's love] in the same way that Christ by his incarnation committed himself to the particular social and cultural circumstances of the men among whom he lived."[82] This declaration has the merit of helping us to focus on the relationship between the theology of Paul Tillich and the project of African Catholic theologians because it echoes the conviction of Tillich and, by the same fact, endorses the quest for correlation in African theology as not only legitimate but imperative. It may not be an exaggeration to state that Tillich's method of correlation and the Second Vatican Council express a common sensitivity to the situation in which local Churches actualize their missionary dimension. This common sensitivity gives an impetus to a task which Robert Schreiter has aptly described by the title of his book as "Constructing Local Theologies." African theology belongs to this family of local theologies.

Pope Paul VI later confirmed the teaching of the council in his famous address to a group of African bishops in Kampala, Uganda, in 1969 when he stated *inter alia*: "The expression, that is, the language and mode of manifesting this one Faith, may be manifold; hence, it may be original, suited to the tongue, the style, the genius, and the culture, of the one who professes this one Faith. From this point of view, a certain pluralism is not only legitimate, but desirable. . . . You may, and you must, have an African Christianity."[83]

Paul Tillich's method of correlation necessarily gives rise to a certain theological pluralism which was not lacking in the early Church. History shows that in that Church there were Jewish, Greek, and Latin Christians. Their linguistic, social, and cultural identities gave expression to a theological pluralism which, in spite of conflicts, was not suppressed. Roman Catholicism rediscovered the courage to promote this pluralism at the Second Vatican Council and through the writings and addresses of Paul VI. This rediscovery was an implicit recognition of the legitimacy of an African theology or any other local theology. Roman Catholicism's explicit recognition of African theology as an expression of legitimate theological pluralism came later in Pope John Paul II's address to the Zairean bishops of the ecclesiastical provinces of Lubumbashi and Kananga on April 30, 1983.[84]

I believe these historical facts permit me to draw my conclusion: if Tillich's method of correlation leads to a certain theological pluralism, and if, like Tillich, contemporary Roman Catholicism encourages theological pluralism, then an African theologian doing theology within the Catholic tradition can see an ally in Paul Tillich.

Notes

[1] My treatment of Tillich's method of correlation in this essay draws from an earlier and more extensive study of the subject. See Anthony A. Akinwale, *La corrélation entre l'histoire et le Royaume de Dieu dans la théologie de Paul Tillich* (Thèse présentée en vue de l'obtention du grade de M. A. Th.; Ottawa: Collège Dominicain de Philosophie et de Théologie, 1991), Ch. 6, "Critique de la méthode de corrélation." In my conclusion, I had highlighted two points of convergence between Tillich's theology and African theology without developing them: the quest for a synthesis between theology and culture, and the focus on existential interrogations. I shall try to say more on the two points in this essay.

[2] Paul Tillich, *Systematic Theology* Vol. 1 (Chicago: University of Chicago Press, 1951) 3.

[3] Tillich believed Karl Barth was in danger of becoming orthodox. But, he admitted: "Barth's greatness is that he corrects himself again and again in the light of the 'situation' and that he strenuously tries not to become his own follower. Yet he does not realise that in doing so he ceases to be a merely kerygmatic theologian" (*Systematic Theology* 1:5). I believe it would be unfair to place Barth in the same camp as the fundamentalists. While fundamentalism could be accused of adopting an antitheological attitude, it would be inaccurate to describe Barth as antitheological.

[4] Paul Tillich, *The Protestant Era* (Chicago, University of Chicago Press, 1948) 55.

[5] Tillich, *The Protestant Era*, 55.

[6] Tillich, *Systematic Theology*, 1:7.

[7] Marc Michel, *La théologie aux prises avec la culture. De Schleiermacher à Tillich*, "Cogitatio Fidei" no. 113, (Paris: Cerf, 1982) 17. Unless otherwise stated, the translations of works with French titles are mine.

[8] Michel, *La théologie aux prises avec la culture*, 14.

[9] Alexander McKelway, *The Systematic Theology of Paul Tillich* (New York: Delta, 1964) 70.

[10] Carl Armbruster, *The Vision of Paul Tillich* (New York: Sheed and Ward, 1967) 293.

[11] See Kenneth Hamilton, *The System and the Gospel. A Critique of Paul Tillich* (London: SCM, 1963).

[12] Read Jean Richard, ''Théologie et philosophie dans l'évolution de Paul Tillich'' *Laval théologique et philosophique*, 42, 2 (juin 1986) 167–216.

[13] Cf. Paul Tillich, *Biblical Religion and the Search for Ultimate Reality* (Chicago: University of Chicago Press, 1955) 29–34. While stating that the method of correlation could be seen as a practical implication of the doctrine of the Word made flesh, one should not overlook the questions raised by Tillich's ''revision'' of the doctrine of incarnation. But that is beyond the scope of this essay. Cf. Paul Tillich, *Systematic Theology*, 2:94–96. See the objections to his reinterpretation in George H. Tavard, *Paul Tillich and the Christian Message* (New York, Charles Scribner's Sons, 1962) 118–24.

[14] Here I reaffirm the position I held in *La corrélation entre l'histoire et le Royaume de Dieu*, 147. Theology's point of departure is faith. Like any Christian theologian, Tillich was a theologian whose point of departure was faith—not necessarily the faith of his audience but his own faith in Jesus as the Christ. But Tillich was realistic in his presentation of the message of this faith. He recognised the fact that he was addressing the Christian message not only to believers but also to an audience of people who no longer accepted, or were yet to accept, the Christian faith and the authority of its message. It would have been futile to use this faith as the point of departure of his message. It might therefore be necessary to speak of a double point of departure in theology: the faith of the theologian in Jesus as the Christ, and the faith of the audience which may not necessarily be in Jesus as the Christ but which, nonetheless, is an ultimate concern. Hence, I see Tillich's theology as one which, in its dialogue with the modern mind (those without *pistis*), begins with *gnosis*, with the aim of arriving at *pistis*.

[15] M. Ngindu, ''The History of Theology in Africa: From Polemics to Critical Irenics,'' in *African Theology en Route*, eds. K. Appiah-Kubi and S. Torres (Maryknoll, N.Y.: Orbis) 23.

[16] Cf. ''Final Communiqué. Pan-African Conference of Third World Theologians, December 17–23, 1977, Accra, Ghana,'' *African Theology en Route*, 189–95. The quotation is on page 193.

[17] Ngindu, ''The History of Theology in Africa,'' 23. My exploration of the history of the concerns of African theologians is informed by Ngindu's article.

[18] Ibid., 23–24.

[19] Ibid., 25.

[20] H. Maurier, quoted by Ngindu, ''The History of Theology in Africa,'' 25.

²¹ Cf. *Lumen Gentium* 13 and *Ad gentes,* chs. 2 and 3, especially 19 and 22.

²² On the Church as community of Churches see J.-M.-R. Tillard, *Eglise d'églises. L'ecclésiologie de communion,* "Cogitatio fidei" no. 143 (Paris: Cerf, 1987).

²³ *Ad gentes,* 22.

²⁴ Cf. Ngindu, "The History of Theology in Africa," 27–31.

²⁵ Vincent Mulago et al., *Des prêtres noirs s'interrogent* (Paris: Cerf, 1956).

²⁶ As I have already indicated above, the missionary theology of the Second Vatican Council, in the light of its positive appreciation of culture, could not be said to have failed in this regard.

²⁷ Cf. Ngindu, "The History of Theology in Africa," 27–28.

²⁸ Ibid., 27.

²⁹ See Vincent Mulago, *Un visage africain du christianisme. L'union vitale bantu face à l'unité vitale ecclésiale* (Paris: Présence Africain, 1965). The proponents of the theology of adaptation were largely inspired by Placide Tempel's writings, particularly *La philosophie bantoue* (Paris: Présence Africain, 1949).

³⁰ L. Hurbon, *Dieu dans le vaudou haitien* (Paris: Payot, 1972) 3, quoted in Ngindu, "The History of Theology in Africa," 28.

³¹ Ngindu, "The History of Theology in Africa," 28–31.

³² Here are some examples given by Ngindu: for a work on fundamental theology see T. Tshibangu, *Théologie positive et théologie positive. Position traditionelle et nouvelle problématique* (Louvain: L'Université; Paris: Beatrice-Nauwelaerts, 1965); in the area of historical theology see K. Ntedika, *L'évocation de l'au-delà dans la prière pour les morts. Etude de patristique et de la liturgie latines, IVe-VIIe S.* (Louvain: Editions Nauwelaerts; Paris: Béatrice-Nauwelaerts, 1971); in the area of biblical theology and exegesis see D. Atal, *Structure et signification des cinq premiers versets de l'hymne johannique au Logos* (Louvain-Paris, 1972) and L. Monsengwo Pasinya, *La notion de nomos dans le Pentateuque grec* (Rome, 1973).

³³ See John Mbiti, *African Religion and Philosophy* (London, 1969); *Concepts of God in Africa* (London, 1970); *New Testament Eschatology in an African Background: A Study of the Encounter Between New Testament Theology and African Traditional Concepts* (Oxford, 1971).

³⁴ L. Mpongo, *Pour une anthropologie chrétienne du mariage au Congo* (Kinshasa, 1968).

³⁵ K. Bimwenyi, *Discours théologique négro-africain. Problème des fondements* (Paris: Présence Africaine, 1981).

³⁶ See James Cone, *Black Theology and Black Power* (New York: Seabury, 1969) and *A Black Theology of Liberation* (Philadelphia: Lippincott, 1970).

³⁷ Ngindu traces its arrival in Africa to a public discussion in March 1971 of James Cone's *Black Theology and Black Liberation.* The Proceedings of this discussion are published in M. Mothabi, *Black Theology: The South African Voice* (London: Hurst, 1973). For a description of the four different approaches in this theology read

Ngindu, "The History of Theology in Africa," 31–32. For a detailed comparison of Black theology with African theology see J. U. Young, *Black and African Theologies. Siblings or Distant Cousins?* (Maryknoll, N.Y.: Orbis, 1986).

[38] See Eloi Messi Metogo, *Théologie africaine et ethnophilosophie. Problème de méthode en théologie africaine* (Paris: L'Harmattan, 1985).

[39] Ibid., part 1.

[40] Ibid., 36.

[41] Ibid., 18.

[42] Ibid., 25.

[43] Ibid., 9, 27–28.

[44] Ibid., 55. Eloi Messi's position and Josiah Young's are identical. According to the latter: "Favouring a theological agenda grounded explicitly in a cultural problem, African theologians give little attention to political problems of postcolonial Africa" (*Black and African Theologies,* 2).

[45] Metogo, *Théologie africaine et ethnophilosophie,* 65.

[46] See ibid., ch. 2 for a critique of Bimwenyi Kweshi's thesis. As Eloi Messi remarked, hardly three of the almost seven hundred pages of the work explicitly address questions related to liberation.

[47] F. Eboussi Boulaga, *La Crise du Muntu. Authenticité africaine et Philosophie* (Paris: Présence Africaine, 1977) 151, quoted in Metogo, *Théologie africaine et ethnophilosophie,* 81.

[48] Metogo, *Théologie africaine et ethnophilosophie,* 81.

[49] See T. Tshibangu, *La théologie africaine. Manifeste et programme pour le développement des activités théologiques en Afrique* (Kinshasa: St. Paul Afrique, 1987) 149.

[50] Tshibangu's *Théologie positive et théologie spéculative* is a classic which provides a solid epistemological foundation for theological pluralism. Mention must also be made of his *La théologie comme science au XXe siècle* (Kinshasa: PUZ, 1980).

[51] See Bakole wa Ilunga, *Chemins de libération* (Kananga: Archdiocèse de Kananga, 1984).

[52] President Mobutu Sese Seko of Zaire, America's most trusted Cold War ally on the African continent, has been in power for close to thirty years.

[53] Metogo, *Théologie africaine et ethnophilosophie,* 80.

[54] Read Cees Hamelink, *Cultural Autonomy in Global Communications* (London: Centre for the Study of Communication and Culture, 1988) ch. 1.

[55] Joseph Ki-Zerbo, *Histoire de l'Afrique noire. D'hier à demain* (Paris: Hatier, 1972) 607.

[56] Ki-Zerbo, *Histoire de l'Afrique noire,* 615.

[57] Cf. Anthony A. Akinwale, *La corrélation entre l'histoire et le Royaume de Dieu,* 184–187.

58 Read Metogo, *Théologie africaine et ethnophilosophie*, 111–14. The author writes: "Only the deep knowledge of the history of Christianity, of her doctrines and of her institutions, will enable Africans to relativise the contribution of missionary Christianity often presented as the unique, true, universal, and eternal Christianity. . . . Apart from the knowledge of the history of Christianity, the other source of African theology is the knowledge, not only ethnological but sociological, of Africa" (111, 113).

59 Since the ambiguities of historical self-creativity and the ambiguities of historical self-transcendence are characterised by the conflict between the old and the new, in this essay both shall be considered together.

60 Paul Tillich, *Systematic Theology*, 3:303.

61 Ibid., 3:339.

62 Ibid., 3:340.

63 Ibid., 3:341–42.

64 Thomas Pakenham, *The Scramble for Africa. The White Man's Conquest of the Dark Continent from 1876 to 1912* (New York: Random House, 1991) xxi.

65 Some cynics have since dubbed the 1960s as the decade when African countries mistook changes of flags for independence.

66 I do not consider this a reason for wanting to repudiate Christianity. A distinction is to be made between the beauty of the Christian message and some of its bearers who entered into an unholy alliance with the colonizers.

67 Tillich, *Systematic Theology*, 3:343.

68 Ibid., 3:344.

69 Ibid., 3:347.

70 Ibid., 3:385.

71 Ibid., 3:397.

72 Ibid., 3:420.

73 Armbruster, *The Vision of Paul Tillich*, 271–73.

74 Tillich, *Systematic Theology*, 3:369–72.

75 An African might retort that in the light of all that has happened and continues to happen in their history, Africans await the *kairos*, the breaking of divine power into the history of the African continent.

76 Tillich, *Systematic Theology*, 3:370.

77 Read ibid., 3:364–69.

78 Armbruster, *The Vision of Paul Tillich*, 272.

79 Read Tillich, *Systematic Theology*, 3:394–423. The first mention of the name "Christ" was in relation to the patripassionist doctrine (404), while the second was in relation to his temptation (405). In this respect, another of Armbruster's remarks comes to mind: "One is more puzzled about what he [Tillich] does not say than about what he says" (*The Vision of Paul Tillich*, 271).

[80] In the introduction to this essay, I have already mentioned how problematic the expression "African theology" is. The expression "African Catholic theology" is even more problematic. The formation of the Ecumenical Association of African Theologians in Accra, Ghana in 1977 testifies to the ecumenical emphasis of African theology.

[81] See Robert Schreiter, *Constructing Local Theologies* (London: SCM Press, 1985) 2.

[82] *Ad gentes*, 10.

[83] "Address at the Conclusion of the Symposium of Bishops of Africa in Kampala, Uganda, July 31, 1969" *Acta Apostolicae Sedis* 61 (September 30, 1969) 573–78 [577]. Cf. also *Africae terrarum* in *Acta Apostolicae Sedis* 59 (December 28, 1967) 1073–1097 and *Evangelii nuntiandi* in which Pope Paul VI explained: "The gospel and, therefore, evangelization cannot be put in the same category with any culture. They are above all cultures. Nevertheless, the kingdom of God which is proclaimed by the gospel is put into practice by men who are imbued with their own particular culture, and *in the building up of the kingdom it is inevitable that some elements of these human cultures must be introduced. The gospel and evangelization are not specially related to any culture but they are not necessarily incompatible with them.* On the contrary, they can penetrate any culture while being subservient to none" (no. 20; emphasis mine).

[84] See *Acta Apostolicae Sedis* 75, 1 (August 1, 1983) 652–58. It is significant to note that this is the first address by a pope in which the expression "African theology" is found. See page 652.

Paul Tillich's Theology of Prayer: An Indian Perspective

Sebastian Painadath, S.J.

Tillich is often called a theologian of the *secular* culture; prayer is universally understood as a *religious* concern. Is it not then paradoxical to look for Tillich's theology of prayer? He has not written elaborately on prayer. But he was aware of its *paradoxical* character, and his insights on prayer scattered throughout his diverse publications do offer valuable material for a systematic theological reflection on prayer. His theology is basically a reflection in terms of "correlation" on the dialectics between the divine and the human, and he places prayer at the core of this dialectical process. "No religious act expresses more obviously the reciprocity between God and man."[1] Tillich defines prayer as the "spiritual longing of a finite being to return to its origin,"[2] and describes it as "the best and most universal example of an ecstatic experience" of union with the divine.[3] For him prayer is not a purely religious act that takes place outside the orbit of secular culture, but the central articulation of the dynamics of self-transcendence that opens up the depth dimension of the integrative and creative process of life in the world. Through prayer one becomes alert to the 'grace and demands' of the 'ultimate concern' operative in the realms of morality and culture.[4] The Church as "the embodiment of the New Being and creation of the Spiritual Presence"[5] has to evolve as "the place where the mystery of the holy should be experienced with awe and sacred embarrassment."[6] Hence Tillich considers prayer to be a "constitutive function of the Church":[7] a Church "in which there is no room for meditation and contemplation, ecstasy and mystical union, is no more a religion."[8] He further condemns the theological endeavour that does not emerge out of meditation and contemplation as a mere "analysis of structures without substance."[9] "We talk and talk and never listen to the voices speaking to our depth and from our depth."[10] In his analysis of contemporary culture Tillich often speaks of the deplorable "inner void,"[11] "loss of the dimension of depth,"[12] and "profanisation of culture'';[13] he calls for a revitalisation of mysticism in spirituality.[14] In meeting this epochal need Christianity has to enter into a process of creative dialogue with the mystical religions of the East.[15]

The question of prayer therefore is not just a peripheral theme in Tillich's theology, but a central issue, though it has not found a *systematic* articulation in his writings. Within the framework of his method of correlation we shall pursue his reflections on prayer in view of synthesizing them into a coherent theology of prayer.[16]

Prayer as Ecstasy at the Heart of Reality

The basis of Tillich's *Systematic Theology* is a keen analysis of the structural polarities of being. At the decisive moments of the evolution of his theological reflection he does make reference to prayer, for it is the central articulation of the dialectics between the divine and the human.

The foundation element of the structure of the finite being is finitude itself. In the very texture of the finite being there is an essential "striving in the vertical direction toward the ultimate and infinite being."[17] This universal dynamics of self-transcendence evolves into a "restlessness of the heart," an "infinite passion"[18] in the human person, for "man alone is able to look beyond the limits of his own being and of every other being."[19] "Man is able to understand in an immediate personal and central act the meaning of the ultimate, the unconditional, the absolute, the infinite."[20] Tillich describes prayer as the concrete articulation of this structural drive in the person: "Prayer is the spiritual longing of a finite being to return to its origin."[21] "In a state of silent gratefulness" we become aware of the divine presence and "we experience an elevation of life that we cannot attain by profuse words of thanks, but that can happen to us if we are open to it."[22] Prayer is "response of our whole being in immediacy" to the Ultimate;[23] it is "presence of the mystery of being," ecstasy at the heart of reality.[24]

The essential dynamics of self-transcendence actualizes itself in the existential process of the life of the spirit as *ultimate concern*. With the word "concern" Tillich means the "existential character of religious experience." That which is "ultimate" demands the "total surrender of our subjectivity."[25] Hence "ultimate concern gives depth, direction and unity to all other concerns and, with them, to the whole personality."[26] It is "the state of being grasped by the ultimate," the "state of being arrested by God."[27] This spiritual experience finds its concrete expression in prayer: "Prayer is the actualization of our ultimate concern."[28] Being the "elevation of the heart, namely, the centre of the personality to God," prayer is a 'revelatory event,' for the 'mystery of being' unfolds itself to the praying person.[29] Through prayer one becomes alert to the ultimate concern that transforms all other concerns into a genuinely integrating and liberating experience.[30]

In the actual evolution of life, essential orientation to the divine and existential estrangement from the divine are "merged in such a way that neither the one nor the other is exclusively effective." The consequent ambiguities of life are manifest "under all dimensions, in all processes and all realms of life." The longing for an unambiguous life is latent in all creatures, but in the human person the ambiguities of life and the *quest for unambiguous life* surface as a matter of 'immediate experience.'[31] Tillich mentions three dimensions of the existential quest that emerge out of the human predicament: awareness of finitude gives rise to the quest for God; experience of existential estrangement engenders the quest for the New Being; confrontation with the ambiguities of life causes the quest for the transforming presence of the Divine Spirit. With this threefold quest one is pushed to the "boundary of one's being," where one can "only stand and wait."[32] It is here that prayer evolves. "God wants us to penetrate to the boundaries of our being where the mystery of life appears, and it can only appear in moments of solitude."[33] Tillich wants the praying person to ask with 'existential seriousness'[34] and 'ultimate honesty'[35] the questions of truth and justice, love and harmony, in a process that transforms "loneliness into solitude."[36] "One hour of conscious solitude," he says, "will enrich your creativity far more than hours of trying to learn the creative process."[37] A genuine transformation takes place in solitude: "The centre of our being, the innermost self that is the ground of our aloneness, is elevated to the divine centre and taken into it; therein we can rest without losing ourselves."[38] Prayer involves a growing sensitivity to the tensions and conflicts of the "boundary situations of life" and a "wrestling of the human spirit with the Divine Spirit" in the midst of existential ambiguities.[39]

Self-transcendence of life in the realm of the spirit finds its universal expression in *religion*. Hence "it is in religion that man starts the quest for unambiguous life and it is in religion that he receives the answer."[40] The correlation between existential quest and revelatory answer finds its most concrete expression in prayer. Tillich points out that "no religious act expresses more obviously the reciprocity between God and man as prayer."[41] However he would not interpret religion as an 'independent function' beside morality and culture, but as the "quality of the two other functions": religion gives to morality "the unconditional character of the moral imperative, the ultimate moral aim'' and ''the religious element in culture is the inexhaustible depth of a genuine creation.''[42] Religion and, at its core, prayer is ''the root-function in which the spirit breaks through all of its forms and penetrates to its ground.''[43] Prayer understood this way will not end up as a pious exercise, nor will it deteriorate into something magical.[44]

Personal Encounter with God in Prayer

Tillich develops the *Systematic Theology* in terms of the dialectics between the human person and God: In self-transcendence the human person can reach for God (yes); but the person cannot grasp God (no), unless the person is first grasped by God (yes).[45] If we examine the process of prayer within this framework the following dimensions could be noticed.

Two basic principles of Tillich's theology are ''in relation to God everything is by God''[46] and ''the Spirit can heal only what is open to the Spirit.''[47] The process of prayer therefore evolves through a dialectic between divine breakthrough and human ecstasy, between revelation and faith, between divine grace and human surrender in love. ''Every prayer and meditation, if it fulfills its meaning, namely, to reunite the creature with its creative ground, is revelatory. . . . The marks of revelation—mystery, miracle and ecstasy—are present in every true prayer.''[48]

The dialectical structure of prayer may be described as follows: Prayer is possible on the basis of structural self-transcendence, 'the potential infinity' of the human person;[49] still it is impossible for the human person to pray, because of the subject-object structure of human perception.[50] With this existential inability the praying person stands ''on the boundary of his being'' with an unconditional openness to the divine.[51] Into this openness the Divine Spirit breaks in and drives the person into a ''successful self-transcendence,'' thus enabling a successful prayer.[52] The first moment of the touch of God in the core of one's being is an experience of an inner perturbance caused by the ''abysmal'' dimension of the divine mystery.[53] The Divine Spirit ''drives the human spirit out of itself''[54] and shatters its tendency to ''rest in the self-sufficiency of the finitude.''[55] ''When the ultimate cuts into the life of a man'' the first reaction is to ''hide one's face,''[56] ''to flee from the attack of that which strikes him with unconditional seriousness.''[57] This is the experience of the Ultimate as the *mysterium tremendum.*[58]

Under the sway of this existential shock one may not be able to pray at all. "We may feel that the abyss between God and us makes the use of his name impossible for us. We may hesitate to speak to God even privately or voicelessly."[59] In this "dark night of the soul" the "Spirit shows us nothing except the absent God, and the empty space within us which is *His* space."[60] Tillich describes this as an inevitable moment in the proper evolution of prayer, for "the Spirit does not give life without having led us through the experience of death."[61]

In this 'sublime embarrassment'[62] and 'silence of awe'[63] of the praying person the Divine Spirit reveals itself as the 'Ground of being,'[64] as the personal God who loves the human person unconditionally; "man is arrested in his hidden flight" by the gracious touch of the divine.[65] This is encounter with the *mysterium fascinosum*, the "state of being grasped by the divine Spirit."[66] This is normally an intense experience of encounter with God in a personal form. Inevitably "every religion calls its God 'thou' in prayer,"[67] because "nothing less than personal"[68] can adequately meet the human person in the existential quest. To the gracious self-revelation of the personal God the praying person responds in faith and love, in "total surrender of the personal centre."[69]

This dialectical process of prayer does not evolve in a vacuum. Tillich repeatedly makes it clear that the encounter between God and the human person takes place in and through symbols: symbol is the language of religious experience, and a fortiori of prayer. "Only symbols can open up the hidden depths of our own being which are otherwise closed for us."[70] Since the human self-experience is that of being a person, the person-to-person relationship between God and the human person is constitutive for religious experience. "A person-to-person relationship to divine power is appropriated through prayer, that is, through an appeal to the personal centre of the divine being."[71] God in his self-manifestation is "dependent on the way man receives his manifestation."[72] Hence the God who grasps the core of the praying person inevitably becomes a personal *thou* for the human *I* in the process of prayer. That God is personal, however, does not mean that God is *a* person. It means that "God is the ground of everything personal,"[73] the "ultimate source of love, power and justice."[74]

Prayer, as we have seen above, is a revelatory process. The transpersonal divine mystery reveals itself as personal God at the core of the human person.[75] But the personal God can be an adequate symbol of the divine only insofar as it participates in the divine Logos, the 'principle of self-manifestation' within the inner-Trinitarian dialectics of divine life.[76] In the Christian faith-experience the "central, decisive and undistorted manifestation" of the divine Logos is in Jesus the Christ:[77] "the face of God manifest for historical man is the face of Jesus as the Christ."[78] Insofar as he is the historical embodiment of the divine Logos, the most concrete and the completely transparent personal symbol of the transpersonal divine,[79] Jesus the Christ becomes the personal *thou* in Christian prayer. Hence Tillich approves of the Christian heritage of "praying to the Christ":

> We cannot pray to anyone except God. If Jesus is someone beside God, we cannot and we should not pray to him. . . . But he who sees *him* sees the Father. There are not two faces. In the face of Jesus the Christ, God "makes his face to shine upon us." . . . Everything in his countenance is transparent to him who has sent him. Therefore and therefore alone, can we sing at Christmas-time: O come, let us adore him![80]

Praying to Jesus the Christ does not mean psychological empathy[81] with the historical Jesus nor prayer to the second person of the Trinity in distinction to the other two persons,[82] but a total personal self-surrender to the Christ in whom the divine pours itself out. It is the silent "elevation of the heart" to him "in whom the Spirit and the Life are manifest without limit";[83] it is "ecstatic participation in the Christ who is the Spirit" whereby one lives in the sphere of this Spiritual Power.[84] In prayer this would mean entry into the solitude of Jesus through which he experienced "complete transparency to the will of the Father."[85]

The Contemplative Dynamics of Prayer

Tillich consistently upholds the mysterious character of the divine reality. He would affirm an inner dynamics of prayer in the dialectical process of encounter between the human person and God: a contemplative movement that takes the praying person beyond personal symbols towards the experience of the transpersonal mystery.

The divine reality is the "unfathomable mystery of the holy," "the inexhaustible ground of being."[86] No personal symbol of God can manifest exhaustively "the God who is the Personal-itself, the ground and abyss of every person."[87] The "holiness of God makes it impossible for man to draw Him into the context of the ego-world and the subject-object correlation" in the process of prayer.[88] Ultimately "I cannot *speak* to God,"[89] for "God is nearer to me than I am to myself."[90] "God can never be an object, unless he is a subject at the same time."[91]

"God stands in the divine-human reciprocity, but only as he who transcends it and comprises both sides of the reciprocity."[92] Hence Tillich upholds with Meister Eckhart a radical openness to the "God above God" as the basic dynamics of prayer.[93] When this mystical dynamics is operative in prayer the divine mystery unfolds itself in the human person.[94] Reflecting on the meaning of biblical personalism he says: "Our encounter with the God who is a person includes the encounter with the God who is the ground of everything personal and as such not a person."[95]

The human person at prayer cannot transcend the I-thou structure of prayer. "We cannot bridge the gap between God and ourselves even through the most intensive and frequent prayers." Hence genuine prayer is humanly impossible![96] "This we should never forget when we pray: we do something humanly impossible; we talk to somebody who is not somebody else. . . ."[97] Tillich finds in St. Paul's pneumatology a liberating message: "We do not know how to pray as we ought; the Spirit helps us in our weakness: the Spirit intercedes for us with sighs too deep for words" (Rom 8:26). Tillich's reflections on this verse form the core of his theology of prayer. In the existential openness of the praying person the divine Spirit generates an ecstatic movement in which a transcendent "union of the human and the Divine" is realized.[98] Pushed to "the boundary of one's being" the praying person suddenly realizes that the Spirit prays in and through herself or himself.

> It is God Himself who prays through us, when we pray to Him, God Himself in us: that is what Spirit means. Spirit is another word for "God present" with shaking, inspiring, transforming power. . . . The essence of prayer is the act of God who is working in us and raises our whole being to Himself.[99]

> In every true prayer God is he to whom we pray and he who prays through us. For it is the divine Spirit who creates the right prayer. At this point the ontological structure which makes God an object of us as subjects is infinitely transcended.[100]

> It is the Spirit which speaks to the Spirit, as it is the Spirit which discerns and experiences the Spirit. In all these cases the subject-object scheme of "talking to somebody" is transcended: He who speaks through us is he who is spoken to.[101]

> God can never be an object, unless he is a subject at the same time. We can only pray to God who prays to himself through us. Prayer is a possibility only in so far as the subject-object structure is overcome; hence it is an ecstatic possibility.[102]

With these reflections Tillich proposes his central thesis on prayer: "The essence of prayer is the act of God who is working in us and raises our whole being to Himself."[103] In the Spirit-created prayer the human person experiences the divine Spirit as the ultimate subject and object of prayer. Successful prayer is "ecstasy in the Spirit."[104]

Having examined the Christological and pneumatological aspects of prayer, we are now in a position to pursue further the dialectical process of prayer described above. Surrender to the personal God evolves "under the impact of the Divine Spirit" into a contemplation of the transpersonal divine mystery. Response in faith and love in relation to Jesus the Christ expands into a grateful awareness of the Spirit of the Father manifest in the Christ event and in the progressive creation of the New Being.[105] Words sink into contemplative solitude. Tillich would describe this process in terms of a Spirit-created movement from *prayer* through *meditation* into *contemplation*.

Prayer is the central religious act of addressing the personal God within the I-thou structure. It could take the forms of "vocally praising the majesty of God," "adoring the divine holiness," "bringing the contents of one's wishes and hopes to God," "calling upon the divine name," or "speaking to God in words of thanks."[106] All these language-bound expressions of inner self-surrender are inevitable elements of prayer because "language is the fundamental expression of man's spirit."[107] Such expressions are also to be taken from revelatory experiences: "God Himself has given mankind names for Himself in those moments when He has broken into our finitude and made Himself manifest. We can, and must use these names."[108] "A name is never an empty sound; it is a bearer of power."[109]

However, there is a certain ambivalence in the use of names and forms in relating ourselves to God; they can "elevate our hearts to God" only insofar as they are transparent to the mystery behind them. Hence Tillich demands that "prayer may be subordinated to meditation."[110] Through meditation one "penetrates the substance of the religious symbols" in order to experience the transforming power inherent in them.[111] At the same time one delves into the depths of one's own self as well as into the deeper dimensions of the social situation.[112] While meditating on the Word of God one experiences the "grasping, shaking and transforming power" of the divine Spirit.[113] In the inner silence of meditation the Word of God strikes in the depth of our being and also in the depth of life situations.[114] The meditating person becomes increasingly receptive—not passive—to the Divine Spirit that leads the person to an ecstatic contemplation.

In genuine prayer, as we have seen above, the subject-object structure of thought is transcended under the impact of the Divine Spirit. This is the meaning of contemplation. It is "participation in that which transcends the subject-object scheme, with its objectifying (and subjectifying) words, and therefore the ambiguity of language as well (including the voiceless language of speaking to oneself)."[115] It could take the forms of "contemplating the mystery of the divine ground, considering the infinity of the divine life, intuiting the marvel of the divine creativity, adoring the inexhaustible meaning of the divine self-manifestation."[116] All this happens within deep silence, for "there is no contemplation without silence."[117] The words of prayer and the symbols of meditation transform themselves in the Spirit-created silence of contemplation. "One may demand that every serious prayer lead into an element of contemplation, because in contemplation the paradox of prayer is manifest, the identity and non-identity of him who prays and Him who is prayed to: God as Spirit."[118] In the Spirit-created silence of contemplation one becomes aware that the prayerful awakening of the human to the divine takes place within the inner-Trinitarian dialectics of life. Through contemplative prayer we are inserted into the power of the divine Logos, in whom "God speaks his word both in himself and beyond himself"; we are brought to the fullness of life through the Spirit "through whom the divine fullness is posited in the divine life."[119] To pray would therefore mean to let the Spirit pray in and through us:

> Better that we remain silent and allow our soul, that is always longing for solitude, to sigh without words to God. This we can do, even in a crowded day and a crowded room, even under the most difficult external conditions. This can give us moments of solitude that no one can take from us. In these moments of solitude something is done to us. The center of our being, the innermost self that is the ground of our aloneness, is elevated to the divine center and taken into it. Therein can we rest without losing ourselves.[120]

The process from personalistic form of prayer to ecstatic contemplation is not a one-way movement. In the actual evolution of prayer there is a to and fro movement: "Often a prayer which starts with addressing itself to God as Lord or Father moves over into a contemplation of the mystery of the divine ground. Conversely, a meditation about the divine mystery may end in a prayer to God as Lord or Father."[121] Prayer addressed to Jesus the Christ would evolve into contemplation of the mystery of the Father and back to invocatory prayer. Prayer as surrender to the Logos would evolve into a contemplative merging with the divine ground and back to encounter with the Logos. In this dialectical process the mediating force is the divine Spirit. Prayer in the Spirit is ecstasy in the Spirit.

Prayer and the Transformation of the World

The main concern of Tillich in his theological reflection is to discover the grace and demands of the theonomous process of transformation in all spheres of life in the world. His understanding of prayer can therefore be interpreted only in terms of a new relationship to the world. We shall now examine the effects of prayer on individuals, communities and on the creation of a new world.

The Spirit-created prayer has a healing power[122] on the human person because of "the elevation of the centre of the personality to God"[123] and "the reunion of the human spirit with the divine Spirit."[124] If "health in the ultimate sense of the word, health as identical with salvation, is life in faith and love,"[125] prayer could be understood as "a most powerful factor" and "a condition of God's directing creativity"[126] in the healing process under the impact of the Spiritual Presence. Prayer engenders in the person "the strength that overcomes the powers splitting world and soul,"[127] the strength "to accept oneself as accepted by God,"[128] in short, the "courage to be."[129] "Devotional life under the Spiritual Presence"[130] is "a process towards Spiritual maturity,"[131] "growth under the impact of the Spiritual power."[132] Tillich speaks of four 'principles of growth,' which could very well be understood as the dynamic factors which express the effects of prayer in the life of a human person: "Both freedom and relatedness, as well as awareness and self-transcendence, are rooted in the Spiritual creations of faith and love. They are present whenever the Spiritual Presence is manifest. They are the conditions of participation in regeneration and acceptance of justification, and they determine the process of sanctification. . . ."[133]

First, *increasing awareness*: Spirit-generated prayer does not strive after Stoic wisdom, but gives expression to a 'belief-ful realism';[134] it does not lead to an esoteric aloofness, but involvement in the "struggle of the Kingdom of God."[135] Prayer creates an awareness which "includes sensitivity toward the demands of one's own growth, toward the hidden hopes and disappointments within others, toward the voiceless voice of a concrete situation, toward the grades of authenticity in the life of the spirit in others and in oneself."[136] Second, *increasing freedom*: Prayer as ecstasy in the Spirit does not degenerate into stereotyped forms of piety or stagnated demands of the law. On the other hand it increases "freedom from the law, power to judge the given situation in the light of the Spiritual Presence and to decide upon adequate action, which is often in seeming contradiction to the law."[137] Third, *increasing relatedness:* Genuine prayer does not cause neurotic introversion or self-exclusion; rather "it drives towards a mature relatedness."[138] Prayer makes one experience "the impact of the power which elevates the individual person above himself ecstatically and enables him to find the other person."[139] Self-alienating loneliness is conquered by self-liberating solitude: "Love is reborn in solitude."[140] Fourth, *increasing self-transcendence:* Through Spirit-created prayer a transformation in the consciousness of the person takes place. "An elevation above average existence . . . is the most important thing in the process of Spiritual maturity. Perhaps one can say that with increasing maturity in the process of sanctification the transcendence becomes more definite and its expressions more indefinite."[141] As a person grows in Spirit-created prayer devotion connected with religious symbols may decrease, "while the state of being ultimately concerned may become more manifest and devotion to the ground and aim of our being more intensive."[142]

What happens to individual persons happens a fortiori to the believing community too. Tillich understands Spirit-created prayer as the "constitutive function" of the Church.[143] In worship "the Church turns to the ultimate ground of its being, the source of the Spiritual Presence and the creator of the Spiritual Community, to God who is Spirit."[144] The two factors of the Church's worship are Word and sacrament. Tillich emphasizes that both should form an integral whole on the basis of a contemplative culture in the Church.[145] The Church would then become "the place where the mystery of the holy should be experienced with awe and sacred embarrassment"[146]; only thus can the regenerative power imbedded in the Church be effectively felt.[147]

If prayer is not to end up as "an affair of the purely inner life,"[148] it has to be related to the theonomous dynamics of history. Tillich himself formulates this perennial question of prayer as the "problem concerning the relationship of the inner contemplative life, the prayer life, to the active life."[149] Genuine prayer as ecstasy in the Spirit enables the person to see the world *ecstatically,* i.e., to perceive it as the milieu in which the Spiritual Presence progressively creates the New Being in all realms of life. The contemplative elevation of the heart in silence and solitude engenders the vision and courage to participate in "the struggle of the Kingdom of God" in the world.[150] Prayer evolves in the dialectic between "the presence and the not-yet presence of the Kingdom of God."[151] Tillich would not advocate a "timeless contemplation of the timeless," but a radical openness to "the presence of the Eternal upon the crowded roads of the temporal."[152] Through prayer the Divine Spirit enables the human person to experience "the infinite depth and eternal significance of the present": "in every moment we stand in face of the eternal."[153] Hence Tillich affirms: "Praying means elevating oneself to the eternal . . . seeing time in the light of the eternal."[154] If this perspective is not upheld in prayer "the forward-looking eschatological fervour of primitive Christianity is paralyzed and the world-transforming aspect of the idea of the Kingdom of God disappears."[155] Hence prayer under the impact of the divine Spirit manifest in Jesus the Christ necessarily leads to transforming action in the world: "faith implies love, love lives in works."[156] Action out of contemplation is participation in the divine work of liberation "from the negative element with which historical creations are entangled within existence."[157] It is participation in the power of the New Being.

It is in this eschatological framework that Tillich interprets the meaning of the various forms of prayer. Through prayer of *supplication* "God is asked to direct the given situation toward fulfilment";[158] "the contents of one's wishes and hopes are elevated into the Spiritual Presence"[159] that breaks through the structures of existential estrangement and creates the New Being in all realms of life.[160] To pray means to look at the world as God sees it, willing "to accept the divine acceptance of prayer whether its overt content is fulfilled or not."[161] Petitionary prayer is personal insertion into the universal providence of God,[162] an ecstatic acknowledgement of "God's directing creativity."[163] Through prayer a concrete "fragment of existence" is "consecrated to the Divine" and thus made transparent to the New Being.[164] The hidden content which is decisive in prayer is "the faith that the person has in God's directing creativity."[165] Prayer of *intercession* is the concrete expression of the healing vocation of all within the Spiritual Community. "There is no greater vocation on earth than to be called to heal."[166] The one who supports others with a genuine concern in one's prayer becomes a priest for them.[167] "The prayers of intercession . . . introduce a change in the relation to the ultimate of the subjects and objects of intercession."[168] Prayer of *thanksgiving* is an ecstatic acknowledgement of the divine goodness and creativity. "Thanksgiving is consecration: it transfers something that belongs to the secular world into the sphere of the holy . . . ; [this] has become a bearer of grace."[169] Thanksgiving means also a responsibility to participate in the sufferings of others. "The fact that others do *not* have changes the character of our having: it undercuts our security and drives us beyond ourselves, to understand, to give, to share, to help.''[170] In all these forms of prayer the Spirit-generated dynamics makes the concrete content of our prayer increasingly transparent to the power and presence of the New Being manifest in Jesus the Christ.

An Indian Perspective

Especially in his later work, Tillich developed his theological reflections with a keen sensitivity to the rich forms of the dialectics between the human and the divine articulated in the diverse religions of humanity. Mircea Eliade remembers Tillich as saying that ''had he time, Tillich would write a new *Systematic Theology* oriented toward, and in dialogue with, the whole history of religions.''[171] In fact, at the base of his theological reflections we could notice a fountain of mystical experience that emerges out of the universal matrix of religions. Towards the end of his life Tillich did show a keen interest in the mystical traditions of Buddhism and Hinduism. Hence it is not out of place to look at his theology of prayer from an Indian perspective. Since this term has a wide range of meaning let me confine it to the understanding of prayer that is found in the primary classics of India's spiritual heritage, namely, Rig Veda, Principal Upanishads, and the Bhagavad Gita.[172] The concern here is to examine some of the areas in which an Indian Catholic theology of prayer is evolving and to explore how it could be enriched by Tillich's theological insights on prayer.

Unlike the Semitic religions, which uphold the inalienable dignity of the person, the responsible insertion of the individual into society, and the creative process of history, the spiritual heritage of India emphasizes the liberative significance of self-realization, the experience of unity with all beings, and the integrative process of cosmic harmony.[173] Hence in the Indian world view prayer is primarily oriented towards an ''ecstatic and integral view of the universe.''[174] The Vedic perception of *Rta*, the Upanishadic intuition into *Brahman*, and the teaching of the Bhagavad Gita on *Dharma* all point to the contemplative experience of one's being as an integral part of the whole.[175] This holistic understanding of reality is having a considerable influence on Indian Catholic theology today. ''What is called for is a conversion away from the quantitative, cybernetic view of nature to a more holistic, reverential one. On the agenda is a revolution of consciousness. For Christian theology this involves a twofold task: discovering the Divine within nature and restoring to human beings their position as children of nature.''[176] In this eco-consciousness prayer receives a cosmic meaning. ''Prayer is a supreme moment of self-realisation. This calls for an awareness of solidarity with the vegetation and animal kingdom, and the experience of harmony with all the planets and stars, especially with mother earth."[177] Through prayer "one experiences the whole creation as one's body";[178] one meets "God playing about us in the breeze."[179] A contemplative attitude towards creation is one of spiritual concern and ethical responsibility to protect the environment. Tillich's unitive vision of reality offers a valuable perspective for developing a Catholic theology of prayer with eco-sensitivity. With his ontological principle, "actualised as life being-itself is fulfilled as spirit," Tillich describes the entire cosmic reality in terms of a polarity and complementarity of the diverse dimensions of life.[180] "All dimensions are present in all realms of life."[181] At the same time there is an inherent movement of self-transcendence, which opens up the horizon of the Ultimate. By defining prayer as the articulation of this self-transcending dynamics of reality, it receives a cosmic dimension: prayer is ecstasy at the heart of reality, actualization of the ultimate concern that elevates and transforms all other concerns related to the world.[182]

According to Indian sages, what happens in contemplative prayer is basically a change of consciousness: transition from the phenomenal feeling of ego (ahamkāra) to the transcendental consciousness of the self (atmabōdha), from the pattern of understanding within the subject-object structure (vyāvaharika) to an intuitive perception of reality beyond the subject-object division (pāramarthika), from a fragmentary grasp of things to a holistic vision of reality.[183] Hence the paradoxical statement of the sage: "It is not understood by those who understand, it is understood by those who do not understand."[184] One of the four "great verses" of Upanishadic spirituality is *prajnānam brahma*, consciousness is brahman.[185] Prayer is awakening to the mystical consciousness at the depth of reality; this awakening, however, is ultimately a gift of divine grace.[186] This Indian understanding of prayer challenges Catholic theology to rediscover its mystical roots. Abhishiktananda (Dom le Saux), a pioneer of Indian Catholic theology, perceived this long ago: "India's experience of God is normally reached by the 'path that leads within,' the path which is 'without return,' as her Scriptures say, since it leads to the point where all distinction and all change is for ever transcended."[187] He clearly states that "the integration of the advaitic experience into his own faith is for the Christian a necessary task."[188] In his beautiful little book, *Prayer*, Abhishiktananda offers an Indian Catholic theology of prayer in terms of a "contemplative entry into Christic consciousness" and awakening to a "universal theophany."[189] The Christian at prayer discovers the divine Spirit "at the heart of being," the Spirit that calls out from within our hearts "Om! Abba!," transforming the advaita experience of non-duality into an experience of communion with God.[190] Tillich too has a mystical understanding of prayer. He rightly demands that the contemplative dynamics of prayer should take the praying person to a deeper level of consciousness, where "the innermost self is elevated to the divine centre" in which the human spirit can rest "without losing itself."[191] His reflections on the paradox of prayer, i.e., "the identity and non-identity of him who prays and Him who is prayed to, God as Spirit," are of great significance for developing an Indian Catholic theology of prayer in creative dialogue with the advaita traditions of India.[192] Tillich does not advocate a monistic subjectivism that destroys the human subjectivity; nor does he accept a dualistic personalism that objectivizes God almost to the point of idolisation and consequently reduces prayer to ritualism. He rightly demands that "the subject-object scheme of talking to somebody is to be transcended" under the impact of the divine Spirit that prays from within our hearts.[193]

In describing the evolutionary process of spirituality the Indian masters widely use the framework of *jnana-bhakti-karma*. *Jnana* is the intuitive perception of reality, *bhakti* means surrender of oneself in love to the divine Lord, and *karma* consists in transformative action. Through contemplative introspection "one sees the self in the Self through the Self," i.e., one sees oneself in the divine Self through the grace of the divine Self.[194] Further, "one sees the divine Self in all beings and all beings in the divine Self," or more exactly, "one sees the divine Lord in all beings and all beings in the divine Lord."[195] This spiritual vision of universal immanence is *jnana*. From within the heart of reality the divine Lord meets the praying person with the words: "you are extremely dear to me . . . I love you . . . surrender yourself to me and take refuge in me with your entire being . . . ; with my grace you will attain the eternal abode of peace."[196] In response to this divine invitation the praying person surrenders his or her entire being and life to the Lord; this total and unconditional self-surrender is bhakti.[197] Transformed through jnana and bhakti one enters the world with a new motivation for transforming action. One no more claims "fruits of action" for the "gratification of one's ego"; one works "with passion for the good of all," for the promotion of the "integration of the world."[198] Karma is active participation in the divine work of establishing dharma, harmony, and justice in the world.[199] In these three paths of spiritual realization the Indian Catholic theologians find a valuable framework for understanding the theological meaning of prayer.[200] The "principle and foundation" as well as the objective of prayer is "to see God in all things'';[201] this is the essence of Christian jnana (gnosis). This theonomous vision motivates a person to self-surrender to God through Christ the Lord, in whom the salvific Love of God was embodied.[202] The consequence is commitment to the liberative work of the divine Spirit in all realms of life.[203] Prayer thus evolves through a progressive integration of all these three factors. For a theological interpretation of this process Tillich's theology of prayer offers much help. We have seen above that a basic framework of contemplation-devotion-action is at work in his understanding of prayer. Through contemplation one experiences the transforming power and presence of the divine Spirit within oneself and in all realms of life. Out of this mystical perception evolves a personal encounter with the divine Lord, surrender in faith and love to Jesus Christ. This communion engenders a holistic vision of reality and an integral motivation to commit oneself to the "struggle of the Kingdom of God."[204] Tillich's theological formula, "faith implies love, love lives in works,"[205] offers an integrated understanding of spirituality.

The perspectives of Tillich and of Indian Catholic theology on prayer seem to converge on a basic intuition: God is the ultimate subject of prayer. "It is God Himself who prays through us, when we pray to Him."[206] Genuine prayer is a receptive process: it is letting the divine Spirit pray within us; it is listening to the divine-human *manthra* "Om! Abba!," which is "eternally prayed by the Son and murmured ceaselessly by the Spirit in the hearts of all saints."[207] This Spirit-generated process takes place not just "in the cave of the heart," but on the "battlefield of life"[208] where the "struggle of the Kingdom of God"[209] ceaselessly takes place. Prayer would then mean alertness to the challenges of *dharma*, to the demands of the Kingdom of God, which emerge from the divine Spirit that *groans* at the heart of the entire creation.

Notes

[1] Paul Tillich, *Biblical Religion and the Search for Ultimate Reality* (Chicago: University of Chicago Press, 1972) 80.

[2] Paul Tillich, *The Eternal Now* (New York: Charles Scribner, 1963) 86.

[3] Paul Tillich, *Systematic Theology*, 3 vols. (Chicago: University of Chicago Press, 1971) 3:119.

[4] Ibid., 3:95–96.

[5] Ibid., 3:168.

[6] Tillich, *The Eternal Now*, 99.

[7] Tillich, *Systematic Theology*, 3:188–93.

[8] Paul Tillich, *Gesammelte Werke*, 14 vols., ed. Renate Albrecht (Stuttgart: Evangelisches Verlagswerk, 1959–75) 7:131.

[9] Tillich, *Systematic Theology*, 3:202.

[10] Paul Tillich, *The Shaking of the Foundations* (New York: Charles Scribner, 1948) 56.

[11] Paul Tillich, *The Protestant Era* (Chicago: University of Chicago Press, 1968) 60.

[12] Ibid.; Tillich, *The Shaking of the Foundations*, 55–56.

[13] Tillich, *Systematic Theology*, 3:97.

[14] Ibid., 3:241–43; Paul Tillich, *Dynamics of Faith* (New York: Harper and Row, 1958) 117–18.

[15] Paul Tillich, *Christianity and the Encounter of the World Religions* (New York: Columbia University Press, 1964) 88–89.

[16] Sebastian Painadath, S.J., Dynamics of Prayer: Towards a Theology of Prayer in the Light of Paul Tillich's Theology of the Spirit (Doctoral dissertation submitted to the Catholic Theological Faculty of the University of Tübingen, 1978) (Bangalore: Asian Trading Corporation, 1980).

[17] Tillich, *Systematic Theology*, 3:86.

[18] Tillich, *Dynamics of Faith*, 9.

[19] Tillich, *Systematic Theology*, 1:186, 206.

[20] Tillich, *Dynamics of Faith*, 9.

[21] Tillich, *The Eternal Now*, 86.

[22] Ibid., 178.

[23] Tillich, *Systematic Theology*, 3:236.

[24] Ibid., 1:127.

[25] Ibid., 1:12.

[26] Tillich, *Dynamics of Faith*, 105.

[27] Paul Tillich, *Ultimate Concern: Tillich in Dialogue*, ed. D. MacKenzie Brown (New York: Harper and Row, 1965) 10; *The Eternal Now*, 103–4.

[28] Tillich, *Systematic Theology*, 1:127.

[29] Ibid.

[30] Tillich, *Dynamics of Faith*, 105–6.

[31] Tillich, *Systematic Theology*, 3:107.

[32] Ibid., 2:13; 3:132; Tillich, *The Eternal Now*, 23.

[33] Tillich, *The Eternal Now*, 23.

[34] Tillich, *Systematic Theology*, 3:223.

[35] Ibid., 3:228.

[36] Tillich, *The Eternal Now*, 22–23.

[37] Ibid., 23.

[38] Ibid., 38.

[39] Paul Tillich, *The Future of Religions* (New York: Harper and Row, 1966) 53; Tillich, *Systematic Theology*, 3:191.

[40] Tillich, *Systematic Theology*, 3:107.

[41] Tillich, *Biblical Religion*, 80.

[42] Tillich, *Systematic Theology*, 3:95; *The Protestant Era*, 57.

[43] Paul Tillich, *What Is Religion?* (New York: Harper and Row) 142.

[44] Tillich, *Systematic Theology*, 1:213; *The New Being* (New York: Charles Scribner, 1955) 136.

[45] Tillich, *Systematic Theology*, 3:112, 133; *Gesammelte Werke* 8:214–15.

[46] Tillich, *Systematic Theology*, 3:133, 224; *Dynamics of Faith*, 105.

[47] Tillich, *Systematic Theology*, 3:190.

[48] Ibid., 1:127.

[49] Ibid., 1:190–91, 258–59.

[50] Ibid., 3:116.

[51] Tillich, *The Eternal Now*, 23.

[52] Tillich, *Systematic Theology*, 3:112, 116, 118–19.

[53] Ibid., 1:110.

[54] Ibid., 3:112.

[55] Ibid., 3:135.

[56] Tillich, *The Eternal Now*, 104.

[57] Ibid.

[58] Tillich, *Systematic Theology*, 1:113.

[59] Tillich, *The Eternal Now*, 98.

[60] Ibid., 88; Tillich, *Systematic Theology*, 1:110.

[61] Tillich, *The Eternal Now*, 90.

[62] Ibid., 95.

[63] Ibid., 99.

[64] Tillich, *Systematic Theology*, 1:112.

[65] Tillich, *The Eternal Now*, 103–4.

[66] Tillich, *Systematic Theology*, 1:113; 3:130–31; *Dynamics of Faith*, 12–13.

[67] Tillich, *Biblical Religion*, 26.

[68] Tillich, *Systematic Theology*, 1:223.

[69] Ibid., 3:134–35.

[70] Tillich, *Dynamics of Faith*, 42–43.

[71] Tillich, *Systematic Theology*, 1:213; *Theology of Culture* (New York: Oxford University Press, 1972) 132.

[72] Tillich, *Systematic Theology*, 1:61.

[73] Ibid., 1:245.

[74] Paul Tillich, *Love, Power and Justice: Ontological Analyses and Ethical Applications* (New York: Oxford University Press, 1974) 109.

[75] Tillich, *Systematic Theology*, 1:127.

[76] Ibid., 1:251; 3:290.

[77] Ibid., 2:175–76; 3:290.

[78] Ibid., 3:290.

[79] Ibid., 1:151; Tillich, *Dynamics of Faith*, 97.

[80] Tillich, *The New Being*, 99–100.

[81] Tillich, *Systematic Theology*, 3:117.

[82] Ibid., 3:289.

[83] Tillich, *The Eternal Now*, 91.

[84] Tillich, *Systematic Theology*, 3:117.

[85] Ibid., 2:134–35; Tillich, *The Eternal Now*, 23–24.

[86] Tillich, *Systematic Theology*, 1:250–51; *Dynamics of Faith*, 14.

[87] Tillich, *Biblical Religion*, 82–83.

[88] Tillich, *Systematic Theology*, 1:272.

[89] Tillich, *The Eternal Now*, 178.

[90] Tillich, *Systematic Theology*, 1:271; *The New Being*, 137; *Shaking of the Foundations*, 43.

[91] Tillich, *Systematic Theology*, 3:120.

[92] Tillich, *Biblical Religion*, 81.

[93] Tillich, *Gesammelte Werke*, 8:69; Paul Tillich, *Ergänzungs-und Nachschlagsbände zu den Gesammelten Werken*, ed. Ingeborg C. Henel (Stuttgart: Evangelisches Verlagswerk, 1971ff.) 1:214-16; *The Courage to Be* (London: Collins, 1973) 183.

[94] Tillich, *Systematic Theology*, 1:127.

[95] Tillich, *Biblical Religion*, 83.

[96] Tillich, *The New Being*, 137.

[97] Ibid.

[98] Tillich, *Systematic Theology*, 3:129; *The Eternal Now*, 24.

[99] Tillich, *The New Being*, 137–38.

[100] Tillich, *Biblical Religion*, 81.

[101] Tillich, *Systematic Theology*, 3:192.

[102] Ibid., 3:120.

[103] Tillich, *The New Being*, 138.

[104] Tillich, *Systematic Theology*, 3:119.

[105] Tillich, *The Protestant Era*, 112.

[106] Tillich, *Systematic Theology*, 1:267, 272; 3:190; *The Eternal Now*, 92–93, 179.

[107] Tillich, *Systematic Theology*, 3:124.

[108] Tillich, *The Eternal Now*, 99.

[109] Ibid., 93.

[110] Tillich, *Systematic Theology*, 3:235.

[111] Ibid., 3:202.

[112] Ibid., 3:119; *Gesammelte Werke*, 4:82–83.

[113] Tillich, *Systematic Theology*, 1:124, 127.

[114] Tillich, *The New Being*, 118.

[115] Tillich, *Systematic Theology*, 3:192.

[116] Ibid., 3:289.

[117] Ibid., 3:192.

[118] Ibid.

[119] Ibid., 1:251.

[120] Tillich, *The Eternal Now*, 24.

[121] Tillich, *Systematic Theology*, 1:289.

[122] Tillich, *The Eternal Now*, 63, 115.

[123] Tillich, *Systematic Theology*, 1:127.

[124] Ibid., 3:280.

[125] Ibid.

[126] Ibid., 1:267.

[127] Tillich, *The Eternal Now*, 153.

[128] Tillich, *Systematic Theology*, 2:178–79.

[129] Tillich, *The Courage to Be*, 180–81.

[130] Tillich, *Systematic Theology*, 3:235.

[131] Ibid., 3:231.

[132] Ibid., 3:232.

[133] Ibid., 3:233.

[134] Tillich, *The Protestant Era*, 76–78, 216.

[135] Tillich, *Systematic Theology*, 3:381.

[136] Ibid., 3:232.

[137] Ibid.

[138] Ibid., 3:234.

[139] Ibid.

[140] Tillich, *The Eternal Now,* 24.

[141] Tillich, *Systematic Theology,* 3:236.

[142] Ibid., 3:210, 237.

[143] Ibid., 3:188–93.

[144] Ibid., 3:190.

[145] Tillich, *The Eternal Now,* 99–100.

[146] Ibid.

[147] Tillich, *Systematic Theology,* 3:168.

[148] Tillich, *The Protestant Era,* 177.

[149] Tillich, *Ultimate Concern,* 201.

[150] Tillich, *Systematic Theology,* 3:381.

[151] Ibid., 3:390–91.

[152] Tillich, *The Protestant Era,* 33; *The Eternal Now,* 24–25.

[153] Tillich, *The Protestant Era,* 78; *Systematic Theology,* 3:395.

[154] Tillich, *The Eternal Now,* 122–23.

[155] Tillich, *The Protestant Era,* 177–78.

[156] Tillich, *Dynamics of Faith,* 115.

[157] Tillich, *Systematic Theology,* 3:397.

[158] Ibid., 1:267.

[159] Ibid., 3:191.

[160] Ibid., 2:176–80.

[161] Ibid., 3:279–80; 2:178–79.

[162] Ibid., 1:266–67.

[163] Ibid.

[164] Ibid., 1:267, 272.

[165] Ibid.

[166] Tillich, *The Eternal Now,* 64.

[167] Ibid., 82–83, 115.

[168] Tillich, *Systematic Theology,* 3:191.

[169] Tillich, *The Eternal Now,* 179.

[170] Ibid., 45.

[171] Tillich, *The Future of Religions,* 31.

[172] An authentic sourcebook of Indian spirituality is Raimundo Panikkar, *Mantramanjari, the Vedic Experience* (London: Darton, Longman and Todd, 1979). See also Mariasusai Dhavamony, S.J., "Hindu Meditation," *Studia Missionalia* 25 (1976) 115–86; "Hindu Prayer," *Studia Missionalia* 24 (1975) 185–222; Ignatius Puthiadam, S.J., *Endlos ist die Zeit in Deinen Händen: Mit den Hindus beten* (Kevelaer: Butzon and Bercker, 1978) 19–68.

[173] Bede Griffiths, *The Marriage of East and West* (London: Collins, 1983) 46–100; Francis X. D'Sa, S.J., *Gott der Dreieine und der All-Ganze* (Düsseldorf: Patmos, 1987) 37–58; Sebastian Painadath, S.J., "Dynamics of a Culture of Dialogue," in *Bread and Breath*, ed. T. K. John (Anand, India: Gujerat Sahitya Prakash, 1991) 279–91.

[174] Panikkar, *Mantramanjari*, 114.

[175] Sebastian Painadath, S.J., "Mukti, the Hindu Notion of Liberation," in *World Religions and Human Liberation*, ed., Dan Cohn-Sherbok (New York: Orbis Books, 1992) 63–77.

[176] Sebastian Kappen, S.J., "The Asian Search for a Liberative Theology," in *Bread and Breath*, 105.

[177] D. S. Amalorpavadass, "Prayer within the New World Vision," *Praying Seminar*, ed. D. S. Amalorpavadass (Bangalore: NBCLC, 1982) 42.

[178] Swami Amaldas, *Yesu Abba Consciousness: Method of a Christian Yogic Meditation* (Bangalore: Asian Trading Corporation, 1982) 8.

[179] Anthony de Mello, S.J., *Sadhana, a Way to God* (Anand, India: Gujerat Sahitya Prakash, 1978) 46.

[180] Tillich, *Systematic Theology*, 1:249.

[181] Ibid., 3:15–28.

[182] See above, "Prayer as Ecstasy at the Heart of Reality."

[183] Panikkar, *Mantramanjari*, 669–74; Swami Nikhilananda, *Self Knowledge* (Madras: Sri Ramakrishna Math, 1947); Swami Sivananda, *Sadhana* (Shivanandanagar, India: Divine Life Society, 1985) 24–62; Bede Griffiths, *Return to the Centre* (London: Collins, 1976) 129–36.

[184] Kena Upanishad 2.3.

[185] Aitareya Upanishad 3.3.3.

[186] Bhagavad Gita 18.56, 58, 62; 11.8.

[187] Abhishiktananda, *Saccidananda: A Christian Approach to Advaitic Experience* (Delhi: ISPCK, 1974) 95.

[188] Ibid., 47. Abhishiktananda, *Towards the Renewal of the Indian Church* (Bangalore: Dharmaram, 1970) 10–14.

[189] Abhishiktananda, *Prayer* (Delhi: ISPCK, 1972) 14–28.

[190] Ibid., 65–70; *Saccidananda*, 77–102.

[191] Tillich, *The Eternal Now*, 24.

[192] Tillich, *Systematic Theology*, 3:192.

[193] Ibid. For a detailed study see Sebastian Painadath, S.J., *Das geistgetragene Gebet: Ansätze für eine systematische Theologie des Gebetes im Rahmen der Pneumatologie Paul Tillichs,* Vortrag zur Jahrestagung der deutschen Paul-Tillich-Gesellschaft, 1983 (Hofgeismar: Evangelische Akademie, 1984).

[194] Bhagavad Gita 13.25; 11.8; 18.56.

[195] Ibid., 6.29–30; 9.6; 18.61. For a theological reflection on the mysticism of the Gita see Sebastian Painadath, S.J., "Die Bhagavad Gita und christliche Spiritualität," in *Bhagavad Gita, Wege und Weisungen,* trans. Peter Schreiner (Zürich: Benziger, 1991) 189–223.

[196] Bhagavad Gita 18.64–66, 62, 56. Bhagavad Purana 2.3; 1.68.

[197] Bhagavad Gita 12.6–12; 9.27; 18.54–58, 62, 66. Robert Zaehner, *The Bhagavad Gita* (Oxford: Clarendon, 1969) 26–28.

[198] Bhagavad Gita 2.47–50; 3.20, 25; 6.1; 12.13. Sebastian Painadath, S.J., "Bhagavad Gita's Vision of Liberative Action," *Towards an Indian Theology of Liberation,* ed. Paul Puthenangady (Bangalore: NBCLC, 1986) 49–65.

[199] Bhagavad Gita 4.7–8. Mary Corona, "A New Society according to Bhagavad Gita," *Indian Church in the Struggle for a New Society,* ed. D. S. Amalorpavadass (Bangalore: NBCLC, 1981) 331–35.

[200] Various Indian theologians offer their reflections on jnana, bhakti, and karma in two books: Amalorpavadass, *Praying Seminar,* 156–246; D. S. Amalorpavadass, *Indian Christian Spirituality* (Bangalore: NBCLC, 1982) 119–82. For a theological synthesis of these three spiritual paths see Sebastian Painadath, S.J., "Towards an Indian Christian Spirituality in the Context of Religious Pluralism," *Indian Journal of Spirituality,* 4 (1991) 299–311.

[201] Ignatius of Loyola, *The Spiritual Exercises,* 23, 230–37; Meister Eckhart, *Sermons,* in *Breakthrough,* ed. Matthew Fox (New York: Image Books, 1980) 75–77, 238–45.

[202] Ignatius of Loyola, *The Spiritual Exercises,* 98, 234.

[203] For an Indian "spirituality of liberation," see Sebastian Painadath, S.J., "Contemplation and Liberative Action," *Vidyajyoti* 52 (1988) 210–23.

[204] Tillich, *Systematic Theology,* 3:381; Painadath, *Dynamics of Prayer,* 247–50.

[205] Tillich, *Dynamics of Faith,* 115.

[206] Tillich, *The New Being,* 137.

[207] Abhishiktananda, *Saccidananda,* 190. *Prayer,* 65–70.

[208] Taitiriya Upanishad, 2:1. Bhagavad Gita, 1:1.

[209] ST 3:381.

Tillich and Contemporary Spirituality

Frederick J. Parrella

The "century of the Church," aptly characterized by a German Lutheran bishop after World War I, is now definitively over.[1] Within the Catholic Church, so concerned with its external structures and its relationship to the world for much of the twentieth century, the Second Vatican Council was the culmination of our period's ecclesiocentrism. This inspired Karl Rahner at the conclusion of the council to inquire in dismay if the Church had nothing more to discuss than how she understands herself.[2] By the 1970s, the "sterile Church-centeredness"[3] had been overshadowed by more foundational questions of faith, by new Christologies, by liberation theology and questions of peace and justice.[4] As the new century and new millennium approaches, spirituality, at both the popular and scholarly levels, has become a much more powerful focal point of Catholic concern.[5] Of course, the interest in spirituality goes far beyond the bounds of Catholicism, even though the word itself has a unique Catholic history. On the contrary, it has become a truly *catholic* issue in recent decades with the term now part of Protestant, non-Christian, and secular vocabulary.[6]

This essay will explore the adaptability and usefulness of Paul Tillich's theology in understanding the new renaissance in spirituality, especially in the Catholic tradition. Since the topic of spirituality in all its present diversity requires more space than the confines of this essay, my objective here is twofold: first, to discuss briefly the current wave in spirituality and Tillich's profound concern for the spiritual situation which informed all of his theology; second, to present some characteristics of a Tillichian spirituality that will direct and guide a modern Christian's understanding of life in the Spirit, especially for Catholics in the post-Vatican II era. In order to understand the relation between Tillich's theology and Catholic spirituality today, we must begin by examining the dramatic evolution of the term *spirituality* to its present expanded ecumenical use and by analyzing the historical and cultural conditions at the genesis of the current "turn to spirituality." In insisting on looking at the signs of the times, the Second Vatican Council taught Catholic theology that it cannot exist above history and culture. Catholicism's greatest strengths as well as its most serious weaknesses are mirrored in the culture in which it lives, and hence the theology that serves the Church has much to learn from its time and place. Spirituality must by its very nature be concrete and experiential since we can seek to fathom God's mystery and respond to the longing in our hearts for the divine only in our own cultural forms. In simple terms, God meets us where God finds us.

The Present Turn to Spirituality

The meaning of the term "spirituality" is hardly self-evident. Few terms are as polysemous in the culture and in the religious and theological milieu today as "spirituality." Karl Rahner describes it as "a mysterious and tender thing."[7] Although programs are devoted to its study, spirituality as an area of academic interest is marked by a distinct difference: it is not simply an objective discipline *alongside of* others such as the study of the Gospels, Christology, or a theology of sacraments. It is by nature a "participative" discipline, described by Sandra Schneiders as one which deals with "spiritual experience as such, not merely with ideas about or principles governing such experience."[8] Spirituality is less concerned with the object of study than with the subjective student, less interested in the doctrinal or moral content of faith than the eyes through which faith is understood and received within the self. Virtually all of its students have come to the discipline of spirituality as a result of their own personal spiritual journey and have as their final goal some aspect of praxis, some pastoral work in which they help in others' spiritual growth.[9]

Different reasons have been suggested for the current cultural and theological interest in spirituality. A steady erosion of the objective order of truth initiated in the post-Enlightenment world of Western philosophy has led to a loss of innocence about objective certainty, whether doctrinal or scientific. In this light, the movement to a post-critical theology proposes, in Avery Dulles's words, that "the contents of faith are known not merely by detached observation but by indwelling and participation, somewhat as we know our own bodies with its powers and weaknesses."[10] Twentieth-century advances in psychology, especially in the works of Freud and Jung, made it possible for modern individuals to discover a new and more creative personal interiority than they had experienced before. This discovery often propelled them on a spiritual journey beyond their own traditional theological paths to spiritual perfection.[11] With the cultural revolution of the 1960s, the outburst of popular interest in non-Western religions and spirituality—Hinduism, Buddhism, Taoism, and Sufi mysticism—inspired many to search for lost dimensions in their own Christian tradition in and through the spiritual traditions of others. Some Christians left their home in the Churches only to return again to their faith—not simply to the institutional faith as they had known it but to a new, deeply experiential commitment to the healing and transforming message of the gospel.[12] The rise of a well-educated class of lay people in American Churches, especially in post-conciliar Catholicism, created more critical minds and hearts searching for both a deeper intellectual foundation and a personal connection with their inherited faith. Many of these people, experiencing both a fresh enthusiasm and excitement over faith and its possibilities and anxiety and uncertainty at the same time, were inspired to inquire more deeply into the meaning of faith and the nature of spiritual life.

Finally, the shallowness of modern culture, especially its translation of the qualitative and spiritual dimension of life to the quantity of one's possessions, the pursuit of material pleasures, and the drive for power and security, took its own toll on many human hearts. Put differently, the utilitarianism of life, its continual purposive drive, swallowed up the realm of meaning and the significance of human existence for many. Because of the pressures and isolation of contemporary society, people were forced, consciously or not, to make their own fulfillment a full-time vocation without the usual support of a traditional community, its cultural mores and moral norms. As Philip Rieff suggests, the modern individual who once felt confined inside a Church now "feels trapped in something like a zoo of separate cages," where the outside world is often constituted as one vast and threatening stranger.[13] In an age of radical transition in which the collective symbols no longer structure and order everyday life, people are forced back onto their own spiritual resources to discover the worthwhileness of life. In Ernest Becker's terms, with the decline of "spiritual ideologies" which made everyone great and small a "cosmic hero," many had no choice but to search for their own "individual ideolog[ies] of justification."[14] Thus, the new "spiritual wave" is both a cry of pain and a search for new wholeness and new depth, a quest for a different self-understanding and new and more inclusive, less rigidly structured and hierarchical forms of community. In short, it is an effort by all people—Christians, non-Christians, non-believers—to return home to transcendence in all of its mystery and simplicity.

Given the wide range of cultural and theological factors involved in the present spiritual renaissance, how is one to understand the term *spirituality* today? Until the Second Vatican Council, *spirituality* was almost exclusively part of the Catholic tradition. The word did not appear in any of the classical Reformed writings, and until very recently most Protestants preferred the older term *piety* (some used *devotion* and others, such as John Wesley, preferred *perfection*) to designate a Spirit-filled life of reverence and love of God.[15] In seventeenth-century Catholicism, dogmatic and moral theology became separate disciplines and moral theology was further divided into ascetical and mystical theology, describing both our ascent to God and God's action of grace in the soul. First popular in French Catholicism and often contrasted with *devotion* because it was "associated with questionable enthusiasm or even heretical forms of spiritual practice,"[16] *spirituality* did not come into common English usage until the 1920s.[17] In recent decades, the word has moved well outside its usual Catholic milieu to describe, in an anthropological sense, something that is available to every human person who seeks to live the full and whole human life. Departing from the traditional Catholic idea of the mystical movement of God to the soul and the soul to God, *spirituality* is now often employed to signify "the whole life of faith and even the life of the person as a whole, including its bodily, psychological, social and political dimensions."[18] Today, spirituality is studied as a component of all the great religious traditions, historical periods, and philosophical schools.[19] Thus, spirituality designates that constitutive part of the human person that searches for an integrative meaning and unrestricted significance to his or her particular life as well as to all of life itself. In John Macquarrie's words, ". . . fundamentally spirituality has to do with becoming a person in the truest sense."[20] As Ewert Cousins writes, "the spiritual core is the deepest center of the person. It is here that the person is open to the transcendent dimension; it is here that the person experiences ultimate reality."[21]

Since *spirituality* is used ecumenically in all religious traditions and is applied to the secular sphere as well, it is perhaps more accurate to speak of spiritualities rather than a single spirituality. Of course, the renewed interest in spirituality also vibrates within its original home, the Catholic tradition. Along with the adaptation of the word *spirituality* beyond Catholicism, the meaning of Catholic spirituality has undergone an enormous shift from the era, more than half a century ago, of Neo-Scholastic manuals on the discipline of Christian holiness and perfection by theologians such as Tanquerey and Garrigou-Lagrange.[22] After the Second Vatican Council, both the style and the substance of American Catholic spirituality underwent dramatic changes. With the virtual collapse of the pre-Vatican II devotional system, including novenas, benediction, private Masses, and the like, Catholic spirituality became much less distinctively Roman Catholic, less focused *in* and *on* the Church and less prescribed and structured by its authority. As Catholics read the Bible for the first time, listened to the liturgy in their own tongue, attended marriage encounters and cursillos, joined civil rights and peace marches, their spirituality became more scripturally grounded, more personal (not private), more communal, experiential, and humanistic. Most important, perhaps, Catholics unearthed sources of spiritual growth and richness not specifically Catholic, or even Christian or religious at all.[23]

The new wave of Catholic spirituality has also been marked by a renewed enthusiasm for the sacramental and the liturgical, by a quest for new prayer forms and smaller, nurturing Christian communities, by an ecumenical concern, and, perhaps most importantly, by its commitment to social justice. At its heart, it searches not only for a new awareness of the self as a child of God but a radically different understanding of God and of the divine gift in Jesus and the Church. Many Catholics in America have encountered the "God of the poor, the human, simple God, the God who sweats in the street, the God with a sunburnt face."[24] They have lost their innocence about the God they once knew, the middle-class God of their catechisms who demanded conformity and obedience, and have discovered instead a God who shares in human suffering, a God who is God of all people. They have wrestled in their souls with difficult issues of public and personal morality and have trusted their consciences often before subscribing to the official position of the teaching Church. Since Vatican II, regardless of the popular confusion and polarization of attitudes within the Church, many Catholics have left the simplistic faith of their childhood and adolescence; even if some of them are less visibly Roman Catholic by their disaffection from the institution, they have grown to be more, not less, Catholic in the true and proper sense of the word. A "second culture" of "Spirit-filled" Catholics, in Eugene Kennedy's terms, has emerged, fewer in numbers but enthusiastic about their faith, and guided not by ecclesiastical norms but by the Spirit of God who makes them God's sons and daughters (Rom 8:14-17).[25]

Spirituality for the Catholic Christian, therefore, is life fully shaped and informed by the Spirit of Christ. The present turn to spirituality is an effort to rediscover the gospel message and the God whom Jesus reveals, to relive "the concrete fullness of Christian experience."[26] The final goal, as Saint Paul tells us, is to become a "spiritual" (*pneumatikos*) person, one who receives revelation through the Spirit and possesses the mind of Christ. Paul contrasts this spiritual person with the "natural" (*psychikos*) person, the individual who has no room for the gifts of God's Spirit and sees them as folly (1 Cor 2:9-16). "Spiritual" in the Pauline sense does not mean a soul distinct from body, but the inner core of the whole person, both body and soul, alive and filled with the Spirit of Christ.[27] Therefore, Catholic spirituality is, by its very nature, centered on the great mysteries of God as Trinity, God as historically present in Jesus, and God *with us* as Spirit in grace and community. Likewise, it is now "inclusive" of all that is human and earthly—that is, nothing lies outside of God's redemptive power and will.[28]

The new Catholic interest in spirituality has also had a significant impact on the style, structure, and direction of the theological discipline. In addition to their recent major work in textual studies and translations of the great spiritual writers and dictionaries in the spiritual traditions,[29] post-Vatican II theologians have made it clear that "only a theology that is rooted in the spiritual commitment of the theologian and oriented toward praxis will be meaningful in the Church of the future."[30] Spirituality as the experience of the full Christian life can serve, as Ewert Cousins has demonstrated, as a fruitful source for theological reflection.[31] William Thompson likewise describes his recent work as "a way of 'testing' the contributions of the experience and the language of Christian spirituality to the realms of theology and christology."[32] In light of Anselm's classic definition of theology as *fides quaerens intellectum,* one must note that in Tridentine Catholic theology the side of *intellectum* (theology) has dominated the *fides* (spirituality) element or at times has submerged the personal element of faith altogether. From the seventeenth century onward, the Catholic understanding of faith shifted from a personal "setting one's heart on" God to the acceptance of truths or beliefs about God and the world. This placed a strong emphasis on the cognitive and intellectual dimension of faith, and further separated the piety and spirituality of Catholics from the reigning theology within the Church.[33] This separation of the *intellectum* and the *fides* was also evident in our classrooms. A decade after the Second Vatican Council, a distinguished professor of Religious Studies suggested this memorable insight at a colloquium: "We teach our students religious studies," he said, "and they want religion instead." He believed that while most undergraduates in Catholic colleges and universities may not understand the philosophical categories and language of spirituality, they are searching for an overarching meaning to their lives. Some may have left their home in the

Church either through their own initiative or because of their parents' prior disaffection from the Church, while others have been raised in a neo-orthodoxy with a prescriptive divine order neatly presented for their acceptance. But all, in their own way and in their own time, are searching for an absolute meaning hidden within all the fragmentary and limited meanings of the world they know. They want this meaning grounded in the Gospels, intimately connected to the liturgy and the sacraments, and understandable in the tradition which nurtured them. They are searching or longing for God in cultural forms they can understand and accept.

Tillich and Spirituality

Before the word *spirituality* emerged beyond its Catholic boundaries to include other religious traditions as well as secular culture, Paul Tillich was deeply aware of the spiritual questions and the spiritual crisis of our times. While he was profoundly concerned with the alienation of people from the Churches, the spiritual crisis for him was much deeper and more complex than the simple rejection of traditional devotion or piety. This crisis was constituted by a loss of meaning which affected the whole of religion and culture, including its political, artistic, and scientific dimensions.[34] Anyone familiar with Tillich's writings should be little surprised by our culture's current turn to spirituality and some might even find Tillich himself a factor in the spiritual renaissance. Like the artist who predicts in aesthetic form the spirit and the texture of the next cultural generation, Tillich read the signs of his own times very well—suffering, meaninglessness, and a world threatened with demonic self-destruction on the one hand, and the shallowness of Christian symbols and the lack of courage within the Christian Churches to properly address this human situation on the other.

Tillich's existential pessimism, present in many of his writings from the 1940s and 1950s, was an indication of his abiding concern for the spiritual anxiety in the post-war experience of emptiness. "We have become a generation of the End . . .";[35] "The foundations of the self-sufficient universe have been shaken . . .";[36] "The catastrophes of the twentieth century have shattered even this limited belief in rational providence. Fate overshadows the Christian world. . . ."[37] He believed modern persons were experiencing their "present situation in terms of disruption, conflict, self-destruction, meaninglessness, and despair in all realms of life."[38] These people sensed "a tragic feeling about the limits of [their] spiritual power," aware of "the confusion in [their] inner life" and "the cleavage in [their] behavior."[39] Twentieth-century persons have "lost a meaningful world and the self which lives in the meanings out of a spiritual center."[40] People were seeking ultimate meaning itself only to discover that all along "it was precisely the loss of a spiritual center which took away the meaning of the special contents of the spiritual life."[41] This loss of a spiritual center grounded in the tradition of the Churches led Tillich to appreciate the values of secular humanist thought. In 1954, he wrote:

> For two centuries, men have experienced the disintegration of the symbols of ultimate concern in their particular religious tradition or they have experienced the change of their ultimate concern without being able to express the new experience in adequate symbols. But there is no vacuum in the spiritual life. . . . The language of those for whom their religious traditions had become obsolete was secular. The alternative was not another religion . . . but secular science, secular art, secular ways of life . . . .[42]

The roots of Tillich's concern for the spiritual emptiness and meaninglessness of modern life are many. Intellectually, his reading of nineteenth- and twentieth-century existential philosophy and his passion for art, sculpture, and literature presented him with a framework to grasp the religious situation and to translate it into his unique interpretive categories of belief-ful realism and *kairos*. Tillich's own personal life also served as a lens through which he could see with sensitivity and compassion the spiritual questions of his contemporaries: his experience of suffering and tragedy while serving as a chaplain in the German army in World War I, his involvement in German politics as a Religious Socialist, his concern about the rise of the demonic with National Socialism, his decision to leave his homeland and immigrate to the United States in 1933, and, finally, his reaction to the Second World War with the Jewish holocaust and emigration. All these experiences opened an abyss in the human condition for Tillich which he termed, in his first volume of serrnons, the "shaking of the foundations."[43]

Tillich's analysis of the human condition and the spiritual situation became the starting point of his theology and found a central place in his formal writings. His basic ontological structure of self and world emphasizes the importance of the subject as well as the object, courage and personal faith as well as being-itself, the quality of one's ultimate concern as well as the Ultimate itself, and the individual's reception of the New Being as well as its universal and objective power. For Tillich, theology as a formal science cannot be separated from the subjective, the historical, and the concrete since the theologian seeks the meaning not only of the universal logos but the concrete Logos which became flesh in history at a certain time and place.[44] Theology by nature is "answering" theology: "My work is for those who ask questions, and for them I am here," he said in an interview just before his death.[45] For Tillich, theology has to be existential, concerning itself with the concrete situation or the spiritual dimension of the person in the Pauline sense of *pneumatikos*. Thus, theology cannot speak about God without also speaking about human persons—it necessarily speaks of both spirit and Spirit. As Tillich says, "whenever an idea of God is enunciated, it is always in correlation with an interpretation of man, and vice versa."[46] On the basis of his concern for the modern spiritual situation as well as his theological method, one could argue that Tillich's theology is, in its deepest import, also a kind of spirituality. If this is the case, then the characteristics of his theology will also mark this spirituality. To construct a spirituality from Tillich's writings adaptable and useful to current Catholic theology and spirituality, I suggest the following four essential characteristics: a spirituality "on the boundary" in its form, ontological in its foundation, mystical in its direction, and sacramental in its substance.

A Spirituality "On the Boundary"

In his classic query, "Can the Christian message be adapted to the modern mind without losing its essential and unique character?," Tillich suggests the inevitable tension that must exist within a contemporary Catholic spirituality.[47] According to his method of correlation, the work of theology is mediation between the eternal message and the human situation. Theology "makes an analysis of the human situation out of which the existential questions arise, and it demonstrates that the symbols used in the Christian message are the answers to these questions." The substance of these questions is the person, an individual concerned about his or her being and meaning. This existential question is "the question he asks about himself before any other question has been formulated."[48] Thus, the foundation of a Catholic spirituality today must be grounded in a specific cultural milieu by observing the "signs of the times"; it cannot float above the present cultural, political, and economic situation nor be used to escape getting one's "hands dirty" by responsible action in the human community. Just like Tillich's method, a spirituality must carefully analyze the human situation so that the form of one's spirituality, one's response to God's invitation to transcendence, conforms to the specific culture in which one lives. Today one's personal growth in the Spirit must also involve the welfare of the whole human community. In Tillich's words, "The divine Spirit's invasion of the human spirit does not occur in isolated individuals but in social groups."[49] As Shirley Guthrie suggests, "True spirituality . . . is not found in the religious *or* in the psychological sphere but in the economic and political sphere which deals with such apparently 'unspiritual' things as hunger, human rights . . . social welfare. . . ."[50] Tillich's own involvement in the political situation before and during World War II testifies to his understanding that the personal presence of the Spirit and peace and justice in the world are intimately related.[51] For him, all Christians are called to be priests, physicians, counselors, and liberators for one another.[52]

In addition to his concern for the existential situation of the human spirit, Tillich's image of his life "on the boundary" creates a helpful model of a "Tillichian spirituality" for Catholicism today. For Tillich, the human person is "infinitely concerned about the infinity to which he belongs, from which he is separated, and for which he is longing."[53] Thus, Catholics seeking to grow in the Spirit today must live in the boundary tension between the finite and the infinite within themselves; between the small, struggling, clutching ego-selves and the rich, expansive children of God enlivened as spirits by God's Spirit; and between their human situation of confusion and struggle, of living in a world of such suffering, inequality, and injustice, and God's eternal promise to be with God's people. And perhaps, most of all, Catholics must live, as Tillich suggested more than a half-century ago, between Church and society, between religion and culture. As Catholics have recently found sources of spirituality outside their tradition, today they know that the spiritual life can no longer be a matter confined to the institutional *ecclesia*. To be spiritual in the full and proper sense of the term is to be part of both Church and society, religion and culture, to stand, as Tillich said, "between alternative possibilities of existence, to be completely at home in neither and to take no definitive stand against either."[54] For Catholics, the boundary image suggests that while the Church is their true home, they do not always have to wear with complete comfort its institutional garb; they are free to trust their own consciences as well as the teachings of the magisterium, and they must submit both their own actions and those of the community as a whole to the scrutiny of the gospel message.

If Catholic spirituality listens to Tillich's classic statement "that religion is the substance of culture, so culture is the form of religion,"[55] it will be pushed to the boundary line of secular culture. Always at home in the culture as long as the culture was the sacramental world of former times, Catholicism has been suspicious of the world and very slow to accept and adapt to secular culture from Trent until Vatican

II. Yet at the center of the Catholic world view remains the belief that *gratia perficit naturam*, that the natural world, the world *as* world, is made complete and is fully realized by the power of grace—not unlike Tillich's belief that culture and religion are inseparably linked, with every cultural form, no matter how muted or distorted, serving as a symbol of religious substance. Through his contact with the de-Christianized masses in Germany after World War I, Tillich affirmed early on that the "Christian substance was hidden . . . within a humanistic framework."[56]

Catholicism's present and future spirituality must likewise make its transcendent substance more accessible in secular political and social forms; it must be more culturally inclusive, and more attuned to its own tradition, which is truly catholic and of the earth. It must seek the depth of God's presence in every cultural expression, including the sacred in other religious traditions, insights into human nature and healing from medicine and the social sciences, new political and economic structures, and secular art and music. True to Tillich's boundary image, however, neither side triumphs over the other; thus Catholicism cannot sacrifice its transcendence to an idolatrous immanence, whether secular or ecclesiastical. Catholicism can offer modern people, either frantically in search of meaning or fanatically convinced of the idolatrous meaning they have, a spirituality which embraces the whole of their lives, a spirituality truly worldly yet pulsating with the transcendent—but only if it continues to have the courage, as Tillich did, to accept the possibilities of *gratia* in many different and perhaps surprising forms of *natura*. In Thomas O'Meara's words: "Although Roman Catholicism, since the end of the baroque era, has frequently suppressed acculturation and diversity, it endures *au fond* as a cultural religious phenomenon: not a mental or verbal articulation of belief, but a tangle of tangible presences of grace."[57] As a Protestant with a strong affinity for Catholicism, Tillich thus continues to remind Catholicism of an essential part of its tradition submerged in post-Tridentine theology and spirituality.

An Ontological and Mystical Spirituality

Ever since the encounter of the gospel message with the Hellenic world, Catholic theology has been grounded in metaphysics. Because Tillich created a comprehensive ontology grounded in Plato, Augustine, and medieval Franciscan philosophy, he tended to be a stranger both in the Protestant mansion of biblical research and preaching and the

Catholic estate of Neo-Scholasticism.[58] This Platonic-Augustinian-Franciscan world view was, of course, deepened and given modern shape and direction through later thinkers, especially Böhme and Schelling. Thus Tillich's passion for ontology made him popular with his earliest Catholic critics, even if they were more likely to see him through the lens of Thomas rather than Bonaventure as well as to underestimate the impact of post-Reformation philosophers on Tillich's thinking.

Catholic spirituality has always had an implicit ontology—to encounter God and the self wholeheartedly, to seek communion with the divine mystery, always contained an encounter with the fullness of being or with Ultimate Reality. This means a metaphysical system, no matter how implicit it is. Since God is at the core of both metaphysics and spirituality, a change in the style and the substance of metaphysics must also affect the spiritual life. The seventeenth-century separation of theology and spirituality resulted in part from the kind of metaphysics in the post-Tridentine Church. Tillich's ontological theology, applied to thoughtful persons of faith, can give a theological foundation for a living spirituality in which the way of the mind and the path of the heart, so long separated, can be reunited.

Once viewed by scholars primarily through existentialist categories, Tillich's thought is now accepted much more in the spirit, as Thomas O'Meara says, of the "romantic-idealist systematician" he was.[59] A "mystical ontology" is one of the most important characteristics of Tillich's thought, perhaps rendered all the more significant because it stands in creative tension with his commitment to a prophetic and kairotic interpretation of history. His special contribution to spirituality today is not in the unusual fact that, as a Protestant, he was an "ontologist par excellence"; rather it is in the *kind* of ontology he propounded.[60] By creating his theology within the Platonic-Augustinian-Franciscan ontology of participation, Tillich retrieves the ontological perspective found in the classical mystics and mystical theologians in which God is immediately knowable and the ground of one's self-knowledge. This theological perspective, which receded in formal theology from the fourteenth century onwards, reaffirms the paradox of God's transcendence and immanence and re-establishes the immediacy of God in human experience.

The fatal flaw in Western philosophy and theology, according to Tillich, was its objectification of God. In late medieval philosophy, especially in Scotus's definition of God as will and Ockham's nominalist thinking, God, who had been the center of everything, became the supreme individual, at a distance from other beings. In Tillich's words:

"God has to know things, so to speak, empirically from the outside . . . not immediately by being the center in which all reality is united." In this way, the unity of all things in God also came to an end since God's "substantial presence" within them no longer had meaning.[61] Although everything that becomes real for us must logically enter the subject-object correlation, when this logical structure also becomes ontological, God is made into an object of thought rather than the prius and ground of thinking itself. For Tillich, "God ceases to be Being-itself and becomes a particular being who must be known *cognitione particulari*. . . ."[62] With the self as an individual separated from God, the supreme individual, persons must necessarily begin with their own existence as the starting point for what is true and real; thus they are forced into what Tillich termed the "half-blasphemous and mythological concept" of proving the existence of God. When God fails to precede the subject-object division, the divine inevitably becomes an object, reduced to a conclusion of an argument initiated within a thinking subject. When God is not immediately present and knowable and instead is mediated and inferred from the cosmos, the absolute certainty of God is lost. The path to God in the finite mind must be completed by authority, which is non-rational, finite, and open to demonic distortion.[63]

Thus, a spirituality based on this cosmological approach to God presupposes separation and distance, not intimacy and communion. Prayer to an objective God "out there" reduces the mystery of God's providence to intrusion into the human situation and places divine omnipotence and omniscience into literal temporal and causal categories. This makes God a distinct being among other beings and, in time, transforms the divine from a distinct supreme being to the most irrelevant being. Likewise, from an ecclesiological perspective, when the unity of all beings in God comes to an end and is replaced by an ontology of individuation, persons "cannot participate in each other immediately in virtue of their common participation in a universal."[64] Authentic community, grounded in participation in a common center, is replaced by a society of individuals bonded by mutual interests. Catholic theology, which is struggling today to understand the Church as a *communio*, must realize that when the Church, like God, is made into an object, no authentic ecclesial community, existing as God's gift prior to an individual's moral decision, is possible. Likewise, the sacraments cease to be windows into God's gracious presence within a community of grace and become instead objective actions which appear as intrusions into an individual's life or serve a magical, not genuinely religious role.

Tillich knew that there is no way from the human to the divine, no path exists from the finite to the infinite, unless the finite in the first place is grounded in the infinite which permits the finite to ask the question of infinity. For Tillich, God is Being-itself, the power of being to resist non-being inherent in everything that has being. God is Being beyond finitude and infinity, transcending every being and the totality of beings.[65] Since God is not only the abyss of being but the ground of everything that has being, God is the source of a person's life and meaning. Every act of self-affirmation is rooted in the affirmation of Being-itself and manifests the ground of Being.[66] Since God is the ground and presupposition of the self, each individual discovers that there is "absolutely no certainty in which the certainty of God is not implicitly present."[67] According to Tillich, all human knowledge presupposes "principles known only in themselves" which are immediately knowable. These principles — the transcendentals of *esse, verum, bonum* — are "independent of the changes and relativities of the individual mind." As the "unchangeable, eternal light," they are not "created functions *of* our mind but the presence of truth itself, and therefore, God, *in* our minds."[68] Put differently, knowledge of God is not like a finite subject knowing a supreme object but a person knowing his or her own infinite depth and ground, what is closer to one than one is to oneself. Simultaneously and paradoxically, the person also encounters that Presence, which, as the abyss of being, infinitely transcends his or her individual life and every other finite reality. If one makes God into an object, this "God" is no longer either abyss or ground and becomes questionable and open to doubt. By establishing God as the ground of the self, however, Tillich renders the "element of ultimacy in God a matter of immediate experience."[69] This makes the mystery of the divine reality self-evident, immediately knowable, and the ground of an individual's self-knowledge.

The mystics and holy people of every century have not prayed to God as an object, to a God of theism, who reigns in some distant realm. Their relationship has been with God who embraces, grounds, and transcends both the personal subject and the objective world, a divine Presence as intimate as it is far away. In Tillich's words:

> If we speak, as we must, of the ego-thou relation between God and man, the thou embraces the ego and consequently the entire relation. If it were otherwise, if the ego-thou relation was proper rather than symbolic, the ego could withdraw from the relation. But there is no place to which man can withdraw from the divine thou, because it includes the ego and is nearer to the ego than the ego is to itself.[70]

Here Tillich's theological anthropology is akin to the experience of the mystics of medieval and post-medieval times. Bonaventure reminds the individual in search of God "to fix his attention first on being itself, and let him see that being itself is so certain in itself that it cannot be thought not to be." Likewise, Meister Eckhart insists that true poverty of spirit requires a person to have no place in the soul where God can act, for this would be to maintain distinctions. Rather, in the unconditional being of God, the "I" of the self and God are one so that this "I" can say, "I have been eternally, I am now, and shall be forever." Thus, the most intimate form of poverty is the identity of God and the human spirit. Finally, Angelus Silesius writes: "I am God's other Self, he can in me behold/What from eternity was cast in his own mold."[71] For Tillich, mysticism—the "union with the unconditional import of meaning as the ground and abyss of everything conditioned"—is not a distinct religious position of its own.[72] Mysticism exists in all living religion and is essential to it. Tillich's ontology is mystical, not merely because it is similar to that of the mystics, but because every encounter with God, with the Christ as the New Being, and with the Spiritual Presence, expresses the paradox of mystical experience in which God remains both the ineffable abyss of being and, at the same time, the ground of a person's essential and true self.

Tillich's approach to God, especially his concept of "God above God," has been criticized by both Protestant and Catholic theologians—for example, Nels F. S. Ferré describes him as "the most dangerous theologian."[73] Yet Tillich's theology and spirituality is really as old as Plato's, in which knowledge is the union of the knower and the known and knowledge and love are one. While Tillich created a theological system, each aspect of this system is relevant to those growing in the Spirit—his theology of personal self-transcendence, God as the inexhaustible depth of reality, sin as estrangement from self and world, Christ as the New Being who brings essential being to existence, the Spirit as God with us—all reach into the souls of modern individuals on the boundary between church and world, faith and its negation, authentic symbolism and idolatry. The goal of much of his theology was to explain life in the Spirit and growth in spiritual maturity to persons who were not seeking objective knowledge of God but union with the divine in knowledge and love.[74] I suspect this spiritual dimension of all his writings, not just the sermons, will endure long after his theological system may seem out of place. Two critics of an earlier generation, one Protestant, the other Catholic, saw Tillich's impact on spirituality very clearly. In Walter Leibrecht's words: "Tillich has been a mystical theologian in the classic sense of the phrase. . . .

His is a theology of the spirit. It is a mystical experience, if we do not misconstrue the meaning of this word, which underlies all his theology.''[75] And the Dominican Christopher Kiesling writes: ''In its basic orientation, Tillich's theological thought is closer to St. John of the Cross than to St. Thomas. . . . If we are looking for counterparts to Tillich's mentality in Catholic theology, we should not go to the books of dogma or even moral theology, but to the books of ascetical-mystical theology, and even to the writings of the mystics themselves.''[76]

A theology grounded in Tillich's mystical ontology offers individuals, whether in the Churches or not, a foundation for a spirituality free of the dualisms plaguing Western culture—subject and object, time and eternity, the finite and the infinite, the concrete and the universal, and the sacred and the secular. Tillich rejects both the Barthian divine no to the human situation as well as the Neo-Scholastic split between nature and the supernatural. Much closer to the spirit of Eastern theology, Tillich affirms that the Holy Spirit can bear witness to our spirit because such witness takes place not beyond our spiritual life but in our human response to the search for God. While he believes that we are God's children not through our humanity but through grace, Tillich insists that our quest for God, our capacity to ask the question and receive an answer comes, not outside of nor in spite of, but *through* our humanity. In his 1935 debate with Barth, Tillich asserts that ''without the antecedent God-likeness of man, no consequent God-likeness would be possible.'' Here the seeds of Tillich's concept of revelation as reason in ecstasy and his Christology as the appearance of the essential God-manhood in existence are clear. The Spirit of the Christ as the New Being even makes our knowledge of one another possible. As Tillich says: ''. . . we know nobody as well as Jesus. In contrast to all other persons, the participation in him takes place not in the realm of contingent human individuality . . . but in the realm of his own participation in God, a participation which . . . has a universality in which everyone can participate.''[77] Thus, without the prior image of God within each person, the witness of the Holy Spirit to our human spirit would make our understanding of God and of one another, as well as true communion among people, impossible or of no concern.[78]

This anthropology is relevant for the ecumenical dialogue between Eastern and Western religions. Tillich's interest in Eastern religions developed in the last two decades of his life, and was expressed in his 1957 dialogue with Hisamatsu Shin'ichi and his trip to Japan four years later. In a 1958 lecture, he foresees the end of Christian provincialism, insisting that other religions are ''realities, not only of power, but also of spirit.''[79] In his final lecture, ''The Significance of the History of Religions for the Systematic Theologian,'' he hopes that systematic theological study of the future might develop and take form in connection with a "Religion of the Concrete Spirit."[80] Tillich's religion of the concrete spirit and his ontology create a window in Western thought to the mysteries of Eastern religion and philosophy. Unlike many of his Western contemporaries, Tillich takes the metaphysical conflict as seriously as Easterners do. His anthropology can also be compared to a number of Buddhist thinkers who share his belief that in order to know the deepest reality of the self, a person must transcend his psycho-physical self or ego.[81] In Christian terms, the real self is the divine self or *imago Dei*—what Tillich would prefer to call the essential self—within each individual. This self has been hidden by layers of self-centeredness, a free separation in one's origins from the divine or essential self.[82] In the passage of time or the "history of forgetfulness," the eye of the human heart which sees and knows God has been covered over by this estrangement from one's true knowledge and vision. In the spiritual journey, one seeks the Sacred not as an objective someone or something strange but as one's estranged other and true self; as both knower and known, as, in Seyyed Nasr's terms, "inner consciousness and outer reality," as "pure immanent Subject and the Transcendent Object."[83] Here we might compare Saint Paul: "the Spirit of God has made a home in [us]" (Rom 8:9). Because the "Spirit of God explores the depths of everything, even the depths of God," when we are filled with the Spirit, we also "have the mind of Christ" (see 1 Cor 2:9-16).

A spirituality grounded in Tillich's mystical ontology offers to moderns an opportunity to grasp and be grasped by their true ultimate concern which is worthy of the ultimate and infinite within them. In theological terms, it offers them the living God who is both gracious immanence and absolute transcendence, a God not reducible to either a third-person object or a first-person subject. When authentic transcendence is lost, so too is authentic immanence; divine presence is replaced by objectification, intimacy by condition, and grace by law. In reaction to a third-person God, many people, without the alternative Tillich offers, have created a kind of first-person idolatry where the divine depth hidden within them is reduced to the pursuit of psychological well-being.[84] Since nothing finite can satisfy the infinite passion within for the infinite itself as both the ground of one's being and the inaccessible Otherness of God, it is no wonder, as the twentieth century draws to a close, that a spiritual quest vibrates within many persons, persons searching for a God beyond the immediate moment and for a self they have almost forgotten.

A Sacramental/Theonomous Spirituality

A spirituality based on Tillich's mystical ontology would also be profoundly sacramental. No matter how the spiritual life is expressed in a mystical dimension which transcends all forms, it remains grounded in the reality of the holy as present in some concrete expression; the "Spiritual Presence cannot be received without a sacramental element however hidden the latter may be."[85] Tillich's classic formula of Protestant principle and Catholic substance describes the tension within the sacramental reality mediating the Spiritual Presence. Catholic substance affirms that every person, place, or thing is capable of becoming a symbol or sacrament of the presence and power of the divine Spirit, while Protestant principle guards the transcendent, insisting that no specific manifestation of the holy can be identified with the holy itself. In an age where sacramental ritual has lost its intelligibility and mysterious power for many, a spirituality grounded in symbol and sacrament is essential: people need a concrete substance in and through which the Holy can grasp and transform life.

For Tillich, the decrease in sacramental thinking within Protestantism is alarming. "Sacraments have lost their spiritual power and are vanishing in the consciousness of most Protestants," he writes. In its place is the tendency to overburden the personal center by defining an individual's relationship with God through continuous experience and by making it dependent on individual conscious moral choice. In this framework, the Christ is seen as just another "religious personality and not as the basic sacramental reality, the New Being."[86] When the Spirit cannot be mediated through visible signs or sacraments, when the unconscious dimension of a person cannot be touched, the power and vitality of the Christian message is concentrated exclusively in one's deliberate moral apprehension, so that either the message or the consciousness suffers seriously. No wonder that more than a half-century ago, Tillich could discern "the longing of youth for new symbols"—in other words, searching for a sacramental world view, a world with windows to the transcendent.[87] The loss of a sacramental mode of thinking in Protestantism and the concomitant objectification and de-personalization of sacraments in post-Tridentine Catholicism has created a modern spirituality which has often been either a quest for individual self-realization (and spiritual good feelings) or an impersonal participation in the objective machinery of salvation.

With reality equated with rational control and conscious choice, prayer, worship, sacraments, and the moral life have lost their compelling power to be transparent and translucent for the divine. Without sacramental realities as windows to transcendence and authentic community, people become alone and isolated from one another, unable to find God within their empirical and self-contained world of spiritual effort, human interpretation, and abundant choice.[88] As Philip Rieff suggests about human choice, "without a parallel range of god-terms from which choices may be derived and ordered, choice itself may become a matter of indifference, or man will become a glutton, choosing everything."[89] These "god-terms" serve as windows which unveil the mystery of ourselves; they are the innumerable sacraments in which the divine Spirit can be embodied in our lives as meaning and wholeness. These sacraments, as Tillich says, are "grace-embodied," the "*Gestalt* of grace"—strange terms for Protestants, he admits.[90] Like all symbols which point to a reality beyond themselves while participating in the reality to which they point, they form what Tillich calls a "*Gestalt* of grace," a grace that is "actual in objects, not as an object but as the transcendent meaning of an object."[91] Put differently, Tillich insists that these "[f]orms of grace are finite forms pointing beyond themselves. They are forms that, so to speak, are selected by grace, that it may appear through them; but they are not forms that are transmuted by grace so that they may become identical with it."[92] Here Tillich misinterprets authentic Catholic sacramentalism, which is understandable in light of his Protestant heritage and his experience of an apologetic post-Tridentine Catholic theology. The spirit of Vatican II, more sympathetic to Tillich's understanding of forms of grace, reaffirmed that the *res tantum*, the ultimate effect of a sacrament, cannot be made final in any temporal expression and is an eschatological grace.[93]

Tillich's sacramental world view parallels much of Catholic theology's renewed interest after World War II in the sacramental principle as a way to define both Christ and Church. In a 1953 essay, Tillich sounds like Semmelroth, Schillebeeckx, or Rahner when he writes: "Christ can be called the *Ursakrament* of the Christian Faith. He is the source of all the sacraments in the church."[94] For Tillich, the sacramental view not only accepts the infinite within the finite; it also means that the finite "has in itself saving powers, powers of the presence of the divine."[95] While he was concerned about Catholicism's tendency toward "sacramental objectification and demonization," he also sought an alternative to an "unstructured, Gestalt-less Protestantism."[96] Grace needs a *Gestalt*, a form, to be present; it needs to be present sacramentally, that is, in an earthly form so that the things of heaven might be visible. This Catholic substance, of course, must also appropriate the

Protestant principle so that no form of grace can be objectified and transmuted into grace itself. But the Holy must first be present before its finite form can be subject to prophetic criticism. Christianity, says Tillich, "lives continuously out of its tradition and Protestantism lives out of the substance of the Catholic tradition."[97] He recommends that Christians "should strive for a fuller reception of the richness, spiritual profundity, and subtlety of the Catholic substance without weakening the critical power of the Protestant spirit."[98]

This sacramental world view—put differently, a visible system of compelling symbols which structure and order human life and personality[99]—is a vital foundation of a contemporary spirituality. In the ferment after Vatican II, the healthy iconoclasm (or better, the critical use of the prophetic principle) of Catholics hungering for change has now run its course. At this juncture, Catholics must take care not to lose sight of their own inner substance by a reductionist thinking that translates the transcendent into secular and psychological categories. Some Catholics, of course, the neo-ultramontanists, still prefer the heteronomous forms of faith and devotion of the pre-Vatican II Church. But many, weaned on both Vatican II and a thoroughly modern consciousness, are looking for new and specifically Catholic "guiding stars," what Tillich might call a "theonomous spirituality," a spirituality that is Spirit-determined and Spirit-directed. A theonomous spirituality sees the presence of the divine Spirit as essentially possible everywhere, not just in the confines of Church or doctrine. Simultaneously, this spirituality establishes a relationship *with* God *through* Christ *in* an ecclesial community whose communal forms and structures reflect a freedom and a transparency to grace. This spirituality provides a home for the pilgrim spirit where depth and meaning are given to one's life through the substance of liturgy and sacraments, doctrines and moral directives, the authority of the apostolic community and service to the world. A theonomous spirituality grounded in Catholic substance takes the Protestant principle seriously, so that all forms of neo-idolatry and heteronomy can be submitted to prophetic criticism. For this very reason, Catholics are free once again to adapt this substance to every new historical *kairos* and to bring with them those forms of piety, both old and new, which reveal the living and transcendent God. As for the old forms, Tillich even believed that the problem of saints needed re-examination by Protestant theology.[100] This sounds like a very good suggestion for Catholics too. Some older forms of piety and devotion, filled with the beauty and poetry of the ages and alive with the Spirit of God, were lost after Vatican II and should be rediscovered.

No less than the *kairos* Tillich saw so clearly after World War I, our own spiritual *kairos* beckons us to explore more deeply into what really matters. Weary of the "usual pastimes and drugs and features of the press," people once again are seeking that point where eternity and time intersect, a place and a substance in which transcendence beckons them out of their self-secluded lives. Because everything can be a revelation of God's kingdom, such a theonomous substance makes it possible for all persons, in the paradox of authentic freedom and unconditional commitment, to find a basis for justice, peace, and a common hope. These people are seeking to renew their spirits, no longer in isolation but in new and creative forms of community filled with both grace and a genuine, demanding discipleship; to rediscover their ties to heaven by living with greater reverence their connections to the earth which God created; to find a God who binds all people together as God's children rather than separates them by race, creed, gender, and sexual orientation; and, most important, to trust and to love wholeheartedly a God who unconditionally shares, accepts, and transforms human suffering so that no time or place or event exists, even in the worst of human conditions, where this God cannot be found.[101]

In this post-critical era, the spiritual dimension of Tillich's theology stands as a sign of hope and a "*Gestalt* of grace" for persons asking questions, for many in distress, for those seeking the simplicity of the Spirit. As epistemologies and theologies have undergone epochal changes, so too is our contemporary spirituality passing through a time of transformation and re-creation as it approaches a new millennium. Tillich's writings may be studied in the decades to come, less under the microscope of historical and philosophical analysis and more for a source of spirituality that is theologically rich, culturally inclusive, and profoundly human. His writings are a little like a theological transcription of the spirit of Taizé, through which many seek rest, reconciliation, and hope. In addition to his passion for philosophy, for culture and politics, for psychology and the existential human question, I imagine the romantic part of Tillich at home in the great medieval cathedrals—perhaps Bourges, that glorious "secluded chapel." Here, as "the light fails on a winter's afternoon," he may have sat preparing a sermon or sketching a lecture on art. Perhaps he was more than a little naïve in idealizing the theonomous period of medieval times, yet he always had a profound sense of what ought to be as well as what is. This sense inspired him, I think, to describe Catholicism in 1929, when the Catholicism of Vatican II and after was at least as unimaginable as a person landing on the moon, in this way:

> The Catholic Church . . . has manifestly been able to preserve a genuine substance that continues to exist, although it is encased within an ever hardening crust. But whenever the hardness and crust are broken through and the substance becomes visible, it exercises a peculiar fascination; then we see what was once the life substance and inheritance of all of us and what we have now lost, and a deep yearning awakens in us for the departed youth of our culture.[102]

This youth of both our "Catholic" and "catholic" culture still awaits us if humanity is to survive and grow in the next millennium.

Notes

[1] Otto Dibelius titled his book *Das Jahrhundert der Kirche* (Berlin, 1926).

[2] Karl Rahner, *The Church After the Council* (New York: Herder and Herder, 1966) 38–39.

[3] Yves Congar, "Do the Problems of Our Secular World Make Ecumenism Irrelevant?" *Concilium* 54 (New York: Herder and Herder, 1969) 21.

[4] The works of Edward Schillebeeckx, Karl Rahner, Hans Küng, Walter Kasper, Gustavo Gutierrez, and Jon Sobrino, among others, are well known.

[5] See Sandra Schneiders, "Spirituality in the Academy," *Theological Studies* 50 (1989) 676–97, for an excellent summary of the new wave of interest in spirituality both inside and outside of the academy. For a summary of the meaning of the term *spirituality*, see Jon Alexander, "What Do Recent Writers Mean By Spirituality?" *Spirituality Today* 32 (1980) 247–56.

[6] The term has worked its way into the business environment: see, for example, Dennis O'Connor, *Spirituality and the Workplace: A Position Paper* (Washington: Cathedral College of the Laity, 1988).

[7] Karl Rahner, "The Spirituality of the Church of the Future," in *Theological Investigations*, vol. 20 (New York: Crossroad, 1981) 143.

[8] Schneiders, "Spirituality in the Academy," 694.

[9] Ibid.

[10] Avery Dulles, *The Craft of Theology. From Symbol to System* (New York: Crossroad, 1992) 8.

[11] Ewert Cousins, "Spirituality: A Resource for Theology," *Proceedings of the Catholic Theological Society of America* 35 (1980) 124.

[12] The idea of leaving home and returning home is discussed in detail in Peter Berger, *The Heretical Imperative. Contemporary Possibilities of Religious Affirmation* (New York: Doubleday-Anchor, 1980) chapters 2, 3, and 4.

[13] Philip Rieff, *The Triumph of the Therapeutic. Uses of Faith After Freud*, 2d edition (Chicago: The University of Chicago Press, 1987) 5ff.

[14] Ernest Becker, *The Denial of Death* (New York: The Free Press, 1973) 160–62.

[15] T. Hartley Hall IV, "The Shape of Reformed Piety," in *Spiritual Traditions for the Contemporary Church*, eds. Robin Maas and Gabriel O'Donnell (Nashville: Abingdon, 1990) 202. See Alexander, 248.

[16] Schneiders, "Spirituality in the Academy," 681.

[17] For a brief explanation of its roots in French Catholicism, see *The Study of Spirituality*, eds. C. Jones, G. Wainwright, and E. Yarnold (New York: Oxford University Press, 1986) xxiv–xxvi.

[18] Schneiders, "Spirituality in the Academy," 682 and 679. See also Robin Maas and Gabriel O'Donnell, "The Theory That Undergirds Our Practice," in *Spiritual Traditions*.

[19] Crossroad's twenty-five volume series, *World Spirituality. An Encyclopedic History of the Religious Quest*, contains volumes on virtually every world culture, philosophy, and religion, whether historically alive or not. Volume 22, for example, is entitled *Spirituality and the Secular Quest*.

[20] John Macquarrie, *Paths in Spirituality* (New York: Harper and Row, 1972) 40; quoted in Alexander, "Recent Writers," 252.

[21] Ewert Cousins, "Preface to the Series," in *World Spirituality* 16:xiii.

[22] See Alexander, "Recent Writers," 255 n.5, or Schneiders, "Spirituality in the Academy," 686 n.43, for full references. Tanquerey divided the spiritual life into the ordinary and the extraordinary or mystical, with the latter reserved for the few. Garrigou-Lagrange, on the other hand, believed that mystical prayer was the goal of every Christian's life (Alexander, "Recent Writers," 249–50.) Thus, he prefigured *Lumen Gentium* in which all are called to holiness and was similar to Tillich in his belief that a mystical element is present in all religion.

[23] For a brief summary, see Margaret Hebblethwaite, "Aspects of Church Life Since the Council: Devotion," in Adrian Hastings, ed., *Modern Catholicism. Vatican II and After* (New York: Oxford University Press, 1991) 240–45.

[24] From the Nicaraguan *Misa Campesina*, quoted in Hastings, *Modern Catholicism*, 244.

[25] See Eugene Kennedy, *Tomorrow's Catholics, Yesterday's Church. The Two Cultures of American Catholicism* (New York: Harper and Row, 1988) in which Kennedy defines first and second culture Catholics.

[26] William Thompson, *Christology and Spirituality* (New York: Crossroad, 1991) 9.

[27] Schneiders, "Spirituality in the Academy," 681.

[28] Thompson, *Christology*, 4.

[29] In addition to works already cited, one must note the *Classics of Western Spirituality* from Paulist Press which contains more than one hundred volumes; *The*

Westminster Dictionary of Western Spirituality (1983) and *The New Dictionary of Catholic Spirituality* (1993) from The Liturgical Press.

[30] Schneiders, "Spirituality in the Academy," 677.

[31] Cousins, "Preface."

[32] Thompson, *Christology*, 14.

[33] See Dermot Lane, *The Experience of God. An Invitation to Do Theology* (New York: Paulist, 1981) 55–62.

[34] Paul Tillich, *The Courage To Be* (New Haven: Yale University Press, 1952) 61–62. See Paul Tillich, *The Religious Situation* (New York: Meridian Books, 1962). Written in 1926 and first translated into English in 1932, this work was an important analysis of the religious dimension of the secular.

[35] Paul Tillich, *The New Being* (New York: Scribners, 1955) 172.

[36] Paul Tillich, *Systematic Theology*, 3 vols. (Chicago: The University of Chicago Press, 1951, 1957, 1963) 1:163.

[37] Ibid., 1:166.

[38] Ibid., 1:49.

[39] Paul Tillich, *The Protestant Era* (Chicago: The University of Chicago Press, 1957) 193, 202.

[40] Tillich, *Courage*, 139–40.

[41] Ibid., 47–48.

[42] Paul Tillich, "Religion in Two Societies," in *Theology of Culture*, ed. Robert Kimball (New York: Oxford University Press, 1959) 178.

[43] Paul Tillich, *The Shaking of the Foundations* (New York: Scribners, 1948).

[44] Tillich, *Systematic Theology*, 1:28.

[45] Cited by Kenneth Bagnell, "Paul Tillich: An Interview," in *The United Church Observer* 27, 15 (November 1965) 24.

[46] Paul Tillich, *The Rediscovery of the Prophetic Tradition of the Reformation* (Washington: Henderson Services, 1950) 11.

[47] Tillich, *Systematic Theology*, 2:7.

[48] Ibid., 1:62.

[49] Ibid., 3:139.

[50] Shirley C. Guthrie, "Narcissism of American Piety: The Disease and the Cure," *Journal of Pastoral Care* 31 (1977) 228.

[51] Ibid.

[52] Paul Tillich, *The Eternal Now* (New York: Scribners, 1963) 115.

[53] Tillich, *Systematic Theology*, 1:14.

[54] Paul Tillich, *On the Boundary* (New York: Scribners, 1966 [1936]) 13.

[55] Ibid., 69–70.

[56] Ibid., 62.

[57] Thomas F. O'Meara, "Tillich and the Catholic Substance," in *The Thought of Paul Tillich*, eds. J. L. Adams, W. Pauck, and R. Shinn (New York: Harper and Row, 1985) 296.

[58] Tillich was especially interested in what he called the second way or second line in Western philosophy. In all of his writings, there is an undercurrent of this mystical second way of thinking and along with it a rejection of the more methodical mainline way—so much so that he makes this startling statement about Jacob Böhme, the seventeenth-century Silesian mystic: "If Protestant theology wants to penetrate the ontological implications of Christian symbols, it would do well to use the ideas of Böhme rather than Aristotle" ("Preface," in J. Stoudt, *Sunrise to Eternity: A Study of Jacob Böhme's Life and Thought* [Philadelphia: University of Pennsylvania Press, 1957] 7-8). See Paul Tillich, "Kairos and Logos," in *The Interpretation of History* (New York: Scribners, 1936) 123-29.

[59] Ibid., 300.

[60] Carl Braaten, "Introduction," in Paul Tillich, *Perspectives on Nineteenth and Twentieth Century Christian Thought*, ed. Carl Braaten (New York: Harper and Row, 1967) xxv, xxxii.

[61] Ibid., 191, 200.

[62] Paul Tillich, "Two Types of a Philosophy of Religion," in *Theology of Culture*, 19.

[63] Ibid., 14, 25.

[64] Paul Tillich, *The History of Christian Thought*, (New York: Harper and Row, 1968) 200.

[65] Tillich, *Systematic Theology* 1:235, 237.

[66] Tillich, *Courage*, 180-91.

[67] Tillich, "Two Types," 25; Paul Tillich, "The Philosophy of Religion," in *What is Religion?* (New York: Harper and Row, 1969) 39.

[68] Tillich, "Two Types," 13. (Emphasis mine.)

[69] Paul Tillich, *Dynamics of Faith* (New York: Harper and Row, 1957) 44. Tillich also states: "Immediacy and 'awareness' stand against the possibility of an argumentative knowledge of God. Awareness of God precedes discursive knowledge of him." In "Appreciation and Reply," *Paul Tillich in Catholic Thought*, eds. T. O'Meara and D. Weisser (Dubuque: The Priory Press, 1964) 308. Thus to say that God is "immediately knowable" does not mean discursive knowledge but human awareness.

[70] Tillich, *Systematic Theology*, 1:271.

[71] Harvey Egan, ed., *An Anthology of Christian Mysticism* (Collegeville: The Liturgical Press, 1991) 504, 298-99, 243.

[72] "The Philosophy of Religion," in *What Is Religion?* 90.

[73] From a review of *The New Being* in *The Presbyterian Outlook*; see Ferré's "Tillich and the Nature of Transcendence," in *Paul Tillich: Retrospect and Future* (New York: Abingdon Press, 1966) 9.

[74] See Tillich's treatment of sanctification in *Systematic Theology* 3:236.

[75] Walter Leibrecht, "The Life and Mind of Paul Tillich," in *Religion and Culture. Essays in Honor of Paul Tillich* (New York: Harper, 1959) 19-20.

[76] Christopher Kiesling, "A Translation of Tillich's Idea of God," in *Journal of Ecumenical Studies* 4 (1967) 708.

[77] Tillich, *Systematic Theology*, 2:116.

[78] Paul Tillich, "What Is Wrong With Dialectical Theology?" in *The Journal of Religion* 15, 2 (April, 1935) 141-42. Note Tillich's argument against what he knows some believe is "a pantheistic trend in my thought." In "Appreciation and Reply," 308.

[79] Paul Tillich, "The Protestant Principle and the Encounter of World Religions," in *The Encounter of Religions and Quasi-Religions*, ed. Terence Thomas (Lewiston, N.Y.: Edward Mellen Press, 1990) 61. Thomas's work contains the text of the 1957 dialogue; Tillich's *Christianity and the Encounter of World Religions* (New York: Columbia University Press, 1963) is well known.

[80] Jerald Brauer, ed., *The Future of Religions* (New York: Harper and Row, 1966) 91. See Terence Thomas for his interpretation of this often-discussed text in his introduction to *The Encounter of Religions and Quasi Religions*, xviii-xx.

[81] Frederick J. Streng, "Selfhood Without Selfishness: Buddhist and Christian Approaches to Authentic Living," in *Buddhist-Christian Dialogue. Mutual Renewal and Transformation*, eds. P. O. Ingram and F. J. Streng (Honolulu: University of Hawaii Press, 1986) 177ff.

[82] Tillich's doctrine of the Fall has also been compared to that of Hinduism and Buddhism in Leroy S. Rouner, "The Meeting of East and West: Paul Tillich's Philosophy of Religion," in L. S. Rouner, ed., *Knowing Religiously* (Notre Dame, Ind.: University of Notre Dame Press, 1985) 177-206.

[83] Seyyed Nasr, *Knowledge and the Sacred* (Albany, N.Y.: State University of New York Press, 1989) 3.

[84] See Frederick J. Parrella, "Spirituality in Crisis: The Search for Transcendence in Our Therapeutic Culture," *Spirituality Today* 35, 4 (1982) 296-97.

[85] Tillich, *Systematic Theology*, 3:122.

[86] Tillich, *The Protestant Era*, xix.

[87] Tillich, *Rediscovery*, 27; *Systematic Theology*, 3:121; *The Protestant Era*, 208.

[88] Parrella, "Spirituality in Crisis," 299.

[89] Rieff, *Triumph of the Therapeutic*, 93.

[90] Tillich, *The Protestant Era*, 209.

[91] Paul Tillich, "Protestantism as a Critical and Creative Principle," in *Political Expectation*, ed. J. L. Adams (New York: Harper and Row, 1971) 25.

[92] Tillich, *The Protestant Era*, 212.

[93] For example, see *Lumen Gentium*, 8, 35, 48-51.

[94] Paul Tillich, *Die Judenfrage—ein christliches und ein deutsches Problem*, cited and translated in Maxwell Johnson, "The Place of Sacraments in the Theology of Paul Tillich," *Worship* 63 (1989) 23–24. See Tillich, *Interpretation of History*, 263–64.

[95] Tillich, *Perspectives*, 147.

[96] Tillich, *The Protestant Era*, 94, 210.

[97] Paul Tillich, *Der Mensch im Christentum und im Marxismus. Protestantische Vision: Katholische Substanz, Protestantisches Prinzip, Socialistische Entscheidung* (Stuttgart and Dusseldorf: Ring Verlag, 1953). In this small work, Tillich suggests three elements in the Catholic substance: sacramental presence, unity in a community of love, and authority.

[98] Paul Tillich, "The Present Theological Situation in Light of Continental European Development," *Theology Today* 6, 3 (1949) 308.

[99] See Rieff, *Triumph of the Therapeutic*, 1–27.

[100] Tillich, *Systematic Theology*, 1:121–22.

[101] See John Dwyer's excellent treatment in his *Son of Man, Son of God. A New Language for Faith* (New York: Paulist, 1983) 180ff.

[102] Paul Tillich "The Protestant Message and the Man of Today," in *The Protestant Era*, 194.

Paul Tillich and the
Future of Interreligious Ecumenism*

Claude Geffré, O.P.

As is well-known, Paul Tillich would have wished to rewrite his *Systematic Theology*, taking into account the newly discovered importance of dialogue with the world's great religions. In any case, in the last lecture he gave, on October 12, 1965, just before his fatal heart attack, he expressed his conviction that the future of theology would depend upon a more intensive "interpenetration" of systematic theology and the history of religions.[1] His hope has been largely realized, and we can truly say that, in the last twenty years, whether in the Catholic Church or in the Protestant Churches, contemporary theology is striving to take seriously the challenge of religious pluralism.

If it is true that theology always exists in correlation with a given stage of culture, certainly the situation has greatly changed since Tillich was writing his *Systematic Theology*. The dominant occupation of his theology was the atheistic criticism of religion, coming from either godless existentialism, Freudianism, or Marxism. This is why he did not hesitate to exercise the specifically apologetic function of theology. Today, Christian thought must confront not only atheism and religious indifference, but the explosion of the religious quest, as seen in the vitality of non-Christian religions, the success of para-Christian sects, or the various forms of New Age religions. In this sense, it is legitimate to say that we have already entered a post-modern age.

In accord with Tillich's bold vision, we can no longer restrict the word "ecumenism" to the dialogue between Christian denominations. Some do not hesitate to speak of a new *planetary* ecumenism. We must agree with them inasmuch as the dialogue between religions coincides with the keener awareness of the unity of the human family and a more acute sense of the common responsibility of religions for the future of humankind and its environment. But it would be absurd to think that the new ecumenism makes ecumenism in the primary sense obsolete or secondary. Within Catholicism at least, the ecumenical dia-

* Translated by Madeleine E. Beaumont and Raymond F. Bulman.

logue begun more than fifty years ago has shattered a certain type of absolutism and has gradually promoted the dialogue of the Church, first with the other two monotheistic religions, and then with the great Eastern religions. The Declaration on the Relation of the Church to Non-Christian Religions (*Nostra Aetate*) promulgated by Vatican II is the charter of the new ecumenism; the meeting at Assisi on October 27, 1986, was, as it were, the consecration of this truly revolutionary attitude of openness. For some thirty years now, the theology of religions has become an important chapter of Catholic theology, thanks chiefly to the influence of Karl Rahner.[2] But, just as it happened at the outset of interconfessional ecumenism, once again we find ourselves stammering because it takes time to shed our old habits and to understand that frank and open dialogue does not necessarily lead to false ecumenism, that is, to religious indifferentism.

A widespread consensus exists today among theologians that any exclusive model for understanding Christianity must be abandoned, whether it be that of ecclesiocentric absolutism as found in some traditional types of Catholic theology or that of the radicalism of Karl Barth, for whom Christianity is the unique religion of grace. On the other hand, it is not enough to adopt an inclusive religious model (Christ fulfills everything that is good, true, and holy in other religions) to believe that we have thereby demystified the absolute character of Christianity as an historical religion. Indeed, a fundamental tension remains between the demands of equality and reciprocity inherent in true dialogue and the legitimate claim of Christianity to be the religion of the absolute and definitive manifestation of God in Jesus Christ. If Jesus himself is only one mediator among others and not God's decisive manifestation for all men and women, then we can seriously question whether we have not already discarded the faith inherited from the apostles.

In other words, it is not at all certain that we yet possess an adequate theological response which takes seriously the implications of interreligious dialogue without sacrificing Christian identity. In any event, I do not think that it is sufficient to go from Christocentrism to theocentrism as the adepts of a pluralistic theology of religion suggest.[3] Every responsible Christian theology must maintain the normative character of Christology. Rather than adopting some general theocentrism, we must start at the very center of the Christian message, that is, God's manifestation in the historical particularity of Jesus of Nazareth, and find there the justification for the dialectical nature of Christianity. This is the only valid way of exorcising Christianity of any totalitarian pretension.

Personally, I fail to see how we can leave completely behind a certain inclusivism, that is, a theology of the *fulfillment* (to use a term present in Catholic theology since Vatican II) in Jesus Christ of all seeds of truth, goodness, and holiness contained in the religious experience of humankind. But my goal is to reinterpret this notion of fulfillment in a non-possessive and non-totalitarian sense. Rather than renounce the confession of Jesus Christ as absolute, I prefer to say that Christians must renounce all claims to absolute truth precisely because they confess Jesus Christ as absolute, that is, as eschatological fullness that will never be revealed in history. It is exactly here that I find the permanent relevance of Paul Tillich's thought. Death prevented him from rewriting the *Systematic Theology* from the perspective of an explicit dialogue with non-Christian religions. But since for him, religion is the "substance" of culture, his theology of culture gives eloquent witness to the non-totalitarian nature of Christianity. Already in the *Dogmatik* of 1925, then in his *Systematic Theology* (especially in the third volume), and in the lectures following his seminar with Mircea Eliade, he never ceases to ponder the paradox of Christianity as a non-absolute religion which nonetheless attests to the final revelation. We certainly can recognize the Catholic resonance in his theology inasmuch as he remains equally removed from the hybris of dialectical theology on the one hand and neo-liberalism, with its readiness to relinquish the Christological norm for the sake of facilitating interreligious dialogue, on the other.

In the following pages, my goal is to demonstrate the fruitfulness of Paul Tillich's intuitions, which enable us to confront the most difficult questions of a theology of religions, and to show how he helps define the rules of interreligious ecumenism. Even though Tillich's system is a coherent whole, I choose to speak first of the Logos made flesh who unites in a single whole the absolutely universal and the absolutely concrete. Subsequently, I shall reflect on the paradox of Christianity as the religion of final revelation. Finally, we shall see how "ultimate concern" furnishes us with a criterion for interreligious dialogue.

The Paradox of the Logos Made Flesh

By virtue of the very demands of interreligious dialogue, we are ready to accept the historical particularity of Christianity. It would be an unwarranted pretension to claim that historical Christianity has been and will be able to encompass all the riches contained in the religious history of humanity, still less in history itself. But we must not confuse the particular character of Christianity as an historical religion with the particular character of Christ as mediator of the Absolute in history. The link between God's presence and the contingent event "Jesus as the Christ" will always remain in the eyes of other religions as the scandal of the Christian claim. By confessing Jesus of Nazareth to be the Christ, the Church claims for Christianity a unique and unrivalled excellence.

In an effort to facilitate dialogue with other religions, certain theologians are tempted today to downplay this extravagant allegation. They say, for instance, that to speak of Jesus' divinity is a "manner of speech," that the incarnation is a "metaphor" expressing his incomparable openness to God (see John Hick). Or else they attempt to loosen the indissoluble link between the Christ of faith and the Jesus of history (see Raymond Panikkar). The human Jesus would be only one historical manifestation, among others, of a transcendent and preexisting Christ. In such a case, one may well wonder whether the uniqueness of Christianity is not jeopardized in the sense that Jesus would only become one of several historical realizations of the Absolute. For it is by the very fact that he is this man Jesus of Nazareth "who gave himself as ransom for all" (1 Tim 2:6) that Christ is the unique and universal mediator between God and human persons.

Thus, in order to firmly establish the dialogical character of Christianity, it is preferable, as I have already said, to return to the very center of Christian faith, that is, to the mystery of the incarnation itself in its most realistic and non-mythical meaning. The paradoxical character of Christianity originates in the paradox of the "Logos made flesh." "There is, in the last analysis, only *one* genuine paradox in the Christian message—the appearance of that which conquers existence under the conditions of existence. Incarnation, redemption, justification, etc., are implied in this paradoxical event."[4] It is well known that Tillich attached great importance to the notion of paradox, in sharp distinction from dialectical theology. In theology, paradox is not contrary to the demands of logical reason. Paradox does not result from logical contradiction, but from the fact that an event transcends all human expectations and possibilities. The doctrine of the Trinity, for example, is neither irrational nor dialectical, but paradoxical. "There is only one paradox in the relation between God and man, and that is the appearance of the essential unity of God and man under the conditions of their existential separation—or in Johannine language, the Logos has become flesh, has entered historical existence in time and space. All other paradoxical statements on Christianity are variations and applications of this paradox, for example, the doctrine of justification by grace alone or the participation of God in the suffering of the universe."[5]

In his *Dogmatik* of 1925, which was only published in 1986,[6] Tillich severely criticized the absoluteness of Christianity not only as Troeltsch did, in the name of the history of religions, but in the name of faith itself and of the principle of justification. The absolute power of faith consists in the absolute "No" and the absolute "Yes" which God pronounces over the same person. This law of absolute paradox is found in every religious experience in which the absolute is taken as the critical, unconditional norm of every concrete determination, but can only become effective through this concrete determination. This law applies to Christianity because the Church, in the very moment in which it depends on faith in the absolute, must accept the "No" pronounced on her by the unconditional. And it is in Christ himself that the absolute paradox finds its concrete fulfillment. In an earlier text (1919), "Justification and Doubt," Tillich sums up his thought in this way: "The struggle for the absoluteness of Christianity is a struggle for the possibility of recognizing in it the pure realization of the Absolute paradox, with its total 'Yes' and 'No' bearing upon itself. This struggle is identified with the history of Christianity in its relation to the surrounding culture and religion."[7]

Tillich always remained faithful to this doctrine of Christ conceived as the identity of the absolutely concrete with the absolutely universal. And in his introduction to the *Systematic Theology*, he does not hesitate to assert that Christian theology is *the* theology inasmuch as it rests upon the tension between the absolutely concrete and absolutely universal: "The Logos doctrine as the doctrine of the identity of the absolutely concrete with the absolutely universal is not one theological doctrine among others; it is the only possible foundation of a Christian theology which claims to be *the* theology."[8] In making this claim, Tillich was conscious of taking his place within the continuum of the early Church's doctrine of the Logos, which derived from her reflection on the "Logos made flesh" from St. John's prologue. In opposition to Harnack, he thought that this doctrine of the Logos was indispensable to safeguard the universal scope of the event "Jesus the Christ." Similarly, if the early Church fought against Arianism, it was because, by making Christ into a cosmic power—albeit the highest one—Arius was divesting him both of his absolute universality (he was less than God) and of his absolute concreteness (he was more than human). "The half-God Jesus of Arian theology is neither universal enough or concrete enough to be the basis of Christian theology."[9]

It is remarkable that Tillich does not speculate on the dialectic of the particular and the universal or of the finite and the infinite when he strives to give an account of the event "Jesus the Christ." He always prefers to speak of the tension between the concrete and the universal, precisely in that it denotes paradox, not dialectic. To speak of the mystery of the incarnation as "God's becoming a human being" is still an inadequate mode of speech because it locks us into the dialectic of the finite and the infinite. The paradox of the Christian message is essentially our confession that Jesus of Nazareth is the Christ. In other words, in the personal life of Jesus, the essence of human nature has appeared under the conditions of existence (that is, marked by finitude, alienation, and ambiguity) without being overcome by them. At least this is how I paraphrase Tillich's condensed formula: "The paradox of the Christian message is that in *one* personal life, essential manhood has appeared under the conditions of existence without being conquered by them."[10]

Such a statement can be understood only in light of Tillich's system, in particular in light of the distinction between essence and existence and the alienation of all historical human existence from its true, essential nature. The essential function of Christ as the New Being is to save humankind from its alienation and to renew the universe. It is in Jesus, confessed as the Christ, that the New Being, which is the principle of the transformation of every historical existence and of the renewal of creation, is manifested. Likewise, it is the New Being in Jesus as the Christ that becomes the material norm of systematic theology.[11] Tillich's whole theology reflects the Pauline doctrine—at once cosmic and eschatological—of the new creation. He thus distances himself from the Pauline theology of the first Reformers and Karl Barth, which is that of justification by faith. He places himself, in an original way, in continuity with the traditional doctrine of the Fathers of the Church on the universal Logos and the "seeds of the Word" scattered throughout creation. In so doing, he establishes the principle of every Christian theology of religions: if Christ is the absolutely concrete, then in a certain way Christianity as a particular religion is already implied in all the other religions. And these religions are themselves particular manifestations of the universal Logos.

The doctrine of Christ as the New Being is nothing more than a theological commentary on the Johannine affirmation of the "Logos made flesh" and on the confession of the early Church of "Jesus as the Christ." The Logos is the principle of the self-revelation of God both in the universe and in history. And the flesh does not designate a material substance, but human historical existence.[12] If we confess Jesus as the Christ, then we identify him with the Logos and he thus becomes the point of identity between the absolutely concrete and the absolutely universal. To the extent that he is absolutely concrete, our relation with him concerns every concrete existence; to the extent that he is absolutely universal, our relation with him includes potentially all possible relations. Moreover, Tillich thinks that one can find a New Testament foundation for this identity of the universal and the concrete, specifically in Paul's letters where the Apostle writes about our "New Being in Christ" (2 Cor 5:17), and about the subjection of the cosmic powers to the Christ (see Rom 8).[13] Despite their different speculative resources, Tillich's approach to this issue invites a close comparison with the provocative teachings of Nicholas of Cusa on Christ as the concrete universal.

Paul Tillich's Christology does not speculate on the union of God and human nature in Jesus Christ. But even though he does not favor the non-biblical term "incarnation" because of its pagan connotations, he would never consent to say that Jesus' divine filiation is only a metaphor. This would threaten the identity of Jesus Christ and Christology would become "Jesusology." If we push the doctrine of Christ as the New Being to its full and logical implications, it is evident that the Christ is the Christ only to the extent that he sacrificed his historical existence as the existence of him who is merely Jesus. As an historical religion, Christianity is not superior to other religions. But it remains a unique religion inasmuch as it attests to the final revelation which is inseparable from the mystery of death and resurrection. "A Christianity that does not assert that Jesus of Nazareth is sacrificed to Jesus as the Christ is just one more religion among others."[14]

In last analysis, therefore, it is in the doctrine of a theology of the cross that the doctrine of Christ as the New Being (which embodies the unity of the absolutely concrete and the absolutely universal) begins to take on ultimate significance. Only a theology of the cross provides a religious basis for the withdrawal of any claim of absoluteness for Christianity as an historical religion. In the dialogue with other religions, we must give up all Christian claims for uniqueness of excellence and integration and claim only a singular and relative uniqueness.[15] The cross is a condition of glory; the renunciation of particularity is the condition of concrete universality. Following Tillich's intuition, we may say that Christ is at once "Jesus" and the "negation of Jesus." This is to say that Jesus as a particular human being sacrifices himself to himself as the Christ. And in the resurrection, there is, in some way, a recovery of Jesus by Christ. The risen Christ frees Jesus' person from a particularism which would make him the property of a particular people. We may therefore assign a symbolic universal value to the cross. The cross is a symbol of universality linked with the sacrifice of particularity. Jesus dies to his own particularity in order to be re-born in the form of universality, the form of Christ.

The Christological paradox is the foundation of the paradoxical con-dition of Christianity as a religion. In order to exorcise any pernicious totalitarianism from our understanding of Christ, we can push Tillich's reflections further by saying that Christianity is always stamped by a certain *lack*. It is Christ's kenosis in his equality with God which al-lows for the resurrection in the widest sense of the term. But it is also the empty tomb, the absence of the founder's body, which is the con-dition of both the body of the Church and the body of Scripture com-ing into being. Christianity is based upon an original absence. And we must add that it is precisely this consciousness of a lack which is the condition of a relation to the other, the stranger, the different. It is for this reason that dialogue with other religious experiences is writ-ten into the original vocation of Christianity. And just as there is no Christian experience without consciousness of an absent origin, there is no Christian praxis without consciousness of a lack in comparison with the religious praxis of other human religions. "For each Chris-tian, each community, and for Christianity as a whole, the goal is to be a sign of what is lacking."[16]

Thus, to conclude the first part of the study, it seems safe to say, in light of contemporary controversies in the field of the theology of religions, that Tillich invites us not to eliminate the Christological para-dox for the benefit of a more ecumenical theocentrism. It is precisely in confessing Jesus to be the Christ that we have some chance to in-sure for Christianity a dialogical rather than totalitarian character. For the Christian faith at any period, Jesus is always to be identified with the personal God, according to Paul's assertion, "In him dwells the fullness of deity in bodily form" (Col 2:9). But this paradoxical iden-tification refers to an invisible God who escapes every identification. Christianity does not exclude other religious experiences which iden-tify in a different manner the transcendent Reality of the universe. Jesus is, indeed, to be recognized as the concrete face of God's absolute love. But against all shades of Docetism—and here is the absolute paradox of the mystery of the incarnation—God can manifest Himself only in non-divine terms, that is, in the contingent humanity of a particular human being. The French theologian Christian Duquoc is therefore quite correct when he writes that by revealing Himself in Jesus, "God does not turn the particular into an absolute: on the contrary, this revelation means that no historical particularity is absolute and that, owing to this relativity, God can be found in our real history."[17]

The Paradox of Christianity as the Religion of Final Revelation

In contrast to Karl Barth's position, which makes Christianity the only revealed religion and regards other religions as false and idolatrous, Catholic theology—in its most commonly accepted form—readily recognizes, beyond the divine revelation which coincides with salvation history, a general revelation immanent in the religious history of humankind. For instance, Karl Rahner distinguishes a transcendental revelation which is coextensive with the spiritual history of humankind (that is, God's self-communication to every human conscience) and a categorical revelation which coincides with the historical phenomenon of biblical revelation. Modern theology strives to retrieve the heritage of the theology of the *semina Verbi* (the seeds of the Word) which are present in all religions and cultures. Vatican II has not taken a very clear stance on the relationship between Christian revelation and general revelation. But it does recognize the universal presence of the Logos, who "enlightens all who come into the world." Without explicitly acknowledging non-Christian religions as "ways of salvation," it accepts them as bearers of "salvational values." Pope John Paul did not hesitate to say, on the occasion of the Assisi meeting, that "every authentic prayer is inspired by God."

Tillich's position is in basic agreement with the Catholic tradition of affirming universal revelation that extends beyond the boundaries of Christianity—a revelation which is based on the universal presence of the Logos and of God's Spirit in humankind as a whole. His inventive thesis on the paradox of Christianity as the religion of the final revelation opens a fruitful way of exorcising the pretension of a Christian religion which would claim to have a monopoly on divine revelation. The paradox consists in declaring that since Christianity is the religion of the final revelation, it denies the claim of unconditionality on the part of any particular religion, beginning with its own. "The final revelation is that in which the demonization of revelation is made impossible by the fact that no way of revelation can make the claim to be unconditional. But this must be understood of the concrete way of salvation; in other words, the concrete and the negation of the concrete must be realized in the way of salvation."[18]

This statement supposes that we clearly distinguish the essence of revelation from its phenomenal form (concrete and historical) and that we never neglect the key to intelligibility which is always at the heart of Tillich's whole system, namely the notion of "ultimate concern," which puts us on guard against the dangers of both demonization and profanization. The essential thesis can be formulated as follows: "A revelation is perfect when its way of salvation supposes the upsetting of every way of salvation."[19] There is no perfect (or final) revelation outside of a concrete way of salvation, for what concerns us unconditionally must be concrete. But at the same time, there exists in this concreteness an element of protest that impugns the concrete way. In this way, the paradox of the perfect revelation consists in the fact that this revelation must reconcile within itself both the element of concrete realization and the disruptive protest that overturns this very realization.

We can imagine what the consequences of this bold vision could be for interreligious dialogue, where the main difficulty consists in the fact that each religion legitimately claims to possess the final revelation, that is, the revelation of the Absolute. Believers attest to the fact that Christianity is really the religion of final revelation. That is, in fact, its very essence. But as a concrete way of salvation, that is, as a particular historical religion, Christianity negates itself. "No historical realization constitutes the essence of Christianity. Christianity is essentially a protest against an historical concept of essence."[20] This is to say that the essence of Christianity does not coincide with any of its historical realizations and that this essence can be found in religions other than Christianity. "The claim of Christianity to be based on perfect revelation can also be upheld by all the other religions."[21] In Tillich's understanding of the basic Christian paradox, we possess a principle that allows us to deflate the hybris that characterizes every particular religion, including Christianity itself. But at the same time, it does justice to the absolute and unconditional commitment that is required for all adherents of a particular religion. In other words, I can respect the absolute commitment of others to their own beliefs without falling into relativism, for my own unconditional commitment to the concrete way of salvation which is mine also falls under the judgment of the unconditional. This perception invites us to go beyond the relativistic viewpoint of the history of religions and to seek a theological foundation for religious pluralism. Religious pluralism is not only *de facto* a pluralism linked to a contingent historical situation. It is also a pluralism *de jure* based on the necessity of divesting every historical religion of its claim to be absolute and to be the embodiment of final revelation. Accordingly, the practical rule which should regulate religious ecumenism in the future is the avoidance of all confusion between the question of the *truth* of Christianity, on the one hand, and the question of its *superiority*, on the other. In the name of the Christian faith, I receive the final revelation about God, the world, and humankind in the concrete way of salvation inaugurated by Jesus Christ. But I leave open whether the final revelation can be attained in other religions.

Lastly, the paradoxical notion of the final revelation should help us in the ongoing debate within the Catholic Church concerning the relationship between interreligious dialogue and the Church's missionary duty. Does not the insistence on dialogue with other religions diminish the urgency of explicit missionary activity? What is necessary is to keep Christianity, along with other religions, under the judgment of the final revelation. Neither historical Christianity nor the earthly Churches are absolute. Only the final revelation as the advent of the kingdom of God is absolute. The mission of the Church is not so much to convert members of other religions to this particular religion which is Christianity as it is to convert them to the unconditional nature of the final revelation. Church mission, then, ought to focus less on the change of religion than on the witness given to the kingdom of God from the very beginnings of humanity and down through the ongoing developments of the religious history of humankind, well beyond the visible boundaries of the Church.

While these liberating perspectives offer genuine promise for the future of interreligious dialogue, they still leave us with the nagging question, "Why grant Christianity the unique privilege of attesting to the final revelation?" Tillich would always answer that this claim results from the unconditional character of faith. But he would add that a Christianity that renounces—whatever its imperfections in the way of demonization and profanization—its claim to be the religion of final revelation has already ceased to exist. Indeed, the origin of the Church rests on this conviction that the final revelation has been revealed to us in Jesus Christ as the New Being, who has sacrificed his historical existence: "Only as he who has sacrificed his flesh, that is, his historical existence, is he Spirit or New Creature."[22] In a manner which differs from all other media of revelation which constitute historical religions (including Christianity), only the Christ is a medium perfectly transparent to the final revelation since he has the power of negating himself without losing himself. Therefore, for Tillich, we see that the refusal to grant absoluteness to Christianity as a means of revelation does not compromise in the least the absolute universality of Christ as the center of history. Christ as the manifestation of the New Being is at the same time the medium and the criterion of final revelation. In this sense, the final revelation is not so much the last as the genuine revelation.[23] In other words, all other revelations, of which the religions of the world can be the bearers, have a necessary relation with Christ as the New Being, who realizes in himself the union of the absolutely concrete and the absolutely universal.

It is especially in the third part of the *Systematic Theology*, whose title, we recall, is *Life and the Spirit: History and the Kingdom of God*, that Tillich reflects on the presence of the New Being in human life, in the religions and in culture, as well as in history. Tillich then speaks in a special manner of the Spiritual Presence. But it is the presence of God's Spirit which has made of Jesus of Nazareth the Christ, that is, the New Being, so that from that point on, he becomes the criterion of every spiritual experience in the past and in the future. "The Spiritual Presence, elevating man through faith and love to the transcendent unity of unambiguous life, creates the New Being above the gap between essence and existence and consequently above the ambiguities of life."[24]

Tillich first studies the manifestation of the divine Spirit in the human spirit. Then he writes at length of the presence of the Spirit in the whole of human history. Even though they are unfortunately very short (pp. 141–46), these texts on the presence of the spirit in the religions of the world give testimony to his growing interest in the history of religions. These passages were written after his trip to Japan, and they remind us of his cautionary remark in the introduction to this third part of the *Systematic Theology*: "Again I must say that a Christian theology which is not able to enter a creative dialogue with the theological thought of other religions misses a world-historical occasion and remains provincial."[25]

In these passages, however brief, Tillich establishes the principles of the Spiritual Presence in other religions by exploring the universal presence of the Spirit and the New Being in the general history of humanity. We could even say that his theology of history is a meditation on the victory of the Spirit seen in the light of the Protestant principle, understood as a methodological principle and not as a confessional imperative. Recognizing that religion is continually tempted by the lures of demonization or of secularization, this principle demands the conquest of the ambiguities of religion through the presence of the Spirit. In any case, Tillich makes a case for the existence of universal revelation and asserts that humankind is never abandoned to itself. Thanks to the presence of the divine Spirit to the human spirit, we may rightly speak of revelatory experiences which have a saving and transforming power. It is reasonable to assume that such experiences are found especially in the world's religions. These revelatory experiences are fragmentary participations in the transcendent unity of unambiguous life. They are, in fact, anticipations of the full possession of the life of the Spirit. "The New Being is fragmentarily and anticipatorily present, but insofar as it is present it is so unambiguously."[26] And it is fitting to add that, in spite of the ambiguities of every human life, those who have a fragmentary experience of faith and a fragmentary practice of love already constitute a "holy community." By carefully distinguishing the "fragmentary" from the "ambiguous," it is possible to say that such and such a particular Church or even such and such a particular religion is an anticipation of the Spirit's victory over life's ambiguities.

Finally, Tillich has recourse to the distinction of the holy community in its latency and in its manifestation in order to explain the relationship between the universal revelation and historical revelation and to stress that the *kairos* of the event "Jesus as the Christ" is coextensive with all the moments of history. "The Spirit who created the Christ within Jesus is the same Spirit who prepared and continues to prepare mankind for the encounter with the New Being in him."[27] The advent of Christ as New Being constitutes the central manifestation of the divine Spirit.

Therefore, there is a "before" and an "after" and we cannot identify the Spiritual Community of human persons during the period of preparation (that is, the Israelite people) with the Spiritual Community of the period of reception (that is, the apostolic Church). The former corresponds to what Tillich calls the "latent" Church and the latter to the "manifest" Church, that is, the Church which is directly related to the central revelation in Jesus Christ. But we must go beyond linear chronology and speak of a Church in a latent state to identify any community before or after Christ that participates in the fullness of the Spirit in a fragmentary and anticipatory manner. This can well be the case with the Spiritual Communities outside the official Churches. And it can be the case with non-Christian religions in which we can recognize fragmentary elements of faith and love, even though they still lack the ultimate criterion of faith and love in Christ. In the following text, Tillich makes this point with particular eloquence:

> There is a latent Spiritual Community in the assembly of the people of Israel, in the schools of the prophets, in the community of the Temple, in the synagogues in Palestine and the Diaspora, and in the medieval and modern synagogues. There is a latent Spiritual Community in the Islamic devotional communities, in the mosques and theological schools, and in the mystical movements of Islam. There is a latent Spiritual Community in the communities worshipping the

great mythological gods, in esoteric priestly groups, in the mystery cults of the later ancient world, and in the half-scientific, half-ritual communities of the Greek philosophical schools. There is a latent Spiritual Community in classical mysticism in Asia and Europe and in the monastic and half-monastic groups to which the mystical religions give rise. The impact of the Spiritual Presence, and therefore of the Spiritual Community, is in all of these and in many others.[28]

"Ultimate Concern" as the Criterion of Encounter Between Religions

Up to now, we have seen that the paradox of Christ as the "Concrete Universal" and the paradox of Christianity as "the religion of the final revelation" can help us to overcome all forms of Christian imperialism without threatening either the uniqueness of the event "Jesus as the Christ" or the originality that belongs to Christianity as an historical religion.

In this, I am justified in saying that Paul Tillich is an ally of Catholic theology whenever the latter—while fully satisfying the demands of interreligious dialogue—seeks to maintain the Christological norm. In this, Catholic theology stands in contrast to the attempts of neo-liberal theology which, for its part, is bent on effecting a Copernican revolution in theology in order to facilitate interreligious dialogue among equal partners. To complete this study, it only remains for us to examine briefly Tillich's view on the criteria for fruitful dialogue with the world's religions. This seems to me of great importance for the future of interreligious ecumenism as distinct from confessional ecumenism. It will provide an opportunity for us to review his unique understanding of religion and to check on the consistency of his insistence upon a complementary balance between Protestant principle and Catholic substance in any authentic expression of religion.

I have already suggested that ecumenism between Christian Churches has served as a kind of apprenticeship for interreligious ecumenism. We have indeed learned that all ecumenism of whatever sort is based on the general principle of "seeking unity in diversity." But in the case of confessional ecumenism, we possess a more specific criterion which, despite the many historical rifts between the Churches, is recognized by all, namely, the absoluteness of the event of "Jesus as the Christ." Beyond this, we also share a certain number of fundamental articles concerning the mystery of Christ and the mystery of the Trinity. Such is not the case with interreligious ecumenism, where we are challenged by an infinite plurality of religious forms. In this case, what will be the common basis on which to establish religious dialogue? Not only do the other religions reject Christianity's claim to be absolute, but they also refuse to accept the absolute mediation of Christ for the salvation of all men and women. And even if it is true that the acknowledgment of a unique God can constitute a common criterion for the dialogue between the three monotheistic religions, what shall we say of the dialogue with the great Eastern religions, which refuse to identify the Ultimate Reality of the universe with a personal Transcendence?

If God, then, understood as personal Transcendence, cannot serve as the common ecumenical criterion, we can still appeal to a criterion of the ethical order, to wit, authentic human nature as it is recognized by universal human conscience. Whatever the diversity of ethical systems, the different religions must nevertheless take into account a certain number of "fundamental convictions" which have been the object of juridical codification, as in the Universal Declaration on Human Rights of 1948. More than forty years afterwards, at the end of the second millennium, it is not rash to assert that all religions which, in one way or another, remain truly inhuman are destined to disappear or at least to undergo radical transformation. In this respect, we do possess a certain number of criteria, at least negative ones, to help us discern whether a religion by its rites, its institutions, its dogmas, and its ethical teaching, violates the dignity of the human person or contradicts the most legitimate aspirations of human conscience.[29] Important as it may be, however, this criterion of genuine human nature is not peculiar to the dialogue between religions. It is of equal concern to all spiritual families as well as ethical programs.

Therefore, it seems preferable to search for an ecumenical criterion in the domains of religious anthropology or philosophy of religion. It is at this juncture that Tillich's notion of the unconditional or of ultimate concern comes into play. On this issue, I cannot but note an obvious convergence between Tillich's thought and that of Mircea Eliade, especially in Eliade's insistence on the universality of *homo religiosus*, in spite of the infinite variety of religious forms. I find the same intuition in the great contemporary theologian of religions, John Hick, especially in his conviction that all religions are characterized by a certain abandonment of self-centeredness for the sake of an ultimate Reality, whether understood through the representations of a personal God or not. [30] According to Tillich's vision, we can distinguish between a "fundamental faith" and an ensemble of "beliefs" which concern particular truths or rules of life. The ultimate Reality can be the personal God of the biblical tradition, the transcendental Absolute of Hinduism—the hidden force of things (Brahman) which coincides with the hidden force in me (Atman)—or even the Void in Buddhism. In the order of fundamental faith, the different religions resemble one another; in their beliefs, they are distinct and even in direct doctrinal opposition.

In his 1958 lecture, "The Meaning of Religion and the Protestant Principle," Tillich strives, within the perspective of a philosophy of religion, to work out a concept of religion capable of affording a basis for the encounter of religions. Not only must this concept allow us to distinguish religion from magic, but it must be broad enough to include religions without God such as Buddhism and Confucianism, as well as the quasi-religions such as humanism, fascist anti-humanism, and communist pseudo-humanism. With this in mind, Tillich arrives at a notion which he believes is at the heart of religion, that is, the sense of the holy, defined as that which is of ultimate concern. It is at this deeper level that we discover a criterion common to all historical religions as well as to the modern quasi-religions. "Religion is ultimate concern or the unconditional in being and meaning. It is ultimate concern, ultimate seriousness." Further on, Tillich argues that "the immediately given in every religion is something that we can approach empirically, phenomenologically, namely the phenomenon of the holy."[31]

There is, then, in every religion, even the most dogmatic, the most legalistic, the most ritualistic, the demand of "going-beyond-self," found in the sense of the holy understood as ultimate concern. From the anthropological viewpoint, this coincides with the irreducibility of *homo religiosus*, whose proper domain is distinct from the cognitive, ethical, and aesthetic realms. But this still remains an abstract analysis. Concretely, within history, every authentic religion which has a sense for the unconditional, that is to say, which does not confuse the Ultimate with all the symbolic material through which the Ultimate is necessarily expressed, is under the judgment of the Protestant principle. The Protestant principle must be understood first of all as a power immanent in all religions, the protest of religion itself against religion in the name of God or Ultimate Reality. It also, secondarily, designates the sixteenth-century Reformation. But this resource in all religions has had other representations in the course of history. We might think, for example, of the prophets of Israel, who in the name of God protested against a false sacralization of the chosen people. Similarly, the first Christian community struggled against pagan religion in the name of the new reality which was manifested in the person of Christ.[32]

In other texts, Tillich gives more details on the contents of the experience of the holy, within which he always distinguishes three elements: the sacramental dimension, the mystical dimension, and the ethical requirement.[33] It is possible to draw up a typology of religions according to the predominance of one or the other of these elements. But we must always remember that these classifications are somewhat misleading, as is exemplified by the often-made distinction between so-called prophetic religions, such as the monotheistic religions, and the so-called mystical religions, such as the Eastern religions. In fact, it is possible to find a mystical dimension in the former and an ethical dimension in the latter. A religion that would embody a harmonious synthesis of all three elements would then be the "Religion of the Concrete Spirit." But Tillich was aware that "we cannot identify this Religion of the Concrete Spirit with any actual religion, not even Christianity as a religion."[34]

There always remains the necessity to fight in the name of the holy (which corresponds to the sense of the unconditional) against the two dangers which threaten all religion, namely, demonization (that is, the perversion of the sacramental dimension to the point of losing all ethical demand) and profanization (which neglects both the sacramental basis and the mystical challenge inherent in all religion). Without this struggle, religion is degraded into a moralistic and finally a secular religion. On the practical level, Tillich is as stern in his criticism of the secular drift of the Protestant Churches as he is of false sacralizations in the Catholic tradition. He notes elsewhere that, having lost their sacramental basis, certain Protestant Churches in the America of his time are comparable to associations of "moral clubs."[35]

Finally, it is the experience of the holy as the experience of ultimate concern that is the point of convergence of all religions and affords us a common criterion for interreligious dialogue. But the future of this new ecumenism depends on the way in which each religion remains open to the critical norm of the Protestant principle. Only this critique of religion in the name of religion itself allows each religion to resist the temptation of self-centeredness and absolutism and, in this way, to remain open to dialogue. It is also the Protestant principle which allows us to denounce the demonic temptation of the quasi-religions which are the modern secular ideologies.

We conclude that Tillich's entire theological enterprise, while correlated to the historical situation of his time, is continually distinguished by the dialectical opposition of the religious and the secular. As the history of religion attests, the religious element becomes heteronomous and therefore a source of alienation when it makes absolutes out of symbols, rites, and ideas, which are only mediations of the ultimate. The history of modern culture, on the other hand, shows that the secular element, in its turn, can become merely autonomous, and therefore profane whenever it abandons the presence of the Spirit. The key word here is "theonomy." A theonomous culture is one that remains under the impact of the presence of the Spirit without sacrificing its autonomy. Far from being alienated, all the resources of culture—in the order of knowledge, beauty, justice, and ethics—find their best fulfillment when they preserve the sense of the ultimate.[36]

Conclusion

At the end of this paper, I trust my readers understand that I do not wish to "make use of" Paul Tillich in the service of a Catholic theology of religions. At present, at least, no such theology exists, and as in many other branches of theology, the lines of demarcation are determined less by denominational boundaries than by the diverse theological trends within each tradition. In this new theological field, Tillich's thought challenges the more timid forms of Catholic theology (for instance, the classical theologies of fulfillment). At the same time, it also challenges the more radical theologies (such as that of Paul Knitter and several Indian theologians).

As far as the Protestant side is concerned, today as yesterday, Tillich continues to confront both neo-Barthian theology and liberal theology, whose main concern is to demystify the uniqueness of Christianity.[37] As the title chosen for this essay indicates, I wanted before all else to show the important contribution of Tillich to what we call "interreligious ecumenism."

But the magnitude of Tillich's vision—beyond all provincial interests—leads me to a more general conclusion concerning worldwide theology. For some time, there have been justifiable reactions against the monopoly of Western theology as the dominant theology within the Church, and it has been encouraging to see theologies rooted in other cultures gain their own autonomy little by little. But it would be absurd for Western theology to go mute on the grounds that it has exercised a kind of cultural colonialism in the past. While there is no such thing as a universal theology, neither can there be a valid particular theology which has no communication with other theologies. All the new theologies participate to some degree in the Western theological heritage. By the same token, Western theology is challenged and enriched by these new theologies. This is why I plead for a worldwide theology which would favor the advent of a multicultural Christianity able to resist the dangers of an increasingly undifferentiated and unidimensional world.

At this juncture, I am struck by both the courageous openness and the balance of Tillich's thought. Protestant principle and Catholic substance are more than slogans depicting the tension between Protestantism and Catholicism within a typically Western theology. The Protestant principle will always be refusal to divinize any element of human or historic reality. And the Catholic substance will always be the affirmation of God's spiritual presence in everything that is. In the same way that it is possible to distinguish, in the history of religions, religions with a prophetic, historical, or ethical emphasis from religions with a mystical, metaphysical, or aesthetic thrust, it is possible to discern this polarity all through the history of Christian thought.[38] From the point of view of the relationship of God with the world, the latter religions belong more to the order of participation, while the former belong to the order of proclamation. It is to Tillich's credit that he understood that we need both these dimensions to express the fullness of the Christian mystery. It is not a question of alternatives, but rather of a dialectical tension between the two. Even the word which negates all idols (demonization) includes and demands an original manifestation. It is of the very nature of Christianity that it should transform the manifestations of nature through the power of the word: such is the very meaning of the sacraments. Following Tillich's own example, we have good reason to hope that interreligious ecumenism, both the current dialogue with the religions of the Book and that with the mystical religions of the East, far from leading to indifferentism, will ultimately bring about a more profound understanding of Christian identity.

Notes

[1] Paul Tillich, "The Significance of the History of Religions for the Systematic Theologian," *The Future of Religions,* ed. J. C. Brauer (New York: Harper and Row, 1966) 91.

[2] I refer my readers to my already old study, "La théologie dans religions non-chrétiennes vingt ans après Vatican II," *Islamo-Christian* 11 (1985) 115-33.

[3] Readers will find in the book by Jacques Dupuis, *Le Christ à la rencontre des religions* (Paris: Desclée, 1989), an excellent typology of the diverse present-day models of theologies of religion.

⁴ Paul Tillich, *Systematic Theology. Vol. 1* (Chicago: The University of Chicago Press, 1951) 57.

⁵ Paul Tillich, *Systematic Theology. Vol. 3* (Chicago: The University of Chicago Press, 1963) 284.

⁶ Paul Tillich, *Dogmatik: Marburger Vorlesung von 1925* (Düsseldorf: Patmos Verlag, 1986).

⁷ Paul Tillich, "Rechtfertigung und Zweifel," (Paul Tillich Archive, Harvard Divinity School) 20, quoted by Jean Richard, "La révélation finale d'après Paul Tillich: une voie théologique pour la rencontre du christianisme avec les religions du monde," *Etudes théologiques et religieuses* 2 (1989) 218. This offers me the opportunity to say how indebted I am to this article by Jean Richard for my own exploration of Tillich's thought in the service of a modern theology of religions.

⁸ Tillich, *Systematic Theology*, 1:17.

⁹ Ibid., 1:17–18.

¹⁰ Paul Tillich, *Systematic Theology. Vol. 2* (Chicago: The University of Chicago Press, 1957) 94.

¹¹ Ibid., 1:48.

¹² Ibid., 2:95.

¹³ Ibid., 1:17.

¹⁴ Ibid., 1:135.

¹⁵ In my use of this vocabulary concerning the various types of Christian uniqueness, I refer to the book of St. Breton, *Unicité et monothéisme* (Paris: Cerf, 1981).

¹⁶ Michel de Certeau, *La faiblesse du croire* (Paris: Le Seuil, 1989) 217. I have developed these ideas in greater length in a study, "La singularité du christianisme à l'age du pluralisme religieux," to be published in 1993 in a work, *Homage à Joseph Moingt*, to which I reply to the concept of "permission" as de Certeau understands it. See also his collected works, *Michel de Certeau où la différence chrétienne*, ed. Claude Geffré (Paris: Cerf, 1991).

¹⁷ Christian Duquoc, *Dieu différent* (Paris: Cerf, 1978) 143.

¹⁸ Tillich, *Dogmatik*, 65. I quote an unpublished French translation, the work of a Canadian team under the direction of Jean Richard.

¹⁹ Ibid., 62.

²⁰ Ibid., 68.

²¹ Ibid., 69.

²² Tillich, *Systematic Theology*, 1:134.

²³ Ibid., 1:132.

²⁴ Ibid., 3:138.

²⁵ Ibid., 3:6.

[26] Ibid., 3:140. In the whole passage preceding this quotation, I have tried to sum up as best as I could the thought of Tillich that seems to me of greatest interest in the establishment of the salvational value of non-Christian religions.

[27] Ibid., 3:147–48.

[28] Ibid., 3:154.

[29] Under the title of "Toward a Hermeneutic of Interreligious Dialogue," my contribution to the Festschrift in honor of David Tracy, *Radical Pluralism and Truth: David Tracy and the Hermeneutics of Religions*, eds. W. G. Jeanrond and J. L. Rike (New York: Crossroads, 1991), I have already expressed my thoughts on this subject.

[30] I refer my readers to his book, *An Interpretation of Religion: Human Responses to the Transcendent* (New Haven, Conn.: Yale University Press, 1989).

[31] Paul Tillich, *The Encounter of Religions and Quasi Religions*, ed. Terrence Thomas, Studies in Theology 37 (Toronto: Edwin Mellen Press, 1990) 12–13.

[32] Cf. ibid., 15–16.

[33] Here I make reference to his last lecture of 1965, "The Significance of the History of Religions for the Systematic Theologian," 80–94.

[34] Ibid., 89.

[35] Ibid., 87.

[36] The notion of theonomy is a frequent theme throughout Tillich's work. Here I am drawing especially from his ideas on the subject as presented under the heading of "Spiritual Presence" in *Systematic Theology*, 3:270.

[37] Here I make explicit reference to the collective work published under the title *The Myth of Christian Uniqueness: Towards a Pluralistic Theology of Religions*, eds. John Hick and Paul F. Knitter (New York: Orbis, 1987). It is well known that Schubert M. Ogden expressed his disagreement with the contributions of Gordon D. Kaufman, Rosemary Radford Ruether, and John Hick. I note in particular that, through other pathways, he concurs with my own criticism of the Christological presuppositions of John Hick's pluralistic option. Cf. Schubert M. Ogden, "Problems in the Case for a Pluralistic Theology of Religions," in *Radical Pluralism and Truth*, 270–85.

[38] This double polarity has been well-described by David Tracy in *The Analogical Imagination: Christian Theology and the Culture of Pluralism* (New York: Crossroad, 1991) 270–85.

A Protestant Response

Langdon Gilkey

It has been a signal and unexpected honor to be invited to write an afterword for the new book on Tillich by Catholic theologians and scholars, more than twenty-five years after the first such volume appeared. It is also an exhilarating task for one long immersed in Tillich's thought, for these writers are intimately and accurately acquainted with his theology. More important, it is a joy to one attached to his theology to find the majority of these authors not only informed about his thought but deeply aware of its relevance to their own projects and hopes as Catholic theologians.

In this regard I cannot but contrast this book with the first Catholic volume on Tillich. There the sense of the importance and possible relevance, certainly the tempting allure, of Tillich to Catholics mixed uneasily with an alert wariness concerning both his modes of thinking and his theological conclusions. One felt that, though he was no longer to be considered a heretic, nevertheless the consciousness remained firmly in place that despite the profundity and fascination of his thought, he was after all *Protestant*. Thus the task of any Catholic theologian was to locate the crucial points at which error and so misunderstanding had begun and so to trace out the effects of these missteps on everything else he said. For this reason even in that volume the deeply Catholic elements of Tillich's theology were muted if not quite overlooked, lest emphasis on his compatibility merely increase the dangers he posed.

These new essays disclose a completely different attitude. Just why is an interesting question. Surely Ray Bulman is right that by now the last vestiges of the "Neo-Scholastic mind-set" are gone (at least among these sorts of Catholic theologians!), and hence Catholics can now view Tillich in his own terms. Only with that new understanding of Tillich has it become possible to see what an immense help much of his thought could be not only for the reformulation but also for the preservation of Catholic theology in the new age. Thus each of these articles in turn is vitally interested in articulating the ways Tillich's methods and categories nurture Catholic thinking at the crucial points where—to these authors—new formulations are called for. In the important enterprise of rethinking Catholic theology, Tillich has become more of an ally than a threat, more of a colleague than a competitor. These were, therefore, not only excellent articles; they were also exceedingly gratifying for a Tillichian who has long maintained that, read correctly, he was at least as Catholic in his theological sensibilities as he was Protestant.

This appropriateness for Catholic theology is not just, as one is at first apt to say, that Tillich loved philosophy and articulated an ontological theology, though that is important. After all, there are other philosophical theologies, for example most process ones, which are built on philosophical speculation and yet are far removed from the concerns and emphases of Catholic theology. Rather, the reasons are (1) that so much of Tillich's strength is also Catholic strength, akin to Catholic concerns; and (2) what is Protestant about him is so conceived as to be capable of becoming a genuine help to Catholics intent on fundamental reform concerning, for example, as several articles insisted, issues of idolatry, ecclesiastical authority, and social liberation. To establish these two points, largely through the inspiration of these outstanding articles (better put: *they* make these points, I reiterate them), will be the purpose of the remainder of this Afterword. That is, I shall try to highlight how both the Catholic elements in Tillich's theology and his more Protestant emphases have each, according to the witness of these articles, become relevant to contemporary Catholic reform. Thus we shall concentrate on the "Catholic" interests of symbol, theonomy, and sacrament; Catholic substance and Protestant principle; *kairos*, heteronomy/autonomy, idolatry, and liberation; and, finally, the most interesting and unexpected topic: prayer and piety.

Religion and Culture: Theonomy

We shall begin where, in the order of being if not of knowing, Tillich would have us begin: with God (incidentally, one of the very best pieces was Julia Lamm's on God). That is, we begin with the central formula of Tillich's thought: God is Being Itself (or the Power of Being in everything). Being Itself is the final object of philosophy, the most general category for understanding nature, history, culture, and the self—the ground, therefore, of all so-called secular culture. God, on the other hand, is the object of religion, of ultimate concern, and so of all witness, sacrament, prayer, and rites, and the referent of all religious reflection. These two are identical (God is Being Itself), though the approaches to each may be different. Hence for Tillich religion and culture are inseparable: religion is the substance of culture and culture the form of religion.

As I have argued elsewhere, for Tillich it is the religious approach, i.e., the apprehension of rescue and renewal, the knowledge through existential participation, and so the witness to revelation in its broadest sense, that is most fundamental in the order of knowing, the "place," so to speak, where the universal and yet elusive reality and power of Being Itself is encountered, known, and celebrated. This direct, participating, and so "religious" experience has diverse modes; it can be in culture through import and ultimate concern, in individual life through courage and self-affirmation, or explicitly in religious experience through acceptance, reconciliation and so "faith." Thus are autonomous culture and dependent religion united inextricably at the most fundamental level, in God as Being Itself.

The basic concepts involved here are, let us note, classically "orthodox": (1) God is the Power of Being, the abysmal ground of all that is; finite being *is* through its participation in its ground and *is not* in separation from its ground. (2) God is the Power of an *autonomous* finitude, one that is its own essential self: autonomous, self-directed, creative, *and* related. (3) The finite, though real, creative, and good, is still always finite (it is not God); it remains, therefore, relative, partial, never absolute—only God is God.

These three points, fundamental to the meaning of *creatio ex nihilo* since the very earliest tradition, form the theological bases for *theonomy*, Tillich's central category and one essential for these Catholic interpretations. Theonomy means that finitude *is* through its participation in God, and that in so participating, each entity becomes most fully itself, autonomous and self-directed. Here also is the root of the religious depth of all finitude, and so of even a secular culture—for all is, and is itself, through participation in God. Correspondingly, religion concerns the finite as finite and so the finite as secular: religion is the depth of the finite. Hence again the formula: religion is the substance of culture, culture the form of religion.

As a consequence, there are not two histories, one secular and the other sacred; nor two kingdoms, of Christ and of the Law; nor the familiar pair of Catholic dichotomies: nature and supernature, Church and world; nor even is there a division between individual and society, person and culture, personal salvation and liberation. Such dualisms have dominated Catholic and Protestant orthodoxies alike; in every line Tillich disputed these dualisms, and so here he is of course of immense help. It is ironic that though Tillich's principles are clearly orthodox, they are also radically "anti-manualist" at every point. And it is even more ironic that these anti-dualist principles were devised by Tillich to counter his own Lutheran background, and yet they function here as the critical and creative principles for a new Catholic theological vision.

These two principles, theonomy and religion as the depth of the finite, form the *ontological* basis for Tillich's central ecclesiological formula: Catholic substance and Protestant principle. Like the finite itself, the religious community on the one hand should maintain unbroken unity with the divine and so be a continuing "symbol" or medium (sacrament) of the empowering divine presence. On the other hand, since it is and remains finite, it must also point beyond itself to its ground, continually be critical of itself, and, if necessary, be prepared to sacrifice itself. If it points to itself for its authority and saving power, it becomes idolatrous and manifests its estrangement as well as its finitude. Although this dialectical symbol for the *ecclesia* is grounded ontologically in theonomy, nevertheless Catholic substance/Protestant principle is, I believe, Christomorphic in its inception, actualized and so known only in the one perfect symbol, the presence of the New Being in Jesus as the Christ. The ontological is disclosed only in the ontic, the philosophical in the religious. This is, I submit, neither Catholic nor Protestant in inspiration, and it is potentially either one of them. In any case, it is clear how relevant this interpretation is for such crucial "Catholic" symbols of divine empowerment as symbol, sacrament, incarnation, *ecclesia*, and sanctification, all cases of theonomy but now interpreted without the seemingly inescapable risk of deification, idolatry, and so heteronomy. No wonder these points appeared over and over in these essays.

This same ontological understanding is, not surprisingly, the basis for Tillich's theology of culture; the unity of religion and culture means that a theology of culture is a part of the responsible and positive role that the religious community and religious reflection should play in the world. If in a world understood theonomously all finitude is religious at depth (each finite *is* through its participation in God), then not only are all religious institutions and forms *culturally* shaped if they are to be in history at all, but conversely all serious cultural problems are in the end *religious* problems, and must accordingly be understood by theological analysis. This is the charter of theology of culture.

If, moreover, cultural ill-health is fundamentally religious estrangement, then all deep cultural resolutions are religious resolutions: courage, faith, repentance, justice, and love. As religion cannot *be* without cultural embodiment, so creative, saving religion cannot *be* without cultural health, i.e., without justice and the reunion of the estranged. Here liberation of the oppressed and rescue of the lost in any cultural setting are essential responsibilities of the Church, as Jean Richard argued. Correspondingly, culture cannot *be* without some analogous form or forms of religious renewal, especially justice, repentance, and reunion or reconciliation. A religious community indifferent to cultural injustice spells not only radical self-misunderstanding but also cultural disaster; likewise, an unhealthy cultural existence threatens any effective religious health. With this powerful union of religion and culture, any dualisms of natural and supernatural, or a conflictual ethic of individual versus society, has disappeared. In theology of culture as in ecclesiology, Tillich provides new ways of resolving older Catholic dilemmas.

The key Tillichian category for this rethinking of Catholic theology is clearly theonomy; it can, therefore, bear a little more discussion. Theonomy, we have said, is the description of essential finitude: finitude in touch with its ground and therefore able to be itself, creative and related. Thus theonomy expresses creation and looks forward to fulfillment in the kingdom; it effectively unites beginning, Christology, history, and fulfillment. This concept we can, I have suggested, all understand theologically as a novel rendition of the classical paradigm set by *creatio ex nihilo*. Nonetheless, theonomy does not become actually meaningful in our experience until it is understood in contrast to its historical deviants which we *do* experience, namely, to autonomy on the one hand and heteronomy on the other. These two describe what is actual in ordinary history, "under the conditions of existence." We can feel their presence and their menace all around us: on the one hand, the relativity, rootlessness, and emptiness, and so in its own way the pride and the greed, of developed autonomy, which leaves life vulnerable to injustice, to fatalism, and so to anxiety and despair. And on the other hand, bred by all of this, its opposite, the heteronomous: the authoritarianism, dogmatism, patriarchy, fanaticism, intolerance, and cruelty of all absolutist attempts to shape existence into one "righteous" mold—as in our own recent experience, Hollywood bred Quayle and relativity breeds Robertson! Our point is that, as in Tillich the presence of Being appears only through the "shock of nonbeing," so the ideal of theonomy appears only in contrast to our experienced anxieties and terrors at meaninglessness (autonomy) and tyranny (heteronomy).

In this sense, autonomy and heteronomy are for Tillich both religious categories, aspects of theological understanding. Autonomy as an ultimate principle is the symbol of religious emptiness, an experience of radical nonbeing, that is, of meaninglessness, lack of ultimate concern, and so the absence of vitality, centeredness, direction, and courage. It is here that we first feel the power of estrangement as the apprehended absence of the sacred and so the destruction of our essential humanity, of self and community. Culture without religious depth is void; this is "autonomy." Heteronomy is also a religious category representing the overpowering presence of the sacred: "religion straight," so to speak, religion without autonomous cultural shaping or cultural and prophetic criticism. Neither category can be understood secularly, as if they were only social or historical categories. On the contrary, autonomy and heteronomy are intelligible only if they are understood theologically, as representing not only the absence of the sacred but also the presence of estrangement, alienation, and, yes, sin. These are the two historical faces of the *demonic,* the sacred as alienated and therefore as infinitely destructive. As in theological understanding grace presupposes sin, so this theology of culture presupposes estrangement, and cannot be understood without it. Yet I found barely a mention of estrangement, alienation, or sin in these articles. Has this side of the Neo-Scholastic mind-set remained in place, so that we can have a theology in which nearly all is clarified except the problem?

Estrangement or alienation (sin) for Tillich is the major cause of social dislocation, expressing itself, as he says, in social as well as individual existence. Sin is thus also injustice, loss of community, and destruction of the other. It is precisely sin that calls for liberation, if sin is properly understood. It is sin that moves history's examples of sacramental presence (in the nobility, in wealth, in whiteness, and in maleness) into radically unjust structures that maim and destroy; and it is sin that makes autonomous culture unbearable, resulting in concupiscence, greed and the empty anxiety that drives on to fanaticism, cruelty, and ultimately heteronomy. Without the shock of nonbeing, the Power of Being becomes pallid, abstract, evanescent at best; without the understanding of estrangement, Tillich's theology of culture lacks touch with actual social existence in its terror as well as its potentialities, its menace as well as its possible goodness. It is in danger theologically of falling back into a grace that completes a relatively sound nature rather than a grace that rescues and then transforms a lost nature. A Catholic understanding of Tillich without the concept of alienation could well lead to the reappearance of the nature/supernature dichotomy.

The same critique, let me say, applies to the other two words associated with theonomy in the theology of culture: *kairos* and empowerment (for this latter category, cf. especially the excellent article of Mary

Ann Stenger). *Kairos* is the appearance of eternity in qualitative, historical time; it is the new and creative possibility of its time and so the demand for its time (for justice and community). This new possibility of theonomy in our time and so in our social forms, this *kairos*, is a foretaste of the kingdom, the appearance in secular history in fragmentary form of the promise (secular history is here understood on the analogy of *Heilsgeschichte*). But *kairos* also presupposes estrangement, the nonbeing of injustice, anxiety, and the possibility of heteronomy. It is a promise manifested in a threatened situation, the New Being disclosing itself amid the travail of the old existence. Again, this historical/cultural category cannot be fully appropriated without a deeper sense of the estrangement of culture (and Church) than these articles showed.

Empowerment is an excellent word for expressing Tillich's sense of power—the power to be—as immanent in things, the principle or driving force within their existence and of their existence, their self-direction, their creative activity. This is Augustinian and Lutheran: God is that power in all things moving all things in *their* way. This, of course, sounds great, inspiring and liberating; its promise can make us feel good, both secularly and religiously, in both cultural and church enterprises. Tillich is, however, very wary of all things heavenly! It is, he reminds us in his early political writings, the very sacramental, semi-divine power in finite beings that breeds, constitutes, justifies, and preserves *injustice*. In fact, he calls these "sacramental demonries," referring to the strange power that remnants of the feudal nobility still had in early twentieth-century German life and that (to continue his analogy) whiteness and maleness still have in our world.[1] Thus, because of estrangement, empowerment invariably calls for repentance, self-criticism, and above all justice. The "powers of origin" and the critical spirit unite only in justice—alone each can become demonic.

The point again is that like theonomy and *kairos*, empowerment is not only an ontological and cultural category. Even more, all are religious categories to be understood theologically, and hence to be comprehended only through a dialectic inclusive of nonbeing or negation as well as being or affirmation, of estrangement as well as grace, of a fallen as well as a religiously grounded culture. Tillich's conceptions of alienation and estrangement are as important to a Catholic understanding of culture as are his more easily appropriable categories of theonomy, *kairos*, and empowerment.

Concerns of Systematic Theology

Again we shall follow the lead of the Catholic articles and discuss those points in Tillich's thought of particular interest to Catholic theology. In this part, however, we are more concerned with the issues peculiar to systematic theology and so *ecclesia* than with those of theology of culture. Of course, as we noted, since religion and culture are for Tillich so closely united—not separable but distinguishable—this shift of concern will be a change of emphasis but not of fundamental principles. As theonomy, *kairos*, and empowerment were the central interests above, so in the area of systematic theology the categories of symbol, sacrament, the menace of idolatry, and finally piety are here our concerns—as they were for so many of these articles. And as we began above with the foundational formula of Tillich's thought, God is Being Itself or the Power of Being, so here again we begin at the most fundamental level, God as *Spirit* as well as Power of Being and Logos. Spirit is, says Tillich, "the most direct and unrestricted symbol for the divine life" (*Systematic Theology*, 1:245), the union, as he put it, of Being and Meaning, that is, fulfillment, and so the symbolic source in God for reconciliation, reunion, in effect for the New Being.

As with the classical tradition itself, in Tillich God acts and appears concretely as a Trinity, as a union of Being, Logos, and Spirit, as a union of Being and Meaning directed at fulfillment. Here, incidentally, in the New Being as the work of the Trinity, is the source of courage throughout human experience, of *kairoi* in the history of culture, and of all forms of religion. Hence, although they appear at the middle and end of the system, the New Being and the Spiritual Presence represent the foundation of the system: God reconciles and reunites as God creates.

Correspondingly, this divine presence in the New Being is fundamental to the possibility of human culture, as the experience of the presence of grace is fundamental to our more explicit awareness and knowledge of God in faith. Although, therefore, in many respects Tillich represents a high humanism, a veneration of the *humanum*, its creative power, its autonomy, and its value, still in another sense he is almost fiercely anti-humanistic. Throughout his understanding, human powers subsist dependently on the religious, on the Spiritual Presence, on the pre-thematic awareness of the divine presence and so of the New Being; as with all else, human powers are theonomous. In effect, Tillich reverses Feuerbach, who laughed at the "superstition" of primeval cultures in believing their crafts had been established by craft gods and goddesses.[2] To Tillich archaic culture was quite right in this "mythological" interpretation, which, correctly read, insisted that the possibility of human cultural powers is grounded in the presence of the divine: autonomy must be theonomy to begin and to persist as autonomy.[3] But let us now continue our effort to understand Tillich's important notion of *symbol*, perhaps the major Tillichian category most often referred to and positively appraised in these articles.

Symbol

Tillich knows that no one, not even a philosopher, can argue to the presence of the divine. This is first because, as we noted above, the presence of the divine is already the basis of all argument; and second, because the divine is only appropriated, experienced, or participated in ontically, in our experience of our own being as finite and as in existence. (Note, in this connection, the important epistemological principles: "Man is the entrance into being" [*Systematic Theology*, 1:168–69] and "finitude [and infinity] is known from the inside" [ibid., 1:191–92].) But how, we must next ask, is the Spiritual Presence "known" for Tillich; what is this "religious knowing"? The initial and most immediate experience of the divine is inward, an experience "from the inside" of our own being. In this experience of our own being we encounter the threat or shock of nonbeing; but we come also to experience *courage*, the overcoming of our own nonbeing in affirmation. (Anxiety concerning our own nonbeing is Tillich's definition of finitude in awareness, of finite being as known from the inside; ibid.) It is this negative awareness of anxiety, common to us all, which sets the stage for, or is the condition for, the positive experience of the Power of Being.

We are, says Tillich, finite being bounded by nonbeing. This nonbeing in us appears to us through the very categories that define our finitude: our precarious being in space, our limited being in time, our involvement in causality, our "reality" as a substance. This essential nonbeing in us is experienced by us in anxiety, through all the anxieties of our life, individual and social alike. This experience of the nonbeing permeating our being would, Tillich is sure, be quite overwhelming were our finitude all there is; our being cannot win over the nonbeing in us. And in estrangement this essential and inescapable anxiety becomes frantic and leads to despair: we realize we have in the end no time, we possess no space, we are merely caused and helpless, and we will soon lose our reality. This sense of the power of negation in experience, of nonbeing, is very heavy in Tillich, quite comparable to similar analyses in Buddhist philosophy; it was not emphasized in these articles.

Tillich's subsequent question is: if this power of nonbeing is so essential, so powerful, and so overwhelming, how are life-affirmation and cultural creativity possible; where does the courageous self-affirmation necessary for them come from? How is it possible to have courage, the power to affirm our life, our powers, and our relations with others despite overwhelming nonbeing (transiency, fragility, vulnerability, and hostility); how is the power to be and to be creatively possible? (Note the sudden, vast difference with Buddhism.) This courage, common throughout finite experience, cannot come from finitude, ours or anyone else's. Finitude is too intertwined with nonbeing to achieve this conquest. Thus courage is the sign of the divine presence within finitude, of the Power of Being in us. Here, as the sole possible ground of courage, God is directly experienced in the conquest of affirmation despite anxiety. Thus God is defined as the Power of Being overcoming our nonbeing, an answer received in the experience and efficacy of courage.[4]

In the courage of self-affirmation, in truly being ourselves through participation in the Power of Being, we each become a *symbol*, the primordial symbol so to speak; in effect, with courage we each represent the primary instance of theonomy, the divine presence enabling our autonomy. In courage finite being is united with its ground (Catholic substance). Courage is thus not only the initial sign of the divine presence; it is also soteriological, a sign of the New Being reuniting us to God. This presence, therefore, represents the internal, universally present "revelation" of God: in courage God is present as Ground or Power of Being. (Tillich names this experience of God as Power of Being "direct" and "immediate.") This experience awakens our awareness of our own infinite dimension and of the presence of the unconditional in existence; it is a condition of creative cultural life. Being Itself, the infinite abyss of Being, appears here against and supreme over nonbeing, through the shock of nonbeing.

This primordial and universal experience of the Divine Ground is, however, not all of revelation and so not the only mode of symbol. Concurrently, God as infinite Being and Meaning discloses Godself through external symbols, in so-called religious experiences: in nature via its wonders and terrors, in society and family, in great heroes, wherever the infinite and unconditional shine through some extraordinary finite entity. The sacred discloses itself as well in all forms of dependent revelation: in rituals, sacraments, scriptures, laws, and holy witness and teaching. Here again finite entities become symbols (really sacraments) of the divine presence, that is to say, manifesting it, communicating it outward to others, and hence giving empowering being, order, norms, and direction (meaning) to communal life. It is, I am sure, through both of these modes of symbol, internal and external, in correlation (miracle and ecstasy), that awareness of the presence of the Infinite, of Being and of Spirit, appears and is appropriately (i.e., in relation to its cultural setting) symbolized. Religion begins with culture, expressed in and through the latter's forms, as on the other side, culture begins through participation in the divine. Since for Tillich the Spiritual Presence grounds, directs, organizes, and reunites at once, Tillich could hardly be more Trinitarian (God is Being, Logos, and re-uniting Spirit).

As we noted, from the empowering presence of this Spiritual Presence comes the possibility of the *humanum:* that is, of the human spirit as centered self, conscious, self-conscious, and conscious of the other— and, most important, conscious of an unconditional obligation to the other and so of a limit to the self and its imperialism. For Tillich it is the unconditional moral consciousness, and awareness of the other as *person,* that limits the self and thus gives rise to the consciousness of the self and of its world through language and organization.[5] Clearly this union of Spiritual Presence with the human is the beginning of theonomy. Hence culture begins with theonomy, the union of the Spiritual Presence with autonomy, with the other and so with community. There is no humanism without the divine presence, no culture without Catholic substance. And, of course, each subsequent *kairos* is an example of the reappearance of this theonomous presence. Here too is the earliest model—a "foretaste"—for Christ and the *ecclesia.* The unconditional in cultural life (import and so ultimate concern, norms and obligations, order and logos) are each of them necessary as conditions for selves, for community, and for culture, as for any religious community. Both culture and religion are consequences, in this sense, of revelation, of the awareness of the Spiritual Presence.

These are the two prototypical examples of symbol, as of theonomy: first, the finite (human) as itself a medium or symbol and hence re-united, empowered, directed, in effect, "saved"; and, second, the finite medium which, participating in the Spiritual Presence, is enabled as a consequence to reveal and communicate the divine to others. Each is an example of theonomy, of the union of religion and culture, of— however minute the scale—a *kairos.* And they are in each case the work of God as Trinity, the reuniting union of Power and Meaning. This fundamental pattern appears possibly with the first sentient, certainly with the first human spiritual life. Theonomy expands and enriches as human culture and religion develop; it finds its fullest form, its decisive and final form, in Jesus as the Christ. Here theonomy is fulfilled, the New Being realized: a finite historical person in unbroken unity with the Spiritual Presence (Catholic substance) and yet one continually pointing beyond himself to God and willing to sacrifice himself in order to retain that unity (Protestant principle). He was not the first or only symbol, for in him all were created, all participate in theonomy, in fragmentary unity with their ground. But he was the disclosive model, the ultimate criterion; on him, as *Ursakrament*, as *Kairos* of *kairoi*, the New Being in existence, the model is based, theonomy is fulfilled, and "originating revelation" is completed.

Ecclesiology

We have followed Tillich's notion of symbol, from its theonomous origin and its revelational appearance to its final and decisive form, because it is the central Tillichian category of immediate interest to Catholic theology. Let us, therefore, conclude this itinerary with a discussion of the primary ecclesiastical application of this notion, namely the definition of the Church as combining a Catholic substance with the Protestant principle. While this formula represents first of all an ecclesiastical symbol, let us note that it also defines the normative notion of society, of "secular" community: such communities—e.g., tribes, states, nations, civilizations, and cultures—have for Tillich an essential "religious substance" that is the source of their power and creativity. But without *criticism* of their pretensions, their self-elevation, their injustice, and their imperialism, societies, precisely because of their religious substance, become idolatrous and self-destructive. As one of the communities responsible among other matters for the religious dimension of society, the religious community (the Church) has as part of its task, along with other groups, to bear this prophetic or Protestant principle in society at large, to criticize the latter's idolatry, its injustice, and its self-destruction. Along with requiring justice from all communities, this prophetic task of the Church represents another ground for the message of liberation theology and for action in its name by the Church. Tillich's "theonomous symbol" thus helps to define society, Church, and history: normatively each represents a historical community characterized, however fragmentarily, by unity with the divine and by prophetic criticism of its own manifestations of estrangement; thus does each represent also a foretaste of the kingdom.

It made good sense for Tillich in the 1920s to name the prophetic, self-critical principle in the *ecclesia* the "Protestant principle"; it was, surely, the way he interpreted Protestantism, applying as he did the latter's central mark of justification by faith to the issue of theological truth as it had formerly been applied to the issue of the virtue of the saints. The Reformation itself, however, (as Tillich well knew) did not make this more radical move: while no person's virtue can justify the Christian, said Luther, still the gospel we preach is absolute and unchanged,[6] and of course Calvin agreed. Hence the self-critical principle in classical Protestantism applied neither to Scripture nor to its theological interpretation, i.e., to the Word as it was understood and preached in the Churches.

What had to be added to the "Reformation" Protestant principle so understood, therefore, in order to bring it to Tillich's level of self-criticism, was the new sense of the historical relativity of all human creative achievements, political, legal, moral, theological, and proclamatory, a historical relativism (the "historical consciousness") that appeared first in the second half of the eighteenth century. According to this historical understanding, all the creative products of church life—scholarship, theology, dogma, preaching; law, customs, requirements, rules, rites, and sacraments—are alike *human* products, relative therefore to their time, place, and culture, and hence not absolute, however much they are (as they are) responses to revelation and however they embody (as they do) the Spiritual Presence. It is this point that completes the definition of theonomy and of the symbol as we have articulated it: all finitude remains finite, and only God is God. Considering its parentage in the late Enlightenment, this principle could more accurately be termed the "Protestant/liberal principle."

Tillich accepted this historical consciousness *in toto* as did all his neo-orthodox colleagues.[7] (Note, even for Barth the role of theology in the Church is to "test" the clearly fallible and faulty preaching and theology of the Church for its fidelity to the Word.[8]) This same principle is implicit in the major documents of Vatican II, and explicit in almost all of these articles. In all of these the Church too has become an example of Tillich's understanding of a theonomous symbol: a finite medium or vehicle of divine grace, but one which retains its finitude—as did Jesus as the Christ himself—and one that adds to that the further burden of "existence" or "estrangement" since in all of us theonomy is only fragmentary. These articles (rightly to my mind) accept all of this with regard to the *ecclesia:* the *ecclesia* is a symbol of grace in which the Spiritual Presence resides but which remains finite and estranged. Only on the presupposition that at no point is the Church as Church absolute can the Church's greatest danger be idolatry, the abandonment of the self-critical principle, and the worship of itself.

Let me refine this point a little more. The move which Tillich consciously made to apply the symbol of justification by faith not only to the problem of personal goodness, virtue, and righteousness—to which it had been confined in the Reformation—but also to the issue of the truth which the Church teaches and preaches, is the result of the new "historical consciousness" and not directly either of the Reformation or of its Protestant successors. It represents, I say, a very radical move for either form of Christian orthodoxy, Catholic or Reformation Protestant. It implies inescapably that the Church's theology, and hence its creeds, its dogmas, and its *ex cathedra* statements, are historically relative, pointers to the truth, to be sure, but by no means absolute or infallible in themselves. And this includes not only stated doctrines authorized by the *ecclesia* (recognized by the Reformers to be relative) but also any interpretation of the Scriptures in preaching, teaching, and confessions, and even the documents of the Scriptures themselves—a point recognized neither by the Reformers nor by many contemporary conservative Protestant groups.

On the contrary, all of these remain human, not divine, and hence they reflect, as do all human creations, their particular place, time, culture, gender, etc. Scripture and tradition alike are, therefore, to be reinterpreted, in fact criticized anew in each age; and in every case, their historical origins are relevant to their meaning. A continually changing theology and Biblical/historical criticism are thus given their charters as necessary to the Church's self-understanding by this Enlightenment and post-Enlightenment principle.

It is because of this relativity of all ecclesiastical creations that the critical principle is ever necessary, lest what is relative, and *as* relative one-sided and biased (e.g., issues of gender in liturgy, doctrine, or law) be "idolized" into something universal, timeless, and so absolute, i.e., as *God's* will. Only if *all* church pronouncements, requirements, and laws are understood in this sense as universally finite, can it be said that the Church is in danger of idolatry. If through its Apostolic Succession (or in its biblical preaching) the Church indeed declares an absolute truth or an absolute law, quite unaware of the shifts, turns, and biases of history (as has been held in the tradition since Ignatius of Antioch!), then it would hardly make sense to accuse the Church of idolatry in its pronouncements. In this way, the late Enlightenment principle of "historical consciousness" has been thoroughly integrated by Tillich as a most important aspect of his larger Protestant principle.

The other, and older, aspect of the Protestant principle is that the Church, *as* Church, *as ecclesia*, is capable of estrangement. Like other estranged communities or institutions, therefore, it can commit idolatry, even when it acts or seeks to act "officially" as Church. That is to say, it can elevate its message—relative because human—into an absolute, timeless, and universal status; it can proclaim its truth as *the* truth, its laws as *the* law, its authority as God's authority. Here the creature claims to be God; or, in Tillich's terms, the sacred spiritual presence given to the religious community as grace is claimed by these creatures—though they be in this way "blessed"—to be their possession. This error was of course recognized by the Reformers as *the* Catholic error, and they protested against it. The Church must recognize its estrangement, confess its sins, and repent, precisely as the first requirement of being the Church. The Catholic tradition has long recognized that all individuals in the church community can sin and must therefore, for their own salvation, repent; but this requirement that the *ecclesia* itself repent is new. As is evident in the mere use of the word *idolatry*, the capacity of the *ecclesia* to sin is an important aspect of the Protestant principle as Tillich formulated it; by the same token, it is implicit in these articles in their discussion of idolatry as the "Catholic temptation." Which one of these aspects of the new Protestant principle (the relativity or estrangement of the ecclesia) poses more difficulties for traditional Catholics, it is hard for an observer to estimate. But certainly at some point this dual issue of relativity and estrangement must be addressed if a genuinely "new" Catholic ecclesiology is to be articulated along these lines suggested by Tillich.

In any case, the concept of symbol in Tillich is radically interpreted, or, better, theonomously interpreted. The finite medium retains its autonomy, hence both its relativity and its freedom, as well as its proneness to estrangement. To Tillich this character of all "sacred" media is universally true, for example, in the social and political exemplars of the German nobility of his youth (which he termed "sacramental demonries") or whiteness and maleness in our time. It is true, moreover, of all historical religions which can use the sacred powers resident in finite media for purposes of power and privilege; thus it has also become true of the historical church itself. This sense of the ambiguity and estrangement of *all* religion characterized all the neo-orthodox, e.g., Barth and Niebuhr as well as Tillich. To him, therefore, the Church's claims to possess absolute truth in its dogmas, its confessions, its theology, or its preaching (whether Protestant or Catholic); its claims that its stated laws were God's laws and its requirements God's requirements; its assumption that its rites and sacraments had unconditional efficacy; and above all its claim that its hierarchy had absolute authority, beyond criticism—this was all to him idolatry, a sign not only of finitude but even more of the estrangement of finitude, in effect an example of the demonic.

The center, in fact, of Tillich's interpretation lies in this category of the demonic. The demonic is the medium of the sacred rendered into its own opposite, into an idol. Concretely, the symbol, and especially the Church as the paradigmatic symbol, is a channel of grace; it is in history the special place of the Spiritual Presence (though it is not the exclusive place). But this is precisely its temptation: if it fails to point always beyond itself and so in repentance to criticize itself, it becomes the demonic. Idolatry is a temptation of the Church *because* the Church is holy, because it is "Catholic substance" if it is to be Church at all. The two poles, therefore, Catholic and Protestant, require each other; the Catholic must be balanced by the Protestant lest it fall into the demonic and the heteronomous. (Interestingly, if our interpretation of the Protestant principle be correct, the Church also seems to require the Enlightenment if it is to be whole!)

Tillich's model of the Church is sacramental and Catholic, a model of a theonomous symbol. Ecclesiologically, however, as this analysis shows, it is a radical interpretation indeed in relation to traditional Catholic ecclesiology. I think these articles well understood these points, though the Enlightenment roots of the Protestant principle may seem unsettling! These articles stress over and over that Catholic Christianity is always in danger of idolatry, and they continuously turn, as an antidote to idolatry, to Tillich's concepts of symbol, theonomy, and sacrament. Here to me lies the greatest strength, and most hopeful promise, of these articles: they envision a Catholicism with a truly Catholic (sacramental) substance, and with a truly Protestant principle, a principle alike of self-criticism and of repentance.

Truly Catholic? On what grounds can this be, if all traces of an Apostolic succession with absolute authority evaporate away? Would Catholicism still be present? Clearly conservatives in the Church say no to this. Thus is raised inevitably the question what authentic Catholicism is, a question surely for another volume! For Tillich, of course (as for me), it is the sacramental principle (the unity of the community with the Spiritual Presence) that is Catholic, not the transformation of the medium—especially the Apostolic hierarchy—into absolute form. This unity with the Spiritual Presence appears in diverse forms in the community: in its liturgy and its sacraments, the center of Catholic life; in its people and their unity in love (cf. Augustine); in its rationality; and in the lives of its saints. Of course, for any number of essential reasons, preaching and teaching are also fundamental, and the Church needs ever more of both. And it will have more of both when it is freed totally from the frozen burden of an absolute authority in its preaching and teaching, and when gender finally ceases to be the criterion of leadership. Such a vision of a renewed Catholicism is implicit in Tillich's ecclesiology though he never witnessed the immense consequences of Vatican II. Such a vision is also surely implicit in these articles. Perhaps, therefore, the next task for this very able group is to make such a Catholic ecclesiology explicit.

Though it be centered in sacrament and liturgy, the sacramental principle in the *ecclesia* is not confined there. For Tillich what is objective must always become also subjective, what is given must be received, if there is to be anything religiously vital and actual. Miracle must be received in ecstasy if there is to be revelation; Spiritual Presence must be received in ultimate concern and responding commitment and trust if we are to speak of grace, etc. Hence the sacramental principle, the Spiritual Presence in the Church, must be actualized in the practices of piety and prayer among the members of the community, or the Catholic substance will not be actual at all. The Spiritual Presence is, to be sure, initiated in Word, sacrament, and liturgy; but it becomes real only when it is received, when personal awareness and assent respond to outer gift and so are experienced inwardly and enacted outwardly. Piety and prayer are thus the essential life blood of the Body of Christ, the essential human response to the presence of grace, the actualization of the Catholic substance so fundamental to the Church. It is, therefore, very appropriate that two of the very best—and most Tillichian—of these articles should have dealt with these important topics, usually gathered under the rubric "spirituality." If the present Churches (Protestant and Catholic) be nearly void of substance at any one point, it is surely here, in the realm of personal and communal piety: reading of Scripture and of meditative texts, meditation, and individual and communal prayer. Without these modes of personal reception and realization, actual Catholic substance is barely possible. It is very important that this realm not be given over entirely to conservative bias and purely traditional practices but be refashioned and reinvigorated as all else in Catholic theology.

One final word. We have stressed the peril inherent in Catholic substance, namely that without the self-critical principle of repentance on the part of the *ecclesia*, a demonic authoritarianism ensues. It is, therefore, only fair to the unusual balance of Tillich's ecclesiology to remind ourselves that to him Protestantism also had its perils, as he saw perhaps even more clearly. If, he said, the Protestant Churches have only a principle of self-criticism (or understand themselves only in that way) and thus lose their own forms of Catholic substance, then they will of necessity seek their substance elsewhere, namely in the surrounding culture; they will be imbued with the culture's religious substance rather than with their own. Thus if the Word ceases to be a living word, a sacramental word, and becomes only a human word; if liturgy and sacrament cease to be media of the Spiritual Presence; and if there be no practice of piety to nourish responsive faith, then the inner life of the Churches will blend with and merely repeat the inner life of the culture. This had, he feared in the 1920s, already happened as the Protestant Churches in Germany became captive to the surrounding bourgeois and nationalistic culture; in our contemporary situation, they are subject to the "American ethos" in liturgy, sermons, everpresent moralism, mild good works, and friendliness, not to mention racism and nationalism. Here the Churches merely reproduce their cultural context and neither nurture themselves with the Spiritual Presence nor prune their lives with the prophetic principle. The problem is, of course, that a reproduction of an estranged culture has within itself no healing depth, no facing of real problems nor any hope of real resolutions of them. Thus for Tillich, as an autonomous culture slowly becomes empty and breeds a heteronomous reaction, so this "culturized religiosity"—though Tillich did not live to see all this work its way out—leads gradually to emptiness, relativity, and irrelevance: emptiness both of the shock of nonbeing and of the reception of grace. Thence in the end it leads also to its polar opposite, to a new search for absolute certainty, certainty of truth and certainty of grace, precisely the Protestant heteronomy of contemporary fundamentalism.

There are many mainline Protestant Churches that have clearly and deliberately eschewed both of these two alternatives, the "liberal-modernist" on the one hand, and the "evangelical-fundamentalist" on the other, and have creatively sought to combine proclamation with genuine piety and both with social criticism and communal action; particularly the Black Churches have (so it seems to me) united in an extraordinarily creative way the reality of Spiritual Presence with a powerful prophetic criticism. With this exception, however, to me the most promising sign remains the sort of union of Catholic substance and Protestant principle implied in each of these clearly "Catholic" articles. Their vision of a sacramental and spiritual community, radically self-critical and so freed of authoritarian and absolutistic temptations, yet one imbued with a passion for the liberation of the oppressed and the rescue of the lost, seems to me to present us with an authentic and promising ecclesiology for our time. Let us hope that these same theologians will increasingly articulate this vision in the years to come.

Notes

1 Paul Tillich, *Political Expectation* (New York: Harper and Row, 1971) 62–79.

2 Ludwig Feuerbach, *Lectures on Religion* (New York: Harper and Row, 1967).

3 This is a good example of Tillich's practice of taking some archaic, even (to modernity) "superstitious" religious category and reinterpreting it "ontologically" as an important aspect of his own contemporary theological understanding; cf. e.g., his use of "miracle" and "ecstasy."

4 Though Tillich does not state (or admit?) the point, he has constructed an argument here: the courage to be is present throughout human life; such courage is not a possibility for finitude; thus the courage to affirm our being against our nonbeing testifies to the presence of the transcendent Power of Being. Cf. Paul Tillich, *Systematic Theology*, 3 vols. (Chicago: University of Chicago Press, 1951–63) 1:192–98, 272–79.

5 For references to these points about the *humanum*, cf. ibid. 3:31, 58, 64–68, 86, 138–40, 159. Cf. also Langdon Gilkey, *Gilkey on Tillich* (New York: Crossroads, 1990) ch. 9.

6 Luther, *Commentary on Psalm 26*.

7 The acceptance of the historical consciousness—with all its consequences for the critical study of Scripture and of church history—and the acceptance of the authority of science with regard to material nature (inorganic and organic) characterizes all the neo-orthodox and sets them sharply apart from their Reformation forebears. Though they were loath to admit it, these were the modern, Enlightenment principles that helped to make them "neo" rather than merely orthodox.

8 Karl Barth, *Church Dogmatics. Vol. 1, 1* (New York: Scribners, 1955) 11ff.

Postscript:
Tillich in the Future of Catholic Theology

This collection of articles by Catholic authors illustrates the wide variety of ways in which Tillich's thought continues to influence Catholic theology today. The context and tone of this current volume is vastly different from that of its 1964 predecessor. The intervening years have witnessed profound changes in Catholic theology, including unheard-of advances in ecumenical openness and receptivity to modern thought. The earlier volume, while enthusiastic, was far more cautious, precisely because it was a pioneering work, opening up very unfamiliar terrain on the Catholic theological landscape. The book was something of an ecumenical milestone in its day, and contemporary theologians can be grateful to its editors and contributors for having been so instrumental in making Tillich's thought available to the Catholic world.

Thomas F. O'Meara, the Dominican scholar, who, while still a student of theology, co-edited the 1964 volume, was gracious enough to write the lead article for the present work. His historical retrospect recreates for the reader the context of the early publication and shows its links—however tenuous—with the present. Tillich's deep concern for the integration of theology with philosophy, as well as his efforts to correlate revelation with culture, were immediately attractive to Catholic theologians of the 1960s and still continue to fascinate their successors today. O'Meara further claims that while the Catholicism of the Vatican II years was still very hesitant to shake off its Neo-Scholastic and juridic mode, even today it "is still not much beyond incipient conversations with modernity." This is why today as in the earlier period Tillich continues to serve Catholic theology as an outstanding "mentor of the modern."

The current volume saliently reflects the pluralistic state of contemporary Catholic theology, bringing to bear new perspectives such as feminism, globalism, and liberation, which would have been quite alien to the horizons of the 1964 work. Nevertheless, despite this striking diversity of perspectives, the present articles have revealed a certain unifying pattern of major motifs or themes. These motifs, we believe,

can be summarized under the following headings: (1) historical responsibility, (2) ecumenical and interreligious concerns, (3) symbolism
and sacramentality, and (4) mysticism and spirituality.

These four unifying themes might very well serve as indicators of
possible future directions in the appropriation of Tillich by Catholic
theology. Accordingly, a brief word on each theme is in order.

Historical responsibility. Both European political theology (e.g., the
work of Johannes Metz) and Latin American theology of liberation have
had an enormous effect on contemporary Catholic theology. These
post-Vatican II developments remind Catholics and other Christians
that the kingdom of God is also *within,* that it makes serious demands
on our responsibility for the historical moment. Within this new context Tillich's notion of *kairos* understandably draws a good deal of
Catholic interest. As an eschatological concept with "socio-political origins and implications" it represents "the specifically historical side of
Tillich's Eternal Now" (Bulman). It is clear from the above articles that
Tillich's *kairos* continues to serve as a powerful theological category,
certainly in Catholic political theology. While some authors have
stressed the transformative power of *kairos* awareness in the social and
political order (Painadath), others have pointed to its value as a safeguard against both human attempts to fabricate utopias and oracular
speculations about the human future (Tavard). Our authors, for the
most part, shy away from outright proclamations of *kairos* situations,
but nevertheless point to important world developments, such as the
new solidarity in African religious consciousness (Akinwale) or the un-
precedented efforts toward interreligious cooperation in India
(Painadath) as signs that the dawn of a new *kairos* might be just on
the horizon. Richard is far less cautious, and in his reflections on the
theme of liberation quietly asserts that we are already in a moment
of *kairos* which requires a "preferential option for the poor." At the
same time, however, he also perceives the *kairos* concept as a warning
against absolutizing any historical moment.

The idea of *kairos* currently captures the Catholic theological imagination and will very likely continue to do so in the decades to come.

Ecumenical and Interreligious Concerns. Here the common denominator appears to be the determination on the part of Catholic authors
to continue to explore the fuller implications of Tillich's famous polarity of Catholic substance and Protestant principle. The working conviction, sometimes made quite explicit (O'Meara), is that these twin
Tillichian categories capture the very core of what both differentiates
and unites Protestant and Catholic thought. Several of the contributors have elaborated on applications of these categories to their own

areas of special theological concern. These applications are often as surprising as they are persuasive. Osborne, for example, argues for the importance of the Protestant principle for preserving an authentic understanding of Catholic sacramentality. Modras, for his part, focuses on the significance of the Protestant principle for helping resolve the frequently bitter struggles over authority in the contemporary Catholic Church. Geffré sees the balance of the two poles as essential for the formulation of a truly global theology. Lamm incisively captures this new Catholic sentiment in her insistence that, when correctly understood, what Tillich calls the Protestant principle is integral to the heart of Catholic thought.

Here also there is good reason to expect to see further developments of Catholic substance and Protestant principle in ongoing Catholic reflection on Tillich's thought.

Symbolism and Sacramentality. In recent decades Catholic theology has become more and more conscious of the symbolic nature of religious and theological language. While Catholic theologians like Karl Rahner have made invaluable contributions to the issue, Tillich still remains unsurpassed among modern theologians in the systematic exploration of the meaning of the religious symbol. In fact, Modras reminds us that Tillich saw the concept of symbol as the center of his theological doctrine of knowledge. Because for Tillich the symbol was the medium of objective divine presence, Modras also argues that his theology of religious symbols provides one of his "closest links" with the sacramentality of Catholic thought. It is not surprising, then, that several of the contributors, including Modras, focus on Tillich's doctrine of symbols in addressing their own theological concerns.

Painadath, for example, in his reflections on Indian spirituality, recognizes the religious symbol as the only language capable of expressing the "ecstasy of prayer" at the core of reality. Both Parrella and Osborne insist that any authentic Catholic sacramental theology will reflect the theonomous quality of the religious symbol. Stenger calls attention to the power of Tillich's own use of symbols to combat the idolatrous absolutizing of male symbols in the Catholic tradition. In a word, we clearly get the sense that in the doctrine of the religious symbol we have a central area of Tillich's thought that will continue to draw intense interest from Catholic theologians, as they clarify their own sacramentality and struggle with the urgent task of theological hermeneutics.

Mysticism and Spirituality. Catholic theology is indebted to Tillich mostly along the lines of his philosophical and systematic thought, as well as in terms of his theological interpretation of culture. An area that is often given far less attention—though not altogether neglected—is his contribution to mystical and spiritual theology. In this present collection this aspect of Tillich's thought is given serious consideration.

As both Parrella and Painadath point out, there is currently a remarkable resurgence of concern for spirituality in the Catholic tradition, both in America and throughout the world. This new brand of spirituality differs sharply, however, from that of the pre-Vatican II Church, especially in its this-worldly understanding of transcendence. This latter emphasis is apparent in its sensitivity to political and social concerns, as well as in the importance it places on a sense of harmony with the environment. We see that among Indian Catholics, for example, Tillich's symbol of "depth" is taken as a source of both prayerfulness and of social commitment. They also find that the "unitive vision" implied in Tillich's notion of the "multi-dimensional unity of life" is a very helpful framework for expressing "a theology of prayer with eco-sensitivity" (Painadath). On this continent, Tillich's holistic, unitary outlook appeals to feminist Catholic theologians (e.g., Stenger) as a bulwark against further hierarchical stratifications. This fresh look at Tillich from the perspective of spirituality has prompted some Catholic theologians to conclude that Tillich's theology is rooted primarily in a "mystical ontology" (Parrella) that is better compared in the Catholic tradition with John of the Cross than with Thomas Aquinas. In this area of spirituality, as in the other three principal motifs to emerge from the collection, we have probably seen only the vanguard of Catholic theological investigation into Tillich's thought.

In response to these articles, Langdon Gilkey has graced the volume with his own frank and probing commentary. His reflections are a model of theological balance, displaying both deep-felt Protestant conviction and genuine ecumenical openness.

It is heartening to find that Gilkey's critique, presented from a different perspective, identifies a very similar pattern of themes running through these various Catholic pieces. He immediately recognizes the important role the notion of *kairos* can play in helping to advance a more historically responsible, truly sacramental Catholic theology. He also calls attention to the rich ecumenical potential in appropriating Tillich's polar categories of Catholic substance and Protestant principle for the ongoing reform of Catholic theology. He clearly concurs with the view that Tillich's doctrine of the religious symbol is very likely the area of greatest Catholic theological interest, whether for the sake of reinforcing sacramental theology or for dealing with the slippery slopes of theological hermeneutics. Finally, Gilkey shares the enthusiasm of several Catholic contributors over the value of Tillich's thought for enhancing the theological understanding of "piety and prayer"—a subject matter Catholic scholars prefer to discuss in terms of "mysticism and spirituality."

Perhaps the greatest service Gilkey renders in his response is his harmonization of the varied elements of Tillich's thought into a coherent, intelligible whole. He shows for example how symbolism is rooted in theonomy and in the depth of spirituality. He makes it clear how both the historical category of *kairos* and the famous Catholic substance/ Protestant principle polarity depend upon a theonomous vision of reality. Finally, he demonstrates that both the prophetic critique of the Reformation and the historical consciousness of the Enlightenment are brought together in Tillich's understanding of the Protestant principle, which on this account, stands in radical tension with the Catholic sacramental principle.

The force of Gilkey's Protestant conviction is felt in his gentle but persistent reminder of the continuous Catholic danger of idolatry and demonization. It is clear that he would like to see even greater evidence of the presence of the Protestant principle in this collection of Catholic scholarship on Tillich. Specifically, he does not find sufficient emphasis on alienation and estrangement among the Catholic authors, despite the fact that these themes were central and foundational to Tillich's whole system. He is particularly concerned about the irresoluteness of Catholic ecclesiology in accepting the real capacity of sinfulness within the official Church, precisely as *ecclesia* or institution. It is very likely that, to a great extent, Gilkey's uneasiness on this score reflects some of the still unresolved tensions between Reformation and Catholic thought, especially in the doctrine of sin. In a similar fashion, Gilkey's radical plea for recognizing the relativity of all church pronouncements points to an inherent antinomy between Catholic and modern thought.

There can be little doubt that the optimism Gilkey has detected in this collection of articles represents to a great extent a reaction (perhaps overreaction) of Catholic theology to the negativity and oppressive guilt that characterized so much Catholic spirituality and theology in the pre-Vatican II era. On the other hand, one could hardly say that the Catholic contributors simply disregard Tillich's stress on sin and estrangement in the course of borrowing his theological insights. The power of sin and alienation, especially in its social and political dimensions, plays a very prominent role in the theological reflections of Richard, Akinwale, Osborne, Stenger, and Modras, and perhaps at the deepest level of all in Dwyer's interpretation of Tillich's theology of the Cross. In his reflections on the grounds for interreligious dia-

logue, Geffré does not hesitate to attribute both finitude and sinfulness to the Church itself, which, he insists, must be ready to "accept
the 'No' pronounced on her by the unconditional." Nor is it likely,
for that matter, that the sense of estrangement is altogether lacking
in any of the other articles, even if this was not their principal focus.

Nevertheless, Gilkey's critique deserves to be taken very seriously.
While it is true that all interpretations of such a complex thinker as
Tillich will necessarily entail significant adaptations of his thought,
Catholic theologians ought to be particularly on guard against creating a "new Tillich" of their own, unrecognizable by their Protestant
colleagues. Catholic theology still exults in the newborn freedom
achieved in Vatican II and expressed so forcefully in Rahner's idea of
a world of grace. But even for this preeminently Catholic thinker, there
is also a dark side of freedom: the reality of radical sin and guilt, an
affliction that all too often strikes at the very heart of church authority
itself. In the long run, however, it may well turn out that the antinomy
of conquering grace and radical evil as well as that of relativity and
religious authority will yield to a higher complementarity, much as has
already occurred in the case of Catholic substance and Protestant
principle.

Gilkey's response, we are convinced, adds an invaluable dimension
to our volume. Even more than that, however, by his enthusiastic and
supportive tone, he provides enormous encouragement to Catholic
scholars dedicated to the difficult but vital ecumenical task of making
the genius of Tillich's thought more available to Catholic theology. For
this encouragement we are deeply grateful.

History has shown that theological prediction is a very risky enterprise, so that what we have suggested in this postscript regarding the
future directions in the Catholic employment of Tillich should be understood as no more than an informed guess. If there is one certainty,
however, that we feel we can draw from this collection of essays, it
is the conviction that the theology of Paul Tillich will continue to exercise a deep fascination for Catholic theologians as we enter the third
Christian millennium.

Raymond F. Bulman
Frederick J. Parrella

Contributors

Anthony A. Akinwale, O.P., studied philosophy in Nigeria, received a B. Th. from the Faculté de Théologie Catholique de Kinshasa, Zaïre, a Lic. Th. and M. A. Th. from the Collège Dominicain de Philosophie et de Théologie, Ottawa, Canada, and is a Ph.D. theology student at Boston College.

Raymond F. Bulman is professor of systematic theology at St. John's University, New York City, and has published widely in the area of Tillich studies. He also chairs the Columbia University Seminar on Studies in Religion.

John C. Dwyer, author of numerous books in Church history and theology, teaches at St. Bernard's Institute in Albany, New York.

Claude Geffré, O.P., is professor of hermeneutics and theology of religions at the Institut Catholique of Paris. He is likewise editor of the collection "Cogitatio Fidei" of Editions du Cerf. He has published *The Risk of Interpretation* (New York, 1987) and many articles about fundamental theology.

Langdon Gilkey, whose most recent book was *Gilkey on Tillich*, is professor of theology emeritus of the Divinity School of the University of Chicago and teaches at Georgetown University and the University of Virginia.

Julia A. Lamm is an assistant professor of theology at Georgetown University. Her primary field of research is the thought of Schleiermacher and his philosophical context.

Ronald Modras is a professor of theological studies at St. Louis University and the author of *Paul Tillich's Theology of the Church: A Catholic Appraisal* (Wayne State University Press).

Thomas Franklin O'Meara, O.P., the co-editor of *Paul Tillich in Catholic Thought* of 1964, has been president of the North American Paul Tillich Society and is at present William K. Warren Professor at the University of Notre Dame.

Kenan B. Osborne, O.F.M., is a professor of systematic theology at the Franciscan School of Theology/Graduate Theological Union, Berkeley, California, and the author of several books on Christian sacraments.

Sebastian Painadath, S.J., author of *Dynamics of Prayer. Towards a Theology of Prayer in the Light of Paul Tillich's Theology of the Spirit,* is the director of the Centre for Indian Spirituality in Sameeksha, India.

Frederick J. Parrella, an associate professor of theology in the religious studies department of Santa Clara University, has published in *Communio, Lumen Vitae,* and *Spirituality Today.*

Jean Richard is professor of systematic theology and director of the research group on Paul Tillich at Université Laval, Québec.

Mary Ann Stenger, a lecturer in the studies of religion at the University of Louisville, is engaged in research in feminism and religious pluralism.

George H. Tavard, the author of some forty volumes in English or French, was conciliar *peritus* at Vatican II, and is now professor emeritus of theology at the Methodist Theological School in Ohio, and distinguished professor of theology at Marquette University.

* * *

Bella Hass Weinberg (Indexer) is a professor in the Division of Library and Information Science at St. John's University, New York City, where she teaches Information Sources in Religion, among other courses. She is a past president of the American Society of Indexers and editor of *Judaica Librarianship.*

Index

Compiled by
Bella Hass Weinberg

The index includes significant subjects, terms, and cited authors—from the notes as well as the text. Reference to notes is by page and note number, e.g., 109n11 refers to note 11 on page 109. Multiple notes on one page are indicated by *nn* after the page number.

Arrangement is word-by-word, i.e., a space is significant. For example, *Ad gentes* files before *Adam, Karl*. A hyphen is treated as a space. Prepositions introducing subheadings are ignored in filing.

Abhishiktananda 231, 239n187–189, 240n207
absolute, the 110n25; Christ as 270–271, 274–275, 279, 281; Christian message 190, 301; in Christianity 272, 277–278, 282; Church teaching 302–305; Eucharist and 83–84; feminist theology 175–177, 185; fundamentalism and 43; God as 53, 60, 63, 159–160, 257, 276, 291; in history 205–206; prayer and 219; spirituality 247, 253; symbols as 37, 39, 284, 301, 310; theonomy and 34; transcendence 193
absolutism 140, 145, 269, 284, 293
abyss: God as 39, 59–64, 70n54; 72n77, n84; 221–223, 254, 291; and spirituality 248, 255, 298
acceptance 74–75, 78–80, 84–86; 88n15, n19; 227, 291
Acerbi, A. 8n19
Ad gentes divinitus 196, 210–211; 214n21, n23; 217n82

Adam, Karl 16
Adams, James Luther 32n51, 111n31, 147n25
adaptation: theology 196–197, 199–200, 202, 208, 214n29
African American theology 94, 197–198. *See also* Black . . .
African theology 5, 189, 192, 194, 196, 198–202, 205, 208, 210–212, 309
agape 78–79
age of confirmation 96
Akinwale, Anthony A. 5, 212, 213n14, 215n57, 309, 312
Alberigo, G. 8n13
aletheia 137
Alexander, Jon 262n5, 263n22
alienation 273, 294–295, 312; ecumenism 284–285; feminist theology 180, 184; God and 63, 76–79, 84; hell and 123; of masses 163–165; sin and 158, 161; spirituality 247
Amaldas, Swami 239n178
Amalorpavadass, D. S. 239n177, 240n200

"Paul Tillich continues to be a major resource for modern, and even post-modern, theology. Among theological scholars and students, Tillich's influence, more than that of any of his Protestant contemporaries, if not also the Catholic, has widened and deepened during the three decades since his death. Some readers of Paul Tillich: A New Catholic Assessment may be unaware of the extensive influence Tillich has had upon Roman Catholic theology during this time. It is arguably greater and more diversified than his impact upon Protestant thought. This volume also makes clear that Catholic thinkers today view Tillich very differently from the response documented in 1964 in a previous symposium on this topic.

"Reading Paul Tillich: A New Catholic Assessment has given me a distinct pleasure. This collection of articles of lasting interest has been put together with intelligence and grace. It provides a bountiful table of food for thought, as tasty and nourishing for the Protestant reader as for the Catholic."

Tom F. Driver
The Paul Tillich Professor Emeritus
of Theology and Culture
Union Theological Seminary

"Paul Tillich's influence on Catholic theological reflection, as this volume ably shows, is not only an historical fact but a continuing source of nourishment. These timely reflections suggest new avenues of research. They point to Tillich's still relevant demand that all authentic theology do its work in close dialogue with that broad range of achievement which we call human culture. Catholic theologians ignore that fact at their own peril. For that reason alone I applaud this careful and provocative collection."

Lawrence S. Cunningham
Professor and Chair of the Department of Theology
The University of Notre Dame